BERYL IVEY LIBRARY

Neighborhood

Neighborhood

EMILY TALEN

OXFORD
UNIVERSITY PRESS

OXFORD
UNIVERSITY PRESS

Oxford University Press is a department of the University of Oxford. It furthers
the University's objective of excellence in research, scholarship, and education
by publishing worldwide. Oxford is a registered trade mark of Oxford University
Press in the UK and certain other countries.

Published in the United States of America by Oxford University Press
198 Madison Avenue, New York, NY 10016, United States of America.

© Oxford University Press 2019

CIP data is on file at the Library of Congress
ISBN 978–0–19–090749–5

1 3 5 7 9 8 6 4 2

Printed by Sheridan Books, Inc., United States of America

This book was made possible in part by a John Simon Guggenheim Memorial Foundation Fellowship.

Also by Emily Talen:
New Urbanism and American Planning
City Rules
Urban Design for Planners
Design for Social Diversity (with Sungduck Lee)

CONTENTS

Now that we are becoming citizens of the world . . . we must take care
that we do not lose our neighborhood feeling.

L. H. Bailey, 1915

People need an identifiable spatial unit to belong to.

Christopher Alexander, *A Pattern Language*, 1977

Neighborhood

‖ 1 ‖

Introduction

This book is written in support of those who believe that neighborhoods should be genuinely relevant in our lives—not as casual descriptors of geographic location but as places that provide an essential context for daily life. Such neighborhoods would be identifiable, serviced, diverse, and connected. Their primary purpose would not be social separation.

By this definition, much of American urbanism is not neighborhood-based. This situation evolved over the course of the past century; before then, neighborhoods were the foundation of urban experience. Centered and sometimes bounded, mixed in land use and people, the neighborhood constituted the basic infrastructure of daily living. Neighborhoods were not always a setting for harmony and should not be sentimentalized. But as physically identifiable places, they functioned as a platform for daily exchange that was distinct from the city of monuments and spectacle. Neighborhoods were the spatial unit that people related to.

This neighborhood-based existence changed fundamentally when cities swelled under industrial capitalism and technological innovations lessened the need for a local urban existence. Urban life became less about localized relationships and more about movement and freedom, and neighborhoods were redefined accordingly. Freed from the requirement of proximity, social connection that required physical contact, and a daily life based on walking, the notion of a neighborhood became open to wider interpretation.

Two responses emerged. One was to try to get the traditional neighborhood back. Early 20th-century sociologists, worried about how the physical and social complexity of the modern metropolis was obscuring the neighborhood and breaking apart the sense of belonging it had long provided, doubled down on what seemed like the most obvious way to reinstate the neighborhood: a definition based on social homogeneity. When urban planners translated these theories to physical form, their neighborhood plans often manifested as explicit enablers of social and land use segregation. This ran counter to the historical experience of the neighborhood, which was mostly mixed in population and use.[1]

But starting in the 1920s, developers, and some government entities, capitalized on the idea of the socially sorted neighborhood as something to be leveraged to sell lots and stoke consumption. It offered a particular understanding of neighborhood that presumably washed away conflict and instead offered a controlled and narrow understanding of urban life. The rapid proliferation of suburban neighborhoods had this kind of identity, an identity rooted in social sameness.

A second, very different kind of response was that, for some urban dwellers, the idea of neighborhood simply lost relevance. It became little more than a convenient geographic locator. For these urbanites, Melvin Webber's "community without propinquity" was not only possible but was preferable, which rendered the neighborhood anemic.[2] Under this new conception, neighborhoods came to be, as Jane Jacobs observed in her landmark treatise, *The Death and Life of Great American Cities* (1961), like valentines. It was an ambiguity that sometimes led to an explicit rejection of the neighborhood as too parochial, in which case the physically prescribed neighborhood seemed disingenuous at best. Ultimately it was a perspective that supported and was supported by academic exploration that heralded the myriad ways neighborhoods could be conceptualized, from cognition to biological analogies about cell structure to rhetorical device. These open-ended definitions reflected a profound reduction in the neighborhood's actual importance.

Neither of these responses was particularly satisfying for anyone hoping that neighborhoods could be sustained—or successfully reinstated—as meaningful dimensions of urban life. Eventually options for living in a neighborhood seemed to be reduced to suburban neighborhoods lacking diversity or undifferentiated urbanism whose neighborhood relevance amounted to being a name on a map. To some segments of the populace, these outcomes did not constitute a problem. But to those living in the ill-defined, formless world of urban ambiguity that had come to characterize much of the American city, the absence of a sense of neighborhood seemed a missed opportunity. Such places lacked what a lucky few well-defined and diverse urban neighborhoods had: a sense of place, local rootedness, social connection, and a sense that the everyday world around them mattered because it was a setting for daily life and that residents had some sense of agency—that is, the ability to effectuate change or play a role in neighborhood life. For those without a neighborhood, what was needed was a reformulation of the neighborhood ideal in a way that was realistic, relevant, and not reliant on exclusion—an experience of neighborhood that went beyond casual description or a marketing selling point.

Might it be possible to constitute neighborhoods that are more than a label, that reject segregation, and that are not hopelessly anachronous? Is it possible to reinstate some version of the historical neighborhood as something real and meaningful in 21st-century urban experience?

While many factors leading to the decline of the traditional neighborhood—e-commerce and the loss of small retailers, suburban exclusivity and gated communities, internet-based social contact—seem to be beyond anyone's control, other factors seem more a product of neglect and confusion about neighborhood definition. I argue that the reinstatement of neighborhoods might be supported if academics and planners finally move past the critiques and countercritiques that have the left the idea of neighborhood muddled and problematized. Historically neighborhoods seemed to just *be*, defined by technological limits and social and economic needs. In modern cities, neighborhoods require more effort. Resolution of entrenched debates—about their design, their ability to be planned, their governance, their social impact, and their social makeup—will help the neighborhood become something more than a valentine or a census tract. And although these debates permeate academic discourse, they are also part of the lived experience of neighborhood residents.

This is mostly an American story. The quest to recapture the neighborhood in its traditional sense—as a localized, place-based, delimited urban area that has relevance, meaning, and some level of personal influence —has long been a part of the American ethos. Alexis de Tocqueville chronicled this spirit in his 1835 treatise, *Democracy in America*. But the idea that neighborhoods can harbor a sense of caring and local participation and not devolve into enclaves seeking social insularity and separation is also fundamental to American life—and to stated American values. That this localized but diverse neighborhood identity has often failed to materialize requires thorough exploration.

While my case for neighborhood is directed at the American experience, the roots of neighborhood extend deeper and wider. There is something hardwired about neighborhood definition that extends far beyond the American industrial city and the response to it.

The historical and global record shows that there are durable, time-tested regularities about neighborhoods. Many places outside of the West were built with neighborhood structure in evidence—long before professionalized, Western urban planning came on the scene. That the American neighborhood can be connected to these traditions, anchored in human nature and regularities of form, is compelling. As the historians David Garrioch and Mark Peel asked, "Is it not possible that proximity and interdependence have produced a local environment that is essentially similar, wherever and whenever it existed?"[3]

The "Everyday Neighborhood"

In the American experience any attempt to reconstitute some version of the historically experienced neighborhood must confront a negative narration: that such neighborhoods are irrelevant in a world of far-flung social relations; that neighborhoods are enablers of gentrification and segregation; that neighborhoods correlate with isolation and exclusion; and that neighborhoods prevent connection to wider networks. There can be no reinstatement of the neighborhood as something genuinely relevant and real without resolving these issues.

Taking stock of these academic but also tangible debates—about how neighborhoods should be designed, whether they can be planned, how they should be governed, how residents within them relate to each other, and how to deal with their segregationist tendencies—I offer a way forward by proposing how each problem might be resolved and how "neighborhood" might be redefined accordingly. What emerges is a proposal for the "everyday neighborhood," an identifiable, serviced, diverse, and connected place.

Why is the reinstatement of the historical neighborhood experience in 21st-century terms a worthy goal? One reason is that our current supply of everyday neighborhoods is scarce, and demand is high. Meeting this demand has become a significant problem over the past few decades, and cities struggle to find ways to sustain whatever supply they are fortunate to have. Urban areas with everyday neighborhood qualities are ground zero for battles waged over gentrification, displacement, loss of small businesses, and the depletion of urban character.

A second reason is that, because everyday neighborhoods are identifiable to the people who live there, they are capable of fostering a sense of ownership and caring. This is less possible under ambiguous definitions, where neighborhood might be a feeling, a mapped polygon, a few houses, or a process rather than a physical place with buildings and centers and public spaces that need to be cared for. Neighborhood tangibility forms the basis of self-governance, evident in the historical record and a century of discourse about the correlation between physical form, neighborhood identity, and sense of local control. In the absence of an explicit definition, neighborhood is an abstraction. Residents lose their ability to control or change it.

Third, the everyday neighborhood cultivates social and economic connection because it roots connectivity in daily experience. From small business success to neighborhood-based surveillance to efforts to combat social isolation among the elderly to increasing success among high-risk children in school, neighborhood-based engagement is regularly cited as a factor in addressing social challenges. The everyday neighborhood provides a meaningful context for such efforts, leveraging sense of place, identity, and the meeting of daily life needs to offer a basis for connection that a more open-ended understanding of neighborhood would not be able to leverage.

Finally, and most important, the everyday neighborhood substitutes place for homogeneity as the basis of neighborhood definition. Neighborhood identity based on race and income has been deeply damaging. Rather than using neighborhood as a marker of social difference, the everyday neighborhood defines neighborhood not as bundles of social data but as physical places where built forms, identity, and social and economic worlds come together. It means using *place* instead of class or race in the formation of neighborhood consciousness and as an alternative basis of collective identity, one capable of transcending the desire for social sameness, the fear of others, and the distrust of institutions.[4]

In all of these ways, the everyday neighborhood is intended as a tool for change. It is not applicable everywhere nor for everyone. But in the vast expanse of amorphous, neighborhood-free uranism that constitutes much of our cities, there is a need to proactively work toward neighborhood definition and reconstitution. Unless we do that, neighborhood cannot be used as a credible resource in the quest to help cities become better places.

The Debates

If we look closely at the main debates that have been litigated at length over the past century—over physical design, planning, governance, social relevance, and segregation—we can start to work our way toward a proposal for resolution and a new definition of neighborhood that does not necessarily throw out the historical experience of neighborhood a priori, but at the same time recognizes that the traditional neighborhood needs to be redefined in certain ways.

Debates about physical design focus on neighborhoods' boundedness and centeredness, their street composition, and their internal and external connectivity. An earlier practice by which neighborhoods were planned all at once on "clean slates" or as whole units in existing urban places has long been discounted, yet it is true that some aspects of the complete neighborhood—particularly its centeredness—help build neighborhood identity. In turn, this identity has local power. When that identity is derived from physical characteristics and not social difference, neighborhood can be a persuasive concept that rejects insularity and disconnection from broader urban forces.

But the second debate turns on the question of whether neighborhoods can be successfully planned at all. Some argue that neighborhoods cannot be planned a priori and that the only potentially meaningful neighborhoods are those that emerge organically. Similarly some people hold that neighborhoods can be designed, but that those designs should focus less on formal plans and more on the social processes that underlie neighborhoods, such as activities and engagement. On the other side of the debate are planners on a quest for a neighborhood structural ideal. The potential resolution of this issue is to embrace both plan and process. Plans without process are top-down affairs that often turn out badly; a neighborhood planning process without a guiding plan can be dispiriting and aimless.

The third kind of debate is about political ideals—specifically, neighborhood governance and the value of and prospects for self-determination and local control. While it might seem obvious that democracy is strongest when it is localized, there are downsides to it; for example, neighborhood-scale democracy might not have much power in any broader context. (Saul Alinsky, the famed community organizer, did not think that geographically defined neighborhoods—as opposed to communities of shared interest—could effect much change.) Neighborhood governance can seem untenable, too, precisely because "neighborhood" has such a weak and ambiguous definition. Moving forward on the question of governance involves building a stronger neighborhood identity and then using that identity to tie into wider political networks, as Jane Jacobs advocated. But it also calls for using neighborhood identity to rally support among residents (and among those currently in power) for more direct control over neighborhood-scale expenditure and regulation. Neighborhood-based capacity-building efforts can be effective, but they can be more effective still if they emphasize leveraging the physical, tangible aspects of neighborhoods to enable collective action.[5]

The fourth debate is the long-standing and still common one over the degree to which the form of a neighborhood influences how residents relate to each other. Many planners, both in earlier generations and today, take it as given that neighborhood form promotes or inhibits social interaction. These planners tend to believe that "traditional" neighborhood design can instill a sense of community. Others characterize this belief as "physical determinism" that misconstrues the social construction of neighborhoods. Moreover, some claim, the entire question has been rendered irrelevant by advances in technology that have enabled communities to take shape in virtual space. Resolving this debate requires shifting the focus away from "community" toward neighborhood functionality—its services, facilities, and institutions and the ways they constitute an embedded social reality. To be sure, social connection is likely enhanced by a neighborhood's functionality. But trying to ascribe social relationship as the neighborhood's primary purpose is both unrealistic and unnecessary.

Finally, there is a debate over the degree to which neighborhoods—or certain kinds of neighborhoods—enable exclusion. There is ample evidence that neighborhoods have often been explicitly or implicitly used to promote social segregation. But the problem can be addressed, either by proactively building for neighborhood diversity or by settling on a neighborhood definition that successfully connects and integrates smaller, homogeneous neighborhoods within larger heterogeneous districts.

Understanding this argumentation is critical because it reveals what matters most about neighborhoods. Having an explicit understanding of where neighborhood ideals have failed and where they have succeeded is essential if there can be any hope of reinvigorating the power of neighborhood in a world dominated by division and detachment. Without this assessment, a century of neighborhood debate is hard to make sense of, although there is no city-related topic upon which more attention has been bestowed.[6] Engaging with and resolving the five neighborhood debates outlined here will help tighten our hold on neighborhood and rescue it from its current domain: caught between planning bureaucracies that depict it as often irrelevant lines on a map, social activists who might disdain its inward focus, academics unable to get past its deterministic antecedents, and residents who are confused about where it ends and where it begins.

Notes

1. Even where neighborhoods were more segregated, the constrained spatial extent of cities meant that neighborhoods were not geographically isolated.
2. Webber et al., *Explorations into Urban Structure.*
3. Garrioch and Peel. "Introduction," 670.
4. For example, loss of a sense of neighborhood is cited as a factor in the decline of police-citizenry relations. See Thale, "Assigned to Patrol."
5. McKnight and Block, *The Abundant Community*, 2010.
6. The Newberry Library's "Chicago Neighborhood Guide" lists 220 books and indices, many of them compendiums in themselves, just on the neighborhoods of one city.

PART I

DEFINITION AND DESIGN

Part I is an overview of neighborhood as an historical and global regularity, as an object of design, and as a concept leveraged by urban reformers. The historical summary draws from all time periods and places, revealing variation but also significant commonality—basic parameters around which our understanding of neighborhood has formed. The objective is to understand when and where neighborhoods were ever identifiable, serviced, diverse, and connected.

The next two chapters summarize the 20th century responses that emerged when neighborhoods came to be seen as in decline. One response was to try to get the neighborhood back by rationalizing its structure and conceptualizing the neighborhood as a spatial "unit". Planned neighborhood units went through various iterations: starting out small and human-scaled, later morphing into large modernist versions, and then later reinstated by New Urbanists as a version of the earlier model. But there was another response to the decline of neighborhood—a recasting of the very basis of what a neighborhood was, or could be. Detached from historical definition, the idea of neighborhood expanded to include political and scientific conceptions that challenged conventional understanding.

The Historical Neighborhood
and Its Decline

Counteracting the often more ambiguous contemporary understanding of neighborhood requires drawing on a broad historical and global perspective. Interconnection, localized identity, human scale, adjacency, access, the need for a graspable spatial unit to belong to—these are the regularities of urban experience that establish a durable foundation for the traditional concept of neighborhood. Historical examples of neighborhood are important precisely because neighborhood form emerged as a regular feature of urban experience all over the globe, despite profound differences in urbanization processes.

What is known about how neighborhoods were laid out and experienced before the city was fundamentally restructured by technological and social changes emerging out of the 19th century? To what degree was the neighborhood ever identifiable, serviced, diverse, and connected?

"Neighborhood" is a word found in nearly all languages (see Table 2.1). The English word originated in the mid-15th century and was initially used to denote areas outside of the city ("And for-to cast my soule from þer neyborowhed"). The Oxford English Dictionary lists a 1425 reference to "myn neghebores," but that is a group of people rather than an actual place. According to the Online Etymology Dictionary, the first use of the word "neighborhood" synonymous to its current meaning as a community of residents living close by was recorded in 1620.[1]

Neighborhoods are a ubiquitous condition of human settlement, found in all time periods, in all cultures, and in both rural and urban contexts (examples from Saudi Arabia, Italy and China are shown in color plates 1, 2, and 3). Even ancient cities have been described as clusters of neighborhoods, "a federation of small locality groups."[2] Plato, writing in the *Republic* (4th century B.C.E.), was an early observer of these spatial groupings.

Spontaneously formed neighborhoods were always more common than deliberately planned ones. The historian Janet Abu-Lughod argued that in premodern times, Islamic neighborhoods were vitalized through state neglect,

Table 2.1 **"Neighborhood" in many languages**

neighbourhood (en)
район (ru)
quartier / circonscription (fr)
barrio (es)
quartiere / vicinato (it)
Nachbarschaft / Wohngegend (de)
近鄰社區 (cn)
bairro (pt)
حي (ar)
квартал (bg)
okolí (cs)
γειτονιά (el)
asum (et)
محله (fa)
asuinalue (fi)
שכונה (he)
पड़ोस (hi)
kvart (hr)
településrész (hu)
район (be)
Miesto rajonas (lt)
mikrorajons (lv)
wijk, buurt(combinatie) (nl)
Nabolag (no)
osiedle/dzielnica (jednostka administracyjna) (pl)
cartier (ro)
susedstvo (sk)
Кварт (sr)
บริเวณใกล้เคียง (th)
mahalle (tr)
район (63) (uk)
vùng lân cận (vi)

Table 2.1 **Continued**

পল্লী (bn)
वस्ती (mr)
அருகாமை பகுதி (ta)
محله (ur)
छर-छिमेक (ne)
അയല്പക്കം (ml)
mikrorayon (az)
kejiranan (ms)
barri (ca)
rukun warga (id)
barrio (54) (gl)
komšiluk (bs)
auzoa (eu)
градски макрореон (mk)
Komunidad (4) (tl)
အိမ်နီးချင်းများ (my)
მიკრორაიონი (ka)
近邻社区 (zh)
comharsanacht (ga)
අසල්-පහළ (si)
rukun warga (jv)
silingan (cb)

Source: "Codes for the Representation of Names of Languages," Library of Congress, http://loc.gov/standards/iso639-2/php/code_list.php.

leaving ad hoc and informal arrangements that strengthened neighborhood-scale cooperation. Other examples of spontaneous neighborhood formation include housing that developed around a church, a university, or, later, a factory. Clusters of related land uses that developed in specific sections of the city created neighborhoods of distinct character.

The history of systematic urban expansion is often a history of growth by neighborhood. There were the colonizing Greek city plans with their uniform

residential quarters (Lewis Mumford praised grid-based Greek planning because it gave neighborhoods "visible boundary lines"[3]); the gridded and partitioned Roman castra military camps; and the clusters of houses outside of an
established city or town that were later absorbed as defined neighborhoods.

Natural geographical barriers like rivers constitute a main category of influencing
factors. A classic case is Rome, whose seven hills formed seven identifiable neighborhoods.[4] In rural settings, neighborhood formation is influenced by topography.
There are also human-made features—streets, utility lines, parcels, buildings—that
may be cause or effect of neighborhood formation. Ann Keating traced the evolution of neighborhoods in the Chicago region and showed that neighborhoods
originated out of distinct settlement types: farm centers, industrial towns, railroad
suburbs, or recreational/institutional centers.[5] Once they were built out, change
slowed, creating the many examples of neighborhoods that no longer seem to match
the social and political contexts behind their creation. Exceptions to slow change
are catastrophes (fire, earthquakes) and massive, government-backed capital investment in pursuit of "modernization" of the kind that occurred in 19th-century
European capitals and in the "urban renewal" period of the mid-20th century.

Our understanding of the neighborhoods of ancient cities comes from archaeologists, whose excavations of ancient urban forms have exposed clear neighborhood patterns. Both Asian and Near Eastern towns are full of examples of tightly
clustered groups of buildings that can be described as neighborhoods. There were
no streets or front doors within these neighborhoods—houses were accessed from
the roof, and thus the roof was probably the main social space. Social interaction is
believed to have been intense. Over time the rooftop social spaces disappeared and
internal open spaces were constructed within the neighborhoods on ground level.
Regardless of where the neighborhood social space was located, these neighborhoods were not part of the public domain; they were tightly bounded and open
only to neighborhood residents. Archaeologists note, however, that the population of each neighborhood was too small to be self-perpetuating, and marriage
kept residents from different neighborhoods interconnected.[6]

Strategies were employed to make sure neighborhoods were for residents
only. For example, neighborhoods had winding, narrow streets, in some cases
with gates or doors that closed at night. Archaeologists describe these tightly
clustered neighborhoods as having "corporate identities." These identities
changed over time, when the same buildings were appropriated by a new group
of inhabitants, but new groups belonged to the same broadly defined society.
That these corporate identities are consistently re-created "bespeaks the central
importance in these societies of living in bounded neighbourhoods."[7]

The earliest neighborhoods were small. In the 4th century B.C.E., The Confucian
philosopher Mencius proposed that the "principles of humanity" could be upheld
by neighborhoods composed of eight families. A neighborhood could be formed
from nine plots of land—one for each of eight families and a ninth for communally

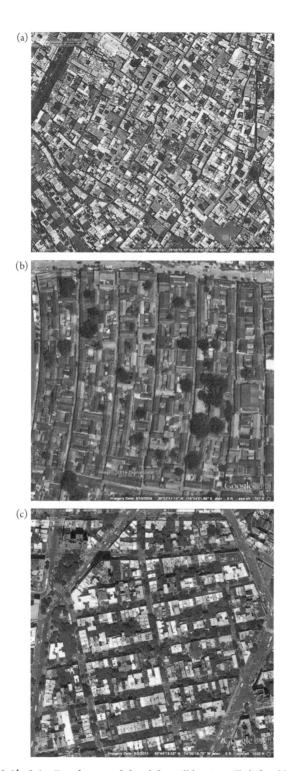

Figures 2.1a, 2.1b, 2.1c People around the globe still live in well-defined historical neighborhoods, even if the localized and self-contained life they once enabled is no longer viable. (a) Shiraz, Iran; (b) hutongs in Beijing; (c) Greenwich Village, New York. Source: Google Earth.

cultivated crops whose proceeds could be used to pay taxes. This neighborhood of eight families would work together, residents keeping each other company "while resting in the evening," guarding against intruders, and attending to the weak or sick. A king would be needed to ensure the success of the system.[8]

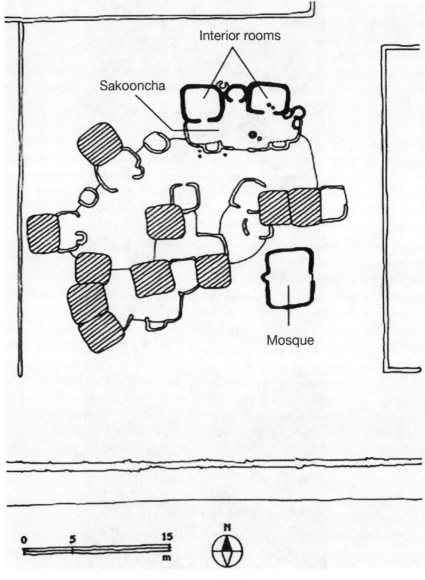

Figure 2.2 In Afghanistan, the neighborhood-like *qawwal* is a cluster of eight family units around an open courtyard with an adjacent mosque, oriented in line with the seasons and the daily cycles of the sun, offering a connection to natural rhythms that has not lost relevancy. The courtyard permits outdoor communal functions, such as workshop, kitchen, or play space. Source: Image redrawn from Kazimee and Mcquillan, "Living Traditions of the Afghan Courtyard and Aiwan."

Some neighborhoods had more than eight families but were constrained in size by what anthropologists believe to be the limit of face-to-face community.[9] If neighborhoods were about face-to-face interaction, then certain thresholds apply: 150 to 250 people can maintain close, personal interaction, while 400 to 600 can maintain a more casual form of interaction. At least six separate studies, cross-cultural and from many time periods, have converged on this range. One author argued that the limit has to do with the size of the neocortex in the human brain.[10] Thus the population of Neolithic settlements (8500 to 5500 B.C.E.) in what is now Turkey was estimated at 250 residents (probably fewer than 70 families or households); these settlements were made up of neighborhoods of 30 to 40 tightly clustered households. The limits of face-to-face social connection might have prompted the Prophet Mohammed's directive that "neighborhood extends to 40 houses in all directions."[11]

Following the Neolithic period, archaeologists have found clear evidence of neighborhoods in an Early Bronze Age (before 2100 B.C.E.) settlement in the Middle East where space was differentiated into compounds of different character, even within relatively small walled settlements.[12] The residential compounds are believed to have been linked not only by kinship but also by "economic relationships and social and ritual responsibilities." Sometimes referred to as the "dynamic corporate village," the grouping of society into differentiated and internally cooperative neighborhoods produced "heterogeneity and complexity" at the village level.[13]

The buildings of Old Babylon (second millennium B.C.E.) reveal a neighborhood form consisting of "one or more very large buildings," probably owned by wealthier families, surrounded by smaller houses. These neighborhoods were economically diverse; within the surrounding houses there were "workshops and commercial facilities" such as bakeries, mills, taverns, chapels, and other kinds of shops. The chapels of Old Babylon seem to have played a strong role in shaping neighborhood identity, as their location and form was locally determined.[14] The temple-based neighborhoods of ancient Mesopotamia were socially diverse in the sense that they included officials and priests, slaves and merchants—"all the people of the god."[15] There is evidence that the ancient city of Ur was socially and economically mixed, with the wealthy living next to "commoners and craft specialists."[16] Elizabeth Stone's excavations of the Mesopotamian city of Nippur (160 km southeast of present-day Baghdad) found evidence of neighborhoods composed of "individuals belonging to all classes."[17]

As the division of labor in cities increased, neighborhood segregation based on occupation might have been more common. Early Mesopotamian neighborhoods were named after ethnic or family groups, but later nomenclature suggests neighborhoods were formed around community or occupational functions.[18] Precapitalist New World cities like Teotihuacan show signs of occupational

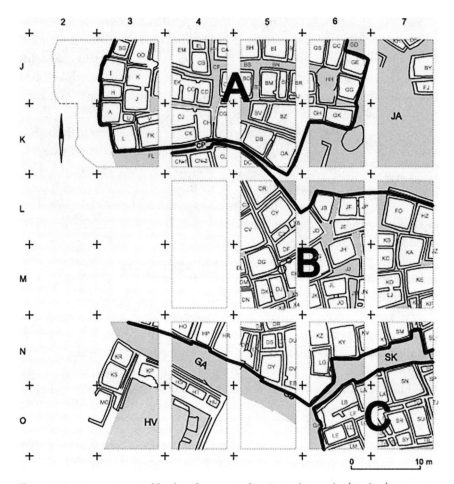

Figure 2.3 Bronze Age neighborhoods excavated in Central Anatolia (Turkey). Source: Image redrawn from Düring, *Constructing Communities.*

segregation, for example, commercial neighborhoods that were created by merchants who settled in discrete enclaves within cities.[19]

Ancient cities were sometimes partitioned by ceremonial streets and main cross streets, and neighborhoods formed around them. The intersection of two main streets would create four "quarters," still the term used for neighborhoods in Western Europe (although the term is misleading, as the number was not limited to four; for example, Venice had six). Alberti wrote that "Babylon was divided into a number of separate quarters" and attributed the practice of dividing cities into quarters to Solon and Plutarch.[20] In the Hellenistic cities of Ancient Greece, neighborhoods were clusters of residences attached to prominent venues, for example, the "bazaar quarter" or the "theatre quarter."[21]

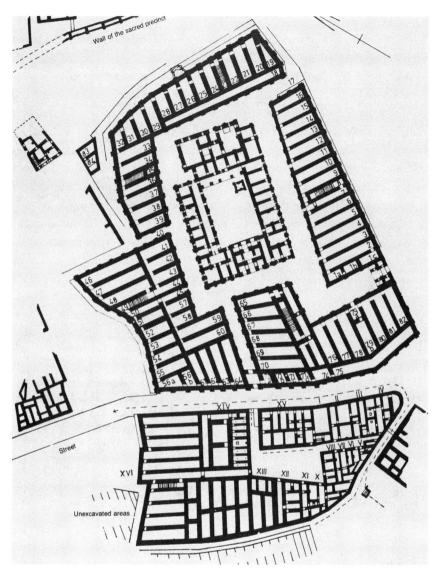

Figure 2.4 Roman numerals indicate 16 housing units clustered around a courtyard in the ancient city of Hattusa in central Turkey. North of the neighborhood lies the temple, surrounded by storage rooms. Source: Image redrawn from Benevolo, *The History of the City*.

Neighborhoods in Augustan Rome, known as *vici* (singular *vicus*), with a population estimated at 2,800 to 3,800, were explicitly identified and officially sanctioned. Augustus was a big supporter of neighborhoods, giving them their own shrines and civic administration. They often had a crossroads at the center, known as a *compitum*, at the intersection of a principal street and a smaller, secondary street. This is where religion was practiced, and the space formed an essential aspect of neighborhood identity, although other kinds of public monuments and neighborhood beautification were also considered essential. As the basis of religious practice, the *vici* had their own local governance that lasted even during the civil unrest of the Late Republic.[22]

Although associated with a street serving as a "platform for communication," the *vici* also included the space around the street, with rows of shops and houses, a distinction that apparently was not appreciated until late in the 20th century.[23] The principal streets kept the neighborhoods connected to the larger town. This is an essential point. Linear organization, in which neighborhoods had a strong attachment to a principal street that connected them to the town center and larger ceremonial and commercial spaces, can be distinguished from neighborhoods that were more internally focused and self-contained. There is at least a conceptual similarity to "ribbon development," a long-standing feature of European cites and not necessarily antithetical to neighborhood formation. London's 18th-century ward maps similarly show how wards, governed by aldermen, were organized around a consolidated street.

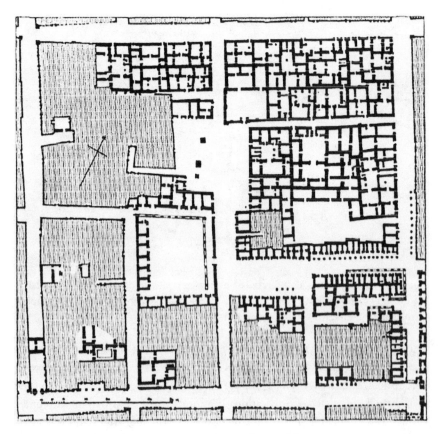

Figure 2.5 The bazaar quarter in the Ancient Greek city of Dura-Europos. Source: Image redrawn after Wycherley, "Hellenistic Cities."

Neighborhoods in ancient China were structured somewhat differently. The earliest period of city development, beginning in 770 B.C.E. and lasting almost 2,000 years, is described as the "closed walled city." Chang'an, the capital of the Tang Empire built starting in 582 C.E., was composed of gated residential wards known as *fang* that were strictly controlled and covered almost 90% of the city (see color plate 3). Neighborhoods were 125 to 200 acres, with densities averaging six households per acre and a typical population of about 4,000. The 109 wards of varying sizes are now buried beneath the existing city, but archaeologists have been able to piece together a picture of what these ancient Chinese neighborhoods were like: walled, gated, and strictly gridded.[24] Another example of a planned neighborhood unit is found in Heian, Japan—present-day Kyoto and the capital of Japan for 11 centuries from 794 to 1868—where the emperor Kwammu laid out the city in 75-acre neighborhood units of about 6,000 residents, each with a superintendent who enforced local rules. Each neighborhood had 16 blocks that were 400 feet square.[25]

Within the walled cities of Ancient China, residential neighborhoods were organized around courtyards. Each self-contained neighborhood unit was enclosed by walls, and there were doors marking their entrances. The purpose of this division was social control: interaction between neighborhood units was meant to be minimized. On the other hand, social mixing in ancient China was driven by control and even state sponsorship, such that when the rules covering wards in Ancient Chinese cities were relaxed, social segregation resulted. (This is the reverse process to the claim that social segregation tends to be state sponsored.)[26] In some Chinese cities, the neighborhoods were highly regularized, embedded in a street grid that kept each neighborhood identical in terms of shape and size. When the next phase in Chinese urban morphology—the "open city"—started in 618, the strict regularity of neighborhood units broke down. Neighborhood walls were demolished as commercial areas expanded along the main urban streets that traversed the city.[27]

Muslim settlement in China involved a merger of large, formalized urban space and organic urban form. Muslims initially settled in small enclaves with markets and mosques located adjacent (and often physically attached to) the outside of the walled Chinese city, forming small "semi-autonomous units" that were spatially distinct but integrated in the urban "superstructure." With their more irregular patterns, they differed morphologically from the adjacent Chinese city, where streets were laid out according to cardinal orientation. Mosques were meant to serve about 2,000 families (which would likely be at least 6,000 residents), beyond which new neighborhoods and mosques were started.[28] These settlements persist even though the walls and many mosques were destroyed in the 20th century.[29]

An organic formation of neighborhood in which individual dwellings started to cluster and communal facilities developed in service to them was the process

Figure 2.6 An organic type of neighborhood is observed in megacities like Kuala
Lumpur, where neighborhoods form around commercial areas extending outward from
the city center. "Business ribbons" along highways have become the neighborhood
centers of newly emerging neighborhoods formed out of resettlement villages that
were established in the mid-20th century. A half-century ago, this business ribbon
was conceived as a neighborhood center. Source: Sendut, "The Structure of Kuala Lumpur."
Image: Google Earth.

of neighborhood formation in Sarajevo. Under Ottoman rule (15th and 16th
centuries), individual dwellings lined meandering streets that led to a market
district, but when 40 or 50 houses and a mosque were built, the settlement became a neighborhood, a *mahalla*, "whereupon a fountain, school, coffeehouse,
bakery and green grocery were built around a square or market-place." There
were 90 *mahalla* in Sarajevo by the 1600s, each neighborhood centered around a
square with a mosque.[30] The tightly clustered groups of houses shown on a 1622

(a)

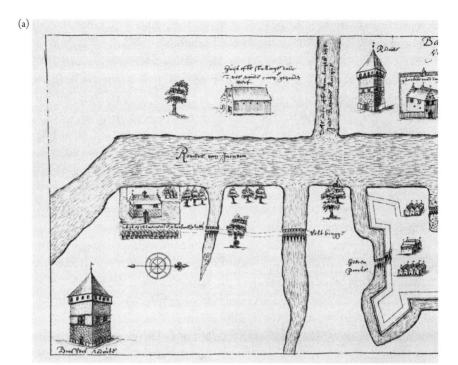

(b)

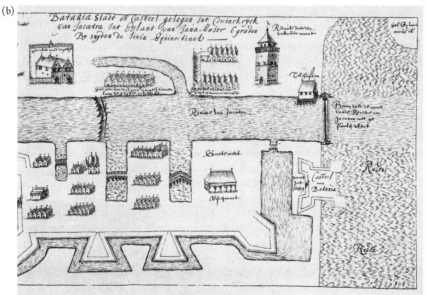

Figure 2.7a and 2.7b Neighborhoods shown on a 1622 map of Batavia, the capital of what was the Dutch East Indies, now Jakarta. Source: Brommer and de Vries, "Historische Plattegronden van Nederlandse Steden."

map of Batavia—the capital of what was the Dutch East Indies, now Jakarta—
can be interpreted as similarly sized neighborhoods.

Neighborhood formation outside of an existing town is also a process that
characterizes some early Jewish neighborhoods, called *shekhunah*.[31] The term
first appeared in Rabbinic literature in the 3rd century C.E. and implied separation from an adjacent area by a physical feature, such as an open field or a street.
Small villages, compact and with no internal form of separation, would be the
same as a single *shekhunah*; only larger towns were separated into more than one
shekhunah. Sometimes it was a process of villages being gradually absorbed by
nearby cities, like that shown in Pierre Lavedan's *Histoire de L'Urbanisme a Paris*,
where three villages in the German town of Rostock had been consolidated by
1265. Lavedan thought it marked "a step towards banality."[32]

Amid the spatial sorting and segmentation that defined neighborhoods,
different cultures had different ways of keeping the population diverse within.
In Islamic cities, religion, rather than the state, sustained the social mix, since
wealth-based social mixing within neighborhoods was the norm under Islamic
religious law. For example, the traditional neighborhoods of Iranian cities
(*mahallehs*) were culturally homogeneous but mixed in terms of class, such that
"the poorest to the richest lived in a neighborhood together." (Some have lamented that in modern times, where these traditional norms have broken down,
monocultural neighborhoods segregated by income have occurred.)[33] Although
neighborhood differentiation was not wealth-based, there was some basis of social differentiation: family, clan, religious sect, occupation, or ethnic identity.
Within the neighborhood, street intersections would have subelements such as a

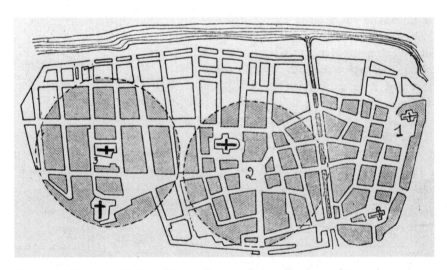

Figure 2.8 The consolidation of three villages in the German town of Rostock,
1265. Source: redrawn after Lavedan, *Histoire de l'urbanisme a Paris*.

mosque, school, *takyeh* (shrine for mourning), and bathhouse, while the neighborhood center itself had a more complete array of services. Self-sufficiency was a necessity: family and clan-based neighborhoods sought to achieve "internal cohesion" and delimitation "against others."[34]

Islamic neighborhoods, described as "cities in miniature," had a poorer servant class surrounding a wealthy family, resulting in mixed-class neighborhoods of 500 to 1,000 people. Each residential quarter of the Islamic city contained a small mosque, a few madrasas (schools), and a few shops for everyday needs like food. The mosque and local market would be situated along a main street with connecting residential cul-de-sacs. Access to the residential areas was by a single street. Neighborhoods backed up to each other, and in times of political strife may have become walled and gated. Each neighborhood had its own leader, who collected taxes and mediated disputes. The lack of a clear archaeological or archival record of citywide administration provides further support for the contention that urban governance was at the neighborhood level.[35]

The form of Islamic neighborhoods was an important source of protection. There were gates barring entry to the *harat* (neighborhood), and there was an

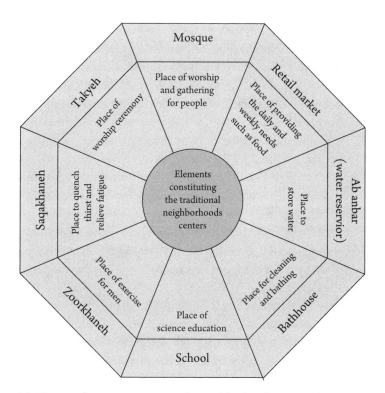

Figure 2.9 Varying elements constituting the neighborhood center in the traditional Islamic neighborhood. Source: Habib et al., "The Concept of Neighborhood."

unambiguous understanding of how space was controlled—which space was private and which was not—not unlike what the 20th-century architect Oscar Newman later termed "defensible space."[36] But this does not mean that social groups did not come into contact. Arab settlements during the Ottoman period (starting in the 16th century) had a neighborhood structure that enabled privacy internally, but the structure supported social mixing within the larger city. A description of Algiers recounts:

> The upper city was comprised of approximately fifty small neighborhoods. As was typical of the decentralized Ottoman urban system throughout the empire, every neighborhood was under the administrative responsibility of religious chiefs and qadis (judges), hence each community was controlled and supervised by its own leaders. The population was mixed. Old families with Andalusian and Moorish roots engaged in commercial and artisanal activities; kabyles formed the working class; Jews, who had three distinct neighborhoods in the upper casbah, were tradespeople. The presence of European consuls and businessmen, Saharans, and Christian slaves made the population of Algiers truly cosmopolitan.[37]

The 18th-century neighborhoods of Aleppo, Syria, were dense and intimate, with high levels of daily social exposure. At the time, Aleppo was a city of only 1.5 square miles, but it had 82 officially designated neighborhoods (mahalla), ranging in size from 1,200 to 1,500 inhabitants, each covering 10 to 12 acres. The neighborhood was responsible for security, upkeep, taxes, and "public morals." These were complex places with a "rich texture" of social life that included not only "warmth" and "familiarity" but also "squabbles," "scandals," "social control," and "limited privacy." Sometimes existing neighborhoods were subdivided in a "process of fission" that was "part of the normal dynamic of the neighborhood system," although these changes were minor. Neighborhood patterns over the centuries are "more striking for their stability than their changes."[38] This is not to say that class-based neighborhood segregation did not occur in Islamic cities. In Cairo gated residential quarters (hara) emerged in the Ottoman period (1517–1798), and they could be poor and at the periphery, or rich and at the center.[39]

According to the historian Lewis Mumford, medieval cities were "composed on the neighborhood principle."[40] They were necessarily pedestrian-based, with populations, at the lower end, of 1,500 inhabitants.[41] A continuous network of streets spaced at approximately quarter-mile intervals, observed in cities like London, was essential for walkability.[42] In smaller towns, inhabitants could readily walk from one end to the other, so that the whole town was the setting for daily life and synonymous with the notion of neighborhood.[43]

Medieval neighborhoods were likely to have developed around a central place, such as a manor, the church, a street, the market, or, in the case of Jerusalem's Jewish Quarter, which started in the early 15th century, a synagogue.[44] Neighborhoods that formed around a manor created a mosaic of "defensible urban compounds" that were socially diverse in that they included servants and tenants clustered around the nexus of a ruling family. Strong families exerted design control on the neighborhood surrounding their residence, which could involve "alignment of facades, the regularization of massive blocks, and the opening of spacious piazzas." In Rome the diversity did not necessarily extend to "undesirables" such as the poor, prostitutes, and religious minorities, who began to be excluded in the 16th century, apparently due to new attitudes about the need to spatially constrain particular social groups.[45]

Some neighborhoods were craft-based. Detailed studies of the social patterning of medieval Marseille show that 70% of craftsmen lived in the neighborhoods associated with their craft.[46] An analysis of maps produced during the period shows the distinct locations of "vicinities," which were sections of streets defined by craft or trade. Neighborhoods in medieval Marseille were thus defined not by parish but by labor and occupation. One map shows 40 of these artisanal and retail vicinities in mid-14th-century Marseille, but there were likely many more.[47]

That preindustrial neighborhoods were highly mixed economically, religiously, occupationally, and, in larger cities, ethnically, has been documented for ancient cities, medieval cities, 15th-century Florence, 17th-century London, and 18th-century Paris, to give just a few examples. As one historian summarized the situation in 17th-century Haarlem in The Netherlands, "bonds between people of the same religion or members of a guild were very important, but so were the bonds of neighborhood."[48] Records of property dispute arbitration in 16th-century Prague show how neighborhood disputes (e.g., over the ownership of a wall) translated not to social segregation but to personal attack and "one's honor in the neighborhood." One neighborhood just south of what is now Wenceslaus Square contained "natives and newcomers, rich and poor," as well as nobility, artisans, laborers, and "individuals practicing a broad array of other trades." The delineated neighborhoods of Renaissance Florence, "whose coordinates linked street corners, bakeries, taverns, the piazza, and the church," constituted approximately 40 "kingdoms," each forging an occupationally mixed world.[49]

In 16th-century Toledo, Spain, although most districts had both rich and poor, predominantly poor districts bordered predominantly wealthy ones. In 17th-century London, "macro-segregation, the location of different social groups in different parts of town, was hardly the rule; meso-segregation—that is, 'around the corner' segregation—was far more common."[50] Homogeneous blocks in the 17th-century Dutch city of Alkmaar were so small that no predominantly rich block was more than a half mile from a predominantly poor one, and most were within a five-minute walk of each other.[51] English cities had a "cellular" social composition, but "the poorest of the poor" were housed "only a few steps away from the self-employed shopkeeper and the small employer."[52]

Neighborhood-scale social mixing in some cities can be verified because of address-specific records showing taxes and rents. For example, this is how historians were able to show a high level of wealth and occupational variation in one ward (*gonfalone*) in 15th-century Florence (alongside "a surprising level of cohesion and unity").[53] Detailed mapping of rent variation by block face in the 17th-century Dutch cities of Alkmaar and Delft revealed a "fine-grained" pattern of differentiation behind what otherwise seemed like homogeneous blocks. Another study of residential segregation in the 16th to 19th centuries in Europe was able to show a complex interweaving of social groups based on data drawn from tax records, rents, and known locations of "recipients of poor relief."[54] In preindustrial Rouen, France, historians mapped the "fine line" separating "producers" (of fine linen, for example) from the "proletariat" living close by on small streets and inner courtyards. Charles Booth's maps showing the streets of London's wealthiest living adjacent to streets inhabited by people "of chronic want" certainly attest to a high level of social mixing still evident in late 19th-century London.[55]

We don't know to what degree residents thought in terms of belonging to an identifiable neighborhood, or whether residents with different wealth statuses were bound together in some way. Certainly the church played a role in defining the neighborhood, not only through common membership but through active participation in small-scale improvements like church decoration. In 15th-century Italy and England, for example, neighborhood residents paid what they could and collaborated in the adornment of their neighborhood church. In Renaissance Florence there was tension between these vernacular, neighborhood-scale efforts and the quest for higher standards of "visual order and clarity," whereby the visual language of Brunelleschi's architecture was pitted against "a neighborhood in social terms."[56] But the chapels and their ornamentation defined the neighborhood in tangible terms, giving residents "a very strong sense of territory."[57]

A few historians have offered specific cases where neighborhood identity did seem to play a role in forging an identity for a diverse population. For example, one study of Georgian towns in England (1680–1840), which were small (rarely more than a 15-minute walk from edge to edge), showed that the towns were organized around neighborhoods with a strong sense of place, attachment to which was elevated by their individual character and distinctiveness. Social networks within each neighborhood were strong, diverse, and essential. Further, neighborhoods did not shut themselves off but instead "depended as much on their exclusivity as on their readiness to welcome incomers."[58] While it is true

that historians have cautioned that the local attachment narrative of the preindustrial city can be overstated, the correction is aimed at changing the source of
attachment and recognizing that solidarity was based on mutual aid rather than
generosity.[59]

But strong neighborhood identity could also coincide with forced social separation. The most conspicuous example is the Jewish ghetto, first established in
Venice in 1516, and a few decades later in Rome. The term "ghetto" later became
the word used for any Jewish neighborhood in Europe, and later of course it
came to mean the segregated realm of poor African Americans.[60] Jewish ghettos
in the 16th century were the result of pure segregation: Jews were not permitted
to reside anywhere except the Jewish quarter, a situation not unlike the formation of black ghettos in the U.S.[61]

Some have challenged the notion that the traditional Jewish quarter was always isolated, arguing that a more integrative Jewish neighborhood identity
was in evidence for centuries prior to the Venetian ghetto. In 13th-century
Trani in southeastern Italy, the Jewish *giudecca* were not walled, and streets
flowed "naturally into the rest of the urban fabric without interruption." There
was regular commercial, political, and social exchange between Christians and
Jews. The *giudecca* were symbolic of a "peaceful coexistence" found around
the Mediterranean, including in medieval Cairo.[62] And in 15th-century Fez,
Morocco, in the Jewish quarter, or *mellah* (estimated to have a population of
about 4,000), residents moved freely, in part because of their role as "middle-
men" linking consumers and producers.[63] The Jewish quarter met the requirements of daily life, but there was fluidity across its boundaries: "Jews entered the
Muslim city for purposes of livelihood, then retreated into their own enclave,
which offered them sanctuary and well-being."[64] This created the ability to transform their "seemingly close quarter into a porous envelope open to the Muslim
city." Although religiously homogeneous, the Middle East Jewish quarter was
diverse on other grounds, where "Jews created their own social pyramid layered
by occupation, family affiliation, and place of origin."[65]

Neighborhood delineation based on religion was capable of producing an
iconic urban pattern. Milan's neighborhoods in the 18th century were relatively small because there was a high density of religious organization, which
was the basis of their definition. There was one religious association for every
650 inhabitants, and a parish served 2,000 (as opposed to Paris, where a parish
served 12,000).[66] The history of Jerusalem is a history of quarters and subquar-
ters, defined by religious sect and ethnicity rather than economic class. Later,
in 19th-century Jerusalem, commercial streets formed the boundaries of each
quarter—Christian, Jewish, Muslim, Armenian—and this had an integrative effect, as individual quarters did not have their own markets. However, this was
unlike other Middle Eastern cities. (Ethnic quarters in Damascus and Shiraz, for

example, had their own markets.) Gradually the names of the old quarters became labels that didn't necessarily match their social makeup. Thus the "Jewish Quarter" contained many Muslims, and the "Kurdish Quarter," according to one census, became majority Christian.[67]

Christianity defined neighborhoods through the Catholic parish.[68] Until the 17th century, properties in London were often identified by parish rather than street address.[69] The parish neighborhoods of Renaissance Venice were immensely important not only as the basis of religious practice but as the boundaries of domestic life. One scholar interpreted Venetian parishes as "female places," distinct from male spaces set in the city's canals and streets. Men did not want their wives and daughters roaming the streets, but within the confines of a parish neighborhood, women enjoyed some ability to venture outside the home. From court documents (covering cases that had to do with the geographic range for exonerating women whose honor had been offended), historians surmise that the male definition of a woman's neighborhood was the parish of residence along with one or two adjacent parishes (in a city with 60 parishes).[70]

In non-Western cities, walls and boundaries had a way of reinforcing social mix. For example, the neighborhoods of 19th-century Shanghai, called *li*, supported wealth-based social mixing through a distinct neighborhood type that combined commercial and residential uses along with "lower-class" and "elite" residents. The "li compound" was bounded by stores facing commercial streets, and at the rear of the shops a wall enclosed the residences. Interior courtyard housing joined the street via a large named portal. The named, mixed-use *li* created a shared collective identity. By the late 19th century, however, the *li* had become a hybrid form that developed in response to the colliding of traditional and modern worlds, Chinese and foreigners. As such it represented a reworking of traditional spaces in which "walls and containment" were replaced with "visibility and openness," and the line between the lower class and the elite was "transgressed."[71]

In the New World, neighborhoods were a distinct feature of the larger seaport cities. The establishment of New York City's neighborhoods has been traced to a 1686 charter that divided lower Manhattan (the settled part) into six wards that were "for the most part" economically and ethnically diverse, until, starting in the early 1800s, a variety of forces worked to differentiate neighborhoods: trade, class, and, above all, race.[72] At a micro-scale, divisions along class lines were evident. In New York City in the late 1700s, there were upper-class neighborhoods near commercial districts, middle-class artisan areas in a middle concentric zone around the core, and poor neighborhoods at the fringes. However, as socially distinct as these neighborhoods might have been, their small size—as witnessed in Europe and elsewhere—meant that they were not far apart, probably no more than a few hundred feet.

There was also a great deal of population churning. In Philadelphia the desire for clusters of social homogeneity worked at cross-purposes with density and real estate value gradients that were pulling people inward toward the center. In other cities, the poor initially lived on higher ground because these areas lacked access (to employment and amenities), and the wealthy lived in higher access locations. Gradually, however, roads and access improved and the wealthy successfully competed for places on higher ground. The spatial juggling of the American city, with groups moving outward and inward, to higher ground and to lower ground, resulted in the mixing of social classes within neighborhoods.[73]

One study of 18th-century New York City identified neighborhoods by combining an archaeological analysis of food remains with variables like wide streets (operating as boundaries), breaks in the street grid, landmarks, and the locations of local services (which, in the 18th-century American city, were limited to taverns, churches, and food markets). The results showed that ethnic and wealth mixing was present, but so was clustering by occupation. The study challenged the more conventional view that neighborhoods were only weakly defined in Western cities prior to the switch from "home-productive" units to a "capital-accumulative" system that gave rise to a neighborhood-seeking labor force.[74]

With the rise of industrial cities in the 19th century, changes in production methods loosened the cultural bonds that had held neighborhoods together for centuries. Industrial capitalism brought division of labor, factory-based employment, and the decline of artisan and guild—changes that complicated neighborhood identity. In Europe the elimination of craft production—weavers, for example—undermined a localized culture that had reinforced neighborhood definition.[75] New practices of land development had a significant impact on neighborhood form, too. An 1835 map of parishes in Lincoln, England, hints at the "astonishing complexity" that resulted when the medieval parishes of the 16th century were overlaid with intervening modern practices of land parcellation.[76]

Urban growth began to stretch out along the roads leading to what had been relatively contained, and often walled, cities (known as *borgate* in Italy, burghs in Northern Europe, and boroughs in England).[77] As boroughs were absorbed into an undifferentiated surrounding sprawl and appeared to be losing their identity, people longed for "true neighborhoods" rather than "peripheral identity."[78] Jerusalem was uniquely successful at transforming its outward growth into distinct neighborhoods. By 1917, 102 neighborhoods had been constructed outside of the Old City—24 Arab, Christian, or mixed, and 78 Jewish. In addition to religious and ethnic sect, each neighborhood was also distinguishable by the initiative that fostered it: philanthropic, private, commercial, or via a "building society." In the British Mandate Period (1920–47), 63 neighborhoods were added outside the Old City, 40 Jewish and 23 Muslim, Christian, or mixed. Some were garden suburbs; some were simple and gridded; some were courtyard-based; all had varying levels of public facilities.[79]

Under industrialization, differences between capital and labor were accentuated, weakening the ability of neighborhoods to "bridge the gulf between classes." New forms of separation and residential differentiation emerged. Previously in the European quarter, shopkeeper and landlord lived alongside their working-class neighbors, creating what has been described as a "collectivist moral economy."[80] But industrialism in the form of factory-based employment increased the distance between work and residence even in the pre-automobile city, and factory workers who had once lived close to their jobs were now burdened by long commutes.[81] The transition "from industrial to finance to corporate capitalism" did not have the effect of producing "higher levels of consumption to successively lower strata" but instead had the effect of differentiating neighborhoods.[82]

Affordable mass transit played a role in this sorting. After 1880 it provided the means for people to segregate into income-defined neighborhoods in a way that had not existed before.[83] Mumford blamed the segregation on "wheeled vehicles" and "the domination of the avenue in planning." Commercialized traffic avenues led to the "sacrifice of the neighborhood" by changing the emphasis in city design "from facilities for settlement to facilities for movement."[84] Wheeled vehicles and avenues made neighborhoods difficult to define and difficult to love, and the city became, according to Mumford, "a nightmare of the undefinable." Lacking definition, the only place neighborhoods held on were in old urban quarters that managed to escape modernization, or where there was deliberate planning: small company towns (see color plate 4), garden cities, and (mostly affluent) designed suburbs.[85] In the planned suburb, attention to design "made people conscious of the neighborhood as an esthetic unit." Rather than dwelling on the elite status of these neighborhoods, Mumford preferred to herald them as raising civic consciousness.[86]

Outside of the planned suburb, expansion enabled by the streetcar in the latter part of the 19th century was not usually in the form of neighborhoods. It was in the form of streets. The result, argues the historian Sam Bass Warner, was "weak and amorphous neighborhood structure," growth not around a commercial or institutional center but arranged around a "historical and accidental traffic pattern." The streetcar metropolis was fragmented and parochial, the result of a physical arrangement based on speculation and class-consciousness rather than community-building. It was the "repetitive habit of little builders" that produced mostly class-based patterns of residential differentiation.[87]

However, within bands of class segregation radiating out from the center city, variation seeped in. Houses in each band were occasionally "mixed in form and finely graded in price," and blocks might have included both "cheap and expensive three-deckers" (structures with three stacked apartment flats). There were exceptions to uniformity: dwellings over stores, cheap parcels of land in undesirable locations (such as next to factory buildings), and the "odds and ends of a subdivision" that resulted in selling some parcels—otherwise destined for single-family housing—for three-decker apartments. The transportation system too sometimes contributed to the mixing, as its irregular growth meant that the "flow of different income groups" was sometimes accelerated and sometimes slowed. The resulting pattern was often variable and mixed.[88]

Throughout the early 20th century, and in some places even later, the neighborhood continued to hold meaning and relevance, despite technological and social change. But such neighborhoods began to be the exception rather than the rule. Freed from an urban form reliant on proximity and walking, neighborhoods were increasingly defined by social homogeneity, or they simply became irrelevant in any traditional sense—that is, as places where neighborhood identity and some degree of social mixing was axiomatic.

Notes

1. "Neighbourhood (n.)," Online Etymology Dictionary, "neighbourhood | neighborhood, n.". OED Online. June 2018. Oxford University Press. http://www.oed.com.proxy.uchicago.edu/view/Entry/125931?redirectedFrom=neighborhood (accessed July 09, 2018).
2. McKenzie, "The Neighborhood II," 344.
3. Mumford, "The City in History," 218.
4. Ibid., 344–63.
5. Keating, "Chicagoland"; Kolb, "Rural Primary Groups."
6. Düring, "Constructing Communities."
7. Ibid., 301.
8. Chen, "Some Ancient Chinese Concepts," 162.
9. For a modern comparison, one team of social network theorists tracing the geography of cell phone calls found that small social groups (fewer than 30 members) tend to be "geographically very tight," but once they exceed 30, the geographical reach expands exponentially; see Onnela et al., "Geographic Constraints," 5.
10. Düring, "Constructing Communities," 302; Dunbar, "Neocortex Size."
11. Cited in Abu-Ghazzeh, "Built Form and Religion," 55.
12. For a review of these ideas, see Chesson, "Households, Houses."
13. Ibid.
14. Keith, "The Spatial Patterns," 66, 77.
15. Mumford, *The City in History*, 74.
16. Keith, "The Spatial Patterns."
17. Stone, *Nippur Neighborhoods*, 3.
18. York et al., "Ethnic and Class Clustering."
19. Keith, "The Spatial Patterns"; York et al., "Ethnic and Class Clustering."
20. Alberti, *The Ten Books*, 000.
21. Wycherley, "Hellenistic Cities."
22. Haselberger et al., *Mapping Augustan Rome*; Lott, *The Neighborhoods*.
23. Lott, *The Neighborhoods*.
24. Kiang, "Visualizing Everyday Life."
25. Adams, *Outline*.

26. As pointed out by York et al., "Ethnic and Class Clustering," who contrast the arguments, for example, of Marcuse in van Kempen. See Xiong, 2000 and Tatsuhiko, 1986, both cited in York et al.
27. Jin, "The Historical Development."
28. Gaubatz, "Looking West."
29. Ibid.
30. Pecar, "Bosnian Dwelling Tradition," 50.
31. Kark and Oren-Nordheim, *Jerusalem and Its Environs*, 21.
32. Lavedan, *Histoire*, 436.
33. York et al., "Ethnic and Class Clustering"; Habib et al., "The Concept of Neighborhood," 2274–75.
34. Mirgholami and Sintusingha, "From Traditional Mahallehs"; Habib et al., "The Concept of Neighborhood," 2274. For more on the *mahallehs* of the Islamic city see Hakim, *Arabic-Islamic Cities*.
35. Stone, *Nippur Neighborhoods*, 4.
36. Abu-Lughod, "The Islamic City." See also Gaube, *Iranian Cities*.
37. Celik, *Urban Forms*, 13–14.
38. Marcus, *The Middle East*, 322.
39. "Cairo's Metropolitan Landscape."
40. Mumford, "The Neighborhood," 257.
41. Ibid., 256–70.
42. Mehaffy et al., "Urban Nuclei."
43. Hohenberg and Lees, *The Making of Urban Europe*, 34.
44. Mumford, "The Neighborhood"; Bar and Rubin, "The Jewish Quarter after 1967."
45. Keyvanian, "Concerted Efforts," 293.
46. Smail, *Imaginary Cartographies*.
47. Ibid.
48. Dorren, "Communities," 177. See also Garrioch, *Neighbourhood and Community*; Boulton, *Neighbourhood and Society*; Warner, *American Urban Form*.
49. Palmitessa, "Arbitration," 125, 129; Rosenthal, "Big Piero," 678.
50. Lesger and Van Leeuwen. "Residential Segregation," 336, 337, quoting Bardet, *Rouen*, 241.
51. Ibid.
52. Mills and Wheeler, *Historic Town Plans of Lincoln*, 20.
53. Eckstein, "Addressing Wealth," 711.
54. Lesger and Van Leeuwen, "Residential Segregation." 335.
55. Charles Booth's maps are available online at "Charles Booth's London: Poverty Maps and Police Notebooks," London School of Economics, http://booth.lse.ac.uk/.
56. Rosenthal, "Big Piero"; Burke, "Visualizing Neighborhood," 707.
57. Garrioch, "Sacred Neighborhoods," 410.
58. Ellis, *The Georgian Town*, 114.
59. Pearson, "Knowing One's Place," 221, 223, 225; Faure, "Local Life."
60. "The ghetto" is a neighborhood type that some consider outdated and not useful; see Small, "Is There Such a Thing as 'the Ghetto'?" See also Duneier, *Ghetto*.
61. Laguerre, *Global Neighborhoods*.
62. Bertagnin et al., "A Mediterranean Jewish Quarter," 41, 44.
63. Miller et al., "Inscribing Minority Space."
64. Ibid., 312.
65. Ibid.
66. Garrioch, "Sacred Neighborhoods," 412, 415.
67. Marcus, *The Middle East*.
68. Worldwide there are now 221,740 Catholic parishes, neighborhoods geographically bound to a particular church and priest. Of those, the U.S. has 17,483, which is virtually unchanged from 1965, when numbers were first reported. A parish can also be secular. England has 10,000 civil parishes, many synonymous with "neighborhood," covering about 35% of the populace. See Center for Applied Research in the Apostolate. "Catholic Data"; U.K. National Archives, Office for National Statistics, "Parishes and Communities."

69. Keene and Harding, *A Survey*, xv, cited in Smail, *Imaginary Cartographies*, 17.
70. Romano, "Gender," 342.
71. Liang, "Where the Courtyard," 482.
72. Scherzer, "Neighborhoods."
73. Abbot, "The Neighborhoods"; Schweitzer, "The Spatial Organization"; Meyer, "The Poor."
74. Rothschild, *New York City Neighborhoods*, 20, 21.
75. Hohenberg and Lees, *The Making of Urban Europe*.
76. Mills and Wheeler, *Historic Town Plans*, 9.
77. Apparently in Italy residents prefer the term "neighborhood" (*quartiere*) rather than "borough" (*borgata*) because the latter implies rural backwardness. See Picone and Schilleci, "A Mosaic of Suburbs."
78. Picone and Schilleci, "A Mosaic of Suburbs," 354–66.
79. Kark and Oren-Nordheim. *Jerusalem and Its Environs*.
80. Pearson, "Knowing One's Place," 223, 225.
81. Faure, "Local Life".
82. Ward, "Environs and Neighbours," 135, 162.
83. Miller, *Visions of Place*.
84. Mumford, *The City in History*, 429.
85. Mumford, "The Neighborhood," 258, 259.
86. Ibid., 260.
87. Warner, *Streetcar Suburbs*, 159, 158, 77.
88. Warner, *Streetcar Suburbs*, 67, 78.

3

Getting the Neighborhood Back

While the opening up of the city and the loss of neighborhood identity was not universally lamented, many planners, sociologists, and social reformers reacted to the decline by trying to plan the neighborhood back into existence. The response to industrial capitalism and the chaotic urbanism it produced (Mumford's "nightmare of the undefinable") was to apportion cities into manageable units and subunits—segmented, patterned, sorted into equal-size circles, squares, or hexagons at regular intervals, nested into hierarchical arrangements, often with mathematical precision. The quest for order and control manifested as the neighborhood unit—an urban partitioning that even ancient cities had practiced.

This had been seen before in the U.S.: the modular growth of James Oglethorpe's early 18th-century plan for Savannah, Georgia, has been described as being in the form of "little neighborhood units" of 40 house lots. (The planning historian John Reps conjectured that these units created a social life driven by "co-operation and neighborly assistance.")[1] In the 19th century, garden cities, model villages, and other idealized units were the more immediate precursors of the 20th-century version: relatively self-contained neighborhoods that had access to services, social life, and nature.

The neighborhood unit proposed by the sociologist Clarence Perry in the 1920s was by far the most famous 20th-century proposal for "getting the neighborhood back." A few developments and planning schemes that immediately preceded him are worth mentioning. One is Forest Hills Gardens, a 1909 development inspired by Ebenezer Howard's Garden City movement and planned by Frederick Law Olmsted Jr.[2] Located on 142 acres in Queens, a short distance from Manhattan, it was here that Perry, while a resident, conceived of his version of the neighborhood unit.

A few years later, in 1912, the City Club of Chicago organized two neighborhood design competitions. One concerned a "micro-community" on an imaginary suburban site a fourth of a mile square (160 acres), and the other focused on designing a neighborhood center. Since the contest rules stipulated

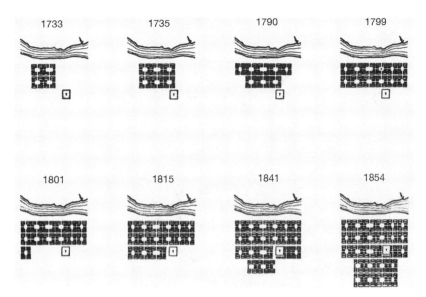

Figure 3.1 Savannah grew by "little neighborhood units" between 1733 and 1856. Source: Image redrawn from Reps, "Town Planning in Colonial Georgia."

Figure 3.2 In the Garden City of Wythenshawe, started in 1929 outside of Manchester, U.K., the neighborhood unit was "as near as possible consummated," a version of the neighborhood unit more like Perry than the later British new towns constructed following World War II. Neighborhoods were bounded by traffic arteries, schools were in the center, and shops were at the intersections of "secondary roads" at intervals of three-fourths of a mile, which meant that each shopping center could draw from four surrounding neighborhoods. Source: Dougill, "Wythenshawe: A Modern Satellite Town." Image: Google Earth.

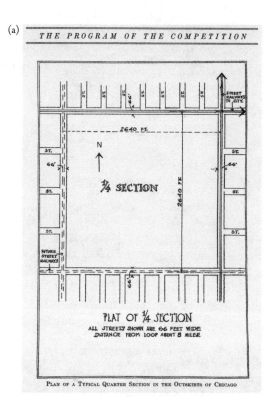

PLAN OF A TYPICAL QUARTER SECTION IN THE OUTSKIRTS OF CHICAGO

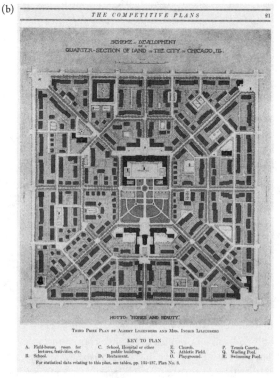

Figure 3.3a and 3.3b Shown is an entry from a 1912 contest sponsored by the City Club of Chicago to design a 1/4 section of land (40 acres or 16 hectares). The entries

that the hypothetical suburban site would have good access to public transit and employment, there was no need to worry about designing a complete community with factories—just a neighborhood. The competitions were an antidote to the Commercial Club's City Beautiful grandiosity, which the landscape architect Jens Jensen (one of the founders of the City Club) was a vocal critic of. The entry by William E. Drummond, an architect who worked for Frank Lloyd Wright (and took over the practice in 1909), which he entitled "Neighborhood Unit," was an inventive proposal that envisioned a whole city interspersed with neighborhood units attached to rail lines and parkland.

In the same year that the City Club of Chicago initiated its neighborhood design contest, 1912, Walter Burley Griffin, a Chicago architect who worked for Frank Lloyd Wright, laid out his neighborhood-based design for Canberra, the new capital of Australia. Griffin had written about neighborhood units well before Perry, arguing for family-oriented, socially segregated "domestic communities" centered on community buildings that should never be more than three blocks away from any household. The neighborhood basis of Canberra is easily discernible in the plan, and as Canberra was built out over the decades, the neighborhoods exhibit a uniform, production-built aesthetic. One critic described the city as a "Sausage Machine that squirts out ready-made neighborhood modules."[3]

In other places around this time, neighborhood proposals were being formed in response to the industrial city. Neighborhood design was conceived as the antidote to the austere rationalism of urban expansion led by developers who had little interest in differentiating space for social purposes. In the Netherlands, for example, progressive leaders tried to stop expansion plans over concerns that the monotonous grid was psychologically and socially harmful. The Dutch architect H. P. Berlage was called in on more than one occasion to redesign neighborhoods in a way reminiscent of Camillo Sitte, with streets terminating in public squares. In this way Dutch planners put Amsterdam's perimeter block in service to the creation of complete and protected neighborhoods.[4]

Also around this time the U.S. government became involved in financing neighborhood-based plans for small communities. In Bridgeport, Connecticut,

---

Figure 3.3a and 3.3b Continued
were the equivalent of neighborhood units and predated Clarence Perry. The object of the competition was to show "the essentials of good housing in the broadest sense." The imaginary sites were to be "on the level prairie about 8 miles distant from the business district of the City of Chicago," 4 miles from industrial plants, and "served by street car lines on two sides." Submissions to the City Club of Chicago's neighborhood design contest achieved everything Perry later sought in terms of boundaries, open spaces, locations of shops and facilities, and an internal street system. Shown (b) is the third prize winner. Source: Yeomans and City Club of Chicago, *City Residential Land Development*.

Figure 3.4 The neighborhood-based plan of Canberra, Australia, by Walter Burley Griffin. Source: Original 1918 plan of Canberra drawn by Walter Burley Griffin (public domain), https://commons.wikimedia.org/wiki/File:Canberra_1918_plan.jpg..

Yorkship Village in Camden, New Jersey, and Wilmington, Delaware, well-serviced planned neighborhoods provided wartime housing within walking distance of industrial sites. The program was short-lived, as the neighborhood quality was believed to be too high to justify further governmental association (in addition to the claim that government involvement was too socialistic), and direct subsidy was ended in 1919, just after the war.

The next neighborhood unit experiment was Sunnyside Gardens in Queens, New York, designed by Clarence Stein and Henry Wright and constructed between 1924 and 1928. The neighborhood principles developed there were subsequently applied to other famous planned neighborhoods in the U.S.: Radburn, New Jersey; Chatham Village outside of Pittsburgh; the Greenbelt Towns; and Baldwin Hills in Los Angeles. The designs were strongly influenced by the writings of Clarence Perry.

Although the neighborhood unit as a concept had earlier roots (historians argue that Perry "appropriated" Drummond's concept),[5] Perry articulated the neighborhood unit's theoretical basis. Following a five-year study of neighborhood concepts (drawing from many sources, including the Russell Sage Foundation's *Social Surveys of American Cities* and Edward Ward's social center movement), Perry published his famous articulation of the neighborhood unit in 1929 as part of the massive *Regional Plan of New York and Environs.*[6] Perry's unit boiled down to six principles: population based on what was needed to support an elementary school, a multipurpose school at the center, local shopping at the periphery along intersecting main streets, arterial streets at the outside forming a boundary, interconnected, pedestrian-oriented internal streets for local traffic, and small parks scattered throughout. (Perry wanted small parks in the quadrant of each neighborhood, ideally making up 10 percent of the total area; there was to be one acre of playground area for every 72 families.)[7] The principles could be applied to new sites as well as the inner city, although the latter, Perry argued, had to be unencumbered, meaning eminent domain would be needed.

Perry's neighborhood extended over 160 acres (the acreage of a half mile square, within which Perry placed a circle with a fourth-mile radius), with a density of 10 units per acre and a population of 5,000—which was the population needed to support an elementary school. At the time the population parameters necessary to support a school could "be fixed with some accuracy," falling between 2,000 and 8,000 residents, with a target size of 5,000 and a "normal" size of 50 to 250 acres. If dwelling types were mixed in order to accommodate variation of family type—a practice that was strongly advocated by planners at the time—the target density for a neighborhood of 5,000 was 10.8 units per acre.[8]

Sunnyside Gardens, where Perry lived, was smaller in terms of acreage, with 1,200 housing units on 56 acres (about one-third of the size of Perry's neighborhood unit). Geographically, 160 acres is the size of one-quarter of one of Thomas Jefferson's land sections laid out in the Land Ordinance of 1785. Based on the number of elementary schools and the approximately 5,000 residents (it was presumed) who surrounded them, one report claimed there were approximately 12,000 Perry-size neighborhoods in the U.S. in 1931.[9] It is worth noting that Ebenezer Howard's Garden Cities were composed of neighborhoods, called "wards," and the six wards of Howard's garden city diagram were each intended for a population of 5,000—exactly the same number Perry was aiming for.

Perry's neighborhood unit idea received special billing at President Herbert Hoover's Conference on Home Building and Home Ownership held in 1931. From there it was rapidly disseminated via government regulations, planning textbooks, chambers of commerce, and social service agencies.[10] The basic outlines of neighborhood as a place of "beauty, convenience, and social opportunity" were reflected in the U.S. housing acts, urban renewal legislation, the new

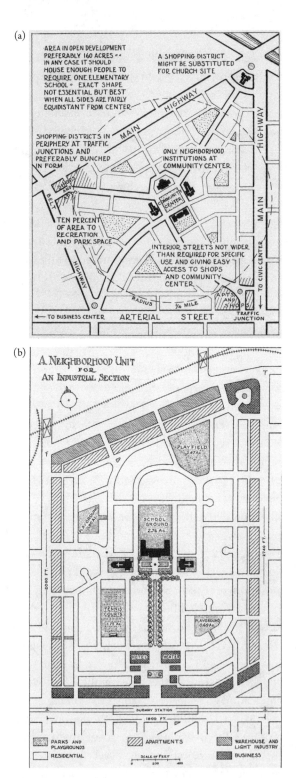

Figure 3.5a and 3.5b Perry devised numerous iterations of the basic neighborhood unit, including one for an industrial area. Source: Perry, *Neighborhood and Community Planning.*

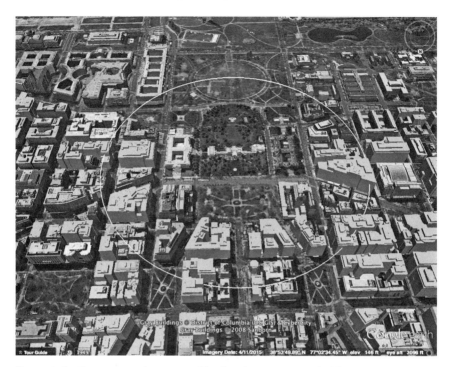

Figure 3.6 Clarence Perry's 1929 neighborhood unit was intended for 5,000 residents on 160 acres. Shown is Perry's neighborhood in relation to the White House in Washington, D.C. Source: Google Earth.

towns movement, and virtually any housing-related program or development proposal that had a wider scope than the individual dwelling unit. As we shall see in subsequent chapters, this brought with it a host of criticisms of insularity, segregation, and social control.

A large part of its popularity and rapid dissemination was its appeal to the real estate community; developers could take it and run with it. And they did, mostly in forms that greatly watered down Perry's principles of unit-type integration, walkability, and self-containment. Some have argued that the neighborhood unit paradigm filled the need for efficient home building on a mass scale, a scale unknown before World War II, when the work of subdividers and home builders were two different operations. When subdividing and home building merged, and the large-scale housing developer was born, the neighborhood unit fulfilled a needed function: building in cellular units.[11] By the low-density standards of this suburban expansion, however, planners realized that Perry's 160 acres would not be enough to sustain schools and commerce. Thus San Jose's 1958 master plan, for example, delineated 154 neighborhoods that had an average size in terms of gross acreage of 480 acres—three times the size of Perry's unit. (Their average population was kept at a Perry-size level of 5,850.)

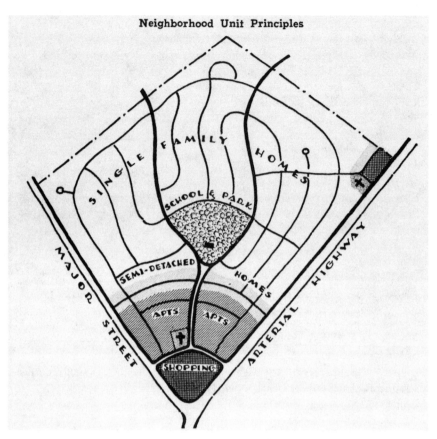

Figure 3.7 The neighborhood unit was popularized by the Urban Land Institute through its publication *The Community Builders Handbook*, which first appeared in 1947. Source: Urban Land Institute Community Builders' Council, *The Community Builders Handbook*.

Radburn, New Jersey, built in 1929, is important in neighborhood planning history because it was iconic and pathbreaking, described as the first implementation of the "modern" idea of the neighborhood. (Clarence Stein, architect of Radburn, called it "The Radburn Idea.") It shows the influence of Perry's neighborhood unit combined with a strong dose of Howard's Garden City: larger, superblock-based neighborhoods that were supposed to form a "complete garden city" for 25,000, a goal that was never achieved. Like Perry's unit, the neighborhoods had a school and playground at the center, but they were overlapping rather than self-contained units, with green spaces rather than streets as boundaries.[12] Stein doubled Perry's size—to half-square-mile neighborhoods (320 acres) for 7,500 to 10,000 people—as a more realistic population threshold for providing neighborhood services.

The next neighborhood unit experiments were FDR's New Deal–era Greenbelt towns—Greendale, Wisconsin; Greenbelt, Maryland; and Greenhills, Ohio. The "towns" had fewer residents than Perry's neighborhood unit, although each was conceived as "in effect, a single neighborhood."[13] In 1941 Stein adapted his "Radburn Idea" for Baldwin Hills Village in Los Angeles. Here the break with Perry's schematic design was carried even further, with its superblocks, complete separation of pedestrian and auto, and the "park as community heart and backbone." Stein hoped that the separated elements would crystallize into a "functional unity."[14] In the decades that followed, neighborhoods conceived as grouped housing around a central open space were imagined by modernist planners a thousand different ways. (The adoption of modernism was unsurprising given the time period and the domination of the Congrès Internationaux d'Architecture Moderne and its affiliated architects: Le Corbusier, José Luis Sert, Walter Gropius, Edmund Bacon, and Louis Kahn.)

Stein's neighborhood unit experiments received widespread, mostly positive reviews. Well-known writers like Lewis Mumford and Catherine Bauer applauded the neighborhood unit in their books. In 1943 the magazine *Architectural Forum* devoted two issues to neighborhood design. Louis Kahn published *You and Your Neighborhood: A Primer for Neighborhood Planning* in 1944 extolling the virtues of neighborhood planning, and Philadelphia's redevelopment under Edmund Bacon was carried out "on a neighborhood basis."[15]

These neighborhood plans were modernist and inspired by the Congrès Internationaux d'Architecture Moderne (CIAM). This means they tended to separate land uses, prioritize the automobile over the pedestrian, reject the street as public space, create superblocks that promoted containment and insularity, treat buildings as isolated objects in space rather than as part of a larger interconnected urban fabric, reject traditional elements like squares and plazas, demolish large areas of the city to make unfettered places for new built forms, and create enclosed malls and sunken plazas that deadened public space. The modernist version of the neighborhood unit was wrapped up in all of these flawed planning ideas.

Planning by neighborhood unit spread across the globe. In Israel, Artur Glikson's successful planning of Radburn-like multiuse, centrally located community buildings and schools as neighborhood focal points throughout the 1950s was prototypical.[16] Versions of the neighborhood unit showed up in such far-reaching places as Kuwait, Brasilia, Sasolburg in South Africa, Elizabeth in Australia, Chandigarh in India, and throughout China, Europe, and the USSR. City-building via cellular unit, with just the right distribution of services and social spaces, seemed the logical answer to post–World War II rebuilding.[17] In India self-contained neighborhoods were thought to have "a special appeal to the people of under-developed countries" because of their ability to facilitate the kind of self-governance rural people moving to cities were used to. As one planner put it, "A village-like neighbourhood makes it easier for them to understand their civic responsibilities than a large amorphous city."[18]

It was the post–World War II British new towns (there were 10 built in the 1940s) that most embraced the neighborhood unit.[19] The theory behind the neighborhood unit was endorsed by a widely disseminated publication known as the *Dudley Report,* followed by official sanction in the 1944 *Greater London Plan.* Despite subsequent criticism by prominent planners, a 1952 survey showed that 79% of British planners were actively implementing neighborhood units. And the British transferred neighborhood-unit planning to other parts of the world, especially Africa and the Middle East, first in the 1920s and then after World War II—in both periods for the purpose of subjugation or, as the leading colonialist of the time, Eric Dutton, put it, to extend "goodwill" and "rule."[20]

Neighborhoods in the British new towns after World War II were also larger than Perry's, set at the 5,000 to 9,000 population range, often with 10,000 and some as high as 12,000 residents.[21] Those closer to 10,000 serviced at least two primary schools instead of one (as in Perry's scheme). Densities were relatively high by American standards, although critics claimed an "absence of urbanity."[22] Densities of a sample of 10 neighborhood units as of 1961, selected from across

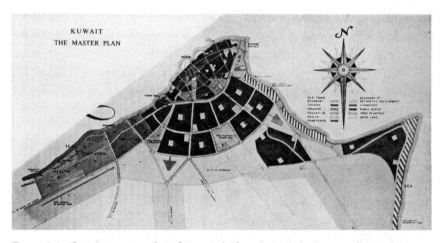

Figure 3.8 The 1952 master plan of Kuwait, laid out by British planners, featured eight neighborhood units of 6,000 residents, each with a mosque, shops, public hall, site for industry, six nursery schools, and two primary schools (one for girls, one for boys). Each neighborhood was to have 160 houses grouped around a nursery school. Source: Macfarlane, "Planning an Arab Town."

the new towns, showed that net density was usually 30 to 50 people per acre. The densities were planned on the basis of travel distance to "social facilities," especially shops and primary schools (see Table 3.1).

New towns in Britain were both new and heterogeneous (since social balance was required); this meant that neither history nor homogeneity could be used to instill neighborhoods with a sense of identity. To address this, neighborhood design was looked at from every which way, and a variety of different schemes were proposed. Variation in street patterns, locations of schools, grouping of housing, and shopping center location was supposed to provide local identity.[23]

European cities outside of the U.K. had their own postwar neighborhood unit experiments. Most of them, as elsewhere, were based on modernist

Table 3.1 **Area, population, and density**

Neighborhood Unit	Size in Area	Planned Population	Net Residential Density (ppa*)	Gross Neighborhood density (ppa)
WEST (Glenrothes)	745	21,000	50.7	28.2
ANDEFIELD (Hamel Hempstead)	570	12,000	30.0	21.0
BEANFIELD (Corby)	440	10,900	40.5	24.8
THE MURRAY (E. Kilbride)	380	10,000	52.0	26.3
BROADWATER (Hatfield)	449	9,650	33.0	21.5
OXLEASE & S. HATFIELD (Hatfields)	353	8,500	33.3	24.0
LANGLEY GREEN (Grawley)	288	8,200	41.5	28.5
PRIESTWOOD (Bracknell)	287	7,800	—	27.2
KINGSWOOD (Basildon)	260	6,00	38.0	23.0
CROES-Y-CEILOG (Cwmbran)	252	5,400	40.0	21.4

*persons per acre

Source: Goss, "Neighbourhood Units in British New Towns," 81.

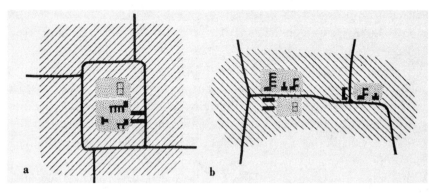

Figure 3.9 This image from Sir Frederick Gibberd's *Town Design* shows "varieties of pattern" in the relationship between housing and social services, patterns "so varied that we can do no more than touch on a few of the more distinctive types." Residential areas are cross-hatched; building outlines show shops and schools. Each neighborhood also has a "sports ground." Source: Gibberd, *Town Design*.

spatial planning principles, especially superblocks. In Sweden the neighborhood unit (*grannskapsenheten*) was popularized by the publication in Swedish of Mumford's exaltation of the neighborhood unit in *The Culture of Cities*, as well as the adoption of the neighborhood unit in the 1944 *Greater London Plan*.[24] The Dutch implemented the neighborhood unit idea vigorously in the 1950s and 1960s under the usual influences: Perry, Mumford, and the Greater London Plan, infused with a heavy dose of CIAM's modernist design ethic of "standardization, repetition and functionality." A highly regularized and hierarchic scheme for neighborhood unit planning throughout the Netherlands was ascribed the usual benefits as an antidote to social anonymity and the unhealthy, chaotic, war-torn country.[25] Greece embraced neighborhood planning in the 1960s and 1970s, when at least 50 government-built neighborhood units were constructed.

Germany's experience with the neighborhood unit was complicated by the neighborhood's prewar association with Nazism, as well as an associated cultural tradition that elevated rural village life over big cities.[26] However, the connection between Nazi ideology and neighborhood form (the Nazis had a natural affinity for controlled settlement cells), which had been inspired by T. Fritsch's nationalistic *The Future of the City* (1896), led to a kind of mothballing of neighborhood planning after World War II, at least overtly. After the war, neighborhood planning was pursued under different guises, including architect Hans Reichow's more ecologically inspired "organic neighborhood." It was not until the 1990s that the neighborhood as a planning unit gained traction again, this time as a hoped-for way of combating social exclusion.[27]

The appeal of urban growth via neighborhood unit extended to Asia. There the 20th-century experience of the planned neighborhood was a blend of historical traditions and Western models. In Japan the notion of small, self-contained and self-governed urban units, connected to or embedded within a larger metropolis, appealed to the Japanese tradition of *machi*, which the planner Nishiyama Uzô called "life units." (The first evidence of a planned neighborhood unit in Japan, the *machi*, is in Kyoto in the year 793.)[28] Theodore Bestor's book *Neighborhood Tokyo* traces the historical roots of the city's unique neighborhood system, which sustains a sense of small-town life in a burgeoning metropolis. Neighborhood associations are run by a minority of residents, dominated by old-timers who hang on to neighborhood traditions and governance as a means of counteracting the influx of wealthier newcomers, yet the compact Tokyo neighborhood is mixed by Western standards, combining apartments and houses, small factories, and a shopping street, all interwoven with a dense network of streets and alleys.[29]

As in Perry's scheme, neighborhoods were often organized around an elementary school. The emulation could be direct: a 1938 proposal for a neighborhood in Datong, Japan, was copied from a neighborhood plan for Detroit.[30] By the 1940s Japanese planners were feeling the influence of Western proposals that included not only Perry's work but that of the German planner and Nazi economist Gottfried Feder.[31]

In China the neighborhood unit gained traction in the 1920s under American influence (although in fact a form of planned neighborhood unit had existed in China for thousands of years). U.S. planners sought to combine "neighborhood planning standards of 20th Century United States with the social institutions of 5th century B.C. China," and the result was a neighborhood unit, or *bao*, of 2,000 people, with 360 families serving one elementary school of 200 to 400 students.[32] One American planner and exporter of the neighborhood unit, Norman Gordon, wrote in 1946 that the neighborhood unit was endemic to Chinese family structure in that it allowed related families to live together in one place. In the postwar period, the neighborhood unit in China was mostly about orderly growth and service efficiency in rebuilding.[33] As elsewhere, the thinking was that Chinese cities were disorganized and unhealthy, and the neighborhood unit was adopted as a method of social organization and reform. Before the war, the Chinese had experienced the quest for neighborhood efficiency when the Japanese redesigned Xinjing (now Changchun) according to neighborhood unit principles during their occupation from 1931 to 1945.[34]

Chinese work units, known as *danwei*, developed after the 1949 Socialist Revolution and were a neighborhood form embodying socialist order. Housing, workplaces, and services were integrated, although there was significant variation and adaptation by workers, making their degree of "preplanning" a somewhat loose characterization. Some regularities in their design were ubiquitous: they were walled; had a flexible, hierarchical, and interconnected street system that "lead to places where people go"; close integration of living and working quarters; and they were modernist in style.[35] Unlike the American and British versions of the neighborhood unit that had green space and arterials as mechanisms of self-containment, with schools and community centers at the center, Chinese work units were surrounded by walls and gates, with the workplace and administrative complex at the center. In addition, the Chinese work unit did not have the same need to use cul-de-sacs to separate automobiles from pedestrians, as the main forms of transportation were biking and walking.[36]

China acquired another version of the neighborhood unit from the Soviet Union: the *mikrorayon*, clusters of five to eight superblock neighborhoods of 8,000 to 12,000 people on about 125 acres (equivalent to a "pedestrian shed," or a circle with a quarter-mile radius). There were at least 1,500 households.[37] In established cities as well as new towns, the highly regularized *mikrorayon* formed the basis of massive residential growth in the postwar period (see color plate 5). In 1961 alone in Moscow, 350 apartment units were built each day.[38] The basis of the communist city was thus the grouped—and neighborhood-based—apartment building; as the authors of *The Ideal Communist City* put it, the apartment building is "unthinkable apart from the existence of the whole."[39] Soviet planners argued that the *mikrorayon* was more organic, egalitarian, collective, and spatially integrated (not isolated in the suburbs) than the American version of the neighborhood unit, and yet the goals were similar: to "help the organization of collective life, facilitate people's commute, and decrease traffic." The scale and form were different, however. Although one level of neighborhood contained superblocks of 50- to 100-meter radius, called *kvartals*, with 1,000 to 1,500 population (and thus small by U.S. standards), the practice of lining the rim of the neighborhood with tall buildings to form a peripheral facade was a significant departure.[40]

Soviet planners, who exerted influence throughout Asia, transferred these superblock-based neighborhood units to Chinese and other cities (notably Vietnamese) as orthodoxy. At first, Chinese planners agreed that superblock neighborhoods were not as wasteful or bourgeois as traditional neighborhood unit design. The neighborhood unit, particularly its self-containment aspect, was considered entirely consistent with Marxism. It made sense in this context, where the emphasis was on connecting residence and workplace. The neighborhood units of China's satellite cities, constructed in the 1950s, were thus clustered around a commercial center or factory, in addition to the standard neighborhood elements of shops, schools, and clinics. Later in the 1950s, however, following Stalin's death, superblock neighborhood units fell out of favor in China, and many considered the Soviet version of the neighborhood unit an unfortunate transfer, especially when people realized that the perimeter blocks meant that some units had poor ventilation, were westward facing (which was undesirable because of too much sun in the summer), and were left unprotected from street noise and pollution.[41]

Figure 3.10 The population in a Soviet-era *mikrorayon* (see color plate 4) is comparable to that of the old town of Lucca, Italy, one of the few remaining cities with Renaissance-era surrounding walls still intact. It has an area of about 250 acres (not including the encircling green space) and a population of 7,500. Source: Google Earth.

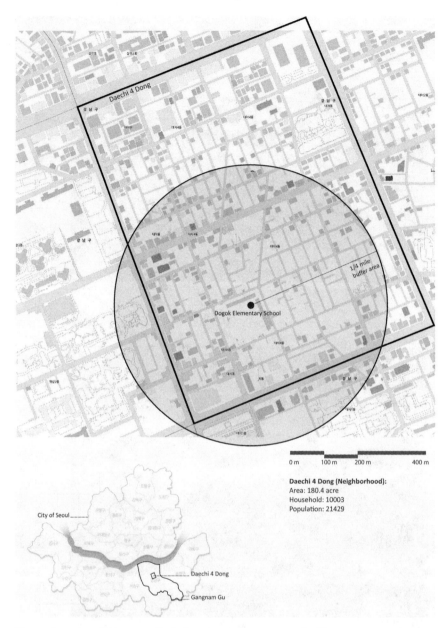

Figure 3.11 Seoul, Korea, is divided into 25 autonomous and self-governing Gu districts and 522 neighborhoods (Dong) that provide "close, first-hand" services for residents. Shown here is a neighborhood of more than 21,000 residents on 180 acres. Source: Seoul City Government, "Administrative Districts." Image: Courtesy of Sungduck Lee.

By the late 1950s the Soviet superblock version of the neighborhood unit in China was replaced by a very high-density Chinese version, the *xiaoqu*, which often had double Perry's population size (5,000) on one-fifth of the acreage (see color plate 6). The design was large-grid superblocks surrounded by arterials, with shopping at the periphery and quieter internal streets designed to keep out through-traffic. The developments were characterized as some variant of work unit, company town, or neighborhood unit, sometimes intertwined. The amalgamation of district, unit, and town was replicated across China.[42]

South America also embraced the neighborhood unit. In Venezuela in the 1960s, planners wanted rapid urbanization to be structured in a neighborhood-like, cellular way (although they used the term "environmental area" rather than "neighborhood unit" because by then the term had taken on negative baggage). But as a system of decentralization, the neighborhood unit did not come close to addressing the problem of poorly serviced and overcrowded cities in South America. (Critics blamed the lack of a British-style New Towns Act that would have provided a larger legal and policy framework with sufficient funding.) In

Figure 3.12 The neighborhood unit in China, the *xiaoqu*, consists of superblocks with apartment towers. They were initially 4 to 8 stories (shown here), but by the 1980s they were over 10 stories. The image is from Wuhan, in central China. Source: Vmenkov, https://commons.wikimedia.org/wiki/File:Wuhan_-_apartment_complex_near_Wuchang_Train_Station_-_P1050164.JPG

Lima, Peru, for example, several neighborhood units, accommodating a total of 3,000 families, were built in the mid-1950s on the outskirts of the city. They were affordable only to the middle class and above. No wonder they commanded that price—the need at the time was housing for 80,000 families.[43]

(a)

(b)

Figure 3.13a and 3.13b Neighborhood units in Lima and Callao, Peru, (a) 1956 and (b) present day. Source: (a) Cole, "Some Town Planning Problems of Greater Lima." (b) Google Earth.

By the latter half of the 20th century, the modernist versions of the neighborhood unit, especially in the U.S., had been thoroughly discounted, most famously by Jane Jacobs. But the appeal of planning by neighborhood unit held on. (It is reasonable to assume that the approximately 870 planned suburbs listed in Robert A. M. Stern's *Paradise Planned* are predominantly based on neighborhood form of one type or another.) In the early 1980s, the New Urbanism movement attempted to resurrect Perry's scheme. The New Urbanists recognized that Perry and those associated with the neighborhood unit had at least been able to present a concrete idea about what a neighborhood was supposed to be, and this still resonated. And it was possible to revise Perry's basic model to address different goals, such as Doug Farr's environmentally-focused version (see color plate 7). The New Urbanists extracted what they considered the most useful parts of Perry's model, boiled

Table 3.2 **The thirteen physical attributes of neighborhoods (paraphrased)**

1. The neighborhood is the increment of planning. A single freestanding neighborhood is a village.

2. The neighborhood is limited in size to a 5-minute walk (.25 miles, 400 meters) from edge to center, where the needs of daily life are available.

3. Neighborhood streets are in an interconnected network, allowing multiple routes to destinations.

4. Neighborhood streets are spatially defined by buildings.

5. Neighborhood buildings are diverse in function but compatible in terms of size and configuration on the lot.

6. The civic buildings of a neighborhood are located in important areas, for example, attached to squares.

7. Neighborhood open space is defined rather than amorphous.

8. Everyone living in a neighborhood has independence of movement, since activities of daily life are within walking distance.

9. Reduced auto trips means less traffic and lower costs.

10. Human-scale streets and squares provide opportunity for social interaction.

11. Transit is made feasible by providing sufficient density near transit stops.

12. There is a full range of housing types and workplaces, allowing age and economic integration.

13. Civic buildings and spaces encourage democratic initiatives.

Source: Thadani, *The Language of Towns and Cities*, 429.

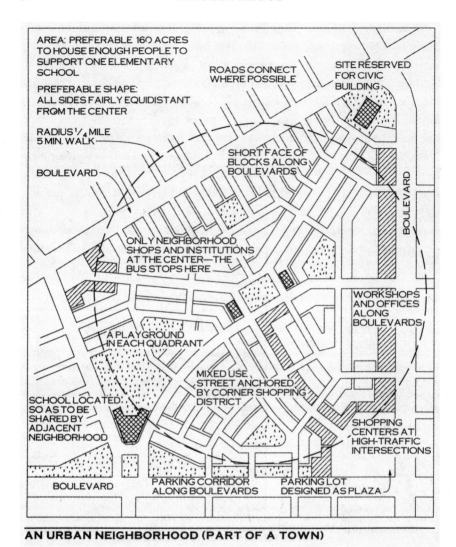

AREA: PREFERABLE 160 ACRES TO HOUSE ENOUGH PEOPLE TO SUPPORT ONE ELEMENTARY SCHOOL

PREFERABLE SHAPE: ALL SIDES FAIRLY EQUIDISTANT FROM THE CENTER

RADIUS 1/4 MILE 5 MIN. WALK

BOULEVARD

ROADS CONNECT WHERE POSSIBLE

SITE RESERVED FOR CIVIC BUILDING

SHORT FACE OF BLOCKS ALONG BOULEVARDS

ONLY NEIGHBORHOOD SHOPS AND INSTITUTIONS AT THE CENTER—THE BUS STOPS HERE

BOULEVARD

WORKSHOPS AND OFFICES ALONG BOULEVARDS

A PLAYGROUND IN EACH QUADRANT

SCHOOL LOCATED SO AS TO BE SHARED BY ADJACENT NEIGHBORHOOD

MIXED USE STREET ANCHORED BY CORNER SHOPPING DISTRICT

SHOPPING CENTERS AT HIGH-TRAFFIC INTERSECTIONS

BOULEVARD

PARKING CORRIDOR ALONG BOULEVARDS

PARKING LOT DESIGNED AS PLAZA

AN URBAN NEIGHBORHOOD (PART OF A TOWN)

Figure 3.14 Perry's model was updated by Duany, Plater-Zyberk & Co. in 1999. The center is replaced with shops and institutions, with the elementary school at the periphery, shared with adjoining neighborhoods. Source: Plater-Zyberk et al., *The Lexicon of the New Urbanism.*

it down to 13 attributes, proclaimed traditional neighborhood form as central to urbanism, and threw out the modernist form that had allowed giantism, car dominance, and isolated buildings to spoil what they believed were the neighborhood unit's time-honored qualities (see Table 3.2).[44] The neighborhood endured, this time forming the central piece of an urbanist trilogy: region, neighborhood, and block.[45]

An URBAN QUARTER
CONtains and PROmotes
all the Qualities of a
CITY

IN – CLUSIVE

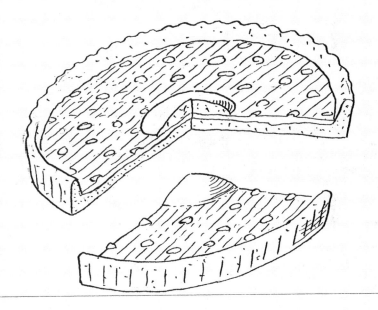

All is Permitted & Promoted
that is not strictly forbidden

Figure 3.15 Leon Krier's notion of the urban quarter, a pedestrian-scaled neighborhood with "an inevitable basis in limits," has all the "pieces of the pie" within it. The ideal was realized in Poundbury, an English new town designed by Krier and built in the 1990s. The urban quarter is meant to have 1,500 people on 35 hectares (86 acres).

Notes

1. Because of the planning work required, as well as Savannah's peripheral location, only one other place—Brunswick, Georgia—followed Oglethorpe's "novel and effective neighborhood pattern." Reps, "Town Planning in Colonial Georgia," 283.
2. The designers were influenced by Raymond Unwin and Barry Parker and their planning innovations in the U.K., especially Letchworth and Hampstead Garden Suburb. For an excellent history, see Klaus, *A Modern Arcadia*.
3. Fischer, "Canberra," 183.
4. Stieber, *Housing Design and Society in Amsterdam*.
5. Johnson, "Origin of the Neighbourhood Unit," 241.
6. Perry, *Neighborhood and Community Planning*. Some of these neighborhood ideas had been published previously in 1926, based on a 1923 lecture he gave at a joint meeting of the American Sociological Society and the National Community Center Association. For an excellent summary of the neighborhood unit's design principles and their antecedents, see Patricios, "Urban Design Principles."
7. Adams, *Recent Advances in Town Planning*.
8. American Public Health Association, *Planning the Neighborhood*, 2.
9. Deering, "Social Reconstruction," 228.
10. Brody, Jason. "The Neighbourhood Unit Concept."
11. Rofe, "Space and Community."
12. Patricios, "Urban Design Principles."
13. Stein, "Toward New Towns for America (Continued)."
14. Stein, *Toward New Towns for America*, 169. On Greendale, see Dahir, "Greendale Comes of Age."
15. Bacon, "Urban Redevelopment"; Ayad, "Louis I. Kahn and Neighborhood Design."
16. Marans, "Neighborhood Planning."
17. Panerai et al., *Urban Forms*. See also Herbert, "The Neighbourhood Unit Principle"; Patricios, "The Neighborhood Concept," 70–90.
18. Koenigsberger, "New Towns in India," 109.
19. Herbert, "The Neighbourhood Unit Principle."
20. Myers, "Designing Power."
21. Bailey and Pill. "The Continuing Popularity."
22. Goss, "Neighbourhood Units in British New Towns," 81.
23. Gibberd, *Town Design*.
24. Nyström and Lundström, "Sweden."
25. Wassenberg, "The Netherlands."
26. Schubert, "The Neighbourhood Paradigm."
27. Eckardt, "Germany."
28. Cowan, *The Dictionary of Urbanism*.
29. Bestor, *Neighborhood Tokyo*, 1. Citizen participation via the *machi* in Japan is thoroughly explored in Sorensen and Funck, *Living Cities in Japan*.
30. Hein, "Machi Neighborhood."
31. Keeble, *Principles and Practice*; Hein, "Machi Neighborhood'"; Sorensen and Funck, *Living Cities in Japan*.
32. Gordon, "China and the Neighborhood Unit."
33. Lu, "Building the Chinese Work Unit"; Lu, "Travelling Urban Form."
34. Liu, "Other Modernities."
35. Lu, "Building the Chinese Work Unit," 64.
36. Ibid., 79. See also Lu, *Remaking Chinese Urban Form*.
37. Herbert, "The Neighbourhood Unit Principle."
38. Frolic, "The Soviet City."
39. Gutnov, *The Ideal Communist City*, 74.
40. Lu, "Building the Chinese Work Unit',', 76.

41. Lu, "Travelling Urban Form."
42. Lu, "Travelling Urban Form."
43. Cole, "Some Town Planning Problems."
44. Many have made this critique. See, for example, Cullen, *Concise Townscape*.
45. See Talen and Congress for the New Urbanism, *Charter of the New Urbanism*.

4

Reinventing the Neighborhood

As the historical experience of neighborhood waned, and as it became clear that reinstating the neighborhood via preset plans was going to be a significant challenge, interest in expanding the definition of neighborhood grew. The approach was to reconceptualize what the neighborhood actually was rather than try to get the neighborhood back through physical planning. Reinvention was thus not a matter of tweaking the size and composition of neighborhood. It was more fundamental than that. It involved opening the door to concepts that, before the 20th century, would have seemed completely alien to what a neighborhood was.

Now detached from any traditional, physical understanding involving centers and boundaries, the idea of neighborhood could be expanded to investigate new modes of inquiry in a whole range of fields, such as biology, computer science, psychology, and physics. And since neighborhood was no longer a matter of local experience in a traditional geographic sense, the definition could be based on cognition, housing markets, police precincts, or social media usage. The newly acquired, open-ended approach to neighborhood definition was liberating, extraneous, or disabling, depending on one's point of view.

This chapter summarizes some of these neighborhood definitions to give a sense of the variety that now exists and to show how many of these definitions challenge conventional understanding of the neighborhood as a relevant and meaningful setting for daily life.

The hundreds of definitions now ascribed to neighborhood vary by how and whether people, home, place, morphology, territory, behavior, perception, or governance is prioritized. Researchers look for a definition that is "theoretically congruent with the dynamics of interest."[1] For example, if the interest is drug trafficking in neighborhoods, then a neighborhood is determined by street intersections. If the interest is neighborhood schools, then school district boundaries define neighborhood. If the interest is social connection, it may be useful to look at resident-defined neighborhoods composed of networks of pedestrian streets along which social interaction occurs.[2] If the purpose of a neighborhood

neighbourhood | neighborhood, *n.*

Text size: A A

View as: <u>Outline</u> | Full entry   Quotations: Show all | <u>Hide all</u> Keywords: On | <u>Off</u>

Pronunciation: Brit. ▶ /ˈneɪbəhʊd/ , U.S. /ˈneɪbər̩(h)ʊd/

Forms: see NEIGHBOUR *n.* and -HOOD *suffix*; also 15 **neghburode**, 15 **neighbrod**; *Sc.* (*Shetland*) 19–**neebrid**. (Show Less)

Frequency (in current use): ●●●●●● ● ●

Etymology: Formed within English, by derivation. **Etymons:** NEIGHBOUR *n.*, -HOOD *suffix*.
< NEIGHBOUR *n.* + -HOOD *suffix*. Compare NEIGHBOURHEAD *n.*, and earlier NEIGHBOURED *n.*, NEIGHBOURSHIP *n.* (Show Less)

I. Concrete uses.

1.

a. The people living near to a certain place or within a certain range; neighbours collectively.   Thesaurus »

> a1425 (▸?a1387) LANGLAND *Piers Plowman* (Cambr. Ff.5.35) C. VII. 98 (*MED*), Neȝburhade [c1400 *Huntington* þenne was ich a-redy..to lacke myn neghebores].
>
> 1686 tr. J. Chardin *Trav. Persia* 73 The Commanders of this Fortress make always Leagues with the Neighborhood.
>
> 1766 O. GOLDSMITH *Vicar of Wakefield* I. iv. 34 The whole neighbourhood came out to meet their minister.
>
> 1802 E. PARSONS *Myst. Visit* III. 204 The neighbourhood had scandalized [her].
>
> 1878 T. HARDY *Return of Native* I. I. ii. 20 Who is she? One of the neighbourhood?
>
> 1955 G. GORER *Exploring Eng. Char.* iv. 55 The neighbourhood, the local group, is not only the area of associations which may be more or less voluntary and more or less friendly; it is also the area in which many annoyances and disagreements can be focused.
>
> 1991 *Daily Tel.* 5 July 19/8 The district auditor recently advised the neighbourhood that it could sell the painting.

(Hide quotations)

Figure 4.1 The Oxford English Dictionary provides a complex definition of "neighborhood," involving 11 "concrete" and 4 "abstract" uses and 19 "compounds," each with a separate meaning—evidencing the magnitude of what is now packed into the definition. There are 250 variants of the word "neighbour" in the OED. Source: Oxford English Dictionary; Painter, "The Politics of the Neighbour," 522, 527.

is to strengthen social bonds, then the neighborhood might be defined as a "communications concept," where spatial boundaries contain "dense and multi-functional" interaction.[3] A police definition of neighborhood is likely based on police workloads.[4]

Sometimes neighborhood definition can be simultaneously vague and concise, such as this one: "any group between the family unit and municipal government."[5] A 1970s-era elementary school curriculum guide offered this succinct definition: "*place, people,* and *purposes,* with the emphasis on *place.*"[6] And there was the painfully uncomplicated definition of neighborhood that was offered in a 1957 editorial published in the *New York Post*: "A neighborhood is where, when you go out of it, you get beat up."[7]

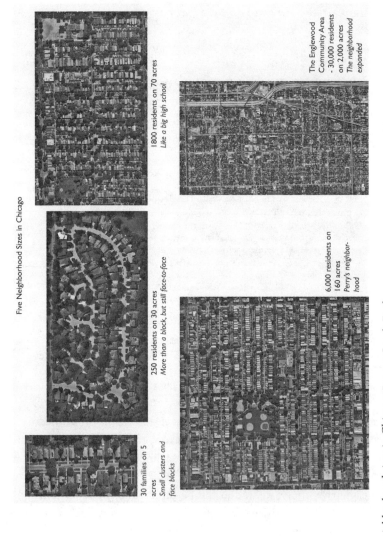

Five Neighborhood Sizes in Chicago

1800 residents on 70 acres
Like a big high school

250 residents on 30 acres
More than a block, but still face-to-face

30 families on 5 acres
Small clusters and face blocks

The Englewood Community Area - 30,000 residents on 2,000 acres
The neighborhood expanded

6,000 residents on 160 acres
Perry's neighborhood

Figure 4.2 Five neighborhood sizes in Chicago. Images: Google Earth.

Neighborhood terms are rarely neutral. A "slum," for example, is a neighborhood suffering from disinvestment, concentrated poverty, and, often, environmental racism.[8] The term "hood" seems to have originated on Chicago's South Side, while "nabe" was used as an adjective for neighborhood services as early as the 1920s—the "nabe gym," for example. "Nabe" dropped out of use by the 1970s ("its decline in sync with that of urban America"), only to reemerge as a more gentrification-friendly version of "hood." One writer explained, "The nabe . . . is a place you try to live. The hood is still a place you try to leave."[9] Social psychology, cultural anthropology, and urban geography have also weighed in with their own neighborhood vocabulary. Relevant terms include "territory," something controlled by an individual, group, or authority (a locale where "the home team always wins"), and "proxemics," the study of how use of space is a "specialized elaboration of culture" comprising a "hidden dimension" of understanding.[10]

The academic understanding of neighborhood as a separate object of study began in the late 19th century. Ferdinand Tonnies, Emile Durkheim, and Georg Simmel, all born in the mid-19th century and active well into the 20th, were the first to understand community in a spatial context[11] (see color plate 8). Although these sociospatial areas were called "communities" they were more in line with a traditional understanding of neighborhood, since the conceptions were formed before "community without propinquity" became an accepted way of thinking about sociospatial relationships. In the 1920s, following on the work of these early sociologists, members of the Chicago School—Ernest Burgess, Homer Hoyt, Roderick McKenzie, Chauncy Harris, Edward Ullman— produced famous diagrams of rings, sectors, and wedges that were not explicitly about neighborhoods but were used as such.

Throughout the 20th century and into the 21st, social scientists continued to cultivate, as they had since the earliest days of the Chicago School, a definition of neighborhood based on social demographics, which mostly meant that neighborhoods were defined as census tracts. In this social data–driven view, neighborhoods were understood through the lens of economic, ethnic, and racial change: assimilation and segregation, prejudice and tolerance, clustering, stratifying, and mobility patterns. Researchers were especially focused on where measures of disadvantage were accumulating, concentrating, or consolidating, and those patterns formed the basis of neighborhood characterization. It was a view of neighborhood that required separating out the extant versus normative view of neighborhood—neighborhoods as they are (or as people think they are), something distinct from neighborhoods as they could be.

For many researchers, to understand neighborhoods as they are is to understand neighborhood *change*. In the U.S., it is not uncommon for 50% or more of residents to change location within three years, and change can mean vitality or

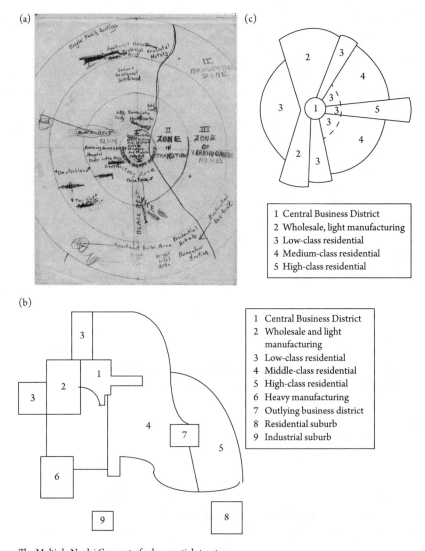

(a)

(c)

1	Central Business District
2	Wholesale, light manufacturing
3	Low-class residential
4	Medium-class residential
5	High-class residential

(b)

1	Central Business District
2	Wholesale and light manufacturing
3	Low-class residential
4	Middle-class residential
5	High-class residential
6	Heavy manufacturing
7	Outlying business district
8	Residential suburb
9	Industrial suburb

The Multiple Nuclei Concept of urban spatial structure

Figure 4.3a, 4.3b, and 4.3c Every city seems to have some aspects of Burgess's concentric rings (a), Harris and Ullman's nuclei, (b), and McKenzie and Hoyt's axials and sectors (c). Variables like age, family structure, wealth and income, and race and ethnicity are used to define the "neighborhoods" that now overlay ring, sector, and nucleus structure. The Burgess image (a) is his original drawing hanging in the Department of Sociology at the University of Chicago. Source: Department of Sociology, University of Chicago; Park et al., *The City*; Harris and Ullman, "The Nature of Cities."

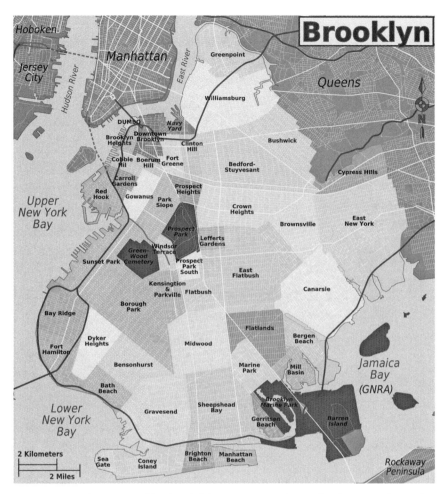

Figure 4.4 In the U.S., neighborhood delineation is mostly unofficial. New York City, for example, has no official neighborhood boundaries, although New York's five boroughs are said to contain more than 400 distinct neighborhoods, down from 725 neighborhoods delineated by the Mayor's Committee on City Planning in 1936, but up from New York City's Planning Commission 2008 report that listed 300 neighborhoods. Separate boroughs in New York have their own neighborhood counts; Brooklyn has at least 90, and Queens has 99. Sources: Manbeck, *The Neighborhoods of Brooklyn*; Copquin, *The Neighborhoods of Queens*. Image: Peter Fitzgerald, CC BY 3.0, https://commons.wikimedia.org/wiki/File:Brooklyn_neighborhoods_map.png.

instability; lack of change can mean stability or lack of options.[12] Three models are often used—life cycle, composition, and arbitrage—which predict change based on variables like poverty status and wealth.[13] In the life-cycle model, neighborhoods go through a natural progression "upward and downward," which could be based on housing age, density, or building type. The arbitrage model uses racial composition and household preferences about socioeconomic

Table VIII

SOURCE OF GROUP NAMES

Name of Source	Total	Eastern	Western
Accident	6	3	3
Economic Institution	1	1	-
Educational Institution	3	2	1
Family Name	32	15	17
Former Resident	8	3	5
Nationality	8	1	7
Natural Phenomenon	39	17	22
Post Office	4	2	2
Social Institution	5	3	2
Township	15	9	6

Figure 4.5 Even as early as the 1920s, the ability to name a neighborhood was seen as an indication of "group consciousness." Relying on a naming methodology in rural Wisconsin, 121 neighborhoods were identified and mapped. Sources were mostly "natural phenomena," followed by family names. Only three neighborhood names were accidental. Source: Kolb, "Rural Primary Groups."

status to predict change. A related "disequilibrium model" predicts neighborhood change based on whether households view their living environment as "sub-optimal."[14] The composition model takes into account the preferences of urban gentrifiers, arguing that the quality of large older homes and their location are essential determinants of change.[15]

Researchers argue that an understanding of these dynamics requires a more complex definition of neighborhood than the historical record or early 20th-century planners allowed. New conceptualizations of neighborhood are needed to explain the social and cultural diversification that expanded in the postmodern, postindustrial world. Alternative lifestyles, family types that far exceed the Ozzie and Harriet household norm, political fragmentation, identity politics, social inequality—all of these social splinters have made traditional notions about neighborhood seem untenable.

The definition of neighborhood is often dictated by data availability, which explains why neighborhoods are sometimes defined as census tracts, sometimes as blocks, sometimes as wards, and sometimes as zip codes. For example, if gentrification is based on changes in housing prices, and those data are available only at the zip code level, then zip codes will be used to define neighborhoods.[16] The Urban Institute's National Neighborhood Indicators Partnership, which has kept track of neighborhood data since 1995, is also data-driven. Student enrollment is collected by school district, and health data are collected by zip code, constituting two definitions of neighborhood. The built environment aspects of neighborhood measurement might be more detailed: property tax delinquencies, foreclosures, building permits, sales—collected at the parcel level and aggregated to form neighborhoods.[17] New technical capabilities have enabled increasingly sophisticated measurement—open data and "big data" using real time sensors of urban movement and other minutiae feeding into urban dashboards.[18] Always lurking in the background of these approaches is the "modifiable areal unit problem," which indicates that the choice of an areal unit boundary (neighborhood), and the aggregated data within it, are arbitrary.

The quest to understand what effects neighborhoods exert—now a key interest in social science—requires this kind of definitional flexibility, where neighborhood varies from a zip code definition to the spatially constrained view of an individual resident (the "egocentric neighborhood," also termed "bespoke" or custom-made neighborhoods).[19] Researchers believe that an individualized view can still involve "cross-cutting networks that connect far-flung areas of the city." As the sociologist Robert Sampson writes, there is no " 'best' or 'correct' operational definition of neighborhood"; there are instead "multiple scales of ecological influence."[20]

One criticism of these data-driven approaches is that neighborhoods are reduced to counts of social variables (or, in the case of "big data," data points), as opposed to viewing urban events, challenges, and people as contextualized within the collectivist-activating platform of neighborhood. Data-driven "urban science" is criticized as leading to a view of cities and neighborhoods as depoliticized collections of variables to be optimized.[21] Missing, critics argue, are the procurement and use of data directed toward the goal of neighborhood empowerment.

There is also a disjuncture between census tract neighborhoods and what residents perceive their neighborhoods to be. Herbert Gans uncovered the disconnection in his study of Boston's West End. To residents, the "West End" was not a neighborhood, although it was labeled as such by urban renewal planners. Instead residents perceived several neighborhoods in the West End, mostly on the basis of housing condition and income level.[22] Claudia Coulton has argued that policies that ignore residents' views on neighborhood—which might include place meaning, sense of ownership, and how the perception of neighborhood boundaries changes when community-building activity occurs—are missing a crucial perspective.[23]

Neighborhood typology potentially avoids some of these definitional and measurement problems.[24] Typologies have been a favorite topic of urban planners, sociologists, and housing developers since the beginning of the 20th century, starting with the Chicago School. Typologies can be tailored to specific purposes; a focus on crime creates one typology, a focus on social interaction creates another. Differentiating neighborhoods for real estate purposes is especially common.

In a well-known approach from the 1950s, Wendell Bell combined census tract and interview data in an attempt to make sense of the "crazy quilt" of American cities; from there a whole industry devoted to neighborhood categorization

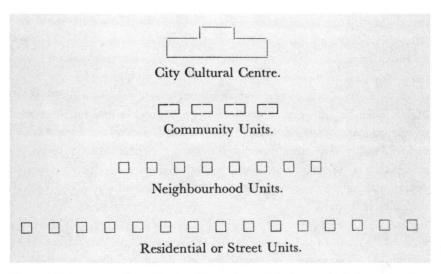

City Cultural Centre.

Community Units.

Neighbourhood Units.

Residential or Street Units.

Figure 4.6 Conventional neighborhood hierarchy, such as this one, included in the 1945 plan for Plymouth, U.K., conceives of the neighborhood as the third tier in a four-part urban hierarchy. Source: Scotland, *A Handbook of the Plymouth Plan.*

emerged. Claritas and PRIZM (Potential Rating Index for Zipcode Markets) use factor analysis and census data to define and classify neighborhoods. Then there are the real estate websites, such as Zillow and Trulia, which characterize neighborhoods of different quality based on crime, socioeconomic profile, schools, and other indicators.[25]

The sociologist Gerard Suttles famously conceptualized four levels of neighborhood, each with an ever-expanding sphere of influence.[26] First is the "face-block," a micro-unit around one's home, perhaps the houses on a single block on one side of a street, where intimate relationships develop. Second is a "defended neighborhood," called a "residential neighborhood" by some, consisting of at least several face-blocks, together with, according to Suttles, stores and daily services. The defended neighborhood is the area within which people "would be called together if a serious crime or social problem occurred close to home" or where residents "share mutual safety problems and concerns."[27] The third level is the "community of limited liability," which has an official boundary and

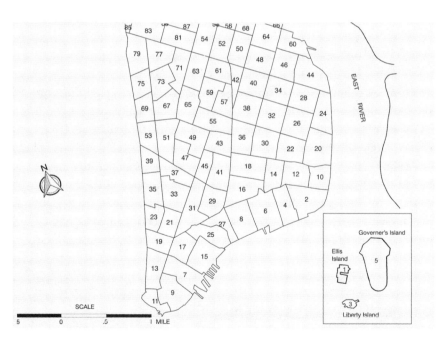

Figure 4.7 The census tract was conceived by Walter Laidlaw in 1906 in New York City and was first applied to eight cities in the 1910 census. There are now about 73,000 tracts in the U.S. Their geographic size varies widely—smaller in dense cities and larger in less populated areas. Tracts are meant to have 4,000 people on average, but their actual range is 2,500 to 8,000. Shown is a map of the census tracts of Manhattan in 1950. Sources: Image redrawn after *Media History of New York*, "Census Tract Map 1950"; Krieger, "A Century of Census Tracts."

is similar to the "institutional neighborhood." The fourth level is an "expanded community of limited liability," which is a much larger version encompassing several subdistricts, for example, "Lower Manhattan." George Galster questioned how valuable Suttle's spatial levels of neighborhood actually were, given the lack of clarity about how one is supposed to move from individual to collective understanding.[28]

Typologies might be based on a neighborhood's degree of collective efficacy. In one proposal, neighborhoods were delineated as "strong," "vulnerable," "anomic," or "responsive" according to their stage of development and level of crime or disorder (see Table 4.1). Policing strategy based on James Q. Wilson and George L. Kelling's seminal "Broken Windows" hypothesis—that neighborhood disorder (graffiti, broken windows, loiterers) leads to crime—was then tailored according to neighborhood type.[29]

But typologies are also easily translated into questionable judgments about neighborhood value or quality. A 1950s article in *Social Forces* very matter-of-factly assessed the desirability of neighborhood types based on percentage of detached housing: less than 30% was "unfavorable"; 30 to 60% was "neutral"; and over 60% was "favorable." (It should be noted that characterizing neighborhoods as "favorable" if they contain 40% attached housing is quite progressive by today's standards, and especially in an American context).[30] This problem was particularly acute during the urban renewal period. One planner, for example, classified neighborhoods as "coming, arrived, going, and gone." This echoed Burgess's succession-invasion and Homer Hoyt's filtering typologies (based on a ranking of racial and ethnic groups), which sought to predict neighborhood change and led decision-makers to enact policies that self-fulfilled the prophecy of decline.[31] The "gone" neighborhoods were "hopeless slums" that needed to be completely wiped out and new neighborhoods formed in their place, from scratch. (In these areas, the planner declared, "neighborhood participation is out.") Most neighborhoods fit the "going" category: not bad enough for urban renewal, but not good enough for a neighborhood protection strategy.[32]

Table 4.1 **Neighborhood types**

1. Integral: cosmopolitan, sharing mutual concerns with larger community
2. Parochial: strong ethnic identity, self-contained, excludes nonconforming
3. Diffuse: homogeneous, some commonality, lacks internal/larger community
4. Stepping stone: active participation for personal, not neighborhood interests
5. Transitory: high population change, separation between new and old residents
6. Anomic: nonneighborhood, no cohesion, unable to mobilize people or issues

Source: Warren and Warren, *The Neighborhood Organizer's Handbook.*

As a final example of neighborhood reinvention, there is the case of defining neighborhood in a way that requires no actual spatial or physical location. This started in the 1960s in the U.S. when neighborhood as *process* surpassed neighborhood as physical design as the focus of professional interest. What replaced design was government-backed neighborhood planning, first under the Community Action Program and the Model Cities Programs of the 1960s, followed by the community development corporations that gained ground in the 1970s, and then the municipal neighborhood planning programs that followed. These forms of neighborhood planning significantly broadened what neighborhood planning up until that time had been. Rather than boundaries, services, centers, street patterns, and mixed housing types, the focus was on resident participation and self-governance in a way that was sometimes strangely detached from the object at hand: the neighborhood.[33]

Thus, by the 1970s, neighborhood planning shifted to a concern for revitalizing existing places through a reconceived political process rather than designing new neighborhoods as an ideal form (although the exception was where neighborhood was applied to suburban expansion by production builders or the American Institute of Architects).[34] President Jimmy Carter's National Commission on Neighborhoods, created in 1977 to recognize the urban neighborhood as a "national resource to be conserved and revitalized,"[35] reflected this new posture. Howard Hallman's 1984 *Neighborhoods: Their Place in Urban Life* benchmarked the new totality of neighborhood definition, which, by then, included economic, political, and personal domains in addition to physical and social ones.

Notes

1. Taylor, "Defining Neighborhoods," 227.
2. Coulton, "Defining Neighborhoods"; Grannis, "T-Communities."
3. Grigsby et al., "Residential Neighborhoods and Submarkets," 21.
4. Buslik, "Dynamic Geography."
5. Cowan, *The Dictionary of Urbanism*.
6. Providence Public Schools and Rhode Island College, *Neighborhoods*.
7. Cited in Bursik and Grasmick, *Neighborhoods and Crime*, 5.
8. Gulyani and Bassett, "The Living Conditions Diamond."
9. Grabar, "Nabe or Hood?"
10. Sommer, "Man's Proximate Environment," 61, 62. On proxemics see Hall, *The Hidden Dimension*.
11. They differed on how much the physical environment mattered for social differentiation. Durkheim saw things in strictly social terms.
12. Coulton et al., "Residential Mobility."
13. Schwab, "Alternative Explanations."
14. Coulton et al., "Residential Mobility."
15. Schwab, "Alternative Explanations."

16. One recent example of defining a neighborhood as synonymous with zip code is found in this study of gentrification: Guerrieri et al., "Endogenous Gentrification."

17. Chaskin, "Neighborhood as a Unit of Planning."

18. Anselin, "Local Indicators."

19. Stein, "Neighborhood Scale."

20. Sampson, *Great American City*, 360.

21. Mattern, "Methodolatry."

22. Gans, "Gans on Granovetter's 'Strength of Weak Ties.'"

23. Coulton, "Finding Place."

24. Hunter, "The Urban Neighborhood," 271; Galster, "What Is Neighbourhood?"

25. Bell, "Social Areas," 63.

26. Suttles, *The Social Construction of Communities*. For a related typology, see Downs, *Neighborhoods*.

27. Nolan and Conti, "Neighborhood Development and Crime."

28. Galster, "What Is Neighbourhood?," 259.

29. Nolan and Conti, "Neighborhood Development and Crime"; Kelling and Wilson, "Broken Windows."

30. Green, "Aerial Photographic Analysis."

31. Bradford, "Financing Home Ownership."

32. Howard, "Democracy in City Planning."

33. Rohe, "From Local to Global."

34. Some groups, such as the American Institute of Architects, still advocated neighborhood-based growth at the periphery since they considered the attempt to renew cities "house by house, problem by problem" ineffective. See American Institute of Architects, *America at the Growing Edge*.

35. National Neighborhood Policy Act, 1977. https://www.gpo.gov/fdsys/pkg/STATUTE-91/pdf/STATUTE-91-Pg55.pdf

PART II

THE DEBATES

Loss of the historically understood neighborhood produced a response that either tried to plan the traditional neighborhood back into existence (although often in nonhistorical and nontraditional forms) or tried to reinvent the neighborhood unrecognizably. Where does this trajectory—the decline of the traditional neighborhood, its subsequent (mostly unsuccessful) replanning, and its wide reinvention—leave us? And what are the prospects for the reinstatement of neighborhood in a more traditional sense now?

To answer this, it is necessary to analyze the protracted debates about neighborhood that occurred over the past century: debates about neighborhood design (e.g., its boundedness and connection), the tension between plan and process, the conflict between self-governance and higher-level control, the social connectedness that neighborhoods had and lost, and the feasibility and desirability of social mix. Understanding these debates and attempting their resolution is necessary if there can be any hope of reinstating a traditional sense of neighborhood in a way that is both real and realistic.

5

Design Debates

This chapter reviews the primary design debates involved in neighborhood formation: whether they can or should be planned all at once and as complete units; their boundedness and centeredness, and their street composition and its effect on internal and external connectivity. All of these debates involve the limits and practicalities of neighborhood identity-building and consciousness, which can be thought of as being on a continuum from most extreme (whole units on clean slates) to more subtle (increasing connectivity via interconnecting pathways). Building a neighborhood on a clean slate and all at once has always been the most extreme case, especially if it involved demolition of existing places. Boundedness is less extreme but criticized as impractical and exclusionary; centers seem an important, less controversial practice capable of instilling a sense of neighborhood. The design of neighborhood streets has long been contentious, as planners have sought to balance internal protection against external connectivity. Moving forward, there is hope for design resolution because the choices are not so black and white. Neighborhood design can maintain the positive aspects of identity-building by emphasizing centers (which also minimizes the need for explicit boundaries) and streets that can be simultaneously well connected and pedestrian based (see color plate 9).

Clean Slates and Whole Units

In the early 20th century, neighborhood was being used to invoke order out of the chaos of the industrial city. By the mid-20th century, neighborhood was being applied at the urban periphery in hopes of making order out of the chaos of sprawl. In either location, neighborhood was seen as something complete and whole—a cell, a unit—capable of turning discord into harmony.

The "whole unit" concept of neighborhood is based on the view that neighborhoods have intrinsic limits. The idea is that neighborhoods that reach a certain size should stop growing and a new neighborhood should be formed to absorb

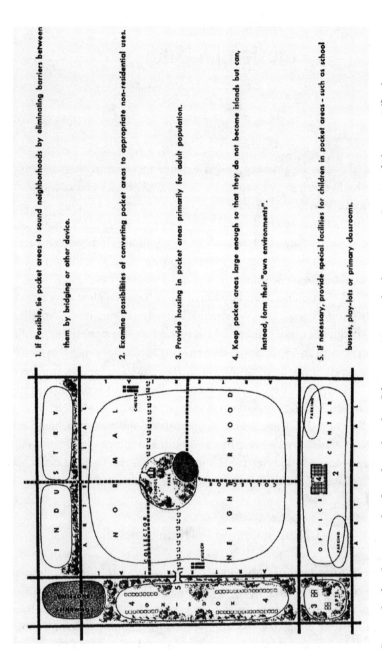

1. If Possible, tie pocket areas to sound neighborhoods by eliminating barriers between them by bridging or other device.

2. Examine possibilities of converting pocket areas to appropriate non-residential uses.

3. Provide housing in pocket areas primarily for adult population.

4. Keep pocket areas large enough so that they do not become islands but can, instead, form their "own environment".

5. If necessary, provide special facilities for children in pocket areas – such as school busses, play-lots or primary classrooms.

Figure 5.1 "Principles for planning isolated residential pockets," from a 1960 report by the American Society of Planning Officials. Source: Image redrawn from Allaire, "Neighborhood Boundaries," appendix A.

new growth. The *Architectural Forum*'s 1943 issue on city planning explained the process: "Once a neighborhood is filled to the edges of its own small park belt, no more building can be done until houses or shops within it are torn down to be replaced. If the population expands, the neighborhoods do not expand, but their number increases."[1] The European architect Leon Krier, making a distinction between ideals and norms, argues that there should be limits on size not because of abstract ideals but because, "like a tree or a man," a human community that exceeds its normal growth becomes a monster.[2]

What are the implications of this notion that neighborhoods should be planned as separate, distinguishable, whole units? In theory, planning by complete unit provided a better understanding of the interrelationship of parts. Radburn, New Jersey's "revolution in planning" was that it combined time-honored urban design strategies to address the problem of the automobile, separating cars and pedestrians, using specialized roads that differentiated between "movement, collection, service, parking, and visiting," turning houses around (front doors faced a park rather than a street), and including a large park as the "backbone" of the neighborhood. Clarence Stein maintained that none of these ideas were new as singular concepts; the innovation was in their combination.[3]

But are neighborhoods as planned "units"—Clarence Perry's version or otherwise—desirable? It is a question that has been raised from the beginning. Robert A. Woods, founder of one of the earliest settlement houses (Boston's South End House), railed in 1920 against the tendency "to consider the neighborhood as a kind of amorphous crystalline unit instead of a highly complex, manifold and ever-changing living organism."[4] Christopher Alexander, especially in his essay "A City Is Not a Tree," was a particularly potent critic of neighborhood plans in places like Columbia, Maryland, and the Greenbelt Towns, which he said were isolating and not at all in keeping with cities as places that interconnect.[5]

Neighborhoods conceived as "villages" in the city were supposed to invoke communal caring, but they simultaneously came to be associated with something much more sinister: the eradication of the existing city and the social diversity it contained. Often this agenda was not disguised. The influential Victorian John Ruskin called for total destruction and replacement wherever cities were less than works of art; Perry advocated the same but called it "scientific slum rehabilitation."[6] The ideal of the unit cast a shadow, associated with urban destruction that complicated and problematized the neighborhood narrative.

Part of the issue had to do with the "clean slate" phenomenon. When the planned neighborhood idea was first circulating in the early 20th century, a good neighborhood, it was thought, could be designed only on vacant land, at the urban periphery, or on cleared land to replace a blighted area. There was no neighborhood design possible for existing places unless those places could be refashioned wholesale. Perry did propose his neighborhood unit for the inner city, but the redevelopment required eminent domain, land assembly, and the creation of an internalized environment whereby "the unpleasantness of the sights and sounds outside the neighborhood could be completely counteracted."[7]

British planners did not impose the same requirements. Sir Patrick Abercrombie's *County of London Plan* applied the neighborhood concept to London, based on Herbert Alker Tripp's *Town Planning and Road Traffic,* to implement the "By-Pass Principle," which actively avoided cutting through existing neighborhoods and tried to make sure that any road development followed existing physical boundaries, such as factories, waterways, and railroads. This was for the explicit purpose of keeping neighborhoods intact and making London a city of villages, since most still had a recognizable "independent spirit."[8]

Homer Hoyt was as unhappy with slums (he called them "jungles of crime") adjacent to the business core as he was with disconnected suburban sprawl at the periphery. Slum clearance within the city was a must, to be replaced with new model neighborhoods. Clearance would need to be total, as new neighborhoods needed to be "entirely free from reminders of the slum." In suburban areas, model neighborhoods of a "garden" quality could be constructed. The only nod to existing context was that they should be within walking distance of "war plants" that could eventually convert to peacetime uses.[9]

Planners were cognizant of the difficulty of delineating complete neighborhood units in existing urban areas. One way to avoid the "clean slate" approach would be to connect "isolated residential pockets" into something resembling a unit. Arguing that such areas could not be ignored, the strategy proposed connecting them to surrounding neighborhoods, whereby they would be "protected and given public services to the extent feasible." Minneapolis conceived of tying together its residual housing areas by way of a "bridge."[10]

But it was hard to deny the appeal of neighborhoods as singular, controllable units on clean slates, whereby the messy, existing urban milieu could be avoided. The neighborhood as complete planned unit created an abstract and unconstrained neighborhood ideal, one in which the parts of a neighborhood could be thought of as constituting "the palette of the architect"—street pattern, land division, and open spaces—to be balanced according to "appropriateness and artistry."[11] It enabled thinking of the neighborhood as an object of pure design—very alluring for architects looking for design license. Freed from the constraints of existing block arrangements and building types, the opportunities for unfettered and innovative thinking about neighborhood form were opened up. In this same spirit, neighborhood planners today use the language of sustainability, claiming that the complete planned unit is essential for figuring out sustainability practices that require coordination at the unit level.

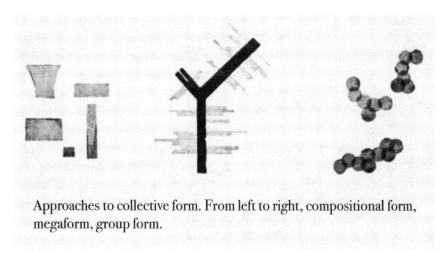

Approaches to collective form. From left to right, compositional form, megaform, group form.

Figure 5.2 An example of the pure design view of neighborhood, with differentiated compositional, megastructure, and group configuration of "collective form." Source: Image redrawn after Maki, *Investigations in Collective Form.*

The downside is that the tabula rasa approach to neighborhood design has left little incentive to learn the methodology or language of incremental neighborhood formation. "Unit thinking" is a conception of neighborhood driven by design experimentation or developer interests, not residents. In the heyday of the neighborhood unit, there seemed little understanding that residents needed to be meaningfully engaged or empowered, that neighborhoods would be fashioned and improved over time, that residents' decision-making powers would advance, and that the wholesale destruction of neighborhoods through urban renewal or gentrification would be mediated. "Neighborhood" became a word attached to redevelopment schemes that, because driven by outside interests, did not have the interests of neighborhood residents at heart. It was an insidious use of the neighborhood ideal.

A succession of government-backed programs, starting with the Neighborhood Improvement Act of 1937, prioritized destruction of existing places and replacement with large-scale housing schemes called neighborhoods. And yet the promotion of the neighborhood unit by government agencies and professional building-related organizations—first President Hoover, then the Federal Housing Administration, then the Urban Land Institute and the National Association of Home Builders—was a story of piecemeal application.[12] Promoters seemed to exclude the one reason planning by complete neighborhood unit made sense in the first place: because it enabled an integrated totality of the neighborhood ideal, especially a size limit related to pedestrian access, serviceability, and building-type variety. Without this backing there was widespread deployment of automobile-based subdivisions and shopping centers—not neighborhoods. In this sense the neighborhood unit proved adaptable, but the result was uniformity.[13] The irony is that the neighborhood unit was conceived as an antidote to the sameness of mass urbanization and the endless grid, but it ended up being a tool of its escalation.

The modernist application of the neighborhood unit during "urban renewal" was thought of as a complete application, but it was undermined by its hyperinsularity. Lakeview Terrace in Cleveland, Ohio, completed in 1937 and one of the first public housing projects in the U.S., is a prime example of a "complete" neighborhood cut off from surrounding neighborhoods. Now government-backed neighborhood planning is trying to mitigate an earlier generation's missteps. Recent modernization of the Lakeview Terrace project has attempted to eliminate security problems by getting rid of common halls and stairways and making smaller communal areas within the larger complex. Choice Neighborhoods, an initiative of the U.S. Department of Housing and Urban Development (HUD), has similarly been trying to remedy the failures of neighborhood unit insularity by embracing integrative—not unit—thinking.

Figure 5.3 The Lakeview Terrace neighborhood was part of a "slum clearance" scheme in Cleveland, Ohio. It was one of the first public housing projects in the U.S. Source: Image courtesy of Cleveland State Library Special Collections. See also Stephenson, "Town Planning"; Cleveland Historical, "Aerial, 1937."

The modernist form of the neighborhood unit seemed especially antiurban. This critique had applied to all forms of complete neighborhoods (modernist or not), including traditional neighborhoods like Forest Hills Gardens—the development that inspired Perry—which was dismissed as "suburban." The criticism seems unfair given that Forest Hills Gardens is actually highly urban in comparison to the vast majority of places in the U.S. (It ranks in the top 3% of neighborhoods when measured on the basis of Walk Score.)[14] But its unit quality had the effect of making it seem more rural than it was. Letchworth, U.K., the first Garden City, was similarly criticized, despite the fact that its lots are the same size as the lots in Greenwich Village. Neighborhoods rendered in pure modernist form, composed of isolated, tall buildings set in open green space, gave an especially rural impression despite having relatively high densities (although it should be noted that their net densities were not necessarily higher than the traditional neighborhood form).

The complete neighborhood units of the architectural avant-garde were unlikely to include single-family housing. Le Corbusier was especially insistent on rejecting the single family house, proclaiming its inhabitants "slaves,"[15] while the Goodman brothers dreamed of a mixed-class neighborhood (juxtaposing even "extreme classes") of about 4,000 people in a "continuous apartment house around an open space of up to ten acres." The motto of their scheme, "the perfection of a valetudinarian environment," was "The style of the whole is anonymous; the cell individualized."[16] From our 21st-century perspective, the modernist rows of identical apartment blocks seem the antithesis of an organic neighborhood.

Although the modernist interpretation of neighborhood could take on a wide variety of forms, the basic, ruralized format was exemplified by Louis Kahn's neighborhood planning proposal: superblocks with an embedded park and elementary school, surrounded by arterials, with residential units fronting the park. José Sert was also a strong advocate of the neighborhood unit as a microcosm of the city ("a whole in themselves"), whose elements could be "precisely determined" based on local factors, which usually meant that elements were separated from each other by green belts. Curvilinearity was the reigning design precept (presumably because there are no right angles in nature). The neighborhood would be protected from through-traffic, while internally, "wide, curving designs ending the parking areas seem the more desirable pattern."[17] It should be noted that 20th century modernists did not invent the superblock. A 19th century version of the superblock neighborhood is shown in color plate 10.

For planners, the ruralized neighborhood worked because it would be self-contained and thus controlled. Pedestrian safety, especially the route children took to school, was a high priority and was used as the rationale for superblocks, as had been the case for Stein and Wright's neighborhood layout at Radburn.

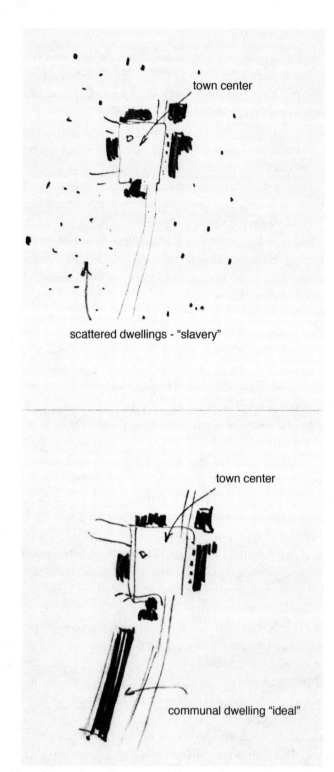

town center

scattered dwellings - "slavery"

town center

communal dwelling "ideal"

Figure 5.4 A neighborhood by Le Corbusier would not include single-family housing. Source: Harbeson, "Design in Modern Architecture."

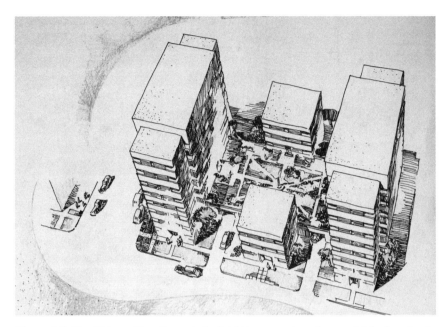

Figure 5.5 The Chicago Plan Commission's 1941 conception of new neighborhoods of grouped apartment blocks. Source: Chicago Plan Commission, *Rebuilding Old Chicago.*

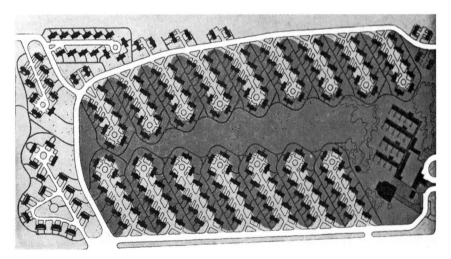

Figure 5.6 Richard Neutra's neighborhood concept, 1942. Source: Image redrawn from Neutra, "Peace Can Gain from War's Forced Changes."

The influence of the traffic engineer could also be seen, as both architect and engineer were synergistically motivated by a desire to propagate internally calm traffic cells (with only locally serving residential streets), surrounded by arterials that would carry the through-traffic.[18] Another variant was Richard Neutra's Radburn-like neighborhood plan, with housing units fronting finger-like parks

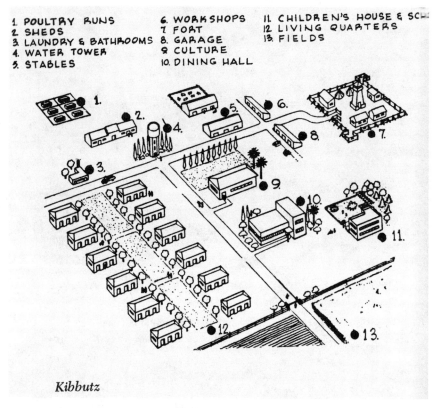

1. POULTRY RUNS
2. SHEDS
3. LAUNDRY & BATHROOMS
4. WATER TOWER
5. STABLES
6. WORKSHOPS
7. FORT
8. GARAGE
9. CULTURE
10. DINING HALL
11. CHILDREN'S HOUSE & SCH...
12. LIVING QUARTERS
13. FIELDS

Kibbutz

Figure 5.7 The kibbutz, as Percival and Paul Goodman drew it in their book *Communitas*, was a face-to-face neighborhood with all the elements of living and working in self-contained harmony. Source: Goodman and Goodman, *Communitas*.

around a large communal green that was emphatically free of cars. Home addresses were to be park locations rather than street numbers. To avoid the charge that such arrangements were just subdivisions in better form, there would be shops, schools, and community buildings for all residents. The result would be "symbiosis" rather than mere "subdivision."[19] Sert's attempt to escape the neighborhood-as-subdivision problem involved grouping units into a "township" in such a way that they would have equal access to high-order functions (junior and senior high schools, light industry, and larger shops).[20]

Even more rationalized was Ludwig Hilberseimer's proposal for an urban hierarchy of various sizes of modular units that could be combined in flexible ways. Each unit was a superblock surrounded by a park and arranged around a "traffic artery" functioning as a "backbone," internally freed from the danger of conventional streets. Some superblocks were to be exclusively commercial and surrounded by parks. The system was meant to be fluid and boundaries

Figure 5.8 An Urban Land Institute publication from the 1970s proposed this neighborhood—Country Club Aventura in Miami—organized around a central open space: a golf course. Source: Jones, *Golf Course Developments*.

could be overlapping.[21] Although Hilberseimer's proposal was labeled "theoretically correct" by Christopher Alexander, it was dehumanizing in the extreme, ultimately elevating the tortuous monotony of the gridded city.[22] Unlike Perry, Hilberseimer envisioned a hypercontrolled "settlement unit" that thrived on the segregation of functions.[23]

These neighborhood concepts were a problem because they tended to thwart the possibility of a bottom-up, naturally occurring (i.e., unsubsidized) socially mixed neighborhood, which thrives on variegation. If subsidized, social mix could survive in neighborhoods of any form: in towers set in superblocks, in low-density suburbs, on blocks with building and housing types that are identical, and on blocks whose building and housing types are highly variegated. But in some of these versions—notably high-rises set in parks—diversity was unlikely to occur without strong public oversight and subsidy. Public dictates and massive subsidies were possible in places like China, but not in the U.S.

In fact planned neighborhoods in any form, modernist or traditional, have struggled to maintain a naturally occurring (i.e., unsubsidized) diversity within them. Variegating housing and lot size within the complete neighborhood unit is a long-standing tradition; mixed housing types were incorporated in Radburn, New Jersey, in the 1920s; in Kentlands, Maryland, in the 1980s; and in most New Urbanist neighborhoods since. These typically include a mix of single-family detached houses, townhouses, and multifamily rental apartments. Radburn has

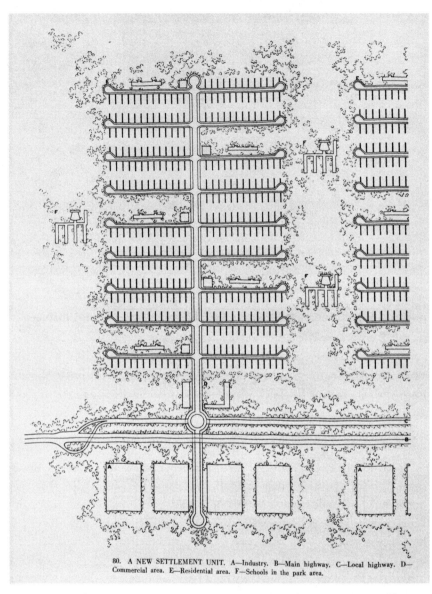

80. A NEW SETTLEMENT UNIT. A—Industry. B—Main highway. C—Local highway. D—Commercial area. E—Residential area. F—Schools in the park area.

Figure 5.9 Ludwig Hilberseimer, one of the main progenitors of modernist urbanism, advocated a highly rationalized "settlement unit." Source: "A New Settlement Unit." Ludwig Karl Hilberseimer. *The New City: Principles of Planning.* Chicago: Paul Theobald, 1944, p. 106, ill. 80. Ludwig Karl Hilberseimer Papers, Ryerson & Burnham Archives, The Art Institute of Chicago. Digital File # 070383.090625-04.

Figure 5.10 Le Corbusier's skyscraper neighborhood, Unite d'Habitation in Marseilles, built in 1946–52, was designed for 337 housing units (1,000 to 1,200 people), with shopping on a central floor, nursery school, and recreational and communal facilities within. The problem with the scheme was predictable: the neighborhood was isolated and removed from the wider network of daily life, and retail services could not be sustained. Source: Lang, *Urban Design*. Image: michiel1972, via Wikimedia Commons, https://commons.wikimedia.org/wiki/File:Unit%C3%A9_d%27Habitation_2_-_panoramio_(1).jpg

duplexes, and Kentlands has multifamily condominiums.[24] But all have experienced a disappointing track record in terms of diversity, despite the fact that, by not relying on public subsidy, their approach is considered more practical.[25] Unfortunately it is a market-based strategy that runs counter to market behavior.

Rather than diversity, the clean slate, whole unit neighborhood is associated more with the uniformly wealthy or the uniformly poor. For the wealthy, designing whole and insular neighborhood units will likely retain its appeal. Gated neighborhoods are a continuing and growing phenomenon of the world's cities, despite protestations from planners that the sequestration is harmful to the broader public.[26] At the other end of the spectrum, with a forced and perverse inward focus, are the housing "projects" of the segregated poor, perhaps originally conceived as neighborhoods but with none of the presumed benefits that the whole neighborhood unit was theoretically supposed to provide.

Boundaries

The issue of whether neighborhoods should be bounded, edged, or otherwise delineated is a debate with well-developed arguments on all sides. Historians, philosophers, and geographers might readily discuss "the edges of the public sphere" in Habermasian ambiguity,[27] but for neighborhood, the edge requires a more specific meaning. These are not just semantics. Although neighborhoods tend to be "ill-defined," boundaries used for the purpose of data collection about neighborhoods are not, and the resulting information has a direct impact on public policy.[28] Even more pragmatically, our understanding of the social makeup of neighborhoods, like their degree of social diversity or homogeneity, would be impossible to understand, quantify, or ultimately realize without explicit boundaries denoting who is to be counted.

In a strictly physical interpretation, a clear boundary is sometimes seen as one of three components that must be present "in order to speak of a neighborhood."[29] Where boundaries are lacking, two other possibilities for neighborhood delineation exist: form homogeneity and a clear focus (provided by a prominent building or civic space, for example). For each type there are alternative means of integration. For boundaries, an "undulating ring road," a "cutting street," or a corner-located square can draw in adjacent areas. Homogeneous streets or buildings can be made to overlap. Focus areas can reach beyond the surrounding neighborhood by way of the "continuation of focusing elements."[30]

Stein and Wright preferred natural buffers for neighborhood boundaries, which were also used in the British new towns and later in the new towns of Columbia, Maryland; Reston, Virginia; Woodlands, Texas; and Irvine, California. The concept was then rekindled in New Urbanist neighborhoods; for

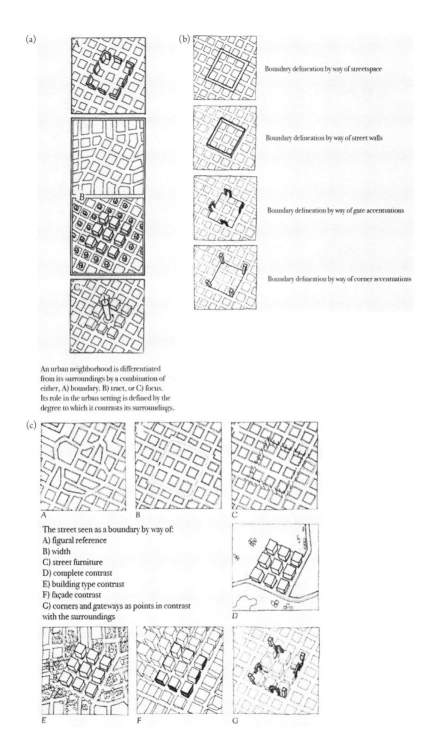

(a)

A

B

C

(b)

Boundary delineation by way of streetspace

Boundary delineation by way of street walls

Boundary delineation by way of gate accentuations

Boundary delineation by way of corner accentuations

An urban neighborhood is differentiated
from its surroundings by a combination of
either, A) boundary, B) tract, or C) focus.
Its role in the urban setting is defined by the
degree to which it contrasts its surroundings.

(c)

A   B   C

The street seen as a boundary by way of:
A) figural reference
B) width
C) street furniture
D) complete contrast
E) building type contrast
F) façade contrast
G) corners and gateways as points in contrast
with the surroundings

D

E   F   G

Figure 5.11 This inventive set of images by Thiis-Evenson (transl. by Campbell) showed
how urban neighborhoods could be both differentiated and integrated. Boundaries are
achieved by one of four methods, in combination or alone: streets, street walls, gates,
or corner accentuations. Integration is achieved by cutting streets, corner incisions, and
overlapping squares, among other strategies. Source: Images redrawn from Thiis-Evenson and
Campbell, *Archetypes of Urbanism*, 62.

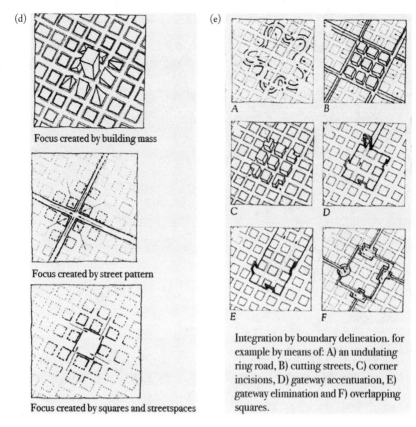

(d)

Focus created by building mass

Focus created by street pattern

Focus created by squares and streetspaces

(e)

A   B

C   D

E   F

Integration by boundary delineation. for example by means of: A) an undulating ring road, B) cutting streets, C) corner incisions, D) gateway accentuation, E) gateway elimination and F) overlapping squares.

Figure 5.11 Continued

example, Kentlands, Maryland, makes use of a lake, wetlands, and green belts to define and differentiate its neighborhoods.[31] Some planners in the 1940s argued against streets as boundaries, not because of potential insularity but because it would create "difficulties in negotiating the cooperation of adjoining land owners." To facilitate each neighborhood (subdivision) looking out for itself, it would be better for the neighborhood to be bounded by another tract of land than a street because street development required negotiation and compromise.[32]

How much does open space versus built environment impact the delineation and boundedness of neighborhoods? Neighborhoods in suburbia, with their open spaces and separated buildings, present very different possibilities for boundedness than neighborhoods in urban places with continuous street walls. The urban morphologist Anne Vernez Moudon looked into the question by studying neighborhood "spatial structure," contrasting the two "structuring elements" of built space and open space. Traditional or vernacular neighborhoods (in the ancient, medieval, and Renaissance eras) are structured around "positive" public open space in the front by way of a continuous building wall,

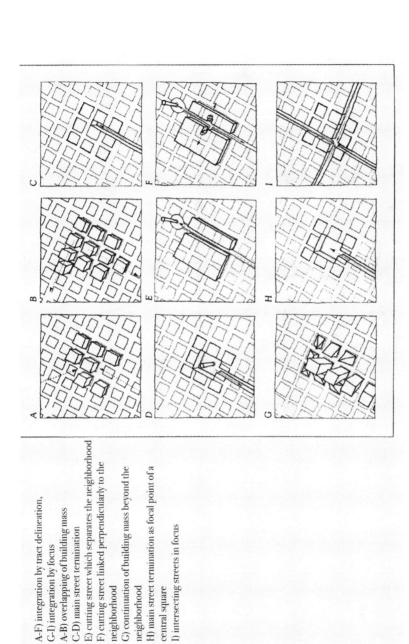

(f)

A-F) integration by tract delineation,
G-I) integration by focus
A-B) overlapping of building mass
C-D) main street termination
E) cutting street which separates the neighborhood
F) cutting street linked perpendicularly to the neighborhood
G) continuation of building mass beyond the neighborhood
H) main street termination as focal point of a central square
I) intersecting streets in focus

Figure 5.11 Continued

with private space in the back. Suburban neighborhoods or detached buildings have a loose definition of public open space, and therefore the built rather than open elements become the primary basis of spatial structure. What this means for neighborhood delineation is that the basis of definition, in the absence of positive open space, is legal lines drawn on a map.[33]

City planners have long advocated the importance of boundaries for aesthetic and efficiency reasons. In one of the earliest defenses, the virtues of edges in human settlement were extolled by the town planner Raymond Unwin in the 19th century; he advocated edges formed by boulevards, playing fields, or belts of parkland, which could prevent "that irregular fringe of half-developed suburb and half-spoiled country which form a hideous and depressing girdle around modern growing towns."[34] Later Perry viewed the "menace" of the automobile as "a blessing in disguise" because, by creating boundaries of traffic arterials, it made self-containment in the form of the neighborhood unit more logical and necessary. These planning sentiments continue; one criterion of the American Planning Association's "Great Neighborhoods" contest is that neighborhoods "should have a definable sense of boundary."[35]

In past times and places cities were physically delineated in many ways. In medieval Europe, for example, there were city walls, church grounds, and market areas—all materially delimited. Town growth in this spatially delineated world translated to neighborhood sub-setting, constraining the possibility of neighborhoods "dissolving in the mass."[36] Physical boundaries were also reinforced by everyday rituals. For example, religious processions would occur in specified areas, making residents "acutely conscious" of neighborhood boundaries.[37] These boundaries were integral to a neighborhood-based "ritual politics" in which an individual's status could be improved through collective participation. Importantly, boundaries were about identity and belonging rather than about social segmentation based on class—an essential point because boundaries are often equated with segregation (especially in connection with the neighborhood unit).

In contemporary American cities, boundaries do not have to be physically recognizable to function as boundaries. Census tracts, for example, are not intended to function as cohesive neighborhoods, but municipal governments regularly use federal census tract designations as official neighborhood boundaries.[38]

Boundaries can be an asset or a problem, depending on how they're used. They have been used to keep people in (ghettos) and to keep people out (gated enclaves). Mostly the concern is whether the boundary is one of exclusion or "the edge of a place that has a welcome at the door." "Boundary scholars" have tried to nuance the differences, assessing whether boundaries are "bright" (firm and well-recognized) or blurred. This might involve an assessment of boundaries expressed as "technologies of racial exclusion": zoning, deed restrictions, sundown laws, redlining, and neighborhood associations.[39] One familiar example is historic district designation, which has a way of rendering neighborhood boundaries exact and official. Planners have been known to ignore the exclusionary implications, arguing, "We must define our neighborhoods as [residents] see them."[40] Unfortunately the 20th-century experience of neighborhood boundaries has sometimes been cast as providing a necessary barrier to "infection," where boundaries were principally a method of containment, confining "blight" to one neighborhood.[41]

Kevin Lynch has defined two types of boundaries: seams and barriers. Perry's boundaries have clearly been interpreted as the latter.[42] Perry believed that major thoroughfares could serve the dual purpose of bounding the neighborhood and directing traffic around rather than through them. This objective obviously doesn't square well with street-based neighborhoods, which many poor and working-class neighborhoods of the early 20th century certainly were. Perry was more interested in the need for articulation, which his neighborhood unit achieved at the expense of continuity.

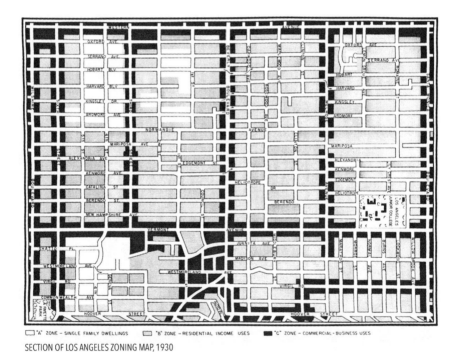

SECTION OF LOS ANGELES ZONING MAP, 1930

Figure 5.12 Zoning for commercial areas contributed to neighborhood delineation. Shown here is a section of Los Angeles's 1930 zoning code. The question is whether commercial zones form boundaries that segregate neighborhoods or function as seams that pull people on either side together. Source: Image redrawn after example in Fogelson, *The Fragmented Metropolis*.

Lewis Mumford defended Perry's street-based boundary ideas. Mumford wrote that the bounded neighborhood unit—with deliberate attention to social diversity within—became necessary because of income segregation wrought by capitalism and the automobile, two forces pulling urbanism apart and requiring a response. The car-based aspect of the modern neighborhood unit meant that the "connective fabric" between neighborhoods was drastically altered, from pedestrian connection across neighborhoods to traffic arteries that encircled and isolated neighborhoods. Perry tried to embrace the surrounding thoroughfare as a blessing in disguise, but others, most especially Jane Jacobs, derailed the "border vacuums" being created.[43]

Heeding Perry, traffic engineers and neighborhood planners conspired to redefine streets as traffic conduits rather than integrative social spaces, especially after the control of streets was transferred from abutting property owners to traffic engineers. The separation wrought by arterials carrying main traffic and smaller side streets carrying local traffic resulted in the loss of the street as a defining social space, because, according to some urban designers, streets are more likely to promote interaction when they integrate both local and nonlocal movement in space. This quality was lost with the neighborhood unit. Separation meant that

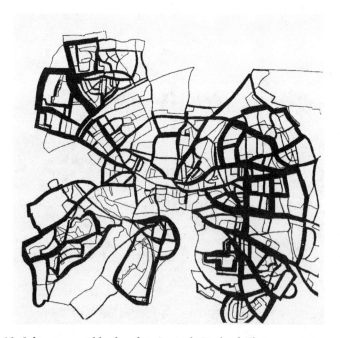

Figure 5.13 Subjective neighborhoods in Ipswich, England. There was strong agreement among respondents on boundaries formed by major streets. From a 1968 study by the British sociologist Peter Willmott. Source: Sims, *Neighborhoods.*

smaller residential streets became unused; segregating the "movement function" of the street had the effect of segregating out their "social functions."

Cognizant of this problem, the attempt was made to redefine street boundaries as "integrators and spines" rather than sharp delineators. Kahn's plan for the Mill Creek neighborhood in Philadelphia exemplifies the approach; there he turned some of the existing streets into "greenways" with street trees and widened sidewalks. These became the "formal backbone" of the neighborhood, integrating cars, pedestrians, and zoning and land use.[44] They were meant to bring people together: a strip of stores as a "social seam," akin to Jan Gehl's "soft edges" or Skjaeveland and Garling's "interactional space."[45] Sociological research has verified the ability of streets to function as seams. A strip of neighborhood stores along a main street can be one of the "social seams" keeping diverse neighborhoods stabilized.[46]

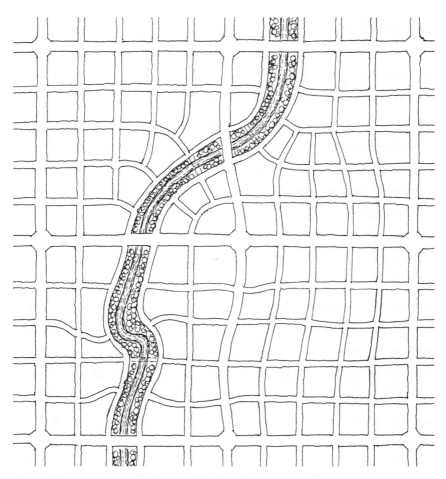

Figure 5.14 A strategy for linking neighborhoods: pathways and greenways. Source: Sketch by Hiroaki Hata, used with permission, in Hess et al., "Pathways and Artifacts."

Bounding streets also need to play a role in connecting (rather than isolating) neighborhoods, because failure to do so weakens the city as a whole. Commercial streets should provide "multiple pathways into a continuous fabric," a condition of urbanism that is easily contrasted with subdivisions isolated by discontinuous streets.[47] Analogously, urban network and "network science" researchers have exposed the economic weaknesses created when service and retail are not integrated within the larger urban system. Translated to physical design, one commonly used idea is to turn bounding arterials into connective seams by transforming them into boulevards. Others argue the importance of positioning neighborhood centers directly on urban thoroughfares, which has the added benefit of making public transit more feasible.[48]

Transforming commercial streets that bound neighborhoods into social connectors was taken up by the American Society of Planning Officials (ASPO) in 1960. Their technical report on the topic of neighborhood boundaries gave the example of Stony Island Avenue in Chicago. The avenue, they acknowledged, separates "an almost 100 per cent Negro population and an almost 100 per cent white population," but they believed that the retailers along the avenue in between could be a kind of social seam ("a local center of pedestrian attraction").[49] Recent development has been working against that. Stony Island Avenue is so antipedestrian—composed of car-dependent strip malls and wide lanes designed to accommodate fast-moving traffic, not pedestrians—that whatever social seaming it provides exists in spite of its design, not because of it.

The ASPO report advanced the argument that boundaries were necessary for delineation, and delineation was necessary for statistics-gathering and funding allocation under urban renewal. Noting that delineation would be easy in suburban areas except "where multiple family development is intermingled in areas predominantly consisting of single and two-family dwellings," the publication was devoted to tackling the problem of identifying neighborhood boundaries in existing cities. Neighborhood unit demarcation in new areas was described as a "design problem" quite different from delineation in existing cities, where it was more of a social, political, and economic problem.

Citing neighborhood delineation work in other cities, the ASPO report's first strategy was to base neighborhood boundaries on physical features: rivers, slopes, railroads, highways, and other natural and built impediments. But by accepting the common use of the word "barrier" to describe these boundaries, the authors easily confirmed the subsequent critique by the sociologist Reginald Isaacs that neighborhood demarcation led to social segregation. The report strained to wave off criticism by arguing that it would be better to use these features "as a cohesive agent encouraging internal social interaction, rather than as a stockade to restrict the entrance of 'undesirables.'" Other variables for neighborhood delineation in the ASPO report were census tracts (although it

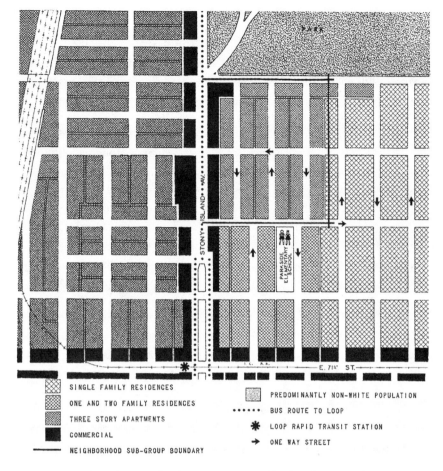

SINGLE FAMILY RESIDENCES
ONE AND TWO FAMILY RESIDENCES
THREE STORY APARTMENTS
COMMERCIAL
NEIGHBORHOOD SUB-GROUP BOUNDARY

PREDOMINANTLY NON-WHITE POPULATION
BUS ROUTE TO LOOP
LOOP RAPID TRANSIT STATION
ONE WAY STREET

Figure 5.15 Chicago's 1960 plan for connecting neighborhoods surrounding Stony Island Avenue. Source: Image redrawn from Allaire, "Neighborhood Boundaries."

Figure 5.16 Stony Island Avenue today. Image: Google Earth.

was acknowledged that they too had their downsides) and "focal points." In the end, the ASPO report recommended a negotiated, multipronged strategy for neighborhood delineation, using a combination of all considerations (physical boundaries, major streets, census tracts, and focal points).

In 1980, under the direction of Assistant Secretary Donna Shalala, HUD issued a guide on how to find the boundaries of neighborhoods. This was described as an "onerous task," but the guide painstakingly stepped through it with the intent, like the ASPO report, to facilitate data gathering. Better data, it was argued, in turn would drive neighborhood revitalization. Citing a Notre Dame study of the process of neighborhood identification in 60 cities, the report recounted a neighborhood delineation process that combined top-down administration and grass-roots initiatives. Most of the report was devoted to procedure: strategies for getting citizens involved in the process, how to mediate disputes over boundaries, legal restrictions, and the proper format for submitting boundaries to the Census Bureau. As far as anyone knows, HUD's interest in collecting data for "real" neighborhoods—not just tracts—was not continued past 1980.[50]

In an effort to introduce flexibility in boundary definition, boundaries have been conceptualized as *soft* if nearby neighborhoods are socially similar and *hard* if nearby neighborhoods are socially different.[51] But even social scientists who prioritize the social data understanding of neighborhoods are unlikely to discount the impact of physical boundaries, whereby "parks, rivers, or major commercial strips or transportation arteries facilitate the process of demarcation."[52] In the absence of bounding by major streets, a close look at street patterns provides the framework for understanding where neighborhoods begin and end.

The argument over boundaries is not just because demarcation can be exclusionary or political (impacting level of service). More theoretically, boundaries conflict with the principle of interdependence drawn from ecological theory. This was the perspective advanced by Jane Jacobs and Rachel Carson, who advocated smallness without boundaries—small ecosystems that are simultaneously interdependent and independent. Under this principle, it is neither necessary nor desirable to bound and delineate neighborhoods.[53]

The biologist and ecological philosopher Alan Rayner offered a "post-dialectic" interpretation of evolutionary process whereby energy flows are part of a "receptive spatial context." In this way, neighborhood (space and boundaries) need not be interpreted as discrete but can instead be thought of as having "natural inclusionality," in which boundaries are simultaneously used to differentiate and to integrate. The "co-creative communion" seems an ethereal idea, but it is a way to view neighborhoods as distinct, diverse, and dynamically continuous, all at the same time.[54] To some mid-20th-century planners, the neighborhood unit was perfectly capable of this kind of evolution if there was variety and flexibility in its application. Abercrombie's 1944 Greater

London Plan tried to achieve it by varying the form of the neighborhood unit from "inner urban" to "outer country." The inner neighborhoods were denser, with more variegated land uses and less open space; the outer neighborhoods went the other way.[55]

In the 1960s George Herbert sorted out the various linkages between organic theory and the neighborhood unit, postulating that the neighborhood unit could be linked, at least partially, to a number of organic analogies: cosmological, natural, systemic, ecological, and cellular. Yet according to Herbert, the neighborhood unit failed because of its insistence on boundaries, limiting the organic principle in the sense of integration with the whole. To be organic means to change and evolve, and the neighborhood unit was not designed to embrace temporal change. Added to this was the problem that additive units are not an organic system of growth; they are mechanical. When nature adds a new part, "the whole" changes too. Perry's bounded neighborhood unit was thus too standardized and simplistic, too static and inflexible. It paid no attention to how the part (the neighborhood unit) related to the whole (the city), thereby elevating the part above the whole. Perry, Herbert thought, was more interested in presenting a universal principle.[56] The irony is that the static simplicity of his approach is one reason the idea spread so rapidly.

The quest to resolve the "problem" of neighborhood boundaries continues to be explored. One researcher labeled the boundedness of neighborhood a "cloistering" process in which demarcation occurs either from the inside, for the purpose of preservation, or from the outside, where enclaving is imposed. However, it is possible to "decloister" such neighborhoods, not through assimilation or boundary dissolution but by engaging fully with "global flows" (while still maintaining local identity). Practically speaking, this happens by helping neighborhoods modernize in terms of communication and transportation infrastructure, as well as repealing laws that segregate housing.[57]

An ongoing argument in support of boundaries is that without them, there is no sense of territory and identity, which are necessary to establish neighborhood meaning. It was a notion articulated by the 20th-century French geographer Chombart de Lauwe, who surveyed Parisians and found that "for most occupational groups the ideal place to live is in a neighborhood that has some kind of identity," an identity that was based on, among other things, "clear-cut physical boundaries."[58] Dolores Hayden wrote that boundaries are essential to ethnic neighborhood identity, and though signifying "both inclusion and exclusion," boundary "enforcement" may be necessary to define economic and political power.[59] There may still be a need to keep boundaries fluid, especially for ethnic neighborhoods, because the population is constantly adjusting. Histories of ethnic groups in American cities tend to reveal inexact boundaries and edges that intermingle ethnic groups.[60]

Boundaries are obviously not the only method for neighborhood identity-building. Developers might try to instill identity through labels and markers, like entranceways and named signs. In Japan a unique numbering system was introduced to try to build neighborhood identity by numbering houses outward from the neighborhood's starting point; house #1 was built first; house #20 was built later and is farther out; and so on. The ability to feel a part of the neighborhood does not require boundaries that emphasize spatial identity; residents can instead be reminded of their place in the neighborhood's temporal identity.[61]

Neighborhood naming is another form of boundary delineation. A writer who uncovered a 110-year-old debate over the boundaries of Brooklyn's Park Slope neighborhood observed that the neighborhood boundary and name game "ends triumphantly for some people, tragically for those less quick, less favored."[62] The naming process can be based on personal fiat more than anything objective: "A neighborhood may endure because no one else wants it, or come to life because someone had a smart idea."[63] Lacking any officially sanctioned protocol, this process is subject to all kinds of power plays. Different groups seek domination, utilizing "symbolic politics in order to prove their claims." Longtime residents are pitted against middle- and upper-class gentrifiers in a battle over neighborhood definition, using "myth making" about neighborhood boundaries and identity based on the competing narratives of history or ethnicity.[64]

Whether boundaries are hard separators or more fluid and overlapping is a matter of perception and is likely to be affected by the characteristics of residents. One study found that the perception of hard boundaries is likely to decrease with age. To adolescent boys in the poor working-class neighborhoods of East London, boundaries were real, strictly delineated, and enforced through regular "confrontation and conflict." Adult men were found to have less understanding of these strictly bounded territories.[65]

Alexander argued in *A Pattern Language* that boundaries for "subcultures"—either "communities of 7000" (pattern 12) or "identifiable neighborhoods" (pattern 14)—needed to be kept separate by at least 200-foot-wide "swaths of open land, workplaces, public buildings, water, parks, or other natural boundaries" as a way of keeping one neighborhood from exerting its values on an adjacent area. This, they argued in the 1960s, is what happened when the "straight" people adjacent to Haight Ashbury in San Francisco wanted that neighborhood to be "cleaned up" by City Hall. A strong physical boundary, Alexander stressed, could release the pressure for conformity, as well as fear about lessening property values. Subcultures or neighborhoods that are cut off "are free to develop their own character."[66] Boundaries are the basis of certain freedoms, then—a somewhat unusual argument in that it could be used to justify the much maligned spatial isolationism of superblocks.

Mary Simkhovitch, an early 20th-century social reformer, embraced boundaries as a form of solidarity and strength. "What made the strength of pioneer life in this country was the sense of boundary," she wrote. Recognizing that modern life was no longer contained within the "compact unit" that organized frontier life, now instead open to "wider fields," it was the working out of a "purposeful fellowship" within the bounded neighborhood that provided meaning and "a pretty good definition of that vast and hazy word democracy." Gerard Suttles's study of social cohesion in a Chicago neighborhood similarly maintained that it was the sense of "turf"—the bounded neighborhood itself that residents identify with—that created social cohesion. One study of children's perception of neighborhood boundaries surmised that a perception of a well-bounded neighborhood had to do with "a well-bounded sense of self."[67]

Centers

Perhaps the argumentation over boundaries can be mitigated by shifting the focus to the heart of the neighborhood rather than its boundary. Historians have documented that centralized civic spaces played an essential role in neighborhood life, reflected in spatial arrangments (see color plate 11), . In an example from 19th-century Sicily, neighborhoods traditionally consisted of households grouped around a partially enclosed courtyard, called a *cortili*, that functioned as an outdoor shared room. The *cortili* was the center of social life, the location of

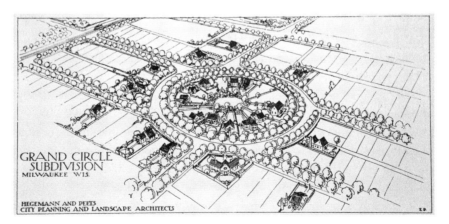

Figure 5.17 In the early 20th century, city planners tried to create neighborhood identity in an otherwise endless grid system by inserting elaborate, centrally positioned civic spaces. Shown here is Hegemann and Peets's "Milwaukee Grand Circle," an effort to "insert a pleasant variation into an existing gridiron." Source: Hegemann and Peets, *The American Vitruvius.*

friendships, and the basis of the Sicilian concept of neighborhood. These were not family compounds. One's extended family lived outside the *cortili*, not within, giving meaning to the Sicilian proverb "Your neighbor is your real relative" and providing a counternarrative to the idea that kinship is all that mattered in southern Italy. However, once immigrants landed in the dense tenement districts of New York City, absent the socializing force of the *cortili*, reliance on kin grew.[68]

Perry maintained that the center should be equidistant from all residents (because that was the best way to maximize access), but he also stressed that center and boundary were mutually reinforcing. Planners later sought to elevate the neighborhood center over its boundary as one of two deviations from Perry (the other being that boundaries could become more accentuated by using green belts to surround and isolate neighborhoods, as in the case of the British New Towns).[69] Then as now, the center is believed to provide a visible, literal focal point, as well as a permanent symbol of the common bond that people living in the same neighborhood share.[70] As Leon Krier put it, in the urban quarter a "beautiful boundary" is a luxury, a "beautiful center" is a necessity.[71] Resident surveys have given this center-over-boundary idea some legitimacy. For example, a survey of 322 people in a hilly area with curvilinear streets in Brisbane, Australia, asked residents about their neighborhood boundaries, and results showed weak agreement on boundaries but strong agreement on the neighborhood's core.[72]

Of course, centers can also be boundaries. In the 1970s it was suggested that neighborhoods could be defined by interviewing a few adolescent boys and understanding their perception of barriers, since it was an age and gender group that represented "a free ranging, diurnally tied, family member with little managerial, sexual or ceremonial restraint or responsibility." The method showed that schools were not really neighborhood centers at all, but were instead neighborhood boundaries.[73] In the adult world, enclaves can be formed from a core location outward, a magnet that attracts by way of goods and services, and that has the same exclusionary outcome as a hard boundary.[74]

Perry's school-centered neighborhood countered the "centerless tendency" of urban expansion prior to the 1920s. It was an attempt to reverse what was mostly a transportation-based method of city-building.[75] Ironically one critique of Radburn (which was based on Perry's neighborhood unit) was that it lacked this centrality and that its green communal space created ambiguity about ownership and control. Herbert implored planners to "worry less about the size and boundaries of neighborhood units and concentrate instead on the institutions and amenities which constitute the focal points of the area," stressing that design was essential for this to succeed. He lauded Walter Burley Griffin's plan for Canberra because he believed it was able to work out a solution involving vague boundaries and strong centers recognizable for their repetitive pattern rather than their functionality.[76]

The QUARTER

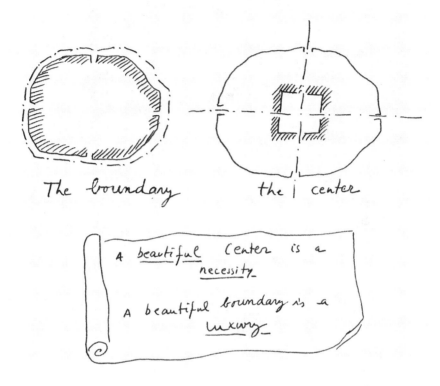

The boundary   the | center

A *beautiful* Center is a *necessity*

A *beautiful* boundary is a *luxury*

Figure 5.18 "The Quarter," by Leon Krier. Source: Krier, *The Architecture of Community*.

Physically the historical precedent for a neighborhood center was the central square. Spanish colonial town planning required them; William Penn established them for Philadelphia, James Oglethorpe for Savannah; and hundreds of courthouse squares embodied the physical expression of community life. In a slightly loosened interpretation, Mumford argued that neighborhoods needed "some point of focus" outside the home, which could be a health center, a settlement house, a school, a community center—these were "all worthy attempts." Patrick Geddes suggested that neighborhoods should set aside a "handsome historic house" that families could rent for parties, while in England a room attached to a pub was considered an appropriate focal point for the neighborhood.[77] French historians pointed to the influence of the "public monument" on defining a neighborhood's layout, life, and "aspect," and public buildings were conceived as the "factor of movement" that helped neighborhoods form around them.[78]

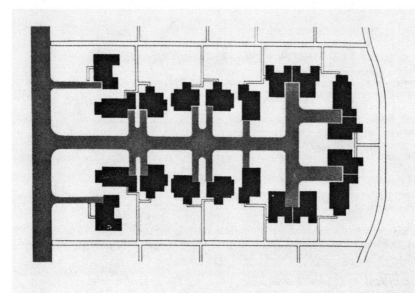

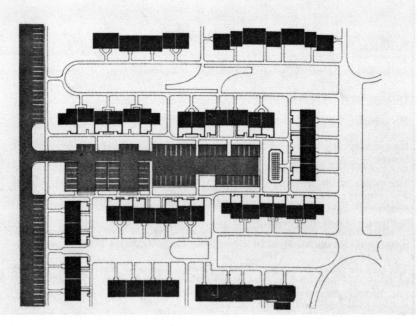

Figure 5.19 The neighborhoods of Radburn, New Jersey, were critiqued by Serge Chermayeff and Christopher Alexander because "the generous provision of communal park space raises new problems of ownership and responsibility." Source: Chermayeff and Alexander, *Community and Privacy*.

Figure 5.20 Public open space anchors housing in the new town of Jakriborg in southern Sweden. Source: Wikimedia Commons, https://commons.wikimedia.org/wiki/File:Jakriborg,_ juni_2005_c.jpg#metadata

In the U.S., centers associated with the settlement house neighborhood took the form of a building or group of buildings. Jane Addams's settlement in Chicago was known as the Chicago Commons Buildings, serving, for example, as neighborhood meeting place, health clinic, school, and communal kitchen. In a manner Jane Jacobs would have approved, it was also a place where the neighborhood connected with the ward alderman and other city politicians in an effort to strengthen its political impact. Above all, the Chicago Commons was "a center for a higher civic and social life" in a diverse industrial district. The Commons was meant to bridge diversity and provide a way "to understand, to interpret and to co-operate" among "strangers in a strange land."[79] Later in the 1960s planners believed that neighborhood centers would be strongest in areas with "concentrations of minority groups," for example, "a Buddhist Church in an oriental neighborhood, a bocce ball court in an Italian area." The "elementary school–common green–community center complex" was an attempt to replicate the magnetism of ethnically specific center functions, with only mixed success.[80]

According to the historian Howard Gillette, the neighborhood center as a deliberate planning idea was launched in St. Louis's plan of 1907. Prior to that, under the reign of the City Beautiful movement, centers were larger, serving the

Figure 5.21 John Daniels published this photo of a neighborhood center in Fitchburg, Massachusetts. The "Finnish Co-operative Center," he wrote, was erected "by the Finns themselves" and contained "a grocery store, meat market, boot-and-shoe shop, bakery, milk-distributing plant, restaurant, and living apartments." Source: Daniels, *America via the Neighborhood*.

needs of an entire city. The St. Louis plan was the first to decentralize, providing a "neighborhood approach to civic concerns," advanced by placing a half-dozen centers throughout the city. Of note is that Henry Wright, who together with Clarence Stein planned Radburn, was instrumental in developing the St. Louis neighborhood civic center concept.[81] The center was supposed to be a neighborhood space that took on "the characteristics of a centrally located magnet that exerts its influence radially."[82] But in a recent turn toward pragmatism, as well as a shift from institutionally based to retail-based centers, some planners now advocate putting the neighborhood center along a busy thoroughfare so that it has a better chance of surviving.

In the 1920s neighborhood centers formed around playgrounds or recreation buildings, famously in Chicago and Washington, D.C., where such venues went beyond the mere provision of equipment and were explicitly intended to "promote neighbourhood consciousness."[83] But it was the school as center that resonated most. Even Ebenezer Howard located a school at the center of each ward in his 1898 Garden City diagram. Perry was under the influence of the social center movement, which advocated in the early 19th century that schools should function as neighborhood centers complete with adult education and town forums. Edward Ward originated the concept in 1907 in Rochester, New York, and was committed to the idea of using neighborhood schools for multiple community functions, an idea also advocated by Jacob Riis. Ward wrote in 1914, "The whole United States is divided into two units of neighborhood. One is the voting precinct, the other is the public school district." The movement sought to merge the two, such that voting would take place exclusively in public schools.[84]

This resonated with Perry. In his 1914 book, *The School as a Factor in Neighborhood Development*, Perry described all the ways that schools were essential for civic life. There was solid evidence, he wrote, that "throughout the country there is a growing tendency to resort to school buildings for deliberation upon matters of civic and political import." Perry detailed the ways in which the "school plant" was being physically altered to accommodate voting booths, museums, employment bureaus, branch libraries, art galleries, and theatrical productions. (Perry pointed out that the novelty of movable chairs was making it easy to transform the school into something else.) In some cases, these school transformations corresponded to neighborhood identity, but if school administration was centralized rather than school-based, the connection to the neighborhood seemed more ad hoc.[85] On the other hand national organizations were supportive: the American Public Health Association's Committee on the Hygiene of Housing published *Planning the Neighborhood: Standards for Healthful Housing* in 1948 to argue that an elementary school–based neighborhood was the source of physical, social, and emotional health.[86]

The centrality of the school in neighborhood identity-building was even more pronounced in rural settings. One 1923 study of rural neighborhoods in New York State delineated areas of "human association" by working with rural schoolteachers. The teachers had their students take a questionnaire home, and each family was asked to identify what their "country neighborhood" was. The teachers then transferred these descriptions and names to a map. Where there was sufficient overlap in the 150 returned questionnaires, a neighborhood was indicated. Using a definition of neighborhood as a "geographic group" beyond the family that "is conscious of some local unity," neighborhood identity seemed mostly based on the school; half of the neighborhoods were identical in name and geographic area to the school district. On the other hand, social functioning was mostly a matter of helping out with farm projects (harvesting) or exchanging tools, as opposed to connection via organized social events. The authors of the study concluded, "In general, the rural neighborhood [is] ceasing to function as a social unit except where its life is centered in some local institution."[87]

But rural schools, abandoned in school consolidations, were increasingly unable to serve that function.[88] Proponents of rural neighborhoods seemed to understand that neighborhoods needed to have centers and that "centers need accommodations, buildings, which even the local farmer can feel are his very own."[89] A Wisconsin plan called for establishing cooperative agricultural communities, called "neighborhoods," and similarly argued that neighborhoods needed to have a physical focal point in the form of a neighborhood center.[90] County employees in rural 1940s North Carolina were specifically charged with identifying neighborhood centers where meetings could take place.[91]

In more urban areas, the historical emphasis on schools as neighborhood congealers now has to be weighed against the reality that schools are not the social integrators they once were. A serious problem in the U.S. is the association of school quality with wealth, where the "good school" attracts affluence and virtually defines neighborhood segregation. Added to this, the ability of a school to function as a center is compromised because many public schools are more school board–based than neighborhood-based, thus losing their incentive for neighborhood connection.[92] Schools today are a far cry from their position as centers of neighborhood life that an earlier generation viewed as fundamental to a child's education. Planners had previously focused on the "school-neighborhood nucleus," arguing that "every neighborhood planner is an educator" and that "the best education is the result of a well-conceived neighborhood plan in which the school has been created as an integral part of the daily life of all the people who reside in the community."[93] Now the interrelation of school and neighborhood is spatially and programmatically ambiguous. School consolidation trends as well as modern site design requirements (having to do with parking and the size of playing fields, for example) have made the connection especially problematic.[94]

Recent proposals have expanded the range of what the neighborhood center should consist of—often a full-blown mixed-use retail destination. The urban planning firm Dover Kohl suggested that the neighborhood center should not only be mixed-use but relatively high-density (although ideally limited to four stories outside of a metropolitan core) and take the form of a square, plaza, or simply the "four corners" of a prominent street intersection. The firm of Duany, Plater-Zyberk & Co. suggested that the neighborhood center should consist of neighborhood shops, institutions, and a bus stop, with the elementary school transferred to the edge to make it accessible to adjoining neighborhoods. Architect Doug Farr provided an update by calling for a "higher intensity transit mode" (bus rapid transit, trolley, light rail) at the center.[95]

If the neighborhood is diverse in terms of housing types and land uses, a neighborhood center is believed to be a good way to link and integrate the mix, which might otherwise lack any deliberate, meaningful connection in terms of physical design. One idea is that if diverse housing types front the neighborhood center equally, they may be more likely to be equally acknowledged as important, even if only symbolically.[96] Related to this are studies documenting the special importance of neighborhood centers—shops, schools, bars, streets, and health centers—in multicultural and multilingual urban neighborhoods.[97]

In heterogeneous neighborhoods social connection via homogeneity can't be relied on, so the emphasis shifts to public space rather than social relationships as a way of countering alienation. In the Netherlands, a sense of neighborhood was found to be especially important for establishing social contacts in unfamiliar terrain, prompting a policy recommendation to create more "meeting places in public spaces."[98]

Neighborhood space as central meeting ground is used to purposefully draw divergent populations together. A project called Barriers Not Included to transform a park in Charlotte, North Carolina, between two very different neighborhoods had the purpose of creating a common area that would use light, sound, and play "to stimulate conversation." The project's designers believed that the transformed park, which sits at the border of the two neighborhoods, would be able to "build relationships and connections."[99]

In high-crime neighborhoods, the neighborhood center takes on the added role of being a safe haven. Neighborhood schools, churches, or other forms of center are protected places that have been shown to be significant factors in a child's ability to cope with violence, reduce anxiety, and increase resiliency.[100] Churches play a special role as neighborhood centers, and their form matters. One study showed that storefront churches, as opposed to freestanding churches, were valuable in poor neighborhoods because, positioned near commercial uses, they offered "a level of continuity and favorable visibility" that was able to provide "material benefit" to other adjacent properties.[101]

There is a certain stability that accompanies the idea that a place of worship is a neighborhood center, especially if the spatial connection between church and churchgoer can be maintained. One study contrasting "resident" and "commuter" churches in Philadelphia found that the former tend to be within neighborhoods that are more stable in terms of household income, homeownership rates, change of residence, population density, and racial makeup. Members' proximity to their place of worship, in other words, is related to neighborhood stability. The obvious challenge is to avoid the situation where overprotection of the church-based neighborhood leads to exclusion.[102]

Another update of the neighborhood center involves connecting multiple centers to create a series of linked focal points. So in addition to drawing residents in, centers facilitate movement through a neighborhood, and potentially enhance the connections between them. One proposal argued for the installation of "artifacts" along "pathways," providing meaningful destinations that not only motivate walking but enhance neighborhood identity.[103]

Focal points can also be a kind of territorial marker that informally regulates and enhances interaction. Conceptually this parallels the decorations on housing units that promote social encounter, like flower boxes and porch decorations.[104] A downscale version of the neighborhood center might similarly be small gardens or renovated houses, or perhaps the result of an urban home-steading program in which vacant property is transferred to communal owner-ship (see color plate 12).[105] Neighborhoods that lack such memorable places are not benign; they can exert negative social effects, like alienation.[106]

Streets

There are boundaries, there are centers, and then there are the internal street patterns of neighborhoods. Streets are important not only for delineation but because neighborhoods might be perceived primarily on the basis of travel along them (by way of sidewalks as well as travel lanes). This movement might include starting at an entrance, traveling along internal pathways, and arriving at various internal destinations. The effects of the physical form of streets is not ambig-uous: neighborhood street patterns determine how people move through space, and therefore the frequency with which people interact. There may still be some debate over the broader implications of this movement and interaction.[107]

In addition, and in complete reversal of neighborhood unit proposals from the 1920s and later, streets are essential public spaces, a view owed largely to the writings of Jane Jacobs. For neighborhoods, streets and sidewalks are not mere conduits; they are outdoor rooms. Streets constitute the largest geographic area of public ownership (by far) and have the ability to create a sense of neighbor-hood based not on social homogeneity but on a shared desire to keep this essen-tial public space desirable and safe.

The important issue about streets in relation to neighborhoods is that dif-ferent street arrangements will create very different experiences of neighbor-hood. It is often argued that the most important point about a neighborhood's internal street pattern is that it needs to be well connected. Neighborhood can be defined as the area around a dwelling, but once positioned in space and at-tached to a street system, a dwelling is no longer just an individual unit; it is part of a network of "spatial practices" that includes people, buildings, landscape, and all the processes and activities associated with them.[108] Connectivity, by way of streets or other kind of pathway, necessarily occurs, which is why neighborhood has been described as a "state of connection."[109] A whole range of meanings and behaviors are then invoked: identity, sense of belonging, social interaction, net-working, and functionality.

The blockage of neighborhood connectivity is often problematized for creat-ing dangerous dead-end streets, loss of "eyes on the street," slower emergency vehicle response times, and ultimately more traffic and more congestion.[110] Donald Appleyard compared the neighborhoods of Radburn, Levittown, and Back Bay in Boston and concluded that Back Bay was the neighborhood with

the strongest imageability because of its strongly defined system of internal pathways (in addition to its compactness and its differentiation).[111] Internal connectivity is likely to improve accessibility too. A study of Calgary's neighborhoods
found that the grid-defined neighborhood type had substantially better connectivity and therefore a much larger "walkshed" than either the warped grid or
curvilinear neighborhood types.[112]

This counters Mumford's contention that Manhattan's strict grid was "con-
trived as if for the purpose of preventing neighborhoods from coming into
existence."[113] Contemporaries criticized the rapid march of undifferentiated,
speculative, grid-based 19th-century urbanism as fostering capitalist greed at
the expense of neighborhood formation. The American planners John Nolen
and Clarence Stein railed against the soul-dispiriting American urban form
characterized by the endless grid (although Nolen seemed more interested
in creative approaches to "land subdivision" than in actual neighborhood
formation).[114]

These "rectilinear urban habits" of American urbanism were well established even in the Colonial period, and the application of Jefferson's 1785
grid across the unsettled territories of the U.S. seemed a logical extension of
the grid culture of U.S. town planning.[115] But in the hands of industrial urbanization, the social value of land was ignored, and the unimproved grid became
the basis of 19th-century expansion, focused exclusively on land speculation
and consumption.[116] Grafting a sense of neighborhood onto the speculative
grid seemed a tall order and out of keeping with most historical accounts of
neighborhood formation. But where it does exist, as "oases of the creative
spirit within the larger desert of the checkerboard mentality," neighborhood
identity and spirit are said to flourish. Two examples are the creative street
and square designs of Ladd's Addition (1891) in Portland, Oregon, and the
radial plan of Perryopolis, Pennsylvania (1814), both of which survive intact
today.[117]

The 19th-century urban designer Camillo Sitte reflected on the relationship between street pattern and neighborhood form from the standpoint of
creating visual interest. In his 1889 classic text, *City Planning According to
Artistic Principles*, he compared an orthogonal neighborhood plan to one laid
out by Friedrich Puetzer, showing how the same neighborhood with a more
curvilinear street pattern could provide street vistas. Dhiru Thadani updated
the argument (beyond visual variety and the creation of vistas) to show the
importance of a neighborhood street hierarchy that naturally limits through-
traffic to only a few streets. These become the logical places for mixed uses (retail, offices, etc.), and the discontinuous streets—the ones requiring a corner
turn or that terminate at a civic space—will, as a matter of course, produce
calmer traffic.[118]

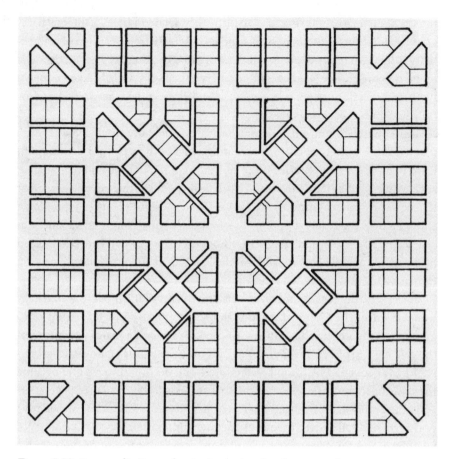

Figure 5.22 Perryopolis, Pennsylvania. Source: Arendt and American Planning Association, *Crossroads, Hamlet, Village, Town.*

The effect of traffic on neighborhoods dominated the thinking of most 20th-century proponents of the neighborhood unit, modernist or not. They lamented the automobile, which was cutting "deep channels" through residential areas and creating "islands around which raging streams of traffic" flowed. Perry pleaded, "Why should we not insist upon equal municipal care and forethought in the interest of the pedestrian and the resident?" The neighborhood unit proposed "a remedy for precisely this emergency" by limiting through-traffic.[119] Perry's street arrangement would also, he argued, lower costs. In the neighborhood unit, street costs per lot were $485, which, Perry estimated, were well below a conventional layout, where street costs were $856 per lot.[120]

But the long-standing and unresolved debate is the relationship between street connectivity, residential life, and wider social and economic connection. Most of the 1912 Chicago Club neighborhood design entries tried to resolve the tension with gridded streets that lined up with the existing Chicago grid. At

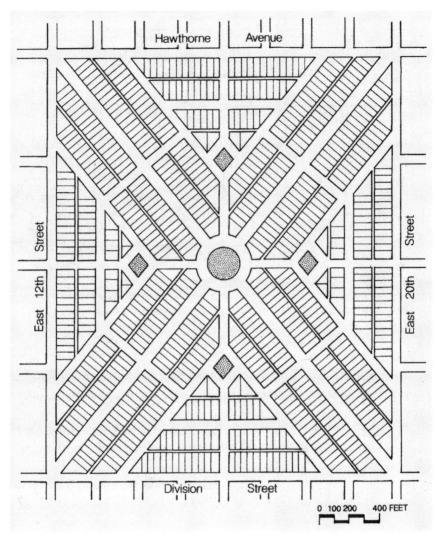

Figure 5.23 Ladd's Addition, Portland, Oregon. Source: Arendt and American Planning Association, *Crossroads, Hamlet, Village, Town.*

the time, planners understood that neighborhoods needed to guard against insularity, that they needed to connect to the city at large and show their relationship to "the whole."[121]

Michael Mehaffy, Sergio Porta, Yodan Rofè, and Nikos Salingaros analyzed the position of the neighborhood center (which they termed its "nucleus") in relation to the street network. They criticized the center in Perry's neighborhood unit scheme for its disconnection, fragmentation, and insularity, lacking connection to the "movement economy," that is, well-traveled streets. Ideally, they argued,

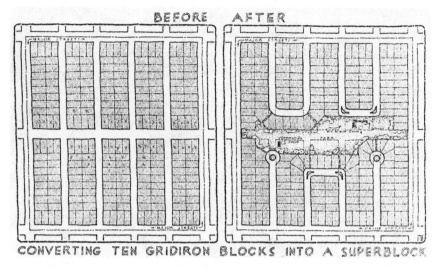

Figure 5.24 This 1920s-era neighborhood redesign argued that the gridiron plan is not suitable for residential neighborhoods because it is "wasteful, expensive, dangerous and unpleasant." Source: Richman and Chapin, *A Review of the Social and Physical Concepts of the Neighborhood.*

centers should be located on streets that are both well-connected and traffic-calmed. They made an additional argument that there is too much confusion between "neighborhood" and "pedestrian shed." A pedestrian shed—the geographic range of access, often conceived as a five-minute walk around an amenity or intersection—may or may not coincide with a neighborhood. Neighborhoods can span more than one pedestrian shed, and people have varying interpretations and perceptions of how neighborhoods are structured. It would be better to dichotomize: pedestrian sheds are about service and social life, and neighborhoods are about something else. And unlike the definition of neighborhood, the pedestrian shed has a regularity to it: 400 meters (equivalent to one-quarter mile or a five-minute walk) between main thoroughfares is a maximum spacing "that traditional, pedestrian-governed urban fabric has always tended to obey."[122]

Between major streets, "sanctuary areas"—areas with quieter and localized streets, which Appleyard called "sanctuary streets"—emerge over time. These sanctuary areas, smaller than neighborhoods and based on the 400-meter rule, are the essential building blocks of cities and were so until modernist urbanism severed the relationship between urban growth and human scale. Both the Jeffersonian grid and the neighborhood unit disrupted this scale and, lacking a connection to the time-honored regularity of 400-meter main streets and intervening sanctuary areas (resulting from "self-organized urban accretion"), became "an abysmal failure based upon a complete misunderstanding of human nature and urban community."[123] The solution is not to try to fix neighborhoods to some predefined

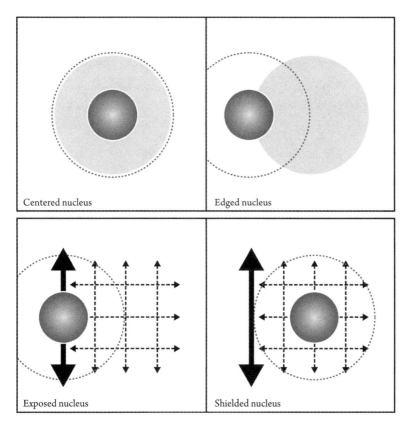

Figure 5.25 In this conception by Mehaffy, Porta, Rofè, and Salingaros, the center or nucleus of a neighborhood can be "centered," "edged," "exposed," "shielded," or some combination. Perry's center is "centered" and "shielded," resulting in insularity, although "edged" and "shielded" would be worse because the center would be disconnected from major streets. The "centered" and "exposed" combination is considered best because nuclei are close to the main movement network (major streets), but nuclei also function as geographic centers. Source: Sergio Porta, published in Mehaffy et al., "Urban Nuclei and the Geometry of Streets," 25–27.

geographic scale but to let them emerge variously—sometimes quiet and sequestered, sometimes centralized and vibrant, sometimes school-centered or focused on a park. Urban nuclei, on the other hand, are fixed because they are based on pedestrian regularity. The upshot is that neighborhoods cannot be designed, but pedestrian sheds can. What is ignored is the limit placed on governance and resident control as it relates to neighborhood functionality. No one is likely to rally around a "pedestrian shed" for proaction, empowerment, and sense of identity.[124]

There would be no need to separate and bound neighborhoods into sheltered units—the way Perry advocated—if disruptors like highways, hospitals, and other large or specialist uses could be made to integrate with smaller and more fine-grained pedestrian networks. All forms of mobility—pedestrian, car, public

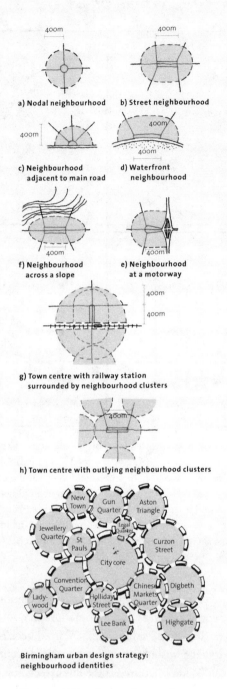

Figure 5.26 A British publication, *Urban Design Compendium*, argues that the neighborhood is successful as an "organizing device" only when overlaid on a "movement framework"—streets, rails, waterways—thereby avoiding the "disconnected enclave" problem. The *Compendium* shows five versions of the neighborhood as a 400-meter mixed-use spatial unit overlaid on various transportation options. Also shown is the neighborhood on a slope and neighborhoods clustered around a town center. Source: Llewelyn-Davies, *Urban Design Compendium*.

transit—are needed and should be combined into "an integrated framework for fluid movement and growth." (In Jacobs's words, the goal should be "city mobility and fluidity of use.")[125] The "emergent neighborhood" model blends in well here, while defined and bounded neighborhood units do not. The former allow "continuity of accessibility across a larger urban field," whereby neighborhoods spontaneously form around central places.[126]

The measurement of neighborhood street connectivity is consequential, as rating systems—like LEED for neighborhood development (LEED ND)—rely heavily on measures of street connectivity as indicators of the sustainable neighborhood. One complication is that, because of the possibility of pedestrian pathways and street blockages, the street pattern might be tree-like, with good connectivity, or grid-like, with poor connectivity. Some measures have been challenged as too loose, where it is possible to "game" the LEED ND street connectivity measure such that streets appear highly connected but through-traffic is actually blocked. Neighborhoods that have a lot of short streets can seem to have high connectivity if the metric used is intersection density. But if those short streets do not connect, perhaps bounded by wider arterials, as in Perry's classic scheme, neighborhood connectivity is actually low.[127]

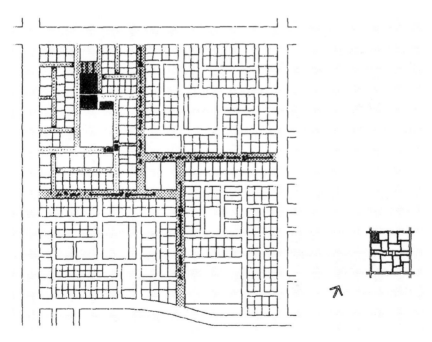

Figure 5.27 This modern gridiron plan in Saudi Arabia is composed of neighborhoods and subneighborhoods: through streets are minimized, but the connectivity is high. Source: Image redrawn from Eben Saleh, "Planning and Designing for Defense, Security and Safety in Saudi Arabian Residential Environments."

Which leads us back to the primary neighborhood design debate: major streets as boundaries of neighborhoods versus major streets as seams around which neighborhoods form. Appleyard, who eloquently summed "around the street lies the neighborhood"—a view shared by Jacobs—argues that if streets were livable, they would be the protectors of neighborhoods, not via encircling boundaries but via good street redesign. For neighborhoods in need of the most protection, this redesign could be in the form of the Dutch *woonerf*, a "street for living."[128]

Those advocating streets as boundaries, as Perry did, might take solace in the fact that it is a neighborhood form that is historical and cross-cultural. Internalizing neighborhoods by surrounding them with larger, busier streets and relegating smaller, pedestrian-oriented streets to the interior of the neighborhood is how Chinese neighborhoods were, and still are, often structured, with surrounding secondary streets connecting to main streets, and internal "lanes."[129] And in the traditional Islamic neighborhood, the interior is quiet and protected, and narrow passages shield the neighborhood from the heavier traffic of outsiders. And yet the centripetal effect of the neighborhood center may be the stronger force supporting neighborhood identification.

Notes

1. "Planning with You," 80.
2. Krier, *Houses, Palaces, Cities*, 79.
3. Stein, "Toward New Towns for America," 224, 226.
4. National Federation of Settlements, "A Letter from Robert A. Woods."
5. Alexander, "A City is Not a Tree."
6. Perry, *Housing for the Machine Age*, 129.
7. Perry et al., *The Rebuilding of Blighted Areas*, 12.
8. Abercrombie and Forshaw, *The County of London Plan*, 28; Tripp, *Town Planning*; Dehaene, "Surveying and Comprehensive Planning," 26.
9. Hoyt, "Rebuilding American Cities," 366, 367.
10. Minneapolis City Planning Commission, "Neighborhood and Community Goals for Minneapolis Living Areas," reproduced in Allaire, "Neighborhood Boundaries," appendix A, 27–28.
11. A summary of neighborhood components was offered by Gulyani and Bassett, "The Living Conditions Diamond"; Spreiregen, *Urban Design*, 78–79.
12. Gillette, "The Evolution of Neighborhood Planning," 439.
13. Brody, "The Neighbourhood Unit."
14. Forest Hills Gardens scores a 90 for both Walk Score and Transit Score; see walkscore.com.
15. Nelson, "Architects of Europe Today."
16. Goodman and Goodman, *Communitas*, 144.
17. Sert and International Congresses for Modern Architecture, *Can Our Cities Survive?*, 70, 234.
18. For example, Kahn's, "Housing in the Rational City Plan" cited in Tyng, *Beginnings: Louis I. Kahn's Philosophy*; See also Ayad, "Louis I. Kahn and Neighborhood Design"; Rofe, "Space and Community."
19. Neutra, "Peace Can Gain," 601.
20. De Chiara and Koppelman, *Urban Planning and Design Criteria*.

21. Herbert, "The Neighbourhood Unit Principle."
22. Chermayeff and Alexander, *Community and Privacy*, 191.
23. Hilberseimer, *The New City*, 104.
24. Lee and Ahn, "Is Kentlands Better Than Radburn?"
25. Talen, "Affordability in New Urbanist Development."
26. For example, the *condominios exclusivos* of Brazilian cities reinforce social segregation and turn the private neighborhood inward, away from the city. See Carvalho et al., "Residential Satisfaction in Condominios Exclusivos."; Snyder, *Fortress America*; Low, *Behind the Gates*.
27. See, for example, Brooke, "On the Edges of the Public Sphere."
28. Graziosi, "Urban Geospatial Digital Neighborhood Areas," 2.
29. Thiis-Evenson and Campbell, *Archetypes of Urbanism*, 62.
30. Ibid.
31. Patricios, "Urban design principles."
32. Federal Housing Administration, "Land Planning Bulletin," 19.
33. Moudon, "Housing and Settlement Design Series."
34. Unwin, *Town Planning in Practice*, 154.
35. Perry, *Neighborhood and Community Planning*, 31.
36. Mumford, *The City in History*, 310.
37. Garrioch, "Sacred Neighborhoods," 410.
38. For example, this is the case in Miami, where the Metropolitan Planning Organization uses Census Designated Places to delineate its neighborhoods. See Hallman, *The Organization and Operation of Neighborhood Councils*.
39. McKnight and Block, *The Abundant Community*, 139; Fox and Guglielmo. "Defining America's Racial Boundaries."
40. Quote from the planning director of Minneapolis, cited in Allaire, "Neighborhood Boundaries."
41. Lewis, *Planning the Modern City*, 3. See also Saarinen, *The City*.
42. Lynch, *Image of the City*.
43. Jacobs, *Death and Life*, 8.
44. Ayad, "Louis I. Kahn and Neighborhood Design."
45. Nyden et al., "Chapter 1"; Nyden et al., "The Emergence." In a similar vein, Jan Gehl, in *Life Between Buildings*, refers to "soft edges" and Skjaeveland and Garling, in "Effects" refer to "interactional space."
46. Rofe, "Space and Community," 109, 120; Nyden et al., "The Emergence."
47. Greenberg, *The Poetics of Cities*, 109.
48. Mumford, "The Neighborhood and the Neighborhood Unit," 257. See also Mehaffy et al., "The 'Neighborhood Unit' on Trial"; Jacobs, *The Death and Life*, 115; Hillier et al., "Natural Movement"; Institute of Transportation Engineers, "Designing Walkable Urban Thoroughfares."
49. Allaire, "Neighborhood Boundaries."
50. Broden et al., "Neighborhood Identification."
51. Hipp and Boessen, "Egohoods."
52. Grigsby et al., "Residential Neighborhoods and Submarkets," 20.
53. On boundary meaning, see Galton, "On the Ontological Status of Geographical Boundaries." On the connection between Jane Jacobs and Rachel Carson, see Kinkela, "The Ecological Landscapes."
54. Wilson, *The Neighborhood Project*, 386, 389, 390; Rayner, "Space Cannot Be Cut."
55. Herbert, "The Neighbourhood Unit Principle."
56. Ibid., 182.
57. Laguerre, *Global Neighborhoods*.
58. Buttimer, "Social Space," 424.
59. Hayden, "The Potential of Ethnic Places," 16.
60. See, for example, Feinstein, *Ethnic Groups in the City*.
61. Hall, *The Hidden Dimension*, 106.
62. Williams, *Blurred Lines*.
63. "New York."

64. Kasinitz, "The Gentrification," 178.
65. Lammers, "The Birth of the East Ender," 334.
66. Alexander, *A Pattern Language*, 78.
67. MOMA Press Release; Suttles, *The Social Order*, 4; Sell, "Territoriality," 298.
68. Gabaccia, "Sicilians in Space" see 59n32 for the source of the Sicilian proverb.
69. Herbert, "The Neighbourhood Unit Principle."
70. See a discussion of this point by Larice, "Great Neighborhoods."
71. Krier, *Houses, Palaces, Cities*, 71.
72. Minnery et al., "Bounding Neighbourhoods."
73. Green, "Aerial Photographic Analysis"; Bowden, "How to Define Neighborhood," 228.
74. Abrahamson, *Urban Enclaves*.
75. Warner, *Streetcar Suburbs*, 158, 159.
76. Herbert, "The Neighbourhood Unit Principle," 184.
77. Mumford, "Planning for the Phases of Life," 12.
78. Bardet, "Social Topography," 249.
79. Chicago Commons Association, *Chicago Commons*, 8, 6, 31.
80. Allaire, "Neighborhood Boundaries," 14.
81. Gillette, "The Evolution of Neighborhood Planning."
82. Allaire, "Neighborhood Boundaries," 14.
83. Peets, "Current Town Planning," 230.
84. Ward, "Where Suffragists and Anti's Unite," 519.
85. Ibid.; Perry, "The School as a Factor," 3.
86. American Public Health Association, *Planning the Neighborhood*.
87. Sanderson and Thompson, "The Social Areas of Otsego County," 27.
88. Holt, "Report," 2, 5, 7.
89. Kolb, "Rural Primary Groups," 105.
90. Williams, "A Plan for a Co-operative Neighborhood."
91. Holt, "Report," 2, 5, 7.
92. Sanchez-Jankowski, *Cracks in the Pavement*.
93. Engelhardt, "The School-Neighborhood Nucleus," 89.
94. See Norris, "*The Neighborhood School*."
95. Plater-Zyberk et al., *The Lexicon of the New Urbanism*; Farr, *Sustainable Urbanism*, 126.
96. Duany, "Chapter 25 Commentary."
97. Blommaert et al., "Polycentricity."
98. Bloem et al, "Starting Relationships," 44.
99. Funded by the Knight Foundation's Informed and Engaged Communities challenge.
100. Osofsky, "The Impact of Violence on Children."
101. Kinney and Winter, "Places of Worship," 348.
102. Sinha et al., "Proximity Matters."
103. Hess et al., "Pathways and Artifacts."
104. See, for example, Greenbaum and Greenbaum, "Territorial Personalization Group Identity."
105. See, for example, "I Grow Chicago" in the Englewood community of Chicago.
106. Ward, *The Child in the City*; Brown et al., "Place Attachment."
107. For example, shared routes and destinations might lead to shared mental imagery about what a neighborhood is, but increased connectivity could lessen a sense of security and control rather than breeding familiarity. See Hillier et al., "Creating Life," 248.
108. For example, Weiss et al., "Defining Neighborhood Boundaries"; De Marco and De Marco, "Conceptualization and Measurement"; Santos et al., "Demarcation of Local Neighborhoods"; Chow, "Differentiating Urban Neighborhoods"; Youssoufi and Foltête, "Determining Appropriate Neighborhood Shapes and Sizes," 12.
109. Wiebe, "People Define a Neighborhood."
110. Zack, "To Connect or Not to Connect?"
111. Appleyard, "Towards an Imageable Structure."
112. Sandalack et al., "Neighbourhood Type and Walkshed Size."
113. Mumford, "The Neighborhood and the Neighborhood Unit," 258.
114. Nolen, *New Ideas*.

115. Kostof, *The City Shaped*, 116.
116. Marcuse, "The Grid as City Plan."
117. Arendt and American Planning Association, *Crossroads, Hamlet, Village, Town*, 20.
118. Collins et al., *Camillo Sitte*; Thadani, *The Language of Towns and Cities*, 76.
119. Perry, "City Planning for Neighborhood Life," 99.
120. Perry, "Neighborhood and Community Planning."
121. Wolfe, "Streets Regulating Neighborhood Form." See more at Wolfe, "Re-visioning Neighborhood and the City."
122. Mehaffy et al., "Urban Nuclei," 25–27.
123. Ibid., 22, 33.
124. Ibid.
125. Jacobs, *Death and Life*, 139.
126. Mehaffy et al., "The 'Neighborhood Unit' on Trial," 12.
127. Stangl and Guinn, "Neighborhood Design."
128. Appleyard, "Livable Streets." On the *woonerf*, see Heeger, "The Dutch Solution."
129. Jin, "The Historical Development of Chinese Urban Morphology."

| 6 |

The Planning Problem

This chapter reviews the debate over predetermination, that is, whether neighborhoods should and can be planned into existence. The planned neighborhood is the result of deliberative action, either through a physical plan or as a set of orchestrated actions, in contrast to spontaneous neighborhood formation. The emphasis here is on the contrast between planning for a specified end state and "neighborhood planning" as a process with no predetermined outcome, especially in physical terms. A common narrative is that top-down neighborhood planning has been harmful, for example when it was used to motivate wholesale destruction of existing neighborhoods in the urban renewal period. To critics, planned neighborhoods will always be too controlling and easily contrasted with more "authentic" neighborhoods that emerge without coercion as part of a generative process. Supporting these arguments are the examples of neighborhood plans rendered half-way (see color plates 13a, b, c), or that failed to hold their form (see color plates 14a,b), creating neighborhood remnants that were at best a waste of effort, and at worst, a degraded urban condition.

But others believe that, despite the challenges and risks, neighborhood formation requires forethought in a world dominated by placelessness, social detachment, and urban sprawl. The resolution of this debate proposes merging the best of both worlds: neighborhoods that do not ignore the importance of bottom-up generation but are still open to the possibility of a planned physical ideal.

Lewis Mumford regarded neighborhoods as simply "a fact of nature" and that to claim they were the "wilful mental creations of romantic sociologists" was "downright absurd."[1] But whether they *do* exist is a different question from whether they *ought* to exist. Are neighborhoods something to be encouraged? And if so, is it possible to plan them? Who benefits and who loses when neighborhoods are deliberately planned?

Over the years, urban planning has moved from a mere sense of the collective spirit (Raymond Unwin's statement that "co-operation will recover for society some organized form, which will find expression in our architecture and the planning of our towns and cities") to, in the minds of some critics, soul-squashing control.[2] In some people's minds, neighborhood planning conjures up a nightmarish manifestation of Fritz Lang's *Metropolis* or perhaps the Neighborhood War Clubs developed during World War II.[3] Is it possible to reconcile this fear with the admonition from sociologists that disorder and physical incivilities reproduce spatial inequality?[4]

If the neighborhood itself stokes feelings of betrayal and loss, the act of deliberately planning for them seems counterproductive. The Federal Housing Administration's "Successful Subdivisions Planned as Neighborhoods for Profitable Investment and Appeal to Owners," published in 1940, popularized the idea that loss of residential value should be pinned on *neighborhood* disintegration,[5] leaving the individual resident feeling somewhat helpless against the wider trajectory of neighborhood decline. Once in full decline, images of the "old neighborhood" and what became of it could be used to incite a sense of injustice. For example, in Los Angeles's Chinatown the original neighborhood of Chinese immigrants was wiped out to make room for Union Station, only to be replaced by inauthentic fragments of Chinese urbanism. Via the neighborhood, the cultural plight of Chinese people in the U.S. was experienced as fragmentation, loss, and eventual rebuilding in the form of enclaves.[6] In a similar way, the story of urban renewal was a story of neighborhood betrayal.

These calamities feed the perception that *authentic* neighborhoods are not really capable of being planned—and so the real tragedy of the lost neighborhood is that it cannot be planned back into existence. Neighborhoods are something that can emerge only spontaneously; they can not be coerced into being.

The Dark Side of Neighborhood Planning

That neighborhood planning has sometimes been disastrous is a well-worn narrative in planning history. Some of the more notorious examples concern the imposition of Westernized neighborhood models in non-Western societies. For example, the neighborhoods built by the British in the 1920s and then after World War II, whether in Nairobi, Cairo, or Zanzibar, were an act of "enframing" that ultimately failed. Not only was there no resident sense of ownership of the imposed schemes, but the spatial layout was often wildly unsuitable. In Zanzibar, clear demarcations between street and house—motivated by the need

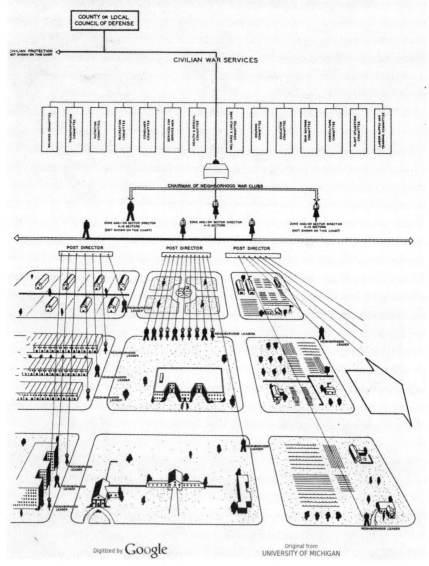

TYPICAL COMMUNITY OF ORGANIZED
NEIGHBORHOOD WAR CLUBS ★ ★ ★

Figure 6.1 Neighborhood War Clubs in Michigan were conceptualized in this 1942 publication. Source: Neighborhood War Clubs, *Michigan's Block Plan.*

Figure 6.2 When marketers try to contrive a sense of "neighborhood," it feels inauthentic. Here, Sprint is invoking "neighborhood" where one does not actually exist. Source: author

for control—conflicted with local social customs that were much more open and fluid.[7] Neighborhood plans under British colonialism appear like geometric aberrations in an otherwise organic urbanism.

The 1952 master plan of Kuwait by British planners is another example of the disjuncture. It was intended to be a model for the Middle East, as cities there were reimagined in the face of spectacular oil wealth. But the plan was a severe alteration of the traditional Kuwaiti neighborhood pattern, with housing units now separated, wide streets, large setbacks, and inadequate amenities. The neighborhood units have been severely criticized as monotonous, inhumane, and disruptive of the family unit.[8]

The modernist, superblock, high-rise, communist version of the neighborhood unit exposed the problem of neighborhood unit planning most starkly. In the USSR the *mikrorayon* was the embodiment of a socialist city based on class unity, public ownership of land (there were no individually sold plots of land), a planned economy, and "equality and friendship" among residents. It was considered the perfect socialist antidote to the "bourgeois necropolis of slums, traffic jams, pollution, noises and hot concrete."[9] What seemed ostensibly positive were the mixed dwelling types—four-story apartments, two-story flats, and hostels (which could be up to 16 stories)—a mix based on assumptions about varying family size as opposed to income variation, as the latter was obviously not an appropriate basis for planning in the socialist city. But while the physical design of the *mikrorayon*s were intended to stimulate "collectivist habits" with their "organic" integration of housing and services, they failed as a system of self-governance. Statistically all the elements of community were there, including centers designed to have schools, playgrounds, small shops, and communal kitchens, few cars, and residential buildings linked via footpaths. But administration was top-down and opaque, public services were often lacking, and there was "too much standardization." By the 1980s the high-minded social principles of the original *mikrorayons* seemed a distant vision, leaving only vast expanses of underserviced blocks of drab and cheaply constructed apartment buildings.[10] Freestanding buildings disconnected from the street, with no attempt to spatially define the public realm, seemed to reinforce the sense of top-down control.

The failure of modernist neighborhood plans played out in other parts of the world. In Sweden the social implication of the neighborhood unit seemed to correspond well with postwar social democratic ideals, but by the 1960s and into the 1970s the "retail lobbyists" took over and the interest was more in commercial units for shopping—planning by "catchment area." Social goals had been subordinated. The standard criticisms of the neighborhood unit were thus applied—that is, that the neighborhood unit promoted social homogeneity, that it lacked services and thus created bedroom communities, and that its modernist designs were anticommunity. Planning by neighborhood "more or less ceased"

Figure 6.3 Vallingby is a famous Swedish example of the modernist neighborhood unit. In design it rejected the spatially defined street, a significant departure from earlier examples of Swedish neighborhood planning that were more pedestrian-scaled. Source: Johan Fredriksson, "Vällingby in Western Stockholm, Sweden," CC BY-SA 3.0, September 20, 2014, Wikimedia Commons, https://commons.wikimedia.org/wiki/File:V%C3%A4llingby,_flygfoto_2014-09-20.jpg#/media/File:V%C3%A4llingby,_flygfoto_2014-09-20.jpg.

in Sweden by 1980, although there have been more recent examples of neighborhood developments along "neotraditional" lines.[11]

Yet the problem of the planned neighborhood is an issue that transcends form, meaning that a more sensitive neighborhood plan would not necessarily be better. Janet Abu-Lughod argues the case vehemently in regard to the traditional Islamic neighborhood. Such neighborhoods were the result of a variety of processes, not a physical product that could be re-created in modern times by planners. These included religious practices having to do with the separation of male and female and of Muslims and outsiders, methods of economic exchange, and the resolution of land use conflict in neighbor-to-neighbor negotiation. Such processes could never be reconstituted as generators of a particular desired neighborhood form.[12]

Neighborhood planning in any form has been accused of rejecting cities and the diversity they contain. Chris Silver, a planning historian, recounts all the ways that neighborhood planning in the U.S. was antiurban and exclusionist: settlement house workers used neighborhood ideals to try to transplant country life to the inner city or disperse the working class to the suburbs; neighborhood associations sought racial exclusion; neighborhood unit advocates sought social uniformity; and groups devoted to highway building and large-scale land development readily co-opted neighborhood planning in support of conformity, control, exclusion, and other nefarious goals.[13]

A who's who of urban planning dignitaries piled on the critique of planned neighborhood units as socially backward, anachronistic, and not reflective of community life.[14] Reginald Isaacs's blistering critique of Clarence Perry's neighborhood unit—or, more exactly, applications of it—boiled down to a denial that neighborhoods exist in the first place. He wrote, "Examples of neighborhoods are few and occur only in some rural areas and suburbs, in some residual and bypassed city areas, and among some cultural groups."[15] In their 1984 book, *Beyond the Neighborhood Unit*, Tridib Banerjee and William Baer wrote an equally scathing critique, arguing that the neighborhood unit was out of touch with the world. Like others, they attempted to redefine the neighborhood idea using the more ambiguous term "environmental area," a strategy that British planners had earlier tried with their 1963 concept of "precinct" or "environmental area," published as the Buchanan Report.

Isaacs, under the influence of the sociologist Louis Wirth, cited the failure of the neighborhood unit on sociological grounds (that it is inconsistent with city life), as a physical concept (that it is impossible for the boundaries of social institutions to coincide), and as a social concept (that neighborhood units are an insidious facilitator of segregation). Isaacs's solution was to abandon any fixed ideas about neighborhood and instead resolve residential problems through "close collaboration among sociologists, social and political scientists, physical

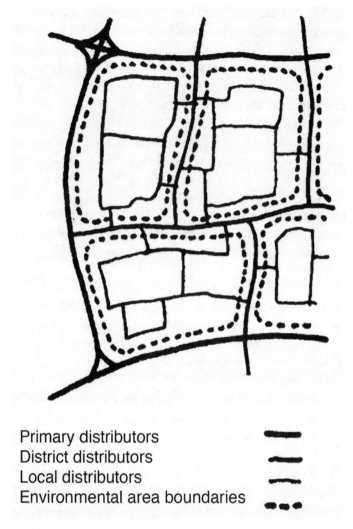

Primary distributors

District distributors

Local distributors

Environmental area boundaries

Figure 6.4 The neighborhood is replaced by "environmental areas" in this 1963 study (known as the Buchanan Report) by the British planner Colin Buchanan. The areas are conceived in terms of access; all social implications were removed. Source: Image redrawn after Appleyard, "Livable Streets."

planners and architects, anthropologists, psychologists, economists," and "the people whose lives are being planned."[16]

Because Isaacs was essentially attacking the idea that place of residence mattered for social and political involvement, the American Society of Planning Officials authored a kind of rebuttal in 1960, arguing that Isaacs and his fellow critics were really critiquing failed implementation, not the idea itself, and that in any case no alternative proposals had been put forth. The rebuttal went on to claim that the neighborhood unit was essential for guiding development in two arenas: suburban peripheral expansion and urban renewal, ironically sealing the fate of the neighborhood unit as forever tied to two of the worst examples of urban planning practice. Fixed to suburban expansion, the neighborhood unit was applied as a simple formula, "tidy, perhaps too tidy," with little differentiation. The modular application of the neighborhood unit across the suburban landscape created a world where "one might feel just as at home, or just as lost, on the curvilinear streets of a 'Desert Mesa' in Arizona, at the neighborhood super-shop in a 'Prairie Estates' in Illinois, or in the centrally located elementary school in a 'Rolling Meadows' in Pennsylvania."[17]

Planners around the world tried to defend the planned neighborhood out of a belief in its higher principles. In India postindependence planners thought that the planned neighborhood unit reflected the indigenous parts of Indian cities, a faith that endured despite the fact that India's most famous application of the neighborhood unit, Chandigarh, had fostered social segregation. Rhetorically the neighborhood unit was an ideal meant to foster socioeconomic equality, and Indian planners wanted to rely on that principle, vowing to house "all income and social groups in a spatially disciplined environment" (although they recognized that India's caste system was making that goal especially challenging).[18] Working in their favor were government guidelines showing target densities and land use tables, specifications that meant that a "one cow Indian town" could apply the neighborhood unit "with the aid of an elementary slide rule."[19] However, in India as elsewhere, there was insufficient political will to enforce the neighborhood unit's lofty, socially integrative idealism. Ultimately the size of neighborhoods in mid-20th-century India was to be governed by whatever was needed to make the local bazaar profitable, estimated at 800 to 1,200 families within 150 to 200 acres (about a half-mile square).[20]

The 1970s produced multiple reports, in the U.S., Britain, and elsewhere, detailing all the ways the neighborhood unit was a failure. Two reports out of the University of North Carolina were especially harsh, drawing on the failure of the neighborhood concept in Columbia, Maryland: that it didn't match activity patterns, that the intent was homogeneity, that spatial identity was mostly an ethnic grouping phenomenon, and that "mental concepts of space" were being overlooked. One of the reports suggested dropping the term "neighborhood" entirely in favor of planning for the "residential environment," by then a well-rehearsed tactic.[21]

In the U.K. neighborhood planning was critiqued for its sentimentality (why were the negatives of "narrowness, gossip and intolerance" in "communal life" being overlooked?) and the sheer impracticality of local association in an age of mobility. It had also become evident that the specifications of the Dudley Report, a British planning document that endorsed the neighborhood unit,

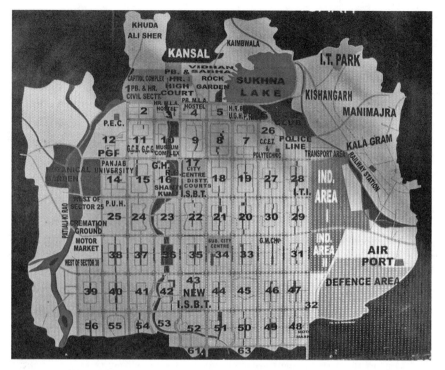

Figure 6.5. The neighborhood unit was widely implemented in India in the decades following independence in 1947. The most famous example was Le Corbusier's neighborhood unit-like plan for Chandighar, the capital of Punjab, planned in the 1950s in several stages. The city hangs on a grid of roads that surround superblocks of four neighborhoods each, one for wealthy residents and three for "lower and middle classes." Park strips connect the neighborhoods to shopping areas along a bazaar street rather than local shopping areas within each neighborhood. Playing into the critique that planned neighborhoods foster exclusion, Chandighar is now the wealthiest city in India. Image: Le Corbusier's Plan of Chandigarh, posted by Ajay Tallam via Wikimedia Commons, https://commons. wikimedia.org/wiki/File:Le_Corbusier_Map.jpg.

were not being lived up to. Shops per person, for example, were about twice the target number; the Dudley Report aimed for 100 to 150 persons per shop; the actual number required was double that.[22]

Arguments against the planned neighborhood were at their peak in the 1980s. Research was showing that residents were not more satisfied; they preferred community facilities and shopping at the periphery rather than at the center; they were skeptical that social interaction could result from neighborhood unit design; they were not all that interested in "community"; and their cognitive maps did not line up with the planned neighborhood.[23] Banerjee and Baer argued that since the sociological baggage of neighborhood could never really be shed, the better approach would be to reject "neighborhood" altogether and provide a "fresh conceptual start" by replacing the term with an "umbrella definition" meant to capture the plurality of "locations, environments, and consumption patterns."[24]

Also delegitimizing the planned neighborhood was the idea that the neighborhood unit produced an inverse correlation between autonomy and deprivation—that neighborhood unit planning meant confinement and being cut off from social and economic networks. Many critics equated the neighborhood plan with the production of "poverty enclaves," isolating and disconnecting in a way that might be fine for rich people, but a disaster for poor people. What poor people needed was the antithesis of the planned, inwardly focused neighborhood; they needed networks, dispersion, and mobility to support integration within the broader urban milieu.

Critical social theorists advance a critique that is even more fundamental and uncompromising, where neighborhood is viewed through the lens of class structure and class identity. Neighborhoods are rejected because they embody and extend the contradictions of capitalism and the injustices they create. An alternative to neighborhood would be to open up the city, engage with a "cosmopolitan ethic" that rejects boundaries and spatial identities, and instead embraces the anarchy and complexity of the city in ways that are about neither social homogeneity nor diversity. According to this view, transcendence based on finding commonalities and embracing multicultural pluralism is as futile as retreat to one of Robert Park's "little worlds" of the urban mosaic. Better to embrace "an ethic of pragmatic tolerance for the contingency and ambiguity of our identities."[25]

To critical social theorists, neighborhoods involve the production and controlling of space to exert power. They are an expression of Lefebvre's "everyday life," but they have been corrupted into a means and expression of capitalist consumption. Every aspect of Harvey's "Grid of Spatial Practices," based on Lefebvre's *The Production of Space* and paraphrased by the sociologist Jerome Krase, is evident in the neighborhood: physical and material flows ("material spatial practices"), signs, codes and knowledge ("representations of space"), the built environment ("spaces of representations"), the "friction of distance" ("accessibility and distanciation"), occupation of space by different social groups ("appropriation of space"), and group control over the production or organization of space ("domination of space"). Any of these cells provides a lens through which the idea of neighborhood is revealed, analyzed, and critiqued as part of the process of spatial production and control.[26]

This puts neighborhood planning efforts aimed at resolving problems like affordable housing or gentrification in conflict with the other urban political struggle coming from the Left: labor and "workers." A focus on neighborhood only elevates consumption over production, which thwarts class-based solidarity and activism. The solution is to embrace a wider political identity, to make use of Richard Sennett's notion of a complex and disordered city and position urban identities as "hybrid, overlapping, mixed up."[27] Conceptions of neighborhood only get in the way of these broadened constituencies.

The question of why neighborhoods exist at all is central to this framing: they exist because of the contradictions of capitalism. Capitalism exploits a false sense of localism, easily replacing traditional meanings of local and neighborhood with business coalitions offering "pseudo-community." Capitalists have become adept at playing on fears about big corporations and big government while at the same time being very much complicit in multinational, capitalist exploitation.[28] Community, and by extension neighborhood, is the basis of social hierarchy and tries to mask what capitalism robs us of.[29] This is why Robert Putnam's plea for "social capital" is seen as a conservative and false attempt at social bonding that relies on social hierarchy and the squelching of difference and dissension. The rhetoric of community, some critics claim, is falsely presented as the humanizing counterforce of capitalism, when in fact it was essential to it. The state's attempt to create socially mixed neighborhoods only makes matters worse by trying to gloss over the divisions wrought by capitalism, employing a false "Love thy neighbor" denial of intrinsic class antagonisms.[30]

Neighborhood is thus primarily in service to the state and the ownership class. For the rich, the neighborhood is a convenient vessel bestowing the "metropolitan milieu" of "higher order cities."[31] The wealthy gentrifier uses the "social cloak" of neighborhood to find like-minded souls with which to "sustain indulgence in specialist forms of consumption, such as a visit to the opera."[32] Although the neighborhood can engender a locally rooted class consciousness that is sometimes effective at resisting capital exploitation (the occasionally successful uprising over big development), the main narrative here is that the differentiated space that neighborhoods help define plays a crucial role in the accumulation of capital.[33] Companies like Nextdoor.com and Everyblock.com pitch their devotion to neighborhood, but, through daily postings of Yelp reviews, building permits, and crime reports, are essentially devoted to managing consumption.

Defending the Planned Neighborhood

There is a counterposition to the neighborhood-as-consumption critique. Rather than looking at neighborhood-based profit-making strategies as inherently debased, a more charitable view is that in an age of extremely limited city budgets, the ability of neighborhoods to position themselves as commercially relevant, or as drivers of economic development, is not a bad strategy for maintaining their long-term viability. The commodified, regulated city is the reality within which neighborhoods fight for existence and find ways to survive. These

Plate 1 The historic Muslim city of Jeddah Al-Qademah in Saudi Arabia still retains the essential neighborhood structure that developed after the spread of Islam started in the 7th century. The city was originally divided into three neighborhoods (*mahelleh*), which were then further divided into "subsections" that "possessed all the institutions required for social life." The local mosque and clusters of shops that occupied the surrounding housing functioned as neighborhood centers; many of them still do. Source: Abu-Ghazzeh, "Built Form and Religion," 54. Image: Google Earth.

Plate 2 The historic quarters of European cities are still recognizable as neighborhoods; for instance, Bologna, Italy, has been described as a "system of neighborhoods" based on a physical differentiation that has been in place for centuries. Source: Thiis-Evenson and Campbell, *Archetypes of Urbanism*, 152. Image: Google Earth.

Plate 3 Digital reconstruction and rendering by Heng Chye Kiang showing the *fang* neighborhoods of 8th-century Chang'an. Source: Image courtesy of Heng Chye Kiang. See also Jin, "The Historical Development of Chinese Urban Morphology."

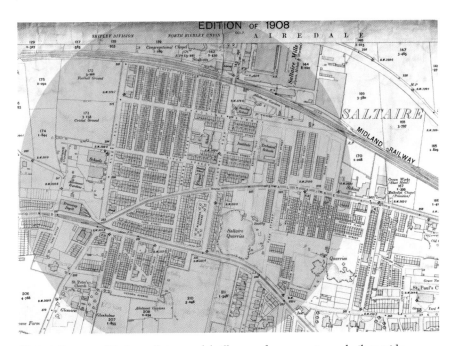

Plate 4 Because of their small size, model villages and company towns built outside of cities are the precursors of complete and self-sufficient neighborhoods. In England, Saltaire, started by Sir Titus Salt in 1850, was intended for a population of 4,356—less than Perry's neighborhood unit of 5,000. The red circle is the size of Perry's neighborhood unit, encompassing the entire village. It shows a complete neighborhood—school, shops, housing, hospital, public space, home for the elderly—with the addition of an employment source, the Salt textile mills. Source: Old Ordnance Survey Maps of Yorkshire, "Saltaire (South), Shipley (West) in 1908-B," Old Towns Books and Maps, http://www.oldtowns.co.uk/Mapshop_Yorkshire/Sheet-201/201-11-1908-b.htm.

Plate 5 A *mikrorayon* in Tbilisi, Georgia (formerly part of the Soviet Union). *Mikrorayons* were 4,000 to 18,000 people, gravitating toward two sizes, one in the 6,000 to 8,000 range and one in the 12,000 to 14,000 range. The buildings grouped into *mikrorayons* were mostly composed of five-story apartment buildings, although many were larger. Sources: Paata Vardanashvili from Tbilisi, Georgia (gldani) [CC BY 2.0 (https:// creativecommons.org/licenses/by/2.0)], via Wikimedia Commons; https://upload.wikimedia.org/ wikipedia/commons/6/6a/Gldani.jpg; Frolic, "The Soviet City."

Plate 6 Caoyang New Village, built in 1951–53 outside of Shanghai (about five miles to the west of The Bund), was designed by the American-trained planner Wang Dingzeng. The neighborhoods of the village were clustered, and each cluster had its own primary schools. Community facilities (co-op shops, post offices, cultural facilities) were at the center, while larger commercial uses and employment were at the periphery. Sources: Pannell, "Past and Present City Structure in China"; Fung, "Satellite Town Development in the Shanghai City Region." Image: Google Earth.

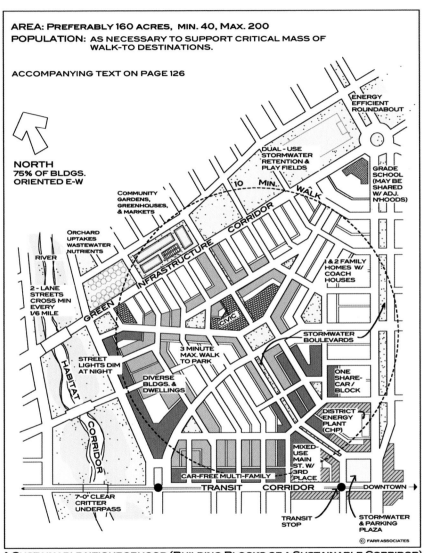

AREA: PREFERABLY 160 ACRES, MIN. 40, MAX. 200
POPULATION: AS NECESSARY TO SUPPORT CRITICAL MASS OF
WALK-TO DESTINATIONS.

ACCOMPANYING TEXT ON PAGE 126

NORTH
75% OF BLDGS.
ORIENTED E-W

ENERGY
EFFICIENT
ROUNDABOUT

DUAL - USE
STORMWATER
RETENTION &
PLAY FIELDS

GRADE
SCHOOL
(MAY BE
SHARED
W/ ADJ.
N'HOODS)

10 MIN. WALK

COMMUNITY
GARDENS,
GREENHOUSES,
& MARKETS

ORCHARD
UPTAKES
WASTEWATER
NUTRIENTS

RIVER

GREEN INFRASTRUCTURE CORRIDOR

1 & 2 FAMILY
HOMES W/
COACH
HOUSES

2 - LANE
STREETS
CROSS MIN
EVERY
1/6 MILE

CIVIC

STORMWATER
BOULEVARDS

HABITAT

STREET
LIGHTS DIM
AT NIGHT

3 MINUTE
MAX. WALK
TO PARK

DIVERSE
BLDGS. &
DWELLINGS

ONE
SHARE-
CAR /
BLOCK

CORRIDOR

DISTRICT
ENERGY
PLANT
(CHP)

MIXED-
USE
MAIN
ST. W/
3RD
PLACE

CAR-FREE MULTI-FAMILY

DOWNTOWN →

TRANSIT CORRIDOR

7'-0" CLEAR
CRITTER
UNDERPASS

TRANSIT
STOP

STORMWATER
& PARKING
PLAZA

© FARR ASSOCIATES

A SUSTAINABLE NEIGHBORHOOD (BUILDING BLOCKS OF A SUSTAINABLE CORRIDOR)

Plate 7 Perry's model was further updated by Doug Farr in 2007. Farr's emphasis is on green infrastructure. The central elementary school is replaced with civic buildings. Source: Farr, Sustainable Urbanism.

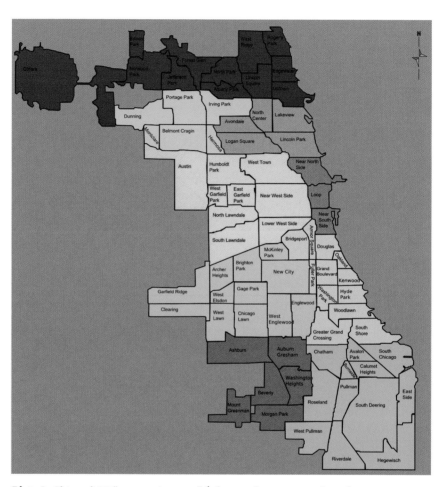

Plate 8 Chicago's 77 "community areas" (often used synonymously with
neighborhoods) were derived by Chicago School sociologists in the early 20th century.
Over the years there have been various attempts to subdivide them into neighborhoods
(their average population size is 35,000): a 1946 plan divided the city into 514
approximately quarter-square-mile self-contained neighborhoods based on elementary
schools, and in 1978 the city designated 178 neighborhoods based on a resident survey.
Later the city's unofficial map contained 228 neighborhoods, based on the work of an
independent researcher. Source: Herbert, "The Neighbourhood Unit Principle and Organic
Theory." Image: Peter Fitzgerald (Chicago_neighborhoods_outline.svg) [Public domain], via
Wikimedia Commons, https://upload.wikimedia.org/wikipedia/commons/b/b3/Chicago_
neighborhoods_map.png

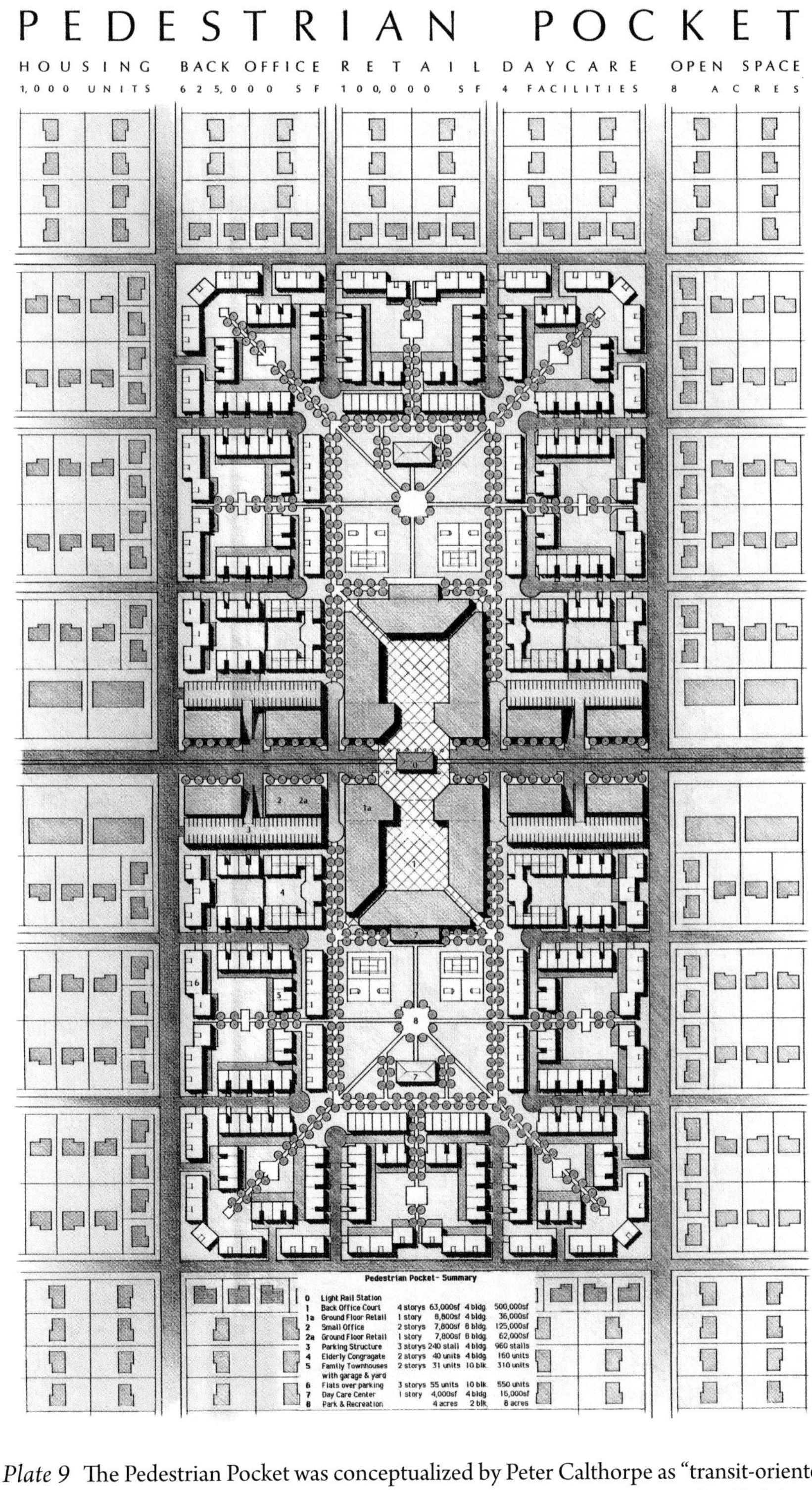

PEDESTRIAN POCKET

HOUSING   BACK OFFICE   RETAIL   DAYCARE   OPEN SPACE

1,000 UNITS   625,000 SF   100,000 SF   4 FACILITIES   8 ACRES

Pedestrian Pocket– Summary

0	Light Rail Station			
1	Back Office Court	4 storys 63,000sf	4 bldg.	500,000sf
1a	Ground Floor Retail	1 story 8,800sf	4 bldg.	36,000sf
2	Small Office	2 storys 7,800sf	8 bldg.	125,000sf
2a	Ground Floor Retail	1 story 7,800sf	8 bldg.	62,000sf
3	Parking Structure	3 storys 240 stall	4 bldg.	960 stalls
4	Elderly Congregate	2 storys 40 units	4 bldg.	160 units
5	Family Townhouses with garage & yard	2 storys 31 units	10 blk.	310 units
6	Flats over parking	3 storys 55 units	10 blk.	550 units
7	Day Care Center	1 story 4,000sf	4 bldg.	16,000sf
8	Park & Recreation	4 acres	2 blk.	8 acres

Plate 9 The Pedestrian Pocket was conceptualized by Peter Calthorpe as "transit-oriented development," combining strategies for mixed-use development, transit, and walkability. It was an idealized neighborhood diagram, with the intention that adjustments would be based on local history, topography, and circumstance. Source: Calthorpe Associates.

Plate 10 Bournville, England, near Birmingham, was started in 1895 and developed by the Cadbury brothers, the chocolate manufacturers. Bournville was an early employer of the "superblock" arrangement in which houses faced an interior greenspace rather than the street, popularized in Radburn's neighborhoods 36 years later. Clarence Stein, planner of Radburn, claimed to have been inspired by something even more historical: New York's 17th-century Dutch patterns of perimeter block housing surrounding gardens at the center of blocks. Source: Eaton, "Ideal Cities." Image: Google Earth.

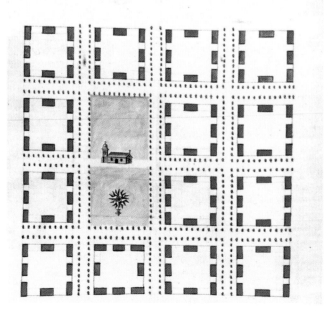

Plate 11 The *Laws of the Indies* (1688) prescribed residential blocks anchored to a central public open space. This example includes 112 houses (families) for a settlement in the Dominican Republic. Source: Carías, La Ciudad Ordenada.

Plate 12 The "Peace House" on Chicago's South Side is a neighborhood center devoted to skill-building and social connection. Source: https://www.igrowchicago.org/

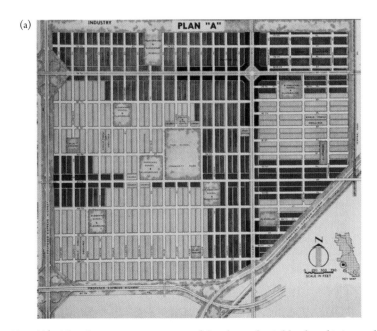

Plate 13a, 13b, 13c One common critique of the planned neighborhood is its tendency to be incompletely realized. In a 1943 publication, the Chicago Plan Commission advocated "Plan B" over "Plan A" for a section of the city. "Plan A" (a) was the conventional practice, without benefit of neighborhood design. "Plan B" (b) was to be an example of a centered and "integrated" collection of neighborhoods, each with a mix of housing types and schools, parks, and stores. Image (c) shows how the area actually developed. A few of the curvilinear streets materialized, but without the centralizing, neighborhood-forming civic and commercial areas. Source: Images (a) and (b) are from Chicago Plan Commission, *Building New Neighborhoods*. The existing image (c) is by the author.

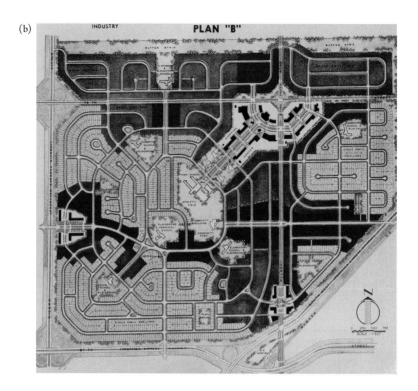

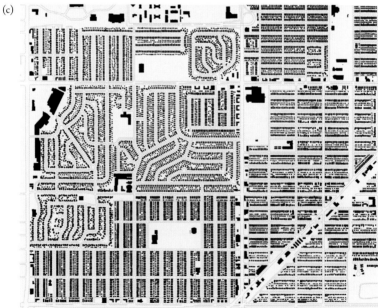

Plate 13a, 13b, 13c Continued

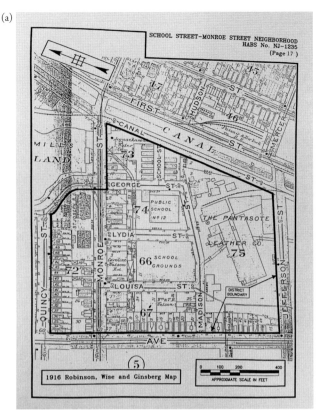

Plate 14a and 14b The "complete neighborhood" attached to a source of employment, such as this school and factory-based neighborhood in Passaic, New Jersey, were rendered vulnerable to redevelopment with the decline of manufacturing. Source 15a: Historic American Building Survey (HABS) No. NJ-1235, School Street–Monroe Street Neighborhood. Source 15b: Google Earth.

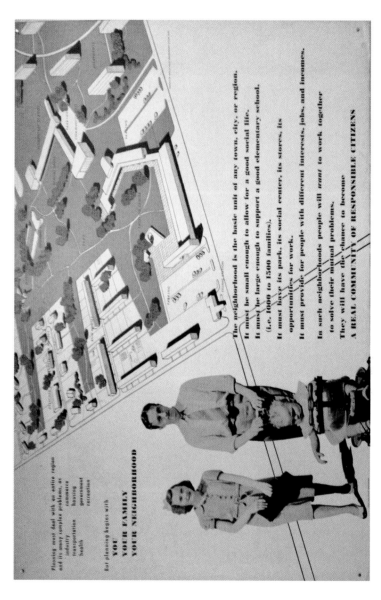

Plate 15 One of the panels from the 1945 Museum of Modern Art's exhibit *Look at Your Neighborhood*. Source: Museum of Modern Art, *Look at Your Neighborhood*.

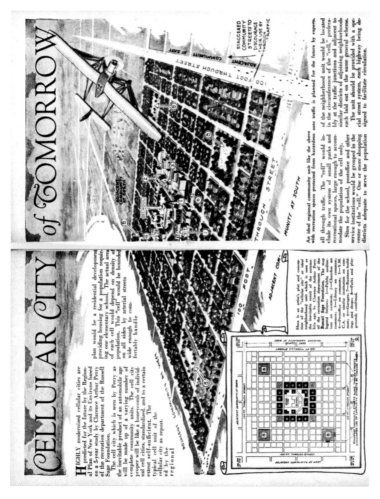

Plate 16 The editors of *Modern Mechanics and Inventions* endorsed Perry's vision in this 1929 article. Source: *Modern Mechanics and Inventions.* "Cellular City of Tomorrow." December, 1929.

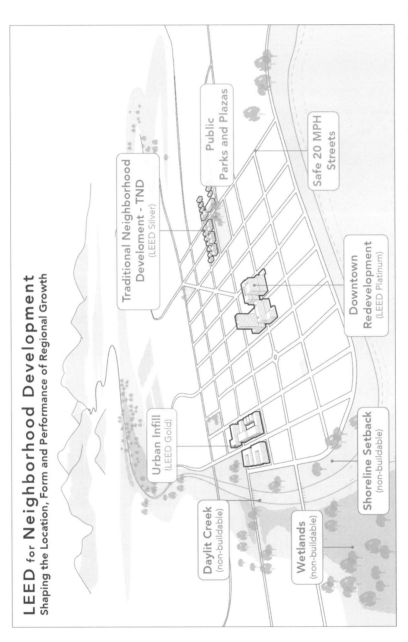

Plate 17 Under the U.S. Green Building Council's LEED rating system for neighborhood development (LEED-ND), different kinds of neighborhoods can be certified if they meet criteria related to location, neighborhood design, and green infrastructure. Shown are three neighborhood types, with silver, gold, and platinum ratings. Source: Image by Farr Associates.

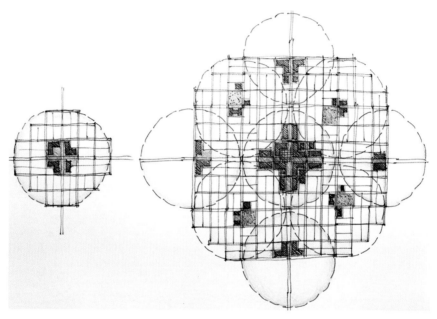

Plate 18 Steve Mouzon, an architect and town planner, argues on his blog *Original Green* that people are "confused about neighborhood centers and edges." Although a self-contained hamlet (left) might have a single commercial center, a city (right) has multiple centers and shopping corners. Neighborhoods are bounded by busy thoroughfares, but multiple layers—centered on civic uses and shopping corners—"weave the city together." Source: Mouzon, *Original Green*.

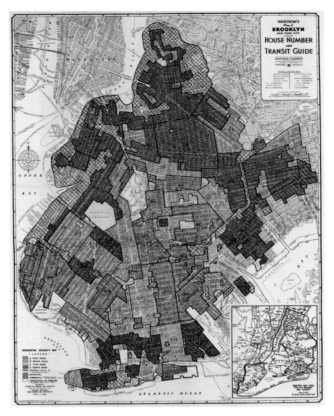

Plate 19 Hagstrom's 1938 map of Brooklyn showed the FHA's redlining districts.
Source: Robert K. Nelson, LaDale Winling, Richard Marciano, Nathan Connolly, et al., "Mapping Inequality,"
American Panorama, ed. Robert K. Nelson and Edward L. Ayers, accessed July 9, 2018, https://dsl.richmond.
edu/panorama/redlining/#loc=9/41.9435/-87.7050&opacity=0.8&text=about&city=chicago-il.

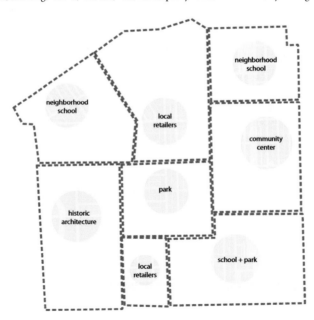

Plate 20 Neighborhood centers and their spatial extents: a beginning proposal for
neighborhood delineation for a section of Chicago. Source: author.

are simply the rules of the game—rules that neighborhoods must play if they want to remain relevant and viable, including for their own residents. That the quest results in targeted marketing strategies and neighborhood branding aimed at consumption is a necessary ploy.

The conflict between big projects aimed at business interests versus small-scale efforts aimed at neighborhood is certainly nothing new. The City Beautiful era's Commercial Club of Chicago viewed the city as an undifferentiated totality in support of the central business district, while women's groups supported the small-scale enterprise of neighborhoods.[34] Now neighborhood efforts are positioned on a larger stage, integrating with global capital flows in an attempt to leverage profits for those inside and outside of the neighborhood. It is no longer a question of far-reaching business interests pitted against the localized domain of neighborhood. Which "side" aligns most with resident interests is not necessarily obvious.

Defense of the deliberately planned neighborhood must begin with a defense of the idea of neighborhood. This starts with the fact that, for millennia, the physical, identifiable neighborhood was a mechanism that "kept society from falling apart" by helping to maintain an organized, place-based social grouping. It makes sense that the neighborhood would matter as a source of local support in a world of high poverty, high mortality, and domination by powerful elites. Sense of neighborhood offered one avenue for the collective joining of forces, a source of mutual aid in societies that offered few sources of support and few avenues for self-advancement. This need for local support constitutes a fundamental contrast between the collectivity of traditional societies and the individuality of modern ones.[35]

The strong sense of neighborhood that formed in poor, ethnic, or working-class neighborhoods in the late 19th century did not necessarily translate to camaraderie and friendship, but residents were often allies, especially when viewed against the outside world. In London's East End, according to one autobiographical account, "natural love and communal instinct" were so strong that residents found ways to overcome poverty, violence, sickness, and other hardships. This is not to dismiss the fact that "the neighborhoods of the East End were divided in almost unnumerable ways," and venturing into different ethnic subneighborhoods, sometimes only a few streets away, "was as if you were in another country."[36] However, although income-based divisions were just as likely to produce "jealousy and competition" over scarce resources, when the "outside world" entered and created a threat, neighbors became allies and closed ranks, based not on friendship but on their shared, localized experience of daily life.[37]

In light of these positive neighborhood associations, where the identifiable, physically prescribed neighborhood promotes neighborhood identity and well-being, why not try to plan for them? Several arguments can be made. First, a

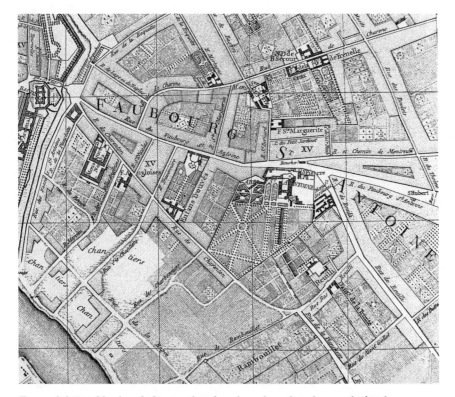

Figure 6.6 Neighborhood identity played a role in the political turmoil of 18th-century Europe, where protests were formed not from an "amorphous crowd" but from a "collectivity" emanating out of specific neighborhoods. Seventy percent of those who stormed the Bastille in Paris were from one specific neighborhood, Faubourg Saint-Antoine. Sources: Mbzt, "Carte de Paris Vaugondy—1760 Faubourg Saint-Antoine," CC BY-SA 3.0, Wikimedia, https://commons.wikimedia.org/w/index.php?curid=14649831; Lis and Soly, "Neighborhood Social Change in West European Cities," 11; Garrioch, Neighbourhood and Community in Paris, 33.

neighborhood plan (as traditionally defined) is a physical plan, and this tangibility has demonstrated value. Above all, it provides a material, visual model for everyday life, a forum for a grounded debate about the link between social values and urban form. This significance is not tied to the particulars of its form and design, but it is tied to its ability to articulate experience, meaning, and change in ways that are not abstract. It was because of the physical plan as an idea—a meme—that the neighborhood unit was able to retain its significance.[38]

The neighborhood unit was especially apt for visual exploration, which is why the New York Museum of Modern Art in 1945 produced *Look at Your Neighborhood*, a traveling exhibit of 12 30-by-40-inch panels of photographs, drawings, charts, diagrams, and text. (They made 200 sets and sold them around the country; see color plate 15) It was the materiality of the planned neighborhood that stimulated dialogue about what neighborhoods needed and currently lacked. The museum took a normative stand, using the exhibit to convey the evils of "haphazard building" and the benefits of planning that would provide a "fuller life" and "make the postwar world a better living place for the individual, the family and the community." An introductory panel personalized the issue, asking viewers to consider the stresses of daily life related to long commutes, the need to "walk miles for your daily shopping," and the constant worry about "children getting run over."[39] The neighborhood model had been thoroughly objectified, and it was having an effect. In 1947 James Dahir published his bibliographic appraisal of the "spread and acceptance" of the neighborhood unit, reporting on its implementation around the world, its design variations, and its many proponents and endorsements.[40]

While the neighborhood unit was criticized as formulaic, in fact it was capable of adaptation. Soviet, Chinese, and Indian planners reworked it in the mid-20th century, trying to find their own, non-Western interpretation, "linguistically and figuratively" altered to find greater acceptance. Chinese scholars argued that the adoption of the neighborhood unit was not a matter of blind repetition but was instead a marvel of adaptation; one observer likened the process to Walter Benjamin's "eddy in the stream of becoming."[41]

A neighborhood plan elevates the importance of context. It was via the neighborhood unit that Perry fought for recognition of a dwelling's surroundings, warning that there was too much focus on "home beautiful" without turning outward to the neighborhood. As Perry analogized, "A gem is of little use without the right setting." Neighborhoods needed tending because maintenance of a good context was a delicate balance, especially when it came to services. A neighborhood unit plan would be able to sustain the necessary balance because, Perry wrote, although "you want assurance that your neighbor will not sell out to a grocer . . . you want a grocery in the neighborhood."[42]

It is especially significant that after Perry made his proposal, city development was conceived in cellular terms, no longer just in terms of platted lots and street grids, which for decades had been the usual method of urban expansion (see color plate 16). The neighborhood provided an expedient way to at least attempt the replication of a superior environment: everything within reach, community facilities on a centralized open space, easy access to shops, and, if designed correctly, the ability to embrace the inevitability of the automobile age without sacrificing quality of life.

The planned neighborhood also created a platform for working out the complexities of mixing housing types, which was necessary to mix income levels and foster social diversity at the neighborhood level. According to Mumford, the first planned neighborhood unit (in 443 B.C.) was "based on the principle of social segregation,"[43] but in the modern era, many planned neighborhood units became models of housing mix, showing that it was possible and even desirable to integrate clustered row houses and apartment buildings with single-family housing. This was pronounced in Yorkship Village (the World War I housing development in Camden, New Jersey, funded by the federal government), for example, where housing was arranged in 243 different groups consisting of 27 housing types in 70 combinations.[44] Radburn too included a mix of unit types, mostly single-family homes but also duplexes, townhomes, and apartment buildings.

At Forest Hills Gardens in Queens, New York, there was a concerted effort to mix housing types and therefore classes, although the initial idea was to limit this mix to a range of middle-income residents (and not day laborers). One strategy for social mix was to place high-density apartment buildings on the same streets as single-family houses. The neighborhood structure of Forest Hills Gardens

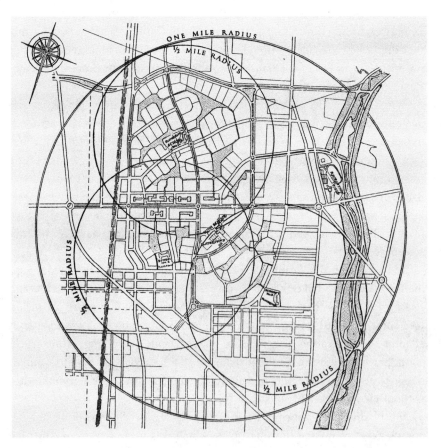

Figure 6.7 The three interlocking neighborhoods of Radburn, New Jersey. Source: Stein, *Toward New Towns for America.*

was such that housing units were arranged in small groups rather than blocks. Streets, although gridded, were kept slightly curvilinear, in direct contrast to Manhattan.

Sunnyside Gardens in Queens also succeeded in the deliberate mixing of housing unit types for reasons of social integration. There the integration was achieved by making the block rather than the individual lot the unit of development. Although the neighborhood was intended to be a unit, it was woven into the existing urban fabric, and within this framework single-family housing easily sat alongside two-family residences and apartment buildings. A possible source for this innovation was Port Sunlight, the 19th-century English company town, which used an array of eclectic styles to build rows of houses that could barely be delimited one from another. Stein's approach at Sunnyside Gardens was to create combinations of rows of single-family, two-family and multifamily dwellings, which, he claimed in his book *Toward New Towns for America*, did not cause "social difficulties."[45] Mumford lived for a time in Sunnyside Gardens and wrote that the mix he experienced—yearly incomes ranging from $1,200 to $12,000, with residents living "side by side"—was, in addition to satisfying loftier principles about educating the young and fostering democracy, "the best kind of community."[46]

Just as the planned neighborhood was a platform for working out the complexities of mixed housing types, it also provided an opportunity to work through the role of civic space in a neighborhood context. Sunnyside Gardens successfully proved that it was possible to plan a neighborhood that was economically viable and could also provide residents with open green spaces without public subsidy. This was accomplished by orienting the housing units around a shared commons, something that the planned neighborhood was able to conceptualize. The layout drew from Raymond Unwin's famous "Nothing gained by overcrowding" doctrine that showed that open spaces, called "green commons," could be preserved at block centers with no additional cost per lot. Equally important, Sunnyside Gardens was able to show that garden city principles could be adapted to a dense urban grid.

Perry and his early 20th-century contemporaries prioritized economy in neighborhood planning and studied intently the monetary implications of lot and street arrangements, particularly the effect of street widths and patterns on the number of lots that could be included. But cost savings were not for the purpose of lining the pockets of developers; they were for the purpose of providing collective space and communal facilities within the neighborhood. One proposal showed how making an internal ring road smaller would mean that 32 additional cottages could be accommodated.[47] One section of the *Regional Plan of New York and Its Environs* worked out all the economic details of what it would cost to build the "complete neighborhood unit"' that included communal

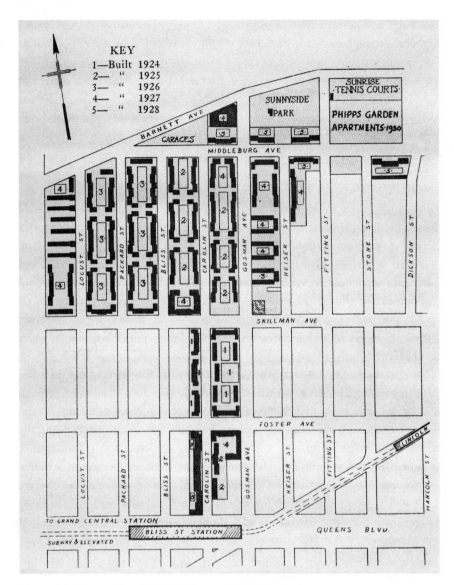

Figure 6.8 Clarence Stein's plan for Sunnyside Gardens in Queens,
New York. Source: Stein, *Toward New Towns for America*, 207.

facilities and medium- or low-cost housing, which was then compared to the
usual subdivision with strictly rectangular lots and no communal facilities. On
most dimensions, the neighborhood plan was the clear winner. Housing in self-
contained neighborhood units of large blocks would save 15 to 30% in costs for
streets and land—savings that could be used to provide parks at the neighborhood's center.[48]

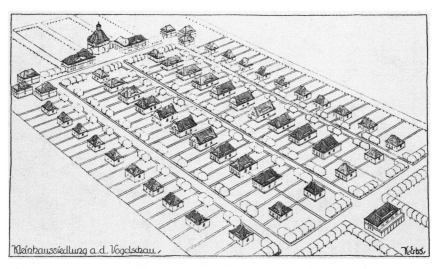

Kleinhaussiedlung a.d. Vogelsbau.   Kebs.

Figure 6.9 This example published in *The American Vitruvius* shows another approach to "neighborhood-izing" the monotonous grid: houses anchored at either end by a school, church, cemetery, and apartments with stores. The neighborhood, located in Lower Silesia (Poland), is composed of two-family and four-family houses. Source: Hegemann and Peets, *The American Vitruvius*.

Lessons Not Learned

Unfortunately the lessons that neighborhood unit planning provided in the early decades of the 20th century were not carried through. The principles of mixed-housing type oriented around communal space were dropped, and most U.S. neighborhoods built in the 1950s and 1960s were watered-down versions of complete neighborhoods—single-use, monolithic suburban developments that were a far cry from Perry's or Stein's ideals. Two influential 1950s-era planning textbooks, Gallion's *Urban Pattern* and Tunnard's *The City of Man*, were especially supportive of Radburn, but, presumably because the attention to planning didn't pencil out, the nuances of the neighborhood unit failed to transfer to the large-scale development that was blanketing the outskirts of Western cities.

Two new towns of the 1960s—Reston, Virginia, and Columbia, Maryland—tried to rectify the neighborhood unit by offering a new articulation, but they were car-based, modernist versions, characterized by separation and hierarchy rather than a more fine-grained urbanism. Their buildings were designed in a dressed-down style that looked as if they were all built by the same architect at the same time, and the commercial components were so antipedestrian that they were later transformed into auto-oriented strip malls. This was bad publicity for the neighborhood unit.

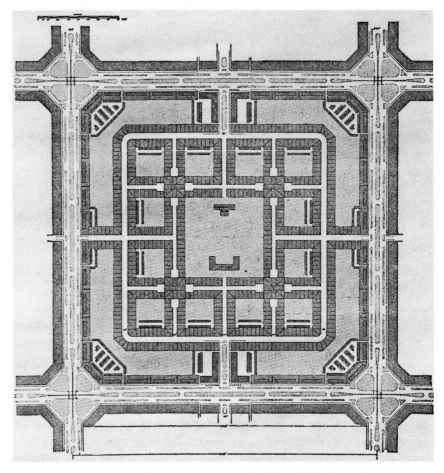

Figure 6.10 In a classic 1931 text, planners considered how block, lot, and open space arrangements—forming neighborhoods of different sizes and patterns—could be constructed in the most economically efficient way. Source: Whitten and Adams, *Neighborhoods of Small Homes.*

Successful emulation of the neighborhood model required an attention to detail that few government agencies have been capable of instituting. The U.S. government, via the Federal Housing Administration (formed after the Housing Act of 1937), ordered that housing be constructed in the form of neighborhoods, but the models were severely diluted. The FHA's hugely impactful 1940 "Land Planning Bulletin" equated "subdivision" with "neighborhood" and directed subdividers to keep lots uniform in size and to "segregate uses," because, despite the benefits for pedestrians, "short blocks are not economical." Listed as causes of depreciated real estate values and the "breakdown of neighborhood character" were business uses "invading residential areas" and "mixtures of apartments and detached dwellings." There was an attempt at nuance: stores were to

Figure 6.11 The Federal Housing Administration used this photograph in its 1940 publication to make the argument that "a shopping center conveniently located, well designed, with off-street parking and service alleys, and restricted in extent is a desirable neighborhood feature." Source: Federal Housing Administration, "Land Planning Bulletin," 16.[49]

be "conveniently located within walking distance" and shopping centers were to be "restricted in extent," but these subtle restrictions were not maintained by developers, and massive shopping centers surrounded by parking lots became the norm.

President Jimmy Carter tried to put neighborhoods on the national scene with his 1977 National Commission on Neighborhoods, but by this time neighborhood definition had become amorphous and there was little agreement about what a neighborhood actually was. This undermined the ability to argue on its behalf. Fundamental rifts in neighborhood agendas were exposed. Grass-roots self-reliance was pitted against those seeking deeper structural changes in social and political institutions. Some sought neighborhood self-protection, while others pushed for diversity and integration. These tensions were added to the usual problems associated with any attempt at a national political movement: underfunding, power conflicts, goal confusion.[50]

By the late 20th century, the whole proposition of normative neighborhood theorizing had unraveled. Even neighborhood proposals that prioritized process over blueprint, as Jane Jacobs's approach had done, were suspect. Attempts to resurrect the neighborhood ideal—with its diverse housing types, mixed uses, centers, focal points, and walkable urban form—were deemed illegitimate based on the assumption that Americans preferred either suburban tranquility or high-rise urbanity. Jacobs's influence was downgraded to a thought experiment. One critic reduced her proposal to "a smaller-than-average home over a candy store in a somewhat rickety old building on a busy city street near a working-class bar," rendered both unrealistic and "not the prevailing American dream."[51]

It was a rejection of the planned neighborhood—of thinking about how neighborhoods *ought* to be rather than affirming their existing form. The planned neighborhood accepts as legitimate—in fact as imperative—that an alternative vision of neighborhood is necessary and valid. That vision applies to the poor ghetto as much as to a wealthy and exclusive neighborhood with gates and guards. Both require a new conceptualization of neighborhood: the poor neighborhood because it lack resources and access, and the wealthy neighborhood because it violates the social contract, hoarding resources and condoning the perverse human instinct to turn inward, away from problems that should be equitably addressed.

But even if there is implicit understanding about what a neighborhood should be, there seems to be a pervasive rejection of the possibility of consensus. This explains why the architect Michael Sorkin labeled New Urbanism a "mimetic project" of fantasy but proceeded to reiterate identical ideals: a neighborhood is "a city reproduced in microcosm," "a place in which all of the necessities of daily life are located within walking distance of home," and where there is "affordable housing for teachers, baristas, shop-keepers, entrepreneurs, musicians, janitors, craftspeople, farmers, policemen, and all the others necessary to make the neighborhood go."[52] These are time-honored, normative neighborhood ideals Clarence Perry himself would have embraced.

Critics of the planned neighborhood assumed that its repeated failures in practice were endemic to the model. But there was a counternarrative: the New Urbanist neighborhood, which emerged just a few years after President Carter's commission. Rather than rejecting the neighborhood unit and reverting to open-ended ideas about the neighborhood, the New Urbanists went completely the other way and offered a model that was unambiguous. There could be only two types of urbanism, they argued: neighborhoods and sprawl.

Neighborhood Alternatives

Around the world the failings of the planned neighborhood, well known by the mid-20th century, were answered with calls for alternative terms and forms that tried hard not to look like neighborhoods. Some planners showed how cities could be planned explicitly without neighborhoods, for example, the Smithsons' "Cluster City," Crane's "Chandigarh Reconsidered," and Braziller's "Ideal Communist City," composed of housing clusters organized around a citywide center or core. In Pakistan in the 1950s, the term "neighborhood" was

not applied to a planned residential area at all because "the sociological content implied is not considered valid." (Instead there were simply groupings of
50 to 100 houses oriented around a play space for small children.)[53] Planners
in Venezuela proposed placing shopping centers with higher-density housing at
the periphery of lower-density housing so that social interaction would occur
between (rather than just within) developments, thus "breaking down any rigid
'neighbourhood' concepts."[54] The Belgian planner Gaston Bardet proposed the
alternative of "micro-groupings," a "social topography" that involved mapping
the locations and activities of the "swarming of individualities" that was meant
to show "the flexibility of living beings."[55]

Other examples of the nonneighborhood include Banerjee and Baer's call for
free-form residential environments with an equitable distribution of resources
(leaving the political basis of facility distribution off the table), achieved by way
of a top-down planning scheme that would produce "an optimal nexus" between
housing and facilities. Corridors and nodes were to contain services and facilities, and residential areas would hover around them.[56] Jonathan Barnett uses the
example of Flower Mound, Texas, which was based on the antineighborhood
planning unit theories of British planner Richard Llewelyn-Davies. It showed
a "calculated ambiguity about the nature of the neighborhood, which might be
within the mile-square grid or on either side of the arterial."[57]

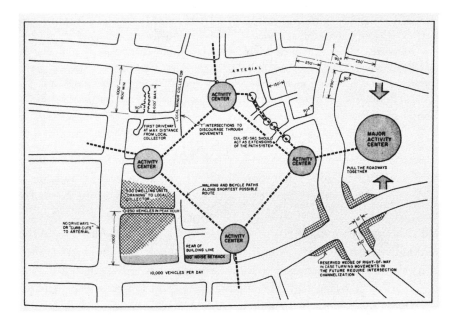

Figure 6.12 "Calculated ambiguity" about neighborhoods is shown on a plan in Flower
Mound, Texas. Source: Barnett, *An Introduction to Urban Design*, 146.

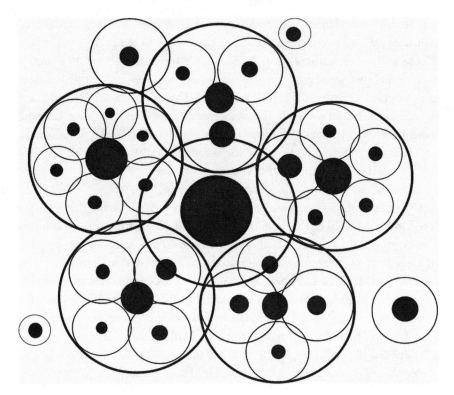

Figure 6.13 In 1963 Gilbert Herbert neatly summarized the numerous permutations of the neighborhood unit that had been devised since Perry. One divergence had to do with the introduction of subunits within the neighborhood, offering a substantial contrast to Perry's monolithic and doctrinaire neighborhood ideal. Examples of subunit proposals include Bardet's 5- to 10-family unit (conceptualized in Bardet's graphic shown here), Herrey's subneighborhood of 30 to 60 families, Gibberd's subneighborhood-level "housing group," Gropius's "super-household," Saarinen's 200-home "basic unit," and Churchill's more loosely defined "social neighborhood." Source: Image redrawn after Bardet, "Social Topography."

Reconceptualized neighborhoods might have cul-de-sacs with buildings arranged for small group interaction along with variations in style and density and planning in housing increments; such strategies were believed to provide both permanence and transience and achieve a "unity in diversity" that permitted integration with the city as a whole. Modernist architects Alison and Peter Smithson were considered exemplars of this new approach to the neighborhood that balanced "permanence and transience" and that above all rejected any notion that social groups had geographical limits. Neighborhood plans emphasized mobility, "a loose, but comprehensible structure" achieved by facilitating all forms of association but tethered to something large-scale and permanent, like road infrastructure.[58]

But designing deviations from Perry's scheme seemed timid compared to the more radical idea that emerged: ennobling the unplanned neighborhood—spontaneous, bottom-up, the result of a process rather than a plan. The social science definition of "neighborhood" aligned well, as neighborhood had become a means to understand dynamic social forces: upward or downward social mobility, succession, filtering, aging, stage in the life cycle—processes that create a constant "churning" of the population and thus variability in neighborhood definition.[59] Social geographers argued that neighborhoods are principally a "social and political product, created through activism," and that the focus ought to be on "how neighborhoods are produced." Under this interpretation, the ambiguity of neighborhood definition is an asset; "blurriness and flexibility" keep neighborhood relevant. Neighborhood can be constructed for the purposes at hand (either for political action or for pure research, for example).[60]

Planners and architects were on board too, as they were seeking a more "sophisticated concept" of neighborhood, a theory capable of unifying "a multiplicity of functional, structural and formal relationships" that existed at different levels and whose "finite solutions" could not "even be postulated." This "fully organic town planning concept" could be found in the process-oriented theories of late modernism.[61] It was an appeal to choice, the basic argument being that a predetermined neighborhood does not happily coexist with freedom. Jacobs's crack that the planned neighborhood was nice if you "were docile and had no plans of your own" reflected this line of thinking.[62]

The unplanned neighborhood seemed part of American lore—that is, that Americans are spontaneous neighborhood self-organizers, a thesis advanced by Alexis de Tocqueville with his observation that "neighbors immediately form themselves into a deliberative body" to address an issue (he used the example of a vehicle blocking a road) rather than consulting a "pre-existing authority."[63] Testaments to "neighborly spirit" as a kind of American, pioneer quality since the 19th century fed into this too. Critics of the planned neighborhood contended that this spirit was capable of thriving independent of place. A 1914 lecture at the University of Pennsylvania entitled "Ethics and the Larger Neighborhood" declared, "The neighborhood long ago ceased to be a matter of physical proximity; a score of scientific agents, methods and instruments have made it a matter, not of space but of time, feeling, imagination."[64] Neighborhood was not an object but an affective feeling: that of neighborliness, meaning unity in a world of division and difference. This required "widening" the idea of neighborhood, not constricting it to a spatial plan.

Urban designers picked up on this fluidity to advocate a more process-oriented neighborhood planning approach. Randy Hester was especially comfortable with the process view, agreeing with Milton Kotler's *Neighborhood Government* thesis that the political definition of neighborhood "supercedes" neighborhood expressed in physical or social terms.[65] This might entail a deliberate rejection of order, with improvised and unregulated public spaces aimed at enabling spontaneity and "authenticity," and neighborhoods formed via a process that has little to do with forethought.[66] A legitimate question is whether neighborhood-based "civic response" (as opposed to "social entrepreneurship"),[67] where people engage, demand action, and work together in collective purpose, is just as easily mobilized.

One example where it has been mobilized is the environmentally infused idea of "ecohousing"—a "family-friendly green neighborhood" that originated in Denmark and has now spread to other parts of the world, especially California and Colorado. Several hundred neighborhoods have been built since the 1990s. It is a bottom-up endeavor: neighborhoods come into being when a small group of dedicated people pool resources, buy a plot of land, and start building in a way that is thoroughly conscious of communal needs. This translates to community gardens, common kitchens, skills bartering, and a "common house" for social events. Cohousing neighborhoods meet a broader range of human needs than Perry ever imagined, from "affection" ("good friends a one-minute walk away") to "creation" ("neighbors co-design new landscaping, aesthetic features and celebrations"). There is also much more antimarket liberalism than Perry would have endorsed. While Perry would have been in agreement with cohousing's motto to "[Build] a better society, one neighborhood at a time," he would have winced at the notion that "each neighbor is a neighborhood citizen" rather than a consumer.[68]

A close cousin of the process neighborhood is the perceived neighborhood— that what is most important to know about neighborhoods is how they are individually understood. The neighborhood is not something to be designed; it emerges based on how residents move through the urban realm. Thus neighborhood theorizing should be based on "individualism and permissiveness," maximizing "pathways for flow and movement," "flux," a "roving neighborhood" that residents design for themselves as individuals.[69]

This is reminiscent of what the sociologist Suzanne Keller had earlier proposed as "alternatives" to the neighborhood unit. First was a personalized "neighborhood circle," which she combined with a larger impersonal "service area." (Keller argued there was an "inverse relationship" between two.) Second was the idea of a "roving neighborhood," centered on "points of interest" rather than one's residence. Next were "service neighborhoods," although Keller found the definition of service areas difficult to manage (because service cut-off distances were too ambiguous). Finally, there was the neighborhood of "collective responsibility," which was more programmatic and in line with the views of Jane Jacobs and Saul Alinsky.[70]

A potential liability—to some, an asset—of the perceived, personalized neighborhood is that the neighborhood becomes anything: a neighborhood of single-family housing and the quest for more space is just as legitimate as a diverse neighborhood of mixed-housing types and pedestrian quality. Cars, single-family homes, and consumer goods—supported by government via road building and tax incentives—create neighborhoods recast as something personally constructed, with limitless access to far-flung social and economic worlds.

Geographically liberated, a dispersed neighborhood can still be "real." Using the Rural Neighborhood Quality Scale, neighborhoods in rural West Virginia were shown to be strong and impactful; that is , a sense of neighborhood was positively correlated with school performance, family stability, and sense of safety. One resident explained that "people [from outside] don't know what neighborhoods are here," but that didn't mean they didn't exist. Rural neighborhoods were not uniform, and their effects varied, but neither were they "socially disorganized, culturally pernicious contexts."[71]

Personally defined neighborhoods are also appealing because residents can belong to more than one. Perceived boundaries can overlap since residents within neighborhoods will not have the same spatial perceptions, networks, or daily movement patterns. Residents are not assigned membership to a spatial group but "exist at the center of their social world." This is verified, some argue, by the fact that people tend to place themselves in the center of their neighborhoods when asked to draw them. One study proposed the "egohood" as a way of accounting for this variation, allowing boundary overlap and conceptualizing each resident as a member of multiple kinds of neighborhoods. Neighborhoods, then, should not be thought of as discrete units but as "waves washing across the surface of the city."[72]

Kevin Lynch and his elements of legibility (paths, edges, districts, nodes, landmarks) are commonly invoked in these explorations.[73] A neighborhood's legibility as well as shared images "born out of repeated movement along its streets," can be the basis of perceived neighborhood structure. A continuous fabric is created because this imagery—of a building, block, park, or facility—is nonhierarchical and overlapping.[74] Harold Proshansky and colleagues showed that distinctiveness (how much a neighborhood stands out as being unique in some way) and continuity (individual or collective memory of place) form the basis of place (and ultimately personal) identity.[75]

Terence Lee was an early documenter of neighborhood perception (which he called "socio-spatial schema"), asking housewives in Cambridge, England, to draw what they considered their neighborhood and recording their perception of spatial organization.[76] Lee argued that neighborhood was delineated based on physical qualities more than the social characteristics of the other residents (although other studies have found the reverse to be the case). Lee was also interested in how neighborhood perception changed depending on a respondent's background. A decade after Lee's work, a survey of Detroit residents led to the

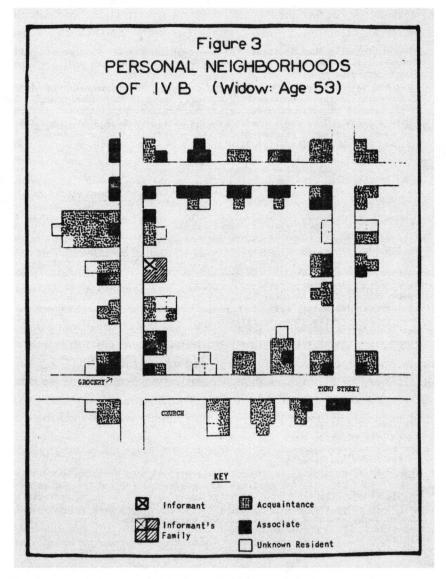

Figure 6.14 Frank Sweetser's 1941 study of 108 personal neighborhoods of 54 residents in Bloomington, Indiana, was a precursor to the "egocentric" neighborhood approach. Source: Sweetser, *Neighborhood Acquaintance and Association.*

conclusion that "neighborhoods play a wider variety of roles in the lives of blacks compared with whites."[77]

The most recent turn in the quest to capture the cognitive neighborhood and make it useful is to crowdsource neighborhood boundaries. A website called Bostonography, devoted to "interesting visual representations of life and land in

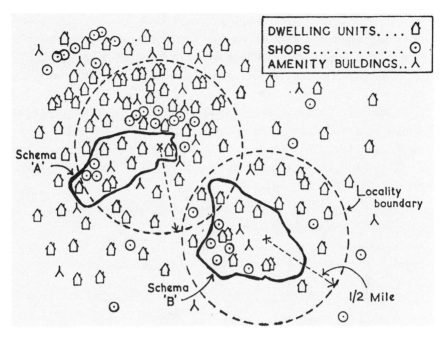

Figure 6.15 Terence Lee's urban neighborhoods conceived as "socio-spatial schema." Source: Lee, "Urban Neighbourhood as a Socio-Spatial Schema."

Greater Boston," used interactive maps to poll people about their neighborhoods. A Chicago group launched a similar app focusing on neighborhood boundaries, exposing wide disagreement over neighborhoods like South Loop and West Loop but stronger agreement on the boundaries of neighborhoods named after iconic or famous features, like "Humboldt Park" and "Wrigleyville."[78]

The problem with the perceptual, crowdsourced neighborhood is that it can become a kind of freewheeling contest devoted to self-interest. Such is the case with the website PlaceIlive.com. The site's founder freely admits, "We just genuinely believe that if there are more educated people, it is a nicer neighborhood, and the same with income." In the same genre are real estate companies specializing in finding the "right" neighbors for potential buyers. For example, neighbors might be "too Republican" to live near, so the idea is to help prospective buyers "be sure that they fit in" and "know who's surrounding them." As it is illegal to ask about someone's race, creed, sexual orientation, marital status, and the like, research on neighbors requires stealth, which some consultants have turned into a niche business.[79] The personal relocation firm Suburban Jungle Realty Group offers prospective homebuyers details on every aspect of neighborhoods so buyers can find one perfectly tailored to their preferences and lifestyle.[80] This is what happens when neighborhood is viewed as a collection of individuals with individualized needs and preferences.

This is not to say that it isn't possible to tap individual views on neighborhood and combine them for some collective, constructive purpose. Trying to put perception to practical use, the Pittsburgh Atlas Project in the 1970s used a combination of consensus mapping and questionnaires to define neighborhoods based on high percentages of agreement on naming.[81] The 1973 Columbus Neighborhood Definition Study tried to align "the existing theory of the neighborhood" with resident surveys to delineate neighborhoods.[82] George Galster's "realist" definition of neighborhood mapped people's "externality space," and then defined neighborhood based on maximizing the "congruence" between individuals.[83]

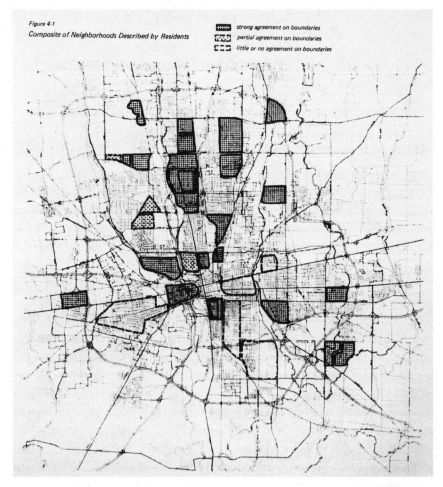

Figure 6.16 The Columbus Neighborhood Definition Study found that 80% of respondents relied on a physical description (house types, level of maintenance, and changes in land use were the strongest predictors), and only 10% gave a "social description." Source: Sims, *Neighborhoods*, 2.

More recently a British group called Common Ground developed a technique called "parish mapping" as a way of encouraging people to think about what makes their local environment unique. Their objective was to help prevent "the march of conforming and homogeneity across Britain." In their open-ended approach, anyone can make a map using any technique to define their neighborhood in any way they want. The point of the project is communication about what people value, about what their "daily round" is, and how the encouragement of active expressions of it can be a basis for action and change.[84]

A final aspect of the perceived neighborhood concerns naming practices. While naming the neighborhood can be an "awareness-raising process" that can foster a "proprietary attitude" (one study found that being able to name a neighborhood correlates with the amount of shared local ties one has),[85] there is a less noble side to it: that tapping perceived names is a way of tapping perceived prejudice. According to one blogger, this is the result of neighborhood naming that springs "from the fertile minds of real estate agents." Names are invented to avoid negative connotations. Since "no one really wants to live in a place called

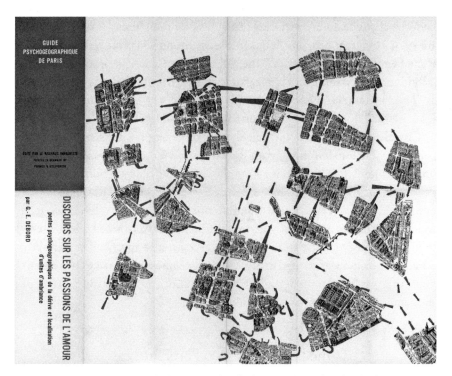

Figure 6.17 "Psychogeography" is the study of urbanism through individual meaning and experience. Although not intended as a depiction of neighborhoods, in this map by Guy Debord, segments of Paris stand out as neighborhood-like cells connected by individual wanderings. Source: Debord, *Guide Psychogeographique de Paris.*

Bushwick," one realtor conjured up the name WeBu (for West Bushwick), although some thought the term was "for sissies."[86] Changing a section of crime-ridden Van Nuys in Los Angeles to Valley Glen was, residents claimed, a boost to neighborhood identity and positive feeling. Elsewhere in California, part of Sepulveda was changed to North Hills; part of Canoga Park was changed to West Hills; and part of North Hollywood was changed to Valley Village. The nature-infused name changes were mostly driven by business associations.[87]

Neighborhood naming can be a commentary on lifestyle with the potential to perpetuate stereotypes. Eric Crum and Dillon Mahmoudi produced a "Badass-ness Neighborhoods" map for Portland, Oregon, that caused a stir since many residents did not appreciate what they viewed as cultural stereotyping. To produce the map, positive factors were discerned: local businesses, pinball houses, food carts, coffee, beer, breweries, strip clubs, light rail stops, and bike networks. Land values were input as a negative factor (the higher the land value, the lower the score). The end result was a map of neighborhoods ranging from "Hella Badass" to "Flannelville" to "Meh," and at the lowest end, "Vancouver-ish."[88]

Drew Hoolhorst tried something similar for San Francisco, creating postcards of that city's neighborhood stereotypes ("This town is fucking weird if you don't know what you're doing"), quickly taking heat for omissions. "It turns out there are 19,429 different neighborhoods to discuss . . . and 398 more were just created while I wrote that last sentence." The author's colorful neighborhood character-izations provoked some outrage—characterizing The Tenderloin neighborhood as "Needles-Landia," Chinatown as "Pink plastic bag–landia," and South San Francisco as "How is this considered San Francisco?–landia."[89]

City planners too are in the neighborhood naming business, often invoking controversy. In Pittsburgh, planners were criticized for renaming neighborhoods on the grounds that the names were arbitrary and caused confusion: "Some people in parts of Oakland, Shadyside and East Liberty may start waking up in a new neighborhood called Baum-Centre," which apparently was foreign to many residents. Planners responded that the name changes were based on an attempt to find "a strategy for the area's identity" based on meetings with stakeholders. Similar confusion was created in Seattle when planners renamed a "hot block of pubs" that was "a gray area between two hoods." Local residents were unaware of the name change, and no one could identify it.[90]

One Part Perry, Two Parts Process

Many are searching for the best of both worlds, a dose of planning, with a heap of flexibility: Ebenezer Howard–type neighborhoods, perhaps even Clarence Perry's school-focused neighborhoods, but without the imposition of top-down plans. One study of 10 Israeli neighborhoods (urban quarters), ranging from highly planned to completely unplanned, showed that highly planned neighborhoods had definite pluses: institutionalized leadership, clearly defined social and spatial boundaries, and a sense of control. The unplanned neighborhoods lacked social and spatial boundaries, in which case social control was a matter of the "abstract mores of society" expressed through the police and courts of law.[91]

Unfortunately, nuancing the plan-process balance that neighborhoods might benefit from has rarely happened. Neighborhood plans have instead been mostly wholesale, all-at-once, expert-driven formulations like Perry's. Missing has been the transfer of the neighborhood ideal in incremental terms, of the kind Henry Wright and Elbert Peets proposed for redeveloping existing places one block at a time.[92] Urban planners never developed a language or methodology that could implement the ideals of neighborhood as a physical and social construct in a way that was not top-down—not about blueprints, but not limited to process, either: plan and process combined.

The complexities of this balancing act come into view in the attempt to rely on incremental change as a way of improving neighborhoods. If there is no understanding of how incremental achievement leads to the gradual building up of something whole, with no tie-in to neighborhood, small improvements may seem like piecemeal shots in the dark, benefiting one landlord, one property owner, one gentrifier at a time. Would these catalytic efforts be that much more effective if they were contextualized within an identified neighborhood? A top-down plan is not necessarily the answer, but a clearer connection to a defined neighborhood may help broaden and deepen these efforts.

Plan versus process reveals the tension between collective input that requires planning protocols and the desire for an agile response in the form of pop-up shops, bench bombing, and painted crosswalks. There is a need for spontaneity and there is a need for representation that is fair and democratic.[93] Perhaps, at least, an explicit understanding of neighborhood and its attendant notions of collective enterprise, responsibility, and ownership could help resolve the two extremes of centralized planning and DIY intervention.

Lack of such a connection might have played a role in the redevelopment problems of Baltimore's 72-block Sandtown-Winchester neighborhood. Famous for being the site of the television serious *The Wire*, and most recently for being the home of Freddie Gray (whose death while in police custody sparked large protests), this area of 8,500 residents has been the recipient of Community Development Block Grants, private housing developer funds from the Rouse company, Habitat for Humanity funds, and other philanthropically motivated partnerships. Since 1989 more than $130 million of public and private investment has been spent on housing upgrades, job training, prenatal care, and revitalization efforts.

But the lack of a strong sense of neighborhood and the lack of meaningful resident decision-making power—plan *and* process—has meant that improvements lack real effect. The *Wall Street Journal* argued that residents should be given vouchers and told to live elsewhere, but longtime residents argued that neighborhood transformation *was* happening and that what the neighborhood needed "more than anything" was "constant attention."[94] Lack of resident empowerment translated to lack of attention, resulting in almost no auditing of what was actually accomplished. Mayor Kurt Schmoke, who launched the initial revitalization effort, said that a significant problem was the lack of follow-up. Researchers documented that there was no informed decision-making and no feedback about how things were going and how investments could be tailored in response to investment effects.[95]

An argument could be made that the lack of on-the-ground accounting in Baltimore reflected a weak neighborhood identity, no sense of neighborhood authority, and no sense of ownership—in short, inadequacies in both plan and process. With residents lacking real decision-making power over the ability to get things accomplished, fountains were left dry, school programming was ignored, and street lights were not turned on. It is the little things of neighborhood life that have catalytic meaning and effect, but they require a neighborhood identity—possibly via a neighborhood plan—as a baseline.

There is always the danger that small-scale efforts combined with a strong sense of neighborhood will be overplayed, resulting in an escalation of housing prices and eventual displacement. But there are deliberate steps that can be taken to thwart potential gentrification problems. One neighborhood group in the Bronx wanted to limit displacement that might result from their neighborhood's environmental cleanup of former brownfields and the addition of new parks and high-line-type revitalization. They worried that it would end up catering to café-seeking gentrifiers and speculative condo developers rather than existing residents, many of them working class. The approach was dubbed "just green enough," whereby amenities were selectively added and the usual upscale accoutrements were purposefully avoided. "Just green enough" strategies tended to be small-scale, scattered, and above all "explicitly shaped by community concerns, needs and desires."[96] This shaping required a plan as well as an explicit understanding of just who and what the neighborhood actually was, or was intended to be.

This kind of intervention does not just seek neighborhood input as a political nicety; the entire strategy—neighborhood improvement without disruption and displacement—is based on the idea that improvements must be defined by residents themselves. Studies consistently document that successful improvement-without-displacement efforts are a matter of "residents rallying together," where they have "mobilized finer scale resistance," constituting a "place-based nature of resilience." Often this mobilization, this ability to organize and activate a constituency, is intertwined with an environmental injustice problem, but the activation is almost always via participation in a neighborhood-based group. In turn, this is activated by a strong understanding of what the neighborhood is in spatial terms.[97]

Narratives surrounding climate change, sustainability, and resiliency could potentially help resolve the dichotomy that pits bottom-up authenticity against neighborhood plans and planning. Neighborhood-scale governance and control is important for environmentalism because neighborhood scale is used as a basis of sustainable practices—for instance, water conservation, groundwater recharge, recycling, energy efficiency, and food production. Individual actions matter too, but many sustainability and resilience goals require local coordination, where the scale of operations is at the neighborhood level.

Do the processes of neighborhood—tactical, empowering, bottom-up, environmentally based—require a defined, to some extent planned neighborhood? When conceived as a collective, deliberative response to unstructured urbanism, might designed neighborhoods be a net positive for human settlement? How can individual possibility be maximized, with minimal limits on opportunity and movement, within the context of bounded urban space? How can both of Georg Simmel's worlds be accommodated: an individualized urban experience composed of varying and unbounded social worlds, against a neighborhood ideal, analogous to Simmel's small town, that is necessarily spatially constrained?[98] And when does the unplanned, authentic spontaneity of the bottom-up neighborhood require some level of planning in order to be "smart" or sustainable?[99] How much is neighborhood identity required for community activism and self-help actualization, and how much does identity correlate with neighborhood as a physical realm? Do the form and design of the neighborhood, if it adheres to certain principles, promote neighborhood identity and, potentially, civic identity and spirit? And by the same token, does a physically deteriorated neighborhood or a widely dispersed neighborhood work against neighborhood and civic identity?

This is the balance between process and plan that has to be found, a sense of neighborhood versus the freedom to engage, small-scale intervention that adds up, neighborhood identity that does not impose too much control and too much order. The good news is that there is broad consensus about the processes needed to support neighborhoods, something that would have seemed alien to Perry and other midcentury neighborhood unit proponents. Two publications do a particularly thorough job of spelling out the method: *Building Better Neighborhoods* and *Planning to Stay*.[100] Both offer detailed instruction on the processes of neighborhood planning, from data gathering to generating support, working through the political process, and adoption of a vision for a neighborhood's future—that is, the neighborhood plan. Both texts provide highly graphic and easy-to-understand examples of the physical features of the neighborhood.

Planning to Stay works through five types of physical features ("neighborhood resources"): homes and gardens, community streets, neighborhood niches, anchoring institutions, and public gardens. Most of the book is devoted to showing residents how they can develop a sense of these elements. Five organizing themes help residents work through the issues involved: location (among neighbors, beyond the front door, on the corner, prominent settings, common ground), scale (visual rhythm, proportions, fit and contrast, visual accessibility), mix (home types, functional balance, mix of services, shared spaces, compatibilities), time (convertible spaces, day/night activities, seasonal markets, traditions, year-round activities), and movement (starting points, enhanced passageways, proximities, orientation, recreation). Being able to "see" these features answers the questions What is it about this place that draws us here? and What could we add to this place that will keep us here? The planning steps are straightforward: neighborhood residents agree to meet, gather the data (on the five physical features), create a vision for the future (using the five physical features and the associated organizing themes as a guide), do some field-testing with public and private sectors, create and implement an action plan, and sustain the plan— that is, find a way to maintain and manage the programs and projects of the plan.

There are two additional ways to achieve a particular neighborhood form that are more about process than blueprint. First, neighborhood ideals might be achieved through regulation—zoning—something an earlier generation of neighborhood unit activists (like Perry) were not particularly concerned about. Now a significant interest is the reform of zoning codes to match a neighborhood perspective, for example by connecting zoning regulation to neighborhood "character." Buffalo, New York's new zoning code lists 12 neighborhood zones, from regional hub to mixed-use center and single-family. Each neighborhood zone has an associated set of building and frontage types that are meant to reflect and strengthen each neighborhood's unique quality.

Second, and absent from earlier proposals, neighborhood plans now might be infused with an environmental ethos that translates to explicit performance measures that operate at the neighborhood scale. For example, EcoDistricts, LEED for Neighborhood Development (LEED-ND, see color plate 17), and the Sustainability Tools for Assessing & Rating (STAR) Communities are all frameworks that include neighborhood-level sustainability assessment. They employ an implicit neighborhood ideal based on performance rather than specific forms. In the case of sustainable energy, for example, there is a movement afoot to decentralize electricity, water, and waste treatment, moving from massive city-wide plants to small, networked, neighborhood-based utility districts.[101]

Economies of scale in public utility provision are increasingly being reversed, whereby smaller is now seen as more efficient, more resilient, and more flexible. It's a way to maximize efficiency and reduce transmission loss, help get individually generated energy (e.g., from solar panels on rooftops) into the grid, and encourage innovation, such as converting compost piles to energy. Such energy localization efforts require an explicit conception of neighborhood.

Notes

1. Mumford, "The Neighborhood and the Neighborhood Unit," 256.
2. Unwin, *Town Planning in Practice*, 383–84.
3. Blumenfeld, " 'Neighborhood' Concept Is Submitted to Questioning," 299.
4. Arguments summarized here, for example: Sampson, "Notes on Neighborhood Inequality and Urban Design."
5. Federal Housing Administration, "Land Planning Bulletin," v.
6. Ward, "Dreams of Oriental Romance."
7. Myers, "Designing Power."
8. Macfarlane, "Planning an Arab Town"; Shiber, *The Kuwait Urbanization*.
9. Frolic, "The Soviet City," 302.
10. Ibid., 285, 292.
11. Marcus, "Social Housing and Segregation in Sweden"; Nyström and Lundström, "Sweden," 49.
12. Abu-Lughod, "The Islamic City."
13. Silver, "Neighborhood Planning in Historical Perspective."
14. In addition to Jane Jacobs, there were Reginald Isaacs, Herbert Gans, Christopher Alexander, and Peter Hall.
15. Isaacs, "Are Urban Neighborhoods Possible?," 177; Bowden, "How to Define Neighborhood," 227.
16. Adams et al., "Panel I," 69, 71, 78.
17. Allaire, "Neighborhood Boundaries," 8.
18. Koenigsberger, "New Towns in India," 105, 109.
19. Vidyarthi, "Inappropriately Appropriated or Innovatively Indigenized?," 260, 264.
20. Koenigsberger, "New Towns in India," 105, 109.
21. Slidell, "The Shape of Things to Come?" Richman and Chapin, *A Review of the Social and Physical Concepts of the Neighborhood*, 32.
22. Collison, "Town Planning and the Neighbourhood Unit Concept," 465. See also Goss, "Neighbourhood Units in British New Towns."
23. Patricios, "The Neighborhood Concept," 70–90.
24. Banerjee and Baer, Beyond the Neighborhood Unit, 33.
25. Tajbakhsh, *The Promise of the City*, xv.
26. Krase, "Italian American Urban Landscapes," 23; Harvey, *The Urban Experience*, 261–64.
27. Tajbakhsh, *The Promise of the City*, xiii; Sennett, *The Uses of Disorder*.
28. Cox and Mair, "Locality and Community in the Politics of Local Economic Development."
29. Joseph, *Against the Romance of Community*.
30. Davidson, "Love Thy Neighbour?"
31. Webber, "The Metropolitan Habitus," 184.
32. Webber, "The Metropolitan Habitus," 184, 206.
33. Whitehead, "Love Thy Neighbourhood," 280. See also Harvey, *Social Justice and the City* and *The Urban Experience*.
34. Belanger, "The Neighborhood Ideal."
35. Schlumbohm, " 'Traditional' Collectivity and 'Modern' Individuality."
36. Cited in Lammers, "The Birth of the East Ender," 336.

37. Ibid., 331, 334.
38. Brody, "Constructing Professional Knowledge."
39. , MOMA, "Press Release," 2.
40. Dahir, *The Neighborhood Unit Plan*.
41. Cody, "American Planning in Republican China," 370.
42. Perry, "The Rehabilitation of the Local Community," 559.
43. Miller, "Legal Neighborhoods"; Mumford, *The City in History*, 193. Mumford was referring to the ancient Greek city of Thurium, laid out in 443 B.C.
44. Ackerman, "Houses and Ships"; Stern and Massengale, *Anglo-American Suburb*.
45. Stein, *Toward New Towns for America*, 35.
46. Mumford, "The Neighborhood and the Neighborhood Unit," 267.
47. Quote from Barry Parker's 1928 article "Economy in Estate Development," in Adams, *Recent Advances in Town Planning*, 297.
48. Whitten, "A Research into the Economics of Land Subdivision," 1.
49. Federal Housing Administration, "Land Planning Bulletin," 11, 12, 16.
50. For perspective on neighborhood planning in the 1970s, see Goering, "The National Neighborhood Movement"; Silver, "Neighborhood Planning in Historical Perspective."
51. Teaford, "Jane Jacobs and the Cosmopolitan Metropolis," 886
52. Sorkin, "Love Thy Neighbor(hood)."
53. Newcombe, "A Town Extension Scheme," 229.
54. Turner and Smulian, "New Cities in Venezuela" 20. See also Healey, "Urban Planning in a Venezuelan City."
55. Bardet, "Social Topography," 247.
56. These cities without neighborhoods were reviewed by Banerjee and Baer. *Beyond the Neighborhood Unit*, 187.
57. Barnett, *An Introduction to Urban Design*, 146.
58. Herbert, "The Neighbourhood Unit Principle," 198, 200, 202, 203.
59. Bailey, "How Spatial Segregation Changes over Time."
60. Martin, "Enacting Neighborhood," 361.
61. Herbert, "The Neighbourhood Unit Principle," 198, 200, 202, 203.
62. Jacobs, *The Death and Life of Great American Cities*, 17.
63. Tocqueville, *Democracy in America*, 187.
64. Mabie, "Ethics and the Larger Neighborhood," 15.
65. Hester, *Planning Neighborhood Space with People*, 13.
66. See, for example, Wolfe, *Urbanism without Effort*. See also Fontenot, "Notes toward a History of Non-Planning."
67. McBride and Mlyn, "Innovation Alone Won't Fix Social Problems."
68. Wann, "Neighborhoods on Purpose."
69. Banerjee and Baer. *Beyond the Neighborhood Unit*, 196.
70. Keller, *The Urban Neighborhood*, 136–46.
71. Bickel et al., "Poor, Rural Neighborhoods and Early School Achievement," 106.
72. Hipp and Boessen, "Egohoods as Waves Washing across the City," 289, 290.
73. Lynch, *The Image of the City*.
74. Rofe, "Space and Community," 118.
75. Proshansky et al., "Place Identity"; Mannarini et al., "Image of Neighborhood, Self-Image and Sense of Community." See also Uzzell et al., "Place Identification, Social Cohesion, and Environmental Sustainability."
76. Lee, "Urban Neighbourhood as a Socio-Spatial Schema."
77. Warren, "The Functional Diversity of Urban Neighborhoods," 171.
78. Woodruff, "Crowdsourced Neighborhood Boundaries"; Ali, "This Is Where Chicagoans Say the Borders of Their Neighborhoods Are."
79. Misra, "The Tricky Task of Rating Neighborhoods on 'Livability'"; Kaufman, "Researching Your Future Neighbors."
80. Prevost, "Using Data to Find a New York Suburb That Fits."
81. Cunningham et al., "The Pittsburgh Atlas Program."
82. Sims, *Neighborhoods*, 2.

83. Galster, "What Is Neighbourhood?," 259.
84. Common Ground, "Parish Maps." See also King, "Mapping Your Roots."
85. Taylor et al., "Neighborhood Naming as an Index of Attachment to Place."
86. "Curbed NY."
87. Manzano, "Community," 2.
88. Crum and Mahmoudi, "Badass-ness Map."
89. Hoolhorst, "Moving to San Francisco."
90. Jones, "Boundaries Blur in Many City Neighborhoods." See also Vinh, "Frelard or Balmont?"
91. Deshen, "Social Control in Israeli Urban Quarters," 166.
92. Walker and Wright, *Urban Blight and Slums.*
93. Lydon et al., *Tactical Urbanism.*
94. Wenger, "Saving Sandtown-Winchester."
95. Ibid.
96. Curran and Hamilton, "Just Green Enough"; Wolch et al., "Urban Green Space, Public Health, and Environmental Justice," 242.
97. Pearsall, "Moving Out or Moving In?," 1014, 1024. See also Curran and Hamilton. "Just Green Enough."
98. Simmel, "The Metropolis and Mental Life."
99. Gopnik, "The Secret Lives of Cities."
100. Greater Minnesota Housing Fund, *Building Better Neighborhoods*; Morrish and Brown, *Planning to Stay.*
101. "Little Grids."

7

The Self-Governed Neighborhood

This chapter picks up where the previous chapter left off, focusing more specifically on the issue of neighborhood self-governance. The previous chapter argued the importance of resident empowerment in neighborhood planning—a bottom-up process working in tandem with the tangibility and forethought of a neighborhood plan. But what about the ongoing management and governance of a neighborhood? Are neighborhoods to be entirely managed and controlled by their own residents?

The debate covered in this chapter is about the pros and cons of self-determination and local control. Strong, self-regulated neighborhoods fit well within a self-help narrative about residents taking control of their own destinies. But the downside, as the debates reveal, is the loss of power and the potential for insularity, which can further deplete power. At the same time, higher-level authorities are often resistant to relinquishing control, putting added stress on the ability of neighborhoods to self-manage. Here again a weak neighborhood identity, in part a result of vague notions about what and where the neighborhood actually is, feed into this problem. With a stronger sense of neighborhood, the debate can be resolved through better connection to wider political networks as well as better application of innovative budgeting and governance procedures that are already in place but not widely in use. Resolution of the self-determination debate, then, capitalizes on existing procedures, regulations, and governing authority that exist at the neighborhood level but have not been activated by an explicit understanding of neighborhood.

The self-governed and self-managed neighborhood controls its own destiny. Theoretically this provides four advantages: efficiency (because of decentralization and subsidiarity), accountability (via greater transparency since local residents are closer to the issues), familiarity (which improves resident interaction and effectiveness at getting things done), and convenience (thus giving neighborhoods instant relevance). Always there are trade-offs and counterfactuals to contend with, such as the well-recognized issue that neighborhood governance does nothing to address structural processes of inequity.[1]

Figure 7.1 Photograph of an "immigrant neighborhood gathering" published in the 1920 book *America via the Neighborhood*. The caption reads, "Over two thousand Bohemian newcomers assembled in the Harrison Technical High School, Chicago, to witness an entertainment and consider local improvements." Source: Daniels, *America via the Neighborhood*.

Attempts to rectify the disparities of urban life tend to be appeals to neighborhood empowerment and local control. This has long been regarded as the antidote to big city machine politics, starting with Mary Parker Follett's 1918 *The New State: Group Organization, the Solution of Popular Government,* where she argues that civic action at the neighborhood level should be the basis of civic involvement in America. Norman Mailer's 1969 "Power to the Neighborhood" mayoral campaign continued the tradition. But it was a double-edged sword. If neighborhoods are in charge of their own destinies, they are also the source of their own problems.

The Village Ideal

In the U.S. the earliest inklings of neighborhood self-determination are rooted in the tradition of 19th-century "village improvement" societies, many of which emerged after the Civil War in small and medium-size cities throughout the country. These were the precursors of neighborhood associations—volunteer efforts with a strong sense of neighborhood, often focusing on its protection. Andrew Jackson Downing was an early advocate, and his devotee, Nathaniel Hillyer Egleston, called for collective organizing for neighborhood improvement in his 1853 *Villages and Village Life: Hints for Their Improvement.* The Laurel Hill Association in Stockbridge, Massachusetts, was born soon after. The movement spread rapidly, especially in New England, and by the 1890s hundreds of mostly women-led village improvement societies had been formed throughout the country.

Although the village ideal was a source of neighborhood identity and civic consciousness, the village life it was based on was a mythical concept. Historians point out that the village model was invented by 19th-century romantics and elites who confused "sentiment with settlement," offering an aesthetic ideology that was "a landscape of corporate construction." Instead of a communally focused, self-governed settlement ideal, it was basically a system of land subdivision. Randall Arendt reviewed the fiction of the New England village from an urban design point of view, showing that the "village" was really more of a "buckshot pattern of farmhouses" than a neatly organized neighborhood around a square.[2]

Whether attached to village idealism or not, rural residents had an interest in promoting a sense of neighborhood because it aligned with Jeffersonian independence and self-determination. In the rural North there were practical implications. Farmers would get together to strategize road maintenance "in their neighborhood," defined by locally maintained road districts. The rural understanding of neighborhood rooted in Jefferson's 1785 Land Ordinance (which had blanketed the country with neighborhood-like sections and quarter-sections) was not only alive and well in the 20th century, but it was used to foster self-governance.[3]

A series of government-backed studies in the early 20th century sought to establish neighborhood identity in rural America for the purpose of stimulating "local responsibility for local neighborhood problems." One neighborhood "reconnaissance survey" in rural North Carolina identified 40 "fairly distinct neighborhoods," where geographical segregation via "creeks and ridges" was believed to generate "considerable local loyalty." The survey tried to gauge the sense of neighborhood that existed among farm men and women, and county employees were charged with finding "neighborhood farmer leaders." (Loyalty and leadership were unlikely to trump race, however. As the report works through each neighborhood identified, a caution is inserted that some areas are "so heavily Negro" that they could "scarcely be included within any white neighborhood.")[4]

The North American rural neighborhood was much more than a cluster of farms with occasional social events. It could function, in some places, as the locale of self-organized economic activity and day-to-day life. One historian showed how the "bee" (whether devoted to cradling, threshing, raking, or quilting) was the basis of a neighborhood's "structural and cognitive order." Though not the physical form of neighborhood found in the industrial city or the suburban enclave, it did manage to impose its own understanding and control of who belonged and who did not.[5]

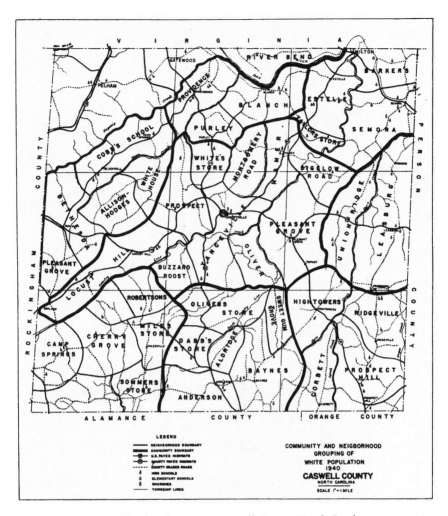

Figure 7.2 Rural neighborhoods in 1940, Caswell County, North Carolina. Source: Holt, "Report of a Reconnaissance Survey of Neighborhoods and Communities of Caswell County, North Carolina with Recommendations."

It was the lack of resident control that exposed a significant weakness of the fabricated village, also known as the company town. Pullman, Illinois, combined housing, factories, stores, and recreational facilities in a model industrial environment intended to benefit workers, their productivity, and, of course, company profits. But following the Depression of 1893, Pullman laid off employees, cut wages, and failed to reduce rents or cut the cost of services. Jane Addams argued that this showed that the model village idea was inferior to the settlement housing approach because it lacked a cooperative effort, one that might have been more attuned to workers' needs. She likened the tragedy of Pullman to the fate of King Lear.[6] As is often the case with the planned-all-at-once neighborhood

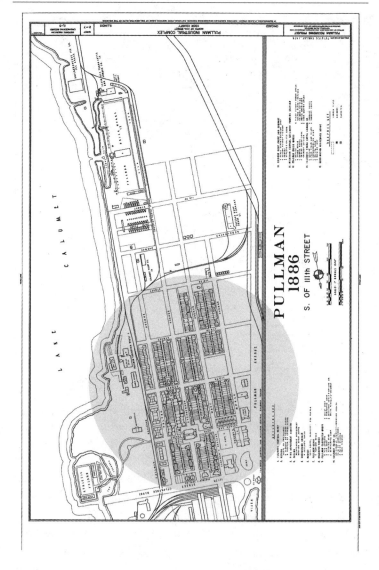

Figure 7.3 Most of Pullman, Illinois, a company town built in 1881, fits within the quarter-mile walking radius of Perry's neighborhood unit, but it was planned for a population of 8,000. Source: "Pullman 1886," Blogspot, http://4.bp.blogspot.com/~6gngIDdac/UII83aJF37I/AAAAAAAASY/8ENomj1pXkg/s1600/Pullman-town-1886-02.jpg.

(or village) scheme, the control (i.e., corporate ownership) made it seem less like a real place and more like an exercise in pure domination.

Kohler, Wisconsin, founded in 1913 and designed by Werner Hegemann and Elbert Peets of *Civic Art* fame, had 2,000 inhabitants within an area of a quarter-mile radius (excluding the Kohler factory). It was an improvement over Pullman in that the village was incorporated and governed by its residents, not the company. By the 1920s similar "villages" were being built to satisfy the industrial workers of factories that were by now proliferating in response to Fordist production techniques. Ford himself was involved in creating "village industries" meant to unite factory and agricultural laborer. Many of these were built with the automobile in mind, signifying not only the capitalist's desire to create an automobile-dependent society but a greater recognition of the American worker's need for independence and individuality.[7]

Associations and Clubs

Neighborhoods became more formalized and proactive in the early decades of the 20th century. By 1906 there were 2,400 neighborhood associations in the U.S.[8] Some were established to advise municipal governments, a practice that made their autonomy (and degree of self-governance) seem questionable. Records from Portland, Oregon, show how carefully delineated neighborhood boundaries, leadership, and meeting schedules were set up to advise the city planning commission on zoning district designation, then a new and progressive reform idea.[9] Other associations were more about managing small-scale physical change—providing rubbish boxes, ornamental lampposts and street trees, and fountains and agitating for litter cleanup, noise and smoke abatement, and the beautification of vacant property. The neighborhood, as Mary Simkhovitch wrote, was a "manageable microcosm."[10] Throughout the Progressive Era there was a strong sense of collective responsibility for the condition of cities via neighborhood-scale improvement, an enterprise the historian Daphne Spain labeled the "voluntary vernacular." Spain used a fabric analogy to characterize the difference between neighborhood improvers and the "White City" of the City Beautiful movement: "While Daniel Burnham was busy trying to create cities from whole new cloth, women volunteers were strengthening the existing urban fabric by focusing not on commerce and large public spaces, but on daily life and the neighborhood."[11]

The settlement house movement endorsed neighborhood self-determination, albeit with a strong message of assimilation. Its chief advocate, Robert A. Woods, declared, "Democracy will never arrive until we all have learned the art of, and grow the mind for fellowship in the small group of the neighborhood."[12] Woods went so far as to write that the neighborhood was a "more ancient and fundamentally causative institution than the family," that there was no equal to the neighborhood (not family, city, or nation) that rivaled its "dignity" and "social self-consciousness." Woods lamented the lack of "precise specifications" about neighborhoods ("a tragic form of negligence") but believed that the growing interest in neighborhood, spurred in large part by the 400 neighborhood settlement houses in operation, would demand better knowledge. The result would be that the "collective power of neighborhoods will be greatly stimulated and developed."[13]

These ideals were conveyed to America's youth. An early 20th-century school textbook entitled *A Course on Citizenship* used the neighborhood to try to instill civic responsibility in children. It defined neighborhood as "the child's city limits," and teaching helpfulness at that scale was seen as a stepping stone to full-scale citizenship. Helpfulness included maintenance of public property: "seeing that papers are picked up, fences and building left undefaced." Through engagement with a variety of neighbors doing a variety of tasks, teachers could show "the real life of the neighborhood" and "break that hard shell of prejudice."[14]

Neighborhood self-governance could lead to neighborhood competitiveness. The struggle unfolded in Baltimore, Maryland, which had a particularly strong tradition of neighborhood associations. Its first neighborhood association, the Catonsville Neighborhood Improvement Association (really a village connected by horsecar line to the city), was started in 1880. By 1900 Baltimore had 30 such organizations. Many of these were businessmen's organizations, formed to promote the interests of—that is, acquire government resources for—their neighborhood over other neighborhoods. The tension among neighborhood associations, and between neighborhood associations and city hall, was legendary. Neighborhood associations "simply intensified the interward rivalries on the city council and thwarted the search for compromise." The problem was chronicled in a famous Sage Foundation sociological study, the 1907–8 Pittsburgh Survey, which showed how the undue influence of strong neighborhood groups meant that some were able to get their streets paved through aggressive tactics, while the more pressing needs of the city were neglected.[15]

Jockeying for resources, the self-governed neighborhood was caught up in the quest for local political power. Rallying around neighborhood causes was believed to be a potent way to exert influence. This quest has come from both the Right and the Left. Neighborhood associations aimed at protecting property rights and excluding unwanted uses were just as interested in bottom-up localized control as neighborhood groups aimed at political empowerment, social justice, or service delivery. Often, however, it was the quest for political power from the Right that was associated with the planned neighborhood. It is emblematic that Radburn's neighborhood association is not elected by residents; its governing board votes other members in. (This was the subject of a lawsuit by residents, but their claim was denied.)

On the question of who should "govern" the neighborhood, the social reformer Mary Simkhovitch thought that the "neighborhood powers" rested
in those servicing the neighborhood day by day: "the doctor, the teacher, the
clergyman . . . the baker, the delicatessen man, the pool parlor proprietor."
Neighborhood governance, she wrote, is about the "interacting relationships
which come both to color and to fix the habits of the population." Formal government, she contrasted, is for people to voice objections, and unless there is
some specific disturbance, people are uninterested in it.[16]

Leaders of the social and civic center movement had high hopes that their
neighborhood civic clubs would take charge of local governance. The clubs were
to be headquartered in the local school or other venue; they would be "non-
partisan, non-sectarian, non-exclusive"; and they would be dedicated to the
"presentation and discussion of public questions." One enthusiast wrote, "You
who have not witnessed it can not understand how party spirit, class spirit, and
even race spirit fade out in the intense civic and community atmosphere of these
neighborhood civic clubs." It was a feeling that was "latent" in every person; it
only needed "an appropriate stimulus to arouse it." Since the government had
failed to develop communally oriented institutions, the neighborhood club was
needed to provide the stimulus and awaken civic spirit.[17]

Cincinnati was famous for one variant, oddly named the Social Unit Plan,
which was operational from 1917 to 1920. The Plan was a system of settlement
houses and centers within neighborhoods through which residents "would be
accountable for the health, safety and welfare of each other."[18] It was to be a form
of participatory, block-level democracy, with neighborhoods as the unit of self-
realization and local control. But maintaining localized control proved especially
difficult. One factor of settlement house decline starting in the 1920s was that
they tended to be governed by outside advocates rather than local residents.[19]

The decline of these early 20th-century neighborhood governance strategies
morphed into an idealism about the symbolic value of neighborhood as the em-
blem of American civility and moral standing. Benjamin Looker's *A Nation of
Neighborhoods* showed how the neighborhood in World War II was a conduit for
expressing American sentiments about national pride, boosterism, friendship,
and a sense of morality. American children have long received "citizenship education" via the neighborhood, with lessons in which the value of police, firefight-
ers, health centers, and schools are all conceptualized and discussed within the
context of neighborhood. A neighborhood K–3 curriculum guide defines the
neighborhood as "a place with a purpose" and a portal through which the values
of "community" should be taught.[20]

During World War II artists were enlisted to use the concept of neighborhood to relate what was best about America: tolerance, local caring, civic idealism. Through the neighborhood, abstract concepts like citizenship and world

harmony were made real. In the wartime appeal to America's unique role in combating fascism and other evils, the "stoop and corner" connected with "grand,
public matters of war and peace, fascism and democracy, ethnic conflict and national pluralism." Thus it was through neighborhood that Americans understood
the broader political economy and America's role in it.[21]

Michigan established neighborhood war clubs because participation in the
war effort, it was argued, required block-by-block organization.[22] Through a
neighborhood war club, every citizen would be given the opportunity to "do
his part," participating in such activities as salvage, child care, labor training, car
sharing, and surveys (of, for example, the number of spare bedrooms available
for war workers). Above all it was a mechanism for boosting morale, "discussion
and common understanding" of civilian war duties, and "the development of the
neighborly spirit of cooperation for war service." Somewhat paradoxical to this
attempt to engender bottom-up neighborhood activism was the way neighborhoods were delineated with military precision. Clubs were to follow the divisions of the air raid warden system, numbered down to the post level, and then
divided into "neighborhood units." On the other hand, the top-down aspect of
this had the added benefit of encouraging neighborhood-scale diversity: neighborhood war clubs were required to be composed "of all residents of a neighborhood, regardless of race, color, or creed."[23]

The Weakness of Neighborhood Governance

In 1940s America, neighborhood planning was tempered with the understanding that "a properly served neighborhood necessarily involves the people
who live in the neighborhood in the planning of their neighborhood." One
needed only "faith enough in democracy" to improve neighborhood quality.[24]
But others argued that democracy via the neighborhood was weak. Jesse Steiner,
president of the National Community Center Association, wrote that the neighborhood was not the right scale for dealing with urban issues; social problems,
he said, should instead be addressed at the regional scale. Hans Blumenfeld had
disdain for "the neighborhood concept" because it rendered so little: "It is hardly
an adequate means to save the city, the nation, and the world from impending
disaster."[25]

The 20th century weakened neighborhood-based political power by instituting citywide elections, city manager forms of government, and regionalism.[26] For
centuries prior, neighborhoods had been the point of entry into wider political
networks, which played out as dramatically in Renaissance Florence as in early
20th-century Chicago and Los Angeles. Alexander Von Hoffman traced what
the changes in neighborhood governance meant for 19th-century Boston, when

political representation went from being neighborhood-based to being more centralized. This was supposedly a Progressive move toward greater equality, but what it really meant was loss of political power. In the process, neighborhoods forfeited their ability to unite a socially mixed clientele that had previously connected over shared, locally based causes.[27]

It is true that the burgeoning metropolis had rendered the neighborhood somewhat powerless. Early 20th-century neighborhood sympathizers blamed large cities for undermining localized political action. According to the sociologist Harvey Zorbaugh, author of the 1929 neighborhood classic *The Gold Coast and the Slum*, it was the mobility of society that rendered neighborhood-based organization weak. Political organization required stability, and an expanding cosmopolitanism undermined that. Expanding social networks did not necessarily mitigate the problem. One study of neighborhood social networks in New York City used data from 1937 to show that social networks were incapable of erasing the "negative effects of adverse social and economic conditions" in New York's neighborhoods.[28]

Some Progressive Era reformers thought that neighborhood-based authority should be controlled at a higher level in any case. George Hooker made the case in a 1917 edition of the *National Municipal Review*. "Real city neighborhoods," he wrote, need a "federal scheme" that conjoined "limited city neighborhood government" to "a well-considered plan."[29] The challenge was that, when neighborhoods were inserted into big city politics, they were caught between grassroots organizing and bureaucratic maneuvering—and they needed to be good at both. The two strategies were often in conflict. Even in cities with a strong tradition of sanctioned neighborhood organization, neighborhoods might be used for legitimacy but ultimately ignored in the name of efficiency.[30]

Initially the "machine politics" of American cities was closely tied to the condensed and centralized ethnic neighborhood. But later, when those voting blocks dispersed, the neighborhood-based voting district gave way to a larger electoral map, and the political power of neighborhoods was channeled through broader community organizations. Such organizations have been described as "reactive," tending to respond to issues that lie well outside of neighborhood boundaries, like school busing. Neighborhood groups might aggregate, but when they do, the tie to neighborhood has a different flavor. Some, like Albert Hunter, welcomed this aggregation. As Hunter saw it, the decisions impacting neighborhoods were being "traced up the vertical hierarchy," whereby "neighborhood politics becomes national politics."[31]

Hunter viewed the "federation of neighborhoods" as a powerful force, "a new urban populism," whereby, paradoxically, increases in scale and mass communication would further the neighborhood cause. Agglomerating forces would help neighborhood activists coalesce and broaden their base, creating "federated national associations" that might have better luck with effectuating real change. Missing was any consideration that these broadened coalitions would further abstract the meaning and physical rootedness of what neighborhoods are supposed to be.

By the 1960s the recasting of neighborhood as an organization with an unspecified physical description was complete, and it paralleled the physical planning side of the equation (see "Neighborhood Alternatives," Chapter 6). Saul Alinsky–style activism was organized around the workplace or ethnic group, not necessarily a geographically constructed, government-defined neighborhood. In fact Alinsky was not supportive of neighborhood as a distinct spatial, physical, or functional place at all, because such delineation held little political advantage. His thinking was more in the tradition of Durkheim and Weber, who pitted emotional sentiments of place against the rational thinking of organizational interests. In this way of thinking, neighborhoods exist not for the purpose of promoting neighborhood-based political activism but to dissipate power and help corporations and politicians avoid action and responsibility. Broader coalitions, not small-area neighborhoods, are a more effective political force.[32]

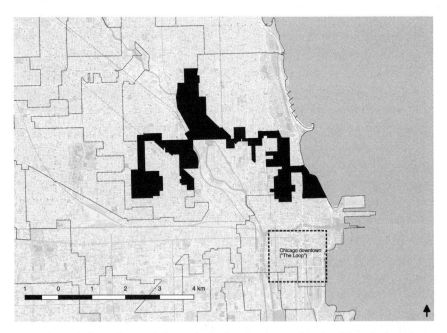

Figure 7.4 The boundaries of Chicago's wards are gerrymandered and have little to do with place-based neighborhoods, as revealed in this map showing the delineation of Ward 2. One could argue, per Jane Jacobs, that Chicago's wards gain their legitimacy as "district" neighborhoods, and that smaller, street-based neighborhoods are enabled by connecting to them. Source: author.

This critique is prominent in Europe, where governments in France, Denmark, and especially the U.K. have adopted the neighborhood as the basis of a social policy that was first more remedial (addressing poverty) but has lately been more strategic (stimulating investment). In the U.K. these are known as ABIs, area-based initiatives. Among academics, this "new localism" is critiqued as merely decentralizing responsibility, not power. It translates to short-term and incremental policies and actions at the expense of long-term and sustainable ones. In the end, neighborhood-based planning and governance seem to be an exercise in political cover, where neighborhood-based service delivery makes possible the "wholesale reform of mainstream services." Such programs are also more easily dismantled.[33]

Progressives thought that spatially unconstrained forms of community organizing, beyond the neighborhood, were especially needed to help the plight of poor residents. This is why the executive director of the Industrial Areas Foundation (the organization created by Alinsky in the 1940s) declared at a 1988 conference called Church and City and held in Philadelphia, "The neighborhood as an organizing mechanism is dead!" Neighborhood-based service delivery and other topics rooted in space and place proximities were subordinated to broader coalitions and agglomerations. One consequence of freeing community activism from the constraints of neighborhood was that it put the focus squarely on housing "projects."[34]

Organizations rooted to the neighborhood idea responded by broadening their definitions. Often this meant obscuring the distinction between "neighborhood" and "community." George Hillery's 1968 study of local societies had claimed that there was an overlap with neighborhood in many of the 94 definitions of community he uncovered[35]—an insight that many neighborhood organizations probably thought was axiomatic. The National Association of Neighborhoods is the oldest (established in 1975) and largest (2,500 members) organization of what it calls "the heart of the nation's community: America's neighborhoods," and to maximize broad-based appeal, the definition of neighborhood it uses is entirely open-ended. Place-bound solidarity is invoked in a way that omits any consideration of spatial concepts like place, proximity, centrality or boundedness. The mission statement of the national nonprofit Neighborhoods USA, or NUSA, also formed in 1975, has a similar quest to "build stronger communities" that have no particular requirement for neighborhood, place-based definition.[36]

And yet it could be argued that a neighborhood is not a community, or even a "place-based community." There are distinctions to be made between neighborhoods as places, as social networks, as parts of the city whole, or as places of "conceptual identity."[37] When "neighborhood" and "community" are combined, the result, "neighborhood community," describes a fairly small subset, given the definition: "a close-knit network of households [that] participate in common social activities" or "an area which contains all or most of the elements of a complete social system."[38] This might lead to the conclusion that neighborhoods without "community" are somehow "deficient, dysfunctional, and doomed."[39] The common theme of "community lost" can spill over to "neighborhood lost" without a clear understanding of the difference. The result is that the neighborhood is just as likely to disintegrate under the weight of Louis Wirth's "mass society" of alienation as "community" is, where the remedy is cosmopolitanism and connection to the world at large, potentially undermining the concept of neighborhood as a physical place.

From the opposite angle, there is the argument that neighborhood should never be equated with "community" because the exclusionary tactics of neighborhoods might infiltrate the more legitimate concerns of community-building. Neighborhoods can be critiqued for being bedroom communities, for having little meaning in people's lives, for being restrictive and exclusionary—but an unplaced, abstract notion of community has the ability to rise above.[40]

The technological, especially internet, basis of social engagement creates an additional strain by making the connection between neighborhood governance and neighborhood as a defined place seem somewhat irrelevant. On the positive side, technology potentially broadens engagement more generally. For example, a recent winner of an "Appmycity!" contest produced a spatially constrained bartering system called Peerby. The app facilitates borrowing among neighbors. Users type in what they need, and the search starts in successive bands, first within a radius of a few hundred feet, expanding outward, mapping each lender's location.[41] This enables some degree of self-determination, but it also defines "neighborhood" in a technical and perceptual way, potentially at odds with the hands-on governance of a place-based neighborhood.

A similar dichotomy pits "smart cities" and "big data" against traditional forms of localized governance. Some view data science as empowering and equalizing, while others see it as authoritarian.[42] Data science would seem to conflict with the goal of the self-governed neighborhood because of the reliance on centralized control-room systems, and because it is ostensibly trying to be apolitical. Neighborhoods are about the working out of daily lives in social terms more than strictly efficiency terms. In this sense, the smart cities movement can be critiqued for masking important issues about neighborhood life that require a political, collective response.[43] In this sense, neighborhood is the antidote to the dehumanizing face of "smart"—or for that matter "sustainable"—cities.

Another take is that a neighborhood's indeterminacy can be used as a method of empowerment. In this approach, the essence of neighborhood is the disagreement over form it incites: opposing views about how boundaries nest, overlap, blur, and change, especially in relation to individualized cognitive understandings of neighborhood. To be proactive, the loaded term "neighborhood" should be avoided altogether and replaced with "place-frames." It would still be possible to build identity, unite residents around a common purpose, downplay differences, and leverage *place* to inform local activism, nested in a macropolitical economy but operating within their own realm. The "territorial sphere" can be activated as "a legitimate and meaningful site for activism." Although potentially undermining "global activist agendas," place-frames would allow residents to make sense of daily life.[44]

The suggested approach shows how far the relationship between neighborhood planning and neighborhood governance has strayed. The solution to the politically weak neighborhood is not to move in the direction of an identity-building and form-specific plan, but to move in the opposite direction: broadening definition, using bigger data, or embracing indeterminacy. Barry Checkoway warned in the 1980s that "the preparation of plans is among the least useful activities undertaken by neighborhood organizations" in part because "such plans can relate poorly to daily concerns."[45] The typical "master plan" of American cities has done much to keep these sentiments alive. Such plans—originating in the 1950s but still in use—imagine the city in terms of discrete functions: the "land use element," the "circulation element," the "recreation element." Missing is planning by neighborhood, especially in ways that bestow real power—self-determination—at the neighborhood level.

Neighborhood planning was not a method by which neighborhoods took control of their own destinies. It was really, Checkoway cautioned, just "subarea planning in disguise." Subarea planning is the top-down decentralization of facilities and an expedient way to satisfy citizen participation requirements set by federal agencies or comprehensive planning statutes; it is not a resident-generated vision in which neighborhoods are assigned real decision-making authority.[46] The attempt to manage services more efficiently by invoking neighborhood is not in the spirit of Jeffersonian bottom-up democracy and self-governance; it is in the spirit of control. Ironically, using the neighborhood as the unit of facility decentralization increases the number of units to be administered, which can create more bureaucracy and cost. However, proponents of neighborhood self-governance cannot take this line of reasoning too far. Neighborhood governance is easily challenged as inefficient and backward in an age when more information age–enabled "subtle and sophisticated tools" to manage a city are superior to governance based on neighborhood.[47]

Neighborhood self-governance seems to be in constant search of authenticity. Practically, it is supposed to involve local resident review of proposals or plans, or development of new plans as a part of a city's comprehensive plan, or neighborhood improvement activities (i.e., cleanup campaigns or housing rehabilitation projects). But all of these forms of involvement require time and energy, and few neighborhood residents might actually participate. Filling the vacuum is "expert knowledge" and other forms of paternalism, leading to what Sherry Arnstein labeled "tokenism."[48] Even where there is a more concerted effort toward neighborhood-level governance it may not be representative. An analysis of Los Angeles's 86 neighborhood councils found "substantial racial bias" against representation by Hispanics, putting the legitimacy of the neighborhood councils "at risk."[49]

Then there is the view that the benefits of formal neighborhood participation do not extend beyond what everyday, informal interaction provides. One study of moderate-income neighborhoods in Akron, Ohio, found that informal social participation, such as frequenting a neighborhood store, had a stronger link to positive feelings about the neighborhood than formal participation in voluntary or government-backed neighborhood associations. Thus, the authors concluded, "formalized kinds of participation do not have any measurable effects on how one feels about his or her neighborhood."[50] An obvious explanation is that participation in formal neighborhood groups is usually very low, gaining traction only when neighborhoods are threatened or in a time of crisis.

Future Prospects

These negations seem rather dark when viewed against the reality that when neighborhoods lack control of their own destinies there can be a severe disjuncture between what residents want in a neighborhood and what governments impose. For Jane Jacobs, the answer was to make neighborhoods part of an interconnected political power framework that integrated smaller neighborhoods into a wider politics. Jacobs observed that small-street neighborhoods, essential for self-governance, lacked the power to control their own destinies (their weak protestations amounting to "pipsqueak protest"); what they needed was a better tie-in to the politically more important district (in her case, Greenwich Village).[51] Optimal neighborhood size depended on the issue being addressed, varying from a street block to a district with 30,000 to 100,000 or more to an entire city, depending on which size would be most effective at addressing a particular type of resident concern. (It is worth noting that Leonardo da Vinci and Ebenezer Howard had each proposed a population of 30,000 to define an optimal self-governing district.)

These political scales are conceptually intriguing, but they have been criticized because the connection between them is unclear. Missing, for example, is consideration of the overall urban street pattern necessary to link the street neighborhood to the district neighborhood.[52] Another criticism is that the district neighborhood is too large to be effective. In the U.K., neighborhood-based governance, necessary for program delivery, was deemed too large if it exceeded 20,000 population.[53]

Jacobs's approach also seemed to assume that neighborhoods were defined and known. Neighborhood self-determination would benefit from, it would seem, an understanding of what and where the neighborhood is, knowing the boundaries and what area and population the neighborhood encompasses. In Jacobs's proposal, the street neighborhood was the first tier in the political structure, resting on a clear understanding of what a healthy street neighborhood consisted of—for instance, eyes on the street, wide-enough sidewalks to accommodate multiple users (engaged in a "street ballet"), networks of small-scale everyday life. This kind of neighborhood definition is usually not so straightforward.

Some cities—notably Albuquerque, Minneapolis, Los Angeles, and Portland—have found ways to wade through the definitional challenges to institute neighborhood-scale governance.[54] Usually the definition of neighborhood that is operationalized is something in between Jacobs's street neighborhood and the district. Philadelphia once convened 45 neighborhood groups to create a six-item "Neighborhood Agenda" after neighborhood leaders demanded the opportunity to be involved in every program having to do with neighborhood needs. It was a governance strategy as much as a quest for funds, as the six items—a neighborhood jobs bank, acquisition of vacant properties, energy conservation, crime prevention, and educational programs—involved direct decision-making by neighborhood groups. (The program has since been abandoned due to the usual power struggles.)[55]

In the past few decades, neighborhood activism has tended to play out as a strategy for poor neighborhoods or a strategy for rich ones. On the one hand, neighborhood improvement and revitalization are focused on neighborhoods with the highest levels of crime and disinvestment. In San Jose, California, for example, using a narrative of making neighborhoods "strong," the city convened neighborhood leaders and came up with a plan to make neighborhoods "cleaner, safer and more engaged." The criteria used to identify neighborhoods that would be targeted for funding included gang-related incidents, code enforcement violations, unemployment, and foreclosures.[56] On the south side of Chicago, The Woodlawn Organization (T.W.O.) embraces a Saul Alinsky–style empowerment approach. The organization today is essentially a social service agency and low-income housing developer.

These efforts are the conceptual offspring of the Community Action Program of the 1964 Economic Opportunity Act, followed by the 1966 Model Cities program (formally, the Demonstration Cities and Metropolitan Development Act). Both acts were part of President Lyndon Johnson's War on Poverty. Some of the features of these programs remain (such as Head Start), but the neighborhood organizing and empowerment initiatives faded out in the 1970s. President Jimmy Carter's 1979 National Commission on Neighborhoods studied the issue of neighborhoods and concluded that they should be empowered, but the federal government ceased to play a lead role.[57]

For wealthy neighborhoods, neighborhood planning is often rooted in NIMBYism. Seattle's Neighborhood Planning Program was accused of this motivation, since the program began after residents complained about a proposal to change zoning to allow the development of pedestrian-oriented, higher-density "urban villages" (complete with multifamily affordable housing) proposed by the city's first black mayor, Norman Rice.[58] It is well documented that neighborhood associations spring to life when the neighborhood perceives itself to be under threat—meaning in danger of socioeconomic change. In direct contrast to poor neighborhoods, their primary purpose is to block change.[59]

Fortunately not all neighborhood associations are based on preserving the status quo and keeping others out. One example is the Neighbors Assisting Neighbors, or NAN, group, an organization of 450 households making up the Bannockburn neighborhood in Bethesda, Maryland. Early on, the group administered a survey to assess needs and willingness to volunteer. There are block coordinators assigned to 15 households who "make sure no one falls through the cracks." Community events and programs are organized, such as the Wise Elder project, which connects seniors to high school students to do oral histories. There are, of course, constant funding stresses, as the "village model" relies on membership dues, a higher tax for low-income neighborhoods.[60]

Sometimes the arts are used as the mechanism of neighborhood empowerment. In Theaster Gates's Dorchester Projects on Chicago's South Side, a cluster of renovated houses provides artist spaces, drawing in people for arts functions, selling art made of locally found objects, and reinvesting money from sales and events back into the community (in line with Luc Boltanski and Eve Chiapello's *The New Spirit of Capitalism*).[61] These can be interpreted as expressions of neighborhood building and engagement—although, as in the process-oriented ideals of neighborhood already reviewed, the activities group loosely, their connection to the wider neighborhood (or its goals) often ambiguous.

Neighborhood empowerment activities aimed at philanthropy have found some success. An example is the Citizens Committee of New York City (www.citizensnyc.org), founded in the 1970s to give small grants to neighborhoods for events, park cleanup projects, cookbook compilations, and nutrition classes. Funds are allocated to street block associations, community councils, garden clubs, schools, and street alliances. Transforming trash-strewn lots into community gardens is a common target of funding.

Where the goal is improving the production capacity of neighborhoods to make them stewards of their own well-being, there are repeated calls to focus on strengthening their institutions. John McKnight and Steve Kretzmann's Asset-Based Community Development (ABCD) approach tries to integrate the organizations of a neighborhood to form an "association of associations" that together become a "unified neighborhood force."[62] Similarly the sociologist Robert Sampson argued the importance of an "organizational infrastructure"— a diversity of nonprofits and collective enterprises, and that where this diversity exists, neighborhoods are better able to break the cycle of decline. Institutional diversity is important because overreliance on one institution, such as a church, is not necessarily a good thing, and can even be a problem.[63] These neighborhood organizations and institutions must be trusted, which is a special challenge in high-poverty neighborhoods that experience "moral and legal cynicism." The importance of a neighborhood's "institutional base" extends to diverse neighborhoods too; it is seen as especially important for creating "strong cross-status ties" in mixed-income areas.[64]

Each decade produces new strategies aimed at helping neighborhoods take control of their own spaces and destinies. Participatory budgeting, which lets residents decide how to spend public money, is gaining traction, although the tie to specifically defined neighborhoods seems underdeveloped.[65] On the legal front, Stephen Miller's review of "legal neighborhoods" shows that "dozens" of tools are already available; they just need to be recognized and leveraged as neighborhood strategies. Miller argues that "because the neighborhood is such a resonant institution in the minds of residents" and there is the added bonus that "neighborhood is a constituency that politicians feel comfortable serving," "failing to structure legal tools for the neighborhood is at best a missed opportunity, and perhaps even perilous." Examples of neighborhood legal tools that can be overlaid include the taxing powers of business improvement districts, code enforcement, neighborhood service centers, schools, neighborhood councils, and zoning. Miller makes the case that the combined power of these myriad, neighborhood-level tools has not been leveraged. Legal structures that operate at the small scale of neighborhood are rarely connected; instead they empower different constituencies in the same neighborhood: business owners, renters, parents. Rather than encouraging fights between these groups, legal neighborhoods could put a priority on visioning: "The more neighbors have the chance to define visions for their neighborhood, the more likely they are to care about where they live." Neighborhood legal tools can then be used to focus on "arbitration and negotiation" rather than litigation.[66]

Perhaps a stronger sense of neighborhood will energize residents to be more proactive about participatory budgeting (the process relies heavily on resident involvement), as well as provide a stronger basis for legal neighborhoods. Connecting and overlapping neighborhood-scale legal tools and budgeting authority requires first knowing what and where the neighborhood is. Even more important, the physically defined neighborhood acts as a counterweight to the conventional association between self-governance and social homogeneity. R. D. McKenzie once wrote that it was of "the utmost importance" that local governance be made to "coincide as near as possible with the natural neighborhood groupings of the population."[67] More defensible is self-governance based on the sharing of space.

Notes

1. Bailey and Pill, "The Continuing Popularity of the Neighbourhood." See also Durose and Lowndes, "Neighbourhood Governance"; Lowndes and Sullivan, "How Low Can You Go?"
2. Wood, "'Build, Therefore, Your Own World,'" 32, 48; Arendt and American Planning Association, *Crossroads, Hamlet, Village, Town*, 13.
3. Barron, "And the Crooked Shall Be Made Straight."
4. Holt, "Report of a Reconnaissance Survey," 2, 5, 7.
5. Wilson, "Reciprocal Work Bees and the Meaning of Neighbourhood."
6. Addams, "A Modern Lear." .
7. Mullin, "Henry Ford"; Stilgoe, *Borderland*.
8. Robinson, "The Remaking of Our Cities."
9. City Planning Commission of Portland, Oregon. "Portland City Planning Commission."
10. Simkhovitch, *Here is God's Plenty*.
11. Spain, *How Women Saved the City* 60.
12. National Federation of Settlements, "A Letter from Robert A. Woods," 1.
13. Woods, "The Neighborhood in Social Reconstruction," 577, 579, 589.
14. Cabot et al., *A Course in Citizenship*.
15. Arnold, "The Neighborhood and City Hall"; Kellogg, *Pittsburgh Survey*.
16. Simkhovitch, *The Settlement Primer*, 12.
17. University of Washington, University Extension Division, "The Social and Civic Center," 7.
18. Bliss, "Forgotten History." See also Mooney-Melvin, "Before the Neighborhood Organization Revolution."
19. Bliss, "Forgotten History." See also Mooney-Melvin, "Before the Neighborhood Organization Revolution."
20. Saginaw (MI) Public Schools, *Elementary Social Studies Curriculum Guide*; Providence Public Schools and Rhode Island College, *Neighborhoods*, 6.
21. Looker, "Microcosms of Democracy," 351.
22. In 1942 the Michigan Council of Defense, Civilian War Service Division published the manual *Neighborhood War Clubs*.
23. Michigan Council of Defense, Civilian War Service Division, *Neighborhood War Clubs*, 10, 14, 16.
24. , MOMA, "Look at Your Neighborhood," 3.
25. Steiner, "Is the Neighborhood a Safe Unit for Community Planning?"
26. Miller, "The Role and Concept of Neighborhood in American Cities"; Campleman, Gordon. "Some Sociological Aspects of Mixed-Class Neighbourhood Planning," 200.
27. Eckstein, "Addressing Wealth in Renaissance Florence"; Garb, "Drawing the 'Color Line'"; Von Hoffman, *Local Attachments*.
28. Kadushin and Jones, "Social Networks and Urban Neighborhoods in New York City," 58.
29. Hooker, "City Planning and Political Areas."
30. Jezierski, "Neighborhoods and Public-Private Partnerships in Pittsburgh."
31. Hunter, "The Urban Neighborhood," 281, 285.
32. McCann, "Framing Space and Time in the City."
33. Bailey and Pill, "The Continuing Popularity of the Neighbourhood," 928.

34. Woods, "Neighborhood Innovations," 474; Simkhovitch, *Neighborhood*, 293.
35. Hillery, *Communal Organizations*.
36. NUSA—Neighborhoods U.S.A., http://www.nusa.org/.
37. Meegan and Mitchell. " 'It's Not Community Round Here, It's Neighbourhood.' " See also Davies and Herbert, *Communities within Cities*.
38. Social Geographies, "Neighbourhoods and Communities."
39. Garrioch and Peel, "Introduction," 665.
40. Agnew, "The Danger of a Neighborhood Definition of Community."
41. Peerby's website is https://peerby.com/.
42. Greenfield, *Against the Smart City*.
43. Graziosi, "Urban Geospatial Digital Neighborhood Areas," 2. See also "Civic Tech," as described in Patel et al., "The Emergence of Civic Tech."
44. Martin, " 'Place-Framing' as Place-Making," 747.
45. Checkoway, "Two Types of Planning in Neighborhoods," 106.
46. Ibid., 102.
47. Madanipour, "How Relevant Is 'Planning by Neighbourhoods' Today?," 180.
48. Arnstein, "A Ladder of Citizen Participation."
49. Jun and Musso, "Explaining Minority Representation in Place-Based Associations," 54.
50. Roach and O'Brien, "The Impact of Different Kinds of Neighborhood Involvement on Residents' Overall Evaluations of Their Neighborhoods," 389.
51. Jacobs, *Death and Life*. .
52. Rofe, "Space and Community."
53. Bailey and Pill, "The Continuing Popularity of the Neighbourhood."
54. Miller, "Legal Neighborhoods."
55. Schwartz and Institute for the Study of Civic Values, *The Neighborhood Agenda*. The program was later critiqued in McGovern, "Philadelphia's Neighborhood Transformation Initiative."
56. "San Jose Strong Neighborhoods."
57. Fisher, *Let the People Decide*.
58. https://shelterforce.org/1999/11/01/seattle-neighborhood-planning/.
59. See the examples reviewed in Hojnacki, "What Is a Neighborhood?"
60. Baker, *With a Little Help from Our Friends*, 29, 35. See also Scharlach, "Creating Aging-Friendly Communities in the United States."
61. Boltanski and Chiapello, *The New Spirit of Capitalism*. See also Reinhardt, "Theaster Gates's Dorchester Projects in Chicago."
62. "A Basic Guide to ABCD Community Organizing," 2, 17.
63. Sampson, *Great American City*.
64. McKnight, "Neighborhood Necessities," 23; Rose, "Social Disorganization"; Clampet-Lundquist, "HOPE VI," 443.
65. Weber et al., "The Civics of Community Development."
66. Miller, "Legal Neighborhoods," 141-142, 165.
67. McKenzie, "The Neighborhood: Concluded," 785, 799.

8

Social Confusion

This chapter focuses on the long-standing debate over the quest to achieve goals about social relationships via the neighborhood. Earlier in the 20th century, it was common for neighborhood proponents to ascribe social outcomes to neighborhoods in the hope that social connection—and at times, conformity—could be instilled, if only neighborhoods were of a particular form. The problem was not that form didn't matter; it was that form did not necessarily matter for engendering particular kinds of social relationships. Later in the century, communications and transportation technologies dealt a further blow to the idea that neighborhoods were a viable source for instilling social outcomes like a sense of belonging and a sense of community. The social prescriptions of neighborhood form have long been problematized, but the argument seems to linger on, fueling critics of neighborhood plans. The most promising avenue for resolving this entrenched debate is to reject outright social relationship–related claims, refocus attention on neighborhood functionality—services, facilities, and institutions—and welcome whatever positive social benefits might be derived.

Overstepping Social Claims

A century ago Charles Horton Cooley, inspired by the German sociologist Ferdinand Tönnies (who thought the condition of urban society was deplorable), instilled the notion that face-to-face local communities were everything. Cooley made the case that neighborhoods, along with family, were on the front line of socialization, and this made neighborhoods important in a fundamental way. Writing in 1912, Cooley argued that family and neighborhood were "ascendant in the open and plastic time of childhood," and this meant that in adulthood they were "incomparably more influential than all the rest."[1]

According to Lewis Mumford, the neighborhood had all but died out by the end of the 19th century before it was rediscovered through the efforts of social thinkers like Cooley, along with social reformers and planners of new kinds of suburbs.[2] Under the influence of Cooley, early neighborhood proponents set in motion misunderstandings and overstatements about the social implications of neighborhoods that ultimately undermined the planned neighborhood ideal. The reaction began very shortly after Clarence Perry first debuted his neighborhood unit in the early 20th century. Looking back, it was the failure to clearly articulate what the neighborhood could or could not achieve in social terms that was one of the most important factors precipitating the dissolution of neighborhood as a prescribed, physical place.

That the neighborhood unit would be village-like and self-contained was always an underlying ethos. John Ruskin had his version, and later William Drummond and Clarence Perry articulated it in American terms. The village-like urban neighborhood was imbued with a pastoral, communal spirit in places that would otherwise be simply "urban." Cities were anonymous and uncaring; neighborhoods as villages, it was argued, counteracted that and enabled closeness and a sense of belonging. If urban neighborhoods could function as villages, they could combine the close bonds of Tönnies's *Gemeinschaft ("community")* villages within a larger *Gesellschaft ("society")*. It was a reform idea with early antecedents: anthropologists believe the practice of villagers re-creating village life in the city by establishing neighborhoods was a feature of ancient cities.[3]

The problem was that early definers of neighborhood based their definition on social *relationships* rather than on mere social or physical contact. Emil Durkheim wrote that if there was low social cohesion in a neighborhood, then it must be a weak and fragmented neighborhood (although Durkheim also hypothesized that too much cohesion was not a good thing either). Building on both Durkheim and Tönnies, sociologists of the 1920s and 1930s seemed obsessed with the idea of the impersonal city. (By 1951 the sociologist C. Wright Mills was writing papers like "The Modern City: Anomic, Impersonal, Meaningless.") Neighborhood was to be the antidote. It would be the means by which social relationships would be reclaimed.

Such claims only caused confusion by overstepping. R. D. McKenzie's four-part series *The Neighborhood*, published in the *American Journal of Sociology* in 1921 and 1922, begins with a definition based on three criteria: spatial proximity, physical or cultural differentiation, and "intimacy of association" of inhabitants. Although neighborhoods, like families, could have hostility, they were places that functioned as "the universal nursery of primary human ideals" like "loyalty, truth, service and kindness."[4] This characterization was ultimately damaging because, if these social qualities were deemed weak or nonexistent, it significantly confused the policy response. Neighborhoods lacking in social intimacy were considered dysfunctional.

The characterizations of neighborhood in social terms created a dissonance between ideals about communal spirit and the reality of urban life, which might produce an antithetical experience involving escape, exclusion, and isolation. With neighborhood identity tethered to feelings and relationships rather than practical functions and settings for daily life, the social challenge of the neighborhood was later abandoned for the social flexibility of suburbia. Social relations in the old urban polyglot neighborhood or a collection of farmsteads took effort; in the low-density, consumer-oriented suburbs, it was the family that ruled, and social interactions could be engaged or not.

The explicit attempt to merge physical and social ideals first surfaced in two early 20th-century campaigns: the settlement house and the community center movements (both termed "social center movements"). Proponents took Cooley's face-to-face community doctrine to heart, giving the concept physical expression in the form of a local meeting place or center embedded in a neighborhood. The center would help give neighborhood communal life tangible structure, and many prominent planners and social reformers (Edward Ward, Jacob Riis, and, of course, Clarence Perry) put great stock in the supportive role played by centralized neighborhood facilities. The social implications of neighborhood and center were profound, as they would function as a gateway through which the larger, impersonal, and chaotic city could be rendered more accessible and less alienating, strengthening social connection and sense of community.

Wanting to be more scientific about these possible effects, Chicago School sociologists met with urban planners at a 1925 meeting of the American Sociological Society to "unravel the social implications" of physical planning for neighborhoods. The sociologists were much more cautious about the value of physical form and its ability to replicate village life, sense of community, social control, and primary association. Robert E. Park and his Chicago School colleagues, especially Harvey Zorbaugh (author of *The Gold Coast and the Slum*), cautioned planners that although the "natural areas" of the city had to be recognized as the defining units of urban growth—populated with "predestined" dwellers of slums, Chinatowns, Gold Coasts, and districts of various kinds— they were not necessarily controllable. Yet, using Perry's neighborhood unit scheme, planners thrust themselves into a campaign that sought "Gemeinschaft ends with Gesellschaft means"—meaning that they wanted to re-create the village (with its means of social control and personalized, primary association) via government planners, regulation, and bureaucracy. Some warned of an evolving "science of social control" that merged the Chicago School's quest for social order with the planner's quest for economic efficiency.[5]

One disconnection that emerged was that sociologists were starting to discover that physical proximity in the neighborhood was having the effect of *increasing* social distance, while planners seemed to be assuming the opposite. Greer and Kube summarized, "As urbanism increases, neighboring declines, as does domestic social participation." Urban dwellers, sociologists argued,

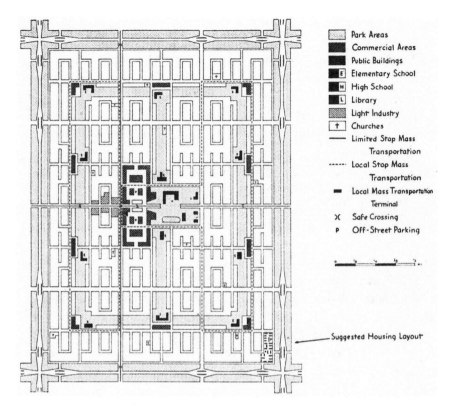

Figure 8.1 Few sociologists were willing to engage in neighborhood planning directly. Louis Wirth was an exception. He helped develop a detailed plan for Chicago consisting of 70 self-governing communities (with 50,000 residents each), divided into 7 to 14 superblock neighborhoods of one-quarter square mile and 3,500 to 6,500 people. Each "neighborhood or super-block" would have its own shopping area and elementary school. Green spaces would separate communities, and street parking, alleys, and restrictive covenants would be eliminated. Source: Grunsfeld and Wirth, "A Plan for Metropolitan Chicago.".

especially people living in apartments, "lack common interests and commitments and, particularly, any commitment to the local area as 'home.'" What urbanites were drawn to, the authors hypothesized, were informal, face-to-face relations, not club membership. This was a direct challenge to the urban anomic theories of Tönnies, Durkheim, and Simmel.[6]

Wanting to retain their socialization goals, planners who caught on to the paradox that more people equals less "community" responded by lowering neighborhood density. Henry Wright, the prolific 1920s-era neighborhood designer, believed that neighborhoods were best composed of single or double family homes, not multifamily housing ("tenements"), because they brought crowding, and crowding meant that people would avoid each other and fail to develop "the neighborhood sense." This would be especially tragic, Wright wrote, because "the neighborhood sense is the basis of responsible citizenship."[7] A related response was to argue that neighborhoods were simply not for everyone. "Of course we can't have the New England village in Manhattan!" one planner lectured.[8] Another wanted to coerce social bonding where it failed to materialize, suggesting that people who were not inclined to socially engage within the neighborhood, "through shyness, impediment, or lack of 'push,'" should be made to participate socially "for their own sake and for the best development of the neighborhood."[9]

Planners lacked nuance. They seemed oblivious to the fact that people in a neighborhood interact in all kinds of ways, ranging from anonymity to instrumental involvement (as in Janowitz's "community of limited liability") to intense daily interaction along the lines of the traditional *Gemeinschaft*. Mumford was one of the few who recognized the differences and wrote that the act of being a neighbor "to be real need not be deep: a nod, a friendly word, a recognized face, an uttered name—this is all that is needed to establish and preserve in some fashion the sense of belonging together."[10] There was even a time—in the teaming ethnic mix of early 20th-century London, for example—when neighborliness meant being left alone.[11] Failing to recognize these variations, neighborhood planning often narrowly revolved around children and women at home, a definition of neighborhood that relied on families coming together for social life.

A few critics contended that planners did not go far enough because their interests were limited to physical neighborhood form and its impact on quality of life and economic viability, not on social connectedness. Social benefits were "afterthoughts," and this was considered a problem. One critic scolded, "Planning should be oriented primarily toward certain established social values which make for satisfactory personal adjustment in an urban environment." The neighborhood unit, in other words, should be directed at solving the problem of *anomie*, Durkheim's description of social maladjustment and disorganization. Planners should address this by using the neighborhood unit as the basis of stability, safe play space, role models, and sense of belonging.[12]

While American sociologists reacted to planners' embrace of Perry's neighborhood unit as a means of producing better neighbors, British sociologists reacted to the Ministry of Town and Country Planning's 1944 Dudley Report, which espoused similar principles.[13] An initial task was to dissect just what "neighboring" and related concepts like "sense of community" actually meant. One sociologist advised planners that there were two forms of neighboring: *manifest*, constituting overt social relationships, and *latent*, constituting attitudes that form over time. Either could exist, or neither could exist, and they could be positive or negative. Combinations of positive and negative forms of neighboring had specific implications. For example, a lot of manifest neighborliness coupled with a low degree of latent neighborliness created "a facile form of relationship" that would not endure. Latent neighborliness was deemed especially important—"the basis of social solidarity"; manifest neighborliness required coupling with "the attitude" such latent neighboring fostered.[14] But in any case, these were not social feelings that could be physically prescribed.

It didn't help that neighborhood advocates sometimes equated neighborliness with morality. This was evident in pre–World War II America especially, although it lingered well afterward. In the 1920s a doctrine of "Christian neighborliness" meant that religious feeling must be expressed through neighborly service: looking in on the elderly, organizing activities for children, mowing lawns, and using slogans like "A good road is a sign of friendliness" to encourage a clean environment. During World War II this took on an imperative tone, so that lack of neighborliness meant ambivalence over fascism: "The fate of a nation and an eventual world peace, it seemed, rested on the everyday actions of millions of individual Americans in thousands of individual neighborhoods."[15] Perry believed that the neighborhood unit would instill morality on the "lower classes," although he initially focused on market-based housing for the middle classes at the neglect of the poor. Later Perry exerted his neighborhood unit ideals in President Herbert Hoover's Committee on Housing and the Community, this time focusing on the need for neighborhood structure in poor areas. The prescriptions remained a frustrating blend of valid serviceability goals and overreaching morality judgment.

This again set the neighborhood up for failure, as it became clear that neighborhood was not the sole basis of friendship, community, or morality, and concepts like neighborliness were not controllable in any case. A possible remedy was to constrain the size of the neighborhood such that social relationships seemed inescapable. This characterized Gerald Suttles's first level of neighborhood: the small, constrained, and single-use (i.e., residential) face-block, a place where intimate relationships develop and a unit of "central importance" because within it, "parochial" levels of informal social control are activated.[16] The neighborhood units of the World War II neighborhood war clubs were kept similarly small in an effort to keep neighborhoods "natural," which translated to neighborhoods of "ten or twenty families," either "a single block, or both sides (facing) a block," or "a small apartment house or part of a large apartment house, or a group of suburban or farm homes."[17]

Urban designers like Donald Appleyard were drawn to the face-block neighborhood idea because, they reasoned, it was likely to enable regular social interaction and feelings of safety. William Whyte, an urbanist and author who famously studied people's behavior in public spaces, believed something in the realm of 12 families was a realistic neighboring group, while the urban designer Kevin Lynch cited 15 to 20 families as an appropriate target. The Belgian planner

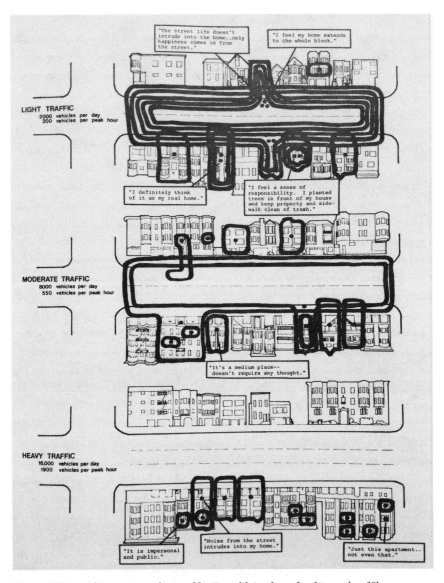

Figure 8.2 Social interaction observed by Donald Appleyard in his study of "home territory" neighborhoods varied by level of street traffic. Source: Appleyard, "Livable Streets."

Gaston Bardet thought of neighborhoods of 5 to 10 families as the ideal size for neighbor helping neighbor.[18] The social psychologist Stanley Milgram put the geographic upper limit of neighborhood at five blocks, which roughly corresponds to Charles Horton Cooley's conception of the "primary group": 50 to 60 adults with some degree of social control, face-to-face interaction, and mutual aid in times of emergency.[19] Christopher Alexander's definition of neighborhood was a maximum of 500 people on seven blocks, which he considered an upper limit if the goal is to actually know everyone in one's neighborhood.[20] Bardet described this size—between 50 and 150 families—as a domestic neighborhood of housewives meeting in shops.[21]

A possible problem with the definition of neighborhood as an "extension of home" is that it feminizes space, bestowing a "nurturing, familiar identity and purpose" in a way that brands women as conveyors of neighborhood while men conduct themselves outside the neighborhood domain. The home-neighborhood-family conflation might instill problematic ideas about women needing to confine themselves to the nurturing of the "home space" and the area around it.[22] It also conjures up the stereotype of a working-class neighborhood in the industrial era that consisted of one or two streets with spatial boundaries "primarily determined by the range of local gossip."[23] Then there is the problem that small, home-based neighborhoods are unlikely to wield much political power.

But in a more urbanized context, small neighborhood size need not translate to intimate social relationship. It might simply be the case that neighborhoods are the block around one's home because that's the area that matters most to people. After New York City's mayor Bill de Blasio gave his State of the City speech in February 2015, the *New York Times* asked people to weigh in on "what's really going on out there." The neighborhood-based responses show how constrained their sense of neighborhood was (see Table 8.1). As the *Times* editorial staff explained, "What people know, in New York City, is their block, that mini-city of brick and mortar, friend and stranger, sidewalk and pothole whose every change, sudden or gradual, we note as we go about our days."[24]

The Defeat of the Social Neighborhood

Through the middle decades of the 20th century, planners continued their quest to give physical context to social relationships via neighborhood planning—but it was starting to take a toll. If they were going to claim that "the basis of the neighborhood is friendship," where neighborhood is defined as "a setting for association among social equals," this was going to lead to a highly constrained view of neighborhood.[25] The uncertainty of social meaning translated to a blanket dismissal of the planned neighborhood.

One irony is that social friendship and intimacy were never something Perry had bargained for in the first place. His interest was in social life in a more functional sense: going to school, shopping, belonging to an identifiable place. He did believe that good design could contribute to the development of a "neighborhood spirit," and he made some morality proclamations, but he wasn't

Table 8.1 **The block as neighborhood: Selected comments from New York City residents**

"The new tenants who are paying the new steep rents are not as friendly as the old ones, leading my son to conclude that rich people are not as friendly and nice."

"Of course the neighborhood is going to appear cleaner and look nicer when people are trying to profit from it. . . . I've never seen my apartment building cleaner or more renovated. It is the intentions of these seemingly beneficial renovations that are questionable. They want to exude the aura of a higher end neighborhood, by smearing a little paint here and there and by altering the aesthetics of the neighborhood."

"My downstairs neighbors blast insanely loud music and have screaming arguments at all hours, and 311 doesn't do anything about noise complaints. The 114th Precinct has been beyond useless. Nevertheless, Astoria remains a great place to live, though I worry about being priced out."

"In 2011, a 328-bed facility for people with mental health, drug and behavior issues opened on our street. Since then, the quality of life has deteriorated, with constant drug use and dealing, public urination, panhandling, ranting, and other anti-social behaviors. A year ago we formed a block association that is working to use green initiatives such as beautifying our block to improve the situation for everybody. We have applied for grants to help us bring the people of the block together to make the block more beautiful. We are a long way from solving our problems, but one result of our work is that our block, which includes businesses and residents, has become a community."

"The state of our block has deteriorated over the last year. Garbage pick-up is erratic and less regular. A speed bump in front of school requested (and promised) for over a year is not delivered. Six-week response for trash/rodent complaints to be addressed by visit from Sanitation Department. Graffiti now increasing and no response from city to complaints. Open drug dealing on our corner increasing over the last year."

"I don't think a crime has ever been performed on my block, to the best of my knowledge at least. Morris Park is practically a suburb, with all the houses and the small town ambiance that takes over the area. Public transportation is the only thing that could be improved. Overnight trips can take as long as two hours to/from Manhattan due to the 5 train's lack of consistency in service and the lack of overnight connecting bus services."

"Pet peeve: out-of-state license plates from homeowners and renters. One example is a family who owns two homes on the block with driveways and car garage in back and have at least six vehicles with Pennsylvania license plates taking up all street parking. This is prevalent in this neighborhood in general."

Table 8.1 **Continued**

"When I moved to my block 25 years ago, we had a heroin dealer two doors down and a crack dealer two doors up. Our car was broken into repeatedly, and we couldn't leave flowers or pots on our front steps, as they would be stolen. Prospect Park was unkempt and scary. The movie theater was closed and there wasn't much variety available in terms of restaurants. Today, the block is safe and beautiful. People build planters and take care of the street trees. There's a vibrant new pub at the end of the block, a refurbished movie theater, and loads of restaurants on Prospect Park West. The park itself is a gem: clean, safe, and alive with runners, bikers, children playing, couples strolling. The downside? Parking has become very difficult, and we get lots of tickets. And the F train has become unbearable at rush hour. But gentrification? I'm all for it!"

"I live on a quaint street in the heart of Queens. It's relatively far from any subway stations, which helps maintain its suburban look. My block is well paved, crime free, and very clean. I can drive from my home on 79th Street to Lower Manhattan in 10 minutes on a good night, yet I can feel like I am hundreds—even thousands—of miles away from the city when I am home."

"My neighbors take great pride in maintaining tradition and culture, so small businesses thrive in our neighborhood."

"The younger generation skips over Middle Village when searching for a new neighborhood to take over because the public commute is simply too long and complicated. But what some might view as Middle Village's shortcomings, we Middle Villagers view as its strengths; we have had little to no trouble maintaining our small town values, and that's the way we'd like for it to stay. We'll sacrifice convenient public transit for it."

"Every year the assessed value increases on my home, but according to Zillow my home decreased in value this year. I read the Real Estate section every week and see homes selling for over $1 million that pay much lower real estate tax than I."

"Potholes—you can't go two blocks in any direction without having to dodge craters in the streets. Two cars had to be towed away having blowouts caused by a deep pothole on Foster Road."

Source: Adapted from "The State of Your New York Block."

especially interested in things like social interaction and sense of community.[26] Clarence Stein went a bit further, declaring that the "neighborhood community" was "a group of people with common interests in which they actively participate."[27] Critics declared that the neighborhood was not a "clearly defined territorial entity corresponding to a group of people with close social ties," and wanted instead a "much looser structure."[28] It is likely that both Perry and Stein would have agreed.

Most critics seemed not to recognize that neighborhood-scale social relations were a misinterpretation of Cooley's idea of the primary group. Stein had argued that "small neighborhoods" should be the basic unit of city building because they provided "eye-to-eye democracy," which was basic not only for "local contentment" but for "national freedom and world-wide security."[29] But as planned, a "small neighborhood" was at least 5,000 people. Small group relationships, not relationships with 5,000 neighborhood residents, were the primary social experiences discussed by Cooley. The idea that neighborhood form related to the face-to-face "primary group" was therefore incongruous.[30] And yet the conclusion drawn was that physical neighborhoods didn't coincide with social interaction, so why bother? As one sociologist put it, the attempt to define a boundary is "sterile" because it doesn't relate to social relationships. Better to "consider the social relationships themselves rather than to worry about where neighbourhoods begin and end."[31]

A critique by the sociologist Gilbert Herbert is an example of how these social confusions led to a rejection of the planned neighborhood. He offered valid criticism about the inflexibility and social exaggeration of the neighborhood unit, but then went further to also dismiss its importance for everyone, including those for whom geographically based communal association was a necessity: old people, the poor, children, newcomers. Such needs were to be addressed by supporting flexibility and "freer patterns of association."[32] A decade later Herbert Gans wrote a particularly strident attack on planners as being overly concerned with buildings (their "physical bias") when they should be focused on helping people "solve their problems and realize their goals" through social and economic programs.[33]

By the 1960s scholars seemed more comfortable treating neighborhood as an ephemeral object of the mind. There was an unwillingness to define neighborhood tangibly for fear that someone's individualized conception would be excluded, or that order was being imposed on something that was fluid and intangible, or that the root objective was exclusion. Equating neighborhood with political organization, some hesitated to define them in a way that would limit jurisdiction and power.

Sociologists were now straddling two definitions of neighborhood, either equating neighborhoods with census tracts or restricting neighborhood to "a relatively bounded and densely knit set of social relations in a commonly identifiable area."[34] The latter definition set a high bar. Few places were capable to being a "container of normative solidarity." The more important goal, then, was *community*, not the place-bound neighborhood, which was not a problem for sociologists because "unlike geographers, spatial distributions are not inherently important variables." Better to focus on "social linkages and flows of resources," wherever they are—within neighborhoods or not.[35] Eventually this way of thinking led to a new urban science devoted to measuring social connection that applied mathematical precision to characterize cities as concentrations of social interactions,[36] but this had little to do with neighborhoods.

Belaboring the neighborhood's social "failure" ultimately undermined the ideal of the physical neighborhood itself, in baby-with-the-bathwater fashion. (There was to be no resolution of the Wirthian problem of urban alienation either, if doing so required sentimental and ruralized notions of neighborliness.) The mid-20th-century definition of neighborhood as "an area within which a spirit of neighborliness exists" was dead, and the subsequent dismantling of this attribution dealt a significant blow to neighborhoods more fundamentally.[37] If neighborhoods are socially defined, then it must be admitted that, unlike infrastructure and buildings, the social world cannot be *built*. There seemed little room for alternative views of neighborhood relevance.

Reflecting this diminished standing, Suzanne Keller's important 1968 book, *The Urban Neighborhood*, questioned whether the idea of a neighborhood was still relevant and whether local ties were something that could be done without. She laid out the many complexities, the conceptual ambiguity, the contradictory research results, the social changes that made the meaning and relevance of neighborhood a moving target. She was especially critical of physical planning, pointing out, as many already had, that "social solidarity and cooperation" as well as "neighborhood loyalty and sociability" seemed not to be responsive to physical design.[38] In the end, her sociological review drew few conclusions. Mel Webber's "community without propinquity," synchronous with Keller, was the end game—the definitive proclamation that social relations were released from any hint of spatial constraint.[39] The social meaning of neighborhood—and the relevance of neighborhood itself along with it—was near extinction by the 1970s.

But there was a resurrection, of sorts. Although many planners, including Webber, were involved in the project of neighborhood dismantling, a new force gained currency in the 1980s that thrust the neighborhood back into vogue: localization. Under the disillusionment of car-based suburbia and the "crisis of connection" it was thought to have caused, a new generation of planners seemed intent on adding the communal notions of neighborhood back in. The New Urbanists, the most visible group, embraced the idea of a sense of community and, not really knowing the history of its social critique, attached it to the neighborhood with impunity. U.K. planners did something similar when they revamped the neighborhood as an "urban village." This launched a new round of criticism, as researchers tried to sort through the contradictory evidence on neighborhood and social life that an earlier generation had debated vigorously. New writings emerged that countered claims about localized social relations.[40]

Meanwhile sociologists picked up on a different thread, this time having to do with neighborhood *effects*, something they had always been concerned with, but now they attended to it with a new spirit of scientific rigor. Whereas earlier sociological studies pointed out relatively straightforward effects (e.g., that neighborhoods were a good source for political contacts or job referrals), research was ramped up in its analytical sophistication and effects were expanded to include a wide variety of outcomes, including health, behavior, life's chances, political views.[41] (Skeptics still argued that neighborhood effects were mere "belief" and "folk concept," in part fueled by media that overreached, such as when it was claimed that "you can drop 15 years of your life just by crossing a few streets.")[42] Social effects were still important, and arguments for or against neighborhood policies (such as income mixing) hinged on social interaction and "community" goals."[43] But there was no longer much concern with the effects of the physical side of neighborhood form, as that issue had mostly been abandoned as irrelevant, at least in the eyes of sociologists and many planners.

Instead the accepted definition of neighborhood was a spatially delimited set of data, such as a census tract. In essence social scientists had responded to the social confusion of neighborhood by engaging with neighborhoods in a way that was scientific, data-driven, and tract-based. They were still interested in the "powerfully enduring impact of place" on individual outcomes, with widespread agreement that residing in a "negative environment" creates problems that "are indisputable,"[44] but the definition of neighborhood bore little resemblance to the neighborhood plans that had been produced in the first half of the 20th century.

Under this new data-driven social science, the social dimension of neighborhood could be dissected not by linking social phenomena to physical neighborhood form but by linking social phenomena to tracts and other quantified data available in spatial units. A few New Urbanist–inspired researchers tried to connect neighboring to neighborhood form, finding that certain (mostly pedestrian-based) neighborhood forms have higher rates of social interaction, a "substantially greater sense of community," stronger place attachment, and higher levels of trust and social engagement.[45] But the bulk of the research focused not on the effects of form but on how social relationships like neighboring could be predicted by other social variables. So, for example, sociologists found that whether a neighborhood was "neighborly" was mostly predicted by crime. Surveys of different kinds of neighborhoods, from "thriving" to "striving," found low levels of "interaction, acquaintance, courtesy and everyday kindness" on the "striving" end of the scale especially.[46] As another example, researchers in New Zealand constructed the NeighFrag index, calculating neighborhood fragmentation based on level of attachment, the social resources the neighborhood had, and shared norms. (The index was found to be inversely correlated with neighborhood cohesion.)[47]

Many studies of the social life of neighborhoods (relying on respondent interpretations of what neighborhoods actually are) now focus on how neighboring has declined. Survey research found that in 1970, 30% of Americans said they interacted with their neighbors frequently; this percentage is now down to 20%. Further, the percentage of people reporting that they had no interaction at all with their neighbors rose from 25 to 33%.[48] Another topic is that the importance of neighborhood social contacts has been found to be stronger for some groups than others. For example, more than other age groups, older adults in particular rely on neighbors for social support. In one Dutch study, older adults were the largest group (39%) that had a key to their neighbor's house. If older adults moved into the neighborhood, triggering a change in their "role setting," neighbors became especially important as a source of knowledge, help, and social contact.[49]

There is also interest in understanding the complexity of neighboring, which has stages: from simple recognition of sharing a geographic space, to nods of acquaintance and unintentional encounter, intentional contact, and purposeful, collective engagement.[50] One scholar claimed that neighboring and neighbors were undertheorized, citing contested "Love they neighbor" biblical roots that, confusingly, vacillate between a universalist (neighbor equals humanity) and particularist (neighbor equals ethnic belonging) notion, both of which can be problematic. Neighboring in modern cities is imbued, it seems, not with hostility and not with warmth but with "awkwardness, embarrassment, wariness, and apparent lack of interaction." Websites devoted to helping residents manage negative neighbors are testimony to that; for example, both Neighbours from Hell and Problem Neighbours provide advice on barking dogs, foul language, shared hedges, and what to do about the neighborhood bully.[51] The modern Western world lacks an accepted cultural practice about neighboring in comparison to the traditional Islamic world, which "urges Muslims to be good neighbors."[52]

Neighborhoods as Service Providers

Trying to interpret the social purpose of neighborhood, one is confronted with paradox, overreach, failed proposals, critiques, and counterresponses. As these issues were being debated throughout the 20th century by social scientists and planners, it sometimes seemed as though the importance of neighborhood in more basic terms was underplayed, its serviceability and livability, involving dimensions like functionality, access, safety, identity, and beauty. Such contributions did not rely on social mechanisms.[53]

Is it possible to stick to the service goals of neighborhood, leaving the complications of the social neighborhood behind? Whether a "friendship ellipse" coincides with a "service ellipse"—in which activity and friendship patterns overlap—is an appealing prospect, but it might be better to build up to that gradually, focusing first on neighborhoods as service providers.[54] This might be the best hope for maintaining neighborhood relevance where neighborhood is defined as a physical, delineated space.

The servicing aspect of neighborhood is appealing because it is less ambiguous. The effects are, in a sense, durable, reminiscent of sociologist Patrick Sharkey's call for a more "durable urban policy."[55] One interpretation of durability has been to prioritize a neighborhood's physical form and land use, its access to facilities, services, and economic opportunities—in short, seeing the neighborhood as a bundle of places and services first; social characteristics come in second. Neighborhoods can be defined by the facilities and services they contain and the distances residents travel to acquire them, in addition to the extent and nature of social and economic interaction.[56] Serviceability can form the basis of planning and policy, not whether the neighborhood is providing positive social experiences.

Defining neighborhoods as service providers escapes the problematic aspects of place-based "community." A British sociologist writing in 1951 in one of the main sociology journals, *Social Forces*, recognized the distinction. He argued that there was great confusion in how neighborhoods were being conceptualized, as there were two concepts working at cross-purposes: neighborhood as "organic" and neighborhood as "amenity." The former was deemed "mystical" and "laden with value judgments," while the latter was "relatively precise in its formulation of planning objectives." The author surmised that the tendency for planners to want to push the organic concept of neighborhood was based on the "occupational needs" of the town planner who was searching for a way "to visualize, as a whole, and in manageable segments, the scope of his duties." While recognizing that the "amenity concept" was also prone to "value judgments," many of which are derived from the organic concept of neighborhood (e.g., the need for a community center), the neighborhood based on amenities had goals that were considered more attainable.[57]

The 1960 "Neighborhood Boundaries" report by the nation's leading planning organization, the American Society of Planning Officials, also came out strongly on the topic of neighborhood serviceability. It included quotes by British planners to argue that "shops and the shopping centre provide the most important elements in the design of neighborhood," and that "the most effective method of generating community life is to use the shops as the basis, and place with them those buildings that serve the community needs, such as the hall, pub, library and health center." It was servicing first, socialization second.

British planners working to implement the neighborhood unit in post–World War II Britain felt immune from the developing social critique of neighborhood

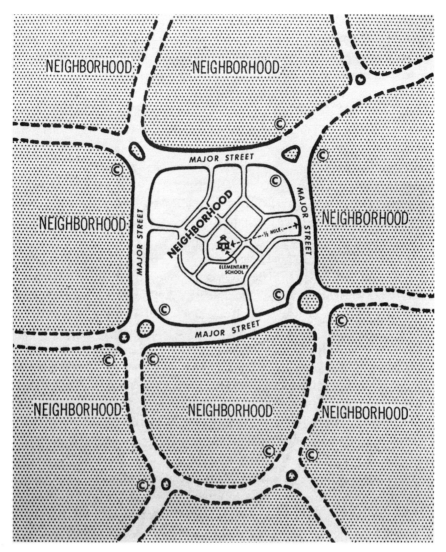

Figure 8.3 This 1955 graphic illustrates how churches could serve more than one neighborhood. Source: Hoover and Perry, *Church and City Planning.*

planning because their interest was in its practical and functional application, especially the integration of housing with amenities. One British planner described the neighborhood unit as a "godsend. . . . One wonders what they would have done without it."[58] Neighborhood-scale shops were likened to "the medieval market place," and the social contact the market engendered was not only far more effective than the community center but provided "the least possible chance of individuals becoming isolated and lonely." The elementary school was considered much less effective for this purpose, limited to the "children's community" and "inadequate" as a neighborhood center.[59]

This servicing definition was recognized as having very different implications for neighborhoods than trying to infuse social intimacies.[60] It was an understanding reminiscent of the regularized pattern of neighborhoods in premodern times, which had always had a functionality basis—churches and their surrounding parishes or guilds and their surrounding members—only this time, goods and services were substituted for religion or occupation. Further, the equal distribution of these goods and services within neighborhoods could be a practical route to a more equitable world. The egalitarianism of utopias, found in plans as divergent as Shaker villages, Le Corbusier's *Ville radieuse*, and Paolo Soleri's Arcosanti, were too radical; the well-serviced neighborhood was an attempt at egalitarianism in a way that was *not* utopian.[61]

The appeal of justifying the neighborhood unit in exactly these terms was realized by planners working in the post–World War II era. There were no shops in Levittown's neighborhoods, but in aspirational planning documents (as opposed to production-built housing manuals) a mix of uses was considered essential. For example, the 1945 Museum of Modern Art exhibit *Look at Your Neighborhood* listed the following as essential for good neighborhoods: "good housing, a park, an elementary school, a community center, a shopping center, service shops and light industries."[62] Keller labeled this straightforward, nonsocial view of neighborhood as "amenity area" planning. The danger, as Keller saw it, was inefficiency and inequity, although this could be attended to by having planners concentrate on the provision of just the basics: shops, clinics, transportation stops.[63]

The sociologist Gerda Wekerle summarized what neighborhoods for the elderly and for working or single-parent women most needed: good public transportation, a range of housing options, and collective services—a distinctly different picture from neighborhood either as "refuge" or as the center of social life. She did not deny the importance of social linkages in the neighborhood, especially for the elderly and single parents, but social connection need not be interpreted as a preference for neighborhood-based social life. It may instead simply be an outcome of "low mobility and heavy time pressures."[64] Jane Jacobs agreed that on the subject of neighborhoods, there was too much emphasis on social relationships and friendship patterns.

Some planners had always considered the "social-network" definition of neighborhood "irrelevant and confusing," advocating a definition that was more about functionality.[65] George Galster later added the practical point that what matters for policymakers is neighborhood operations, investment, movement, behaviors—and these are not necessarily determined by social meaning.[66] Residents of mixed-income neighborhoods were known to express similar pragmatism. Robert Chaskin and Mark Joseph interviewed residents of HOPE VI housing and found that residents were not looking for social solidarity, just a decent neighborhood with a lack of problems between neighbors.[67] Recommendations for making diversity work was oriented around services: shared governance for regulating public areas and more attention to "third spaces" such as coffee shops, stores, and recreational facilities.[68]

These tangible benefits may be why residents who are dissatisfied with the social attributes of a neighborhood are still able to have positive, optimistic feelings about their neighborhood.[69] Functionality is what underlies the somewhat dissonant finding that long-term residents of gentrifying neighborhoods are able to see positive gains, despite rising rents and the threat of displacement.[70]

The Social Value of Neighborhood Services

The service-based neighborhood is fundamentally about functionality, but the social experience it engenders is not ignored. Exchange dynamics are key. People come together to buy or sell, teach or learn, greet or glance.[71] These points of exchange are not devoid of social meaning. To the extent that service provision is based on social and demographic desires (some argue that this extends to racial groups, e.g., that African Americans have a special need for integration with neighborhood institutions like schools and churches),[72] the social dimension will never be entirely tangential. But on the topic of social interaction and relationships, the social implications do not really go further than providing spaces for contact.

It was on this basis that Mumford called Le Corbusier's plan for Nemours in North Africa "socially intelligent," because (in addition to it's Radburn-like separation of traffic, which Mumford endorsed) it provided for "social life in specially spotted civic nuclei" like schools and civic centers. Mumford argued that without this "deliberate local nucleation" one was simply trusting that the "mere massing of population" would produce the right "social drama."[73] But there were no assumptions about friendship, intimacy, or morality. In this it presaged Robert Sampson's argument that "thick" social ties are not needed for a healthy neighborhood with good collective efficacy (and that in fact such ties might even produce worse outcomes for individuals).

The social value of services has been poignantly described. A 1914 textbook for elementary school children included a chapter called "The Neighborhood" that opened, "Neighborhoods give us minute but characteristic worlds to enter day by day, till we are enlarged in sympathy and comprehension." By "doing good turns" in the neighborhood, children could learn to understand "the rights and feelings of the Chinese laundryman, the Italian fruit-dealer, the Jewish tailor." The valuing of diversity, in other words, was rooted in retail and occupation. Teachers were instructed to ask their students, "If you walk down a street of shops, what signs do you see over the door? Provisions, groceries, furniture, drug-store, shoemaker, painter, carpenter, lunchroom, dressmaker, tailor, topshop, books and stationery, moving-picture show, police station. Could we do without any of these stores? What things does everybody need?"[74] Historians verified how sentiments toward neighborhood services had a strong impact on neighborhood identity, countering, at least for a time, Hawley's claim that neighborhoods were being "absorbed and stripped of their identities by the larger universe of activities."[75]

The British were explicit about the social value of commerce, and this made the new town neighborhoods fundamentally different from American examples. As prescribed in the Dudley Report, British neighborhood units were to have shops connected to internal neighborhood centers, not the periphery; public open space was to be a surrounding buffer rather than civic space at the center. Both the open spaces and the neighborhood centers "were supposed to encourage the formation of social groupings."[76] Locating light industry adjacent to neighborhoods was also deemed socially important. (The British planner Sir Frederick Gibberd remarked, "Work is one of the strongest social ties.")[77] While the elementary school was important—it improved safety and the chance for contact between parent and child, and it helped children accept the school "as a natural part of their existence"—shops were more important, especially for "generating community life" in a way "far more effectively than any community centres."[78]

But there were adaptations. Sometimes the shops had to be consolidated. One of the British new towns, Harlow New Town, proposed a "neighborhood cluster," where three neighborhood units, each with their own primary schools and "a few local shops," shared a larger neighborhood center.[79] And cultural differences could have an effect on what kinds of services could be expected to have social value. For example, in post–World War II Scotland, pubs could not be used as ready-made neighborhood centers as they were in England, because in Scotland the pub was "mostly reserved for serious and prolonged masculine drinking in upright position."[80]

As a form of informal neighborhood participation, the use of neighborhood services has been shown to correlate with positive feelings toward the neighborhood more than belonging to a formal organization.[81] R. D. McKenzie had observed in the 1920s that organizations seemed to rely on the contributions of only a few individuals, so that interest in neighborhood affairs was being "artificially sustained." Rather than a government-supported organizational apparatus, reliance on small retail establishments may be both economical and more effective as a means of engaging. As one researcher put it, "The old fashioned mechanisms of community organization, especially informal interaction and neighborhood shops, are as effective today in building neighborhood cohesion as they were generations ago."[82]

In many of these idealizations about the value of services, neighborhoods are mixed in use and mixed in population. This was for practical reasons, one of which was that business owners needed to be near their place of business. Serviceability was therefore much more than neighborhood-scale convenience; it was about economic interdependence. The interconnection created social bonds, not because of friendship but because one's livelihood depended on it. Writing in 1939, Carol Aronovici surmised that wealthy families living in poor neighborhoods must be due "either to a lag in their aspirations for better conditions, or to business interests which are located in the poorer sections of the city."[83] McKenzie's 1922 study of a centrally located neighborhood in Columbus, Ohio, found a similar dynamic. He chronicled the diversity as "a collectivity of very unlike family groups" where "superior wholesome families are frequently found living next door to disorderly worthless people." These "superior wholesome families" were unable to move "on account of property ties."[84] And in early 20th-century Baltimore, at a time when whites were leaving the city on the streetcar lines, blacks were immigrating from the South, and neighborhoods were becoming increasingly segregated, it was the merchants—owners of small corner grocery stores—who constituted the remaining whites in otherwise black neighborhoods.[85] The fact that the concept of the "ethnic neighborhood" persisted even where the ethnic population of a neighborhood was barely one-third can be attributed to the visibility of a particular ethnic group's business and religious institutions—more durable markers of a neighborhood's character than a mobile population.[86]

This role played by services in enabling the socially diverse neighborhood has fundamentally changed, however. New methods of retailing have undermined local ownership, and while the services and facilities necessary for everyday life are widely shared by many social groups, whether defined by race, ethnicity, age, or income (according to one observer, there is "complete consensus across racial and economic lines" for a "core" set of services),[87] except in the densest cities, the heterogeneous neighborhood lacks critical mass to support tailored services. The result is that neighborhoods are not well supported by the necessary service diversity required. The problem is especially acute in suburban areas, which tend to have lower functional variety to begin with, because of their decreased density.

One social implication of services that cannot be avoided is that social status often determines service quality. Thus, on the topic of adequately servicing a neighborhood, social segregation is often the root cause of inequity. Poor neighborhoods lack quality stores, public spaces, and facilities, while wealthy neighborhoods either have these services or, in the case of wealthy suburban neighborhoods, residents have the means to acquire services from far-flung locations, making proximity irrelevant or at least lack of proximity easier to live with.

This servicing problem is avoided completely by reverting back to the social definition of neighborhood, so that serviceability is rendered moot. For example, one study showed that racial and economic segregation was lower in suburban neighborhoods as compared to more centrally located ones, concluding that the suburbs offered a "better neighborhood condition." Specifically, an African American household living in a newer suburb was more likely (by 13 percentage points) to live in a higher-income neighborhood than an African American living in the central city. But "better neighborhood condition" was strictly a condition of social status, using variables like poverty and education rates. Service functionality had no bearing.[88]

And yet neighborhood businesses—services and employment—whether or not for a diverse population, are considered essential for neighborhood stability. Between 1930 and 1970, before de-industrialization gutted urban neighborhoods, sociologists showed that the proximity between workers and jobs translated to stable neighborhoods (defined as the percentage of adults living in the same residence), especially for neighborhoods of workers who could walk to their industrial jobs. In neighborhoods that were able to provide local services and facilities—small groceries, retail stores, churches, and bars and restaurants—these too were shown to be more stable.[89] A study in San Francisco found that those neighborhoods that coalesced around commercial main streets had a "significantly higher sense of community" than those without.[90] Research on Dutch neighborhoods concluded that the strongest predictor of community was the sharing of resources and common activities, which fostered mutual interdependence.[91] And in Birmingham, U.K., neighborhood boundaries are formed from a service-based identity built on the "codes of conduct" of everyday existence—"constellations" of activities and relations.[92]

The most recent and potentially very hopeful chapter in the social benefits of neighborhood services story is the informal barter economy. Collaborative services might be "time banks" (e.g., Timebank.org, whose mission is to promote equality and "caring community through inclusive exchanges of time and talents") and DIY blogs (e.g., snapgoods.com, whose motto is "Own less. Do more"). Putting in a neighborhood system of sharing, collaborating, and exchanging, perhaps creating a "cul-de-sac commune" in the process, has been aptly described as "extreme neighborliness." In more urban situations, some even hope that the negative side of gentrification can be offset by getting gentrifiers more involved in service exchanges and issuing "gentrification offsets" through stoop sitting, bike sharing, or "trade lessons."[93]

Self-Containment and Service Hierarchies

Unlike community and other aspects of social life, the servicing dimension
of neighborhood is deemed unequivocally more successful if it is spatially
constrained—that is, if services are accessed within the neighborhood. This prioritizes a particular kind of neighborhood form—pedestrianism—a condition
of neighborhood that Perry, Stein, and Wright had only assumed but never explicitly advocated. There was no need; they were proposing their neighborhood
ideal at a time when walking was the assumed modality. Still, the planning of

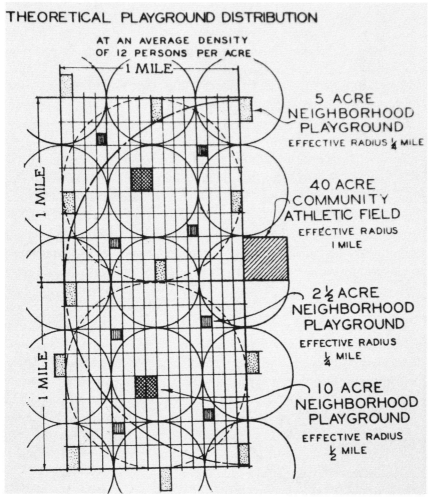

Figure 8.4 Neighborhood service distribution based on the quarter-mile walk was an
accepted metric in the 1930s. Source: Hegemann et al., *City Planning, Housing*.

neighborhood services was required because the industrial city had undermined human scale and the servicing of daily life.

This pedestrian basis is the underlying ethos of the New Urbanist neighborhood and its European counterpart, the urban quarter, which, the architect Leon Krier pronounced, "must have its own center, periphery and limit." Ideally such neighborhoods are meant to be "complete," with the functions of daily life contained within. The idea harkens back to late medieval and early modern European cities, when neighborhoods were relatively self-sufficient, each with its own water supply, church, and markets.[94] Self-containment was furthered by the presence of walls: "The walls enclosed a single space, a community more concerned with protecting itself against outsiders than with dividing inhabitants among themselves."[95] In analogous fashion, although without walls, the modern urban quarter, according to Krier, is to be a "a city within a city," complete with employment and leisure. This has been quantified. The "complete neighborhood," by one measure, is "excellent" if 70% of neighborhood services are within the neighborhood; "satisfactory" if there are 30 to 70%; "minimal" if there are 10 to 30%; and "poor" if there are fewer than 10%.[96]

For New Urbanists, the pedestrian basis of neighborhood has been categorical: without neighborhood structure based on pedestrian access, and without a structural limit, there can be no quality urbanism. Under this proximity-based assessment, the most profound dismantling of the neighborhood came from the automobile. The proposal for neighborhoods then boils down to this: rather than design *around* the automobile, as Stein and the modernists had done, the neighborhood is to be designed *in spite of* the automobile. And there is something else: without a structural limit to the neighborhood, imposed by the proximity requirements of pedestrianism, there can be no meaningful concept of diversity.

Pedestrianism obviously complicates the goal of neighborhood self-sufficiency. One response is to limit the goal to a single service, like education. In the early to mid-20th century, the service delivery of education was analyzed with mathematical precision. Neighborhood service provision, starting with the elementary school, was the very definition of neighborhood in the Urban Land Institute's 1960 *Community Builders Handbook*. The elementary school initially controlled the discourse because the service area of an elementary school seemed like an especially efficient way to organize dwellings. It was also considered more egalitarian. A British review of the *Regional Plan of New York and Its Environs* pointed to the inherent equalizing function of the elementary school in the U.S. because it "caters for all social classes."[97]

In search of a "total educational program" connected to neighborhood structure, schools and neighborhoods were thought to form a hierarchical, nested pattern, with multiple nursery schools and playgrounds within the neighborhood, one elementary school at the center of a neighborhood, middle schools between

A circle of ½ mile radius = 500 acres.

Deduct 50 acres for open spaces = 450 acres.

At 9½ houses per acre = 4,200 houses.

At 1 school child per house = 4,200 children.

Possible distribution :   *A.*   Senior Boys,   600

Senior Girls,   600   1,200

B,C,D.   each 500 Infants

and   500 Juniors   3,000

——————

4,200

——————

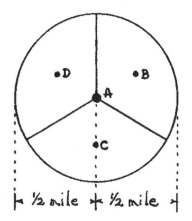

Figure 8.5 The distribution of houses and schools in a neighborhood was worked out mathematically in this 1934 article in a British planning journal. Source: Dougill, "Educational Buildings."

two neighborhoods, and high schools or junior colleges at the center of four or more neighborhoods. Perry's centralized, multipurpose elementary school was to be equidistant from all residents, an idea he earlier argued in his book *Wider Use of the School Plant.* The idea endured for a time, but there was increasing recognition that to "catch" a sustaining population, either the geographic range or the density of the neighborhood had to increase, or both.

The lower density of Radburn created servicing challenges, which is why Stein and Wright overlapped neighborhoods to accommodate the sharing of larger facilities like high schools and theaters at the edges. Each neighborhood was supposed to have its own shopping center, but, for all the usual monetary reasons, these did not materialize. A 1943 proposal for the "school-neighborhood nucleus" increased Perry's distances: one-fourth mile to a nursery school or playground, one-half mile to an elementary school, 1 mile to the middle school, and one and a half miles to the high school. Transport by bus was another option, although it was considered "not entirely satisfactory."[98] Radburn now has about 3,000 residents on 149 acres, roughly the geographic size of one of Perry's neighborhood units, but with 2,000 fewer residents.

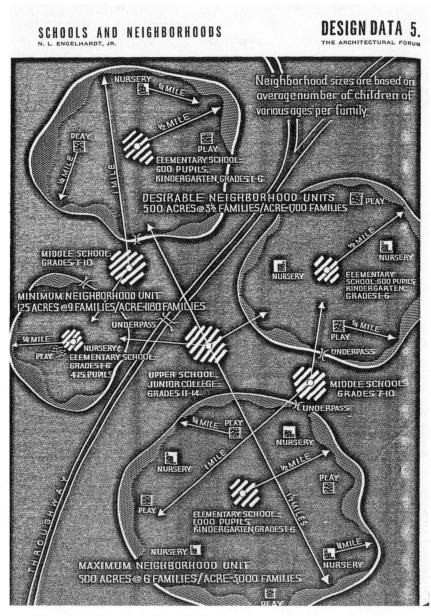

Figure 8.6 Figure adapted from a 1943 proposal in *Architectural Forum* for optimal school and neighborhood arrangement. Source: Engelhardt, "The School-Neighborhood Nucleus."

The interest in neighborhood servicing is not limited to schools, of course. The hope has always been that manipulation of the arrangement of schools, shops, and their service areas, if highly regularized, could mean a "high degree of accessibility." In volume 7 of the *Regional Plan of New York and Its Environs*, every resident in a neighborhood unit was supposed to be within one-half mile of all the shops needed for daily life, and 50 feet of business frontage for every 100 residents was considered ideal. In Europe in the 1940s, complete servicing of the neighborhood was accepted as "just the way of doing things."[99] It mirrored what planners were advocating for the ideal communist city too. Complicated formulations and varying neighborhood arrangement ("units of settlement") were based on assumptions about levels of service, nuclei, density, transit, and population—all worked out precisely.[100]

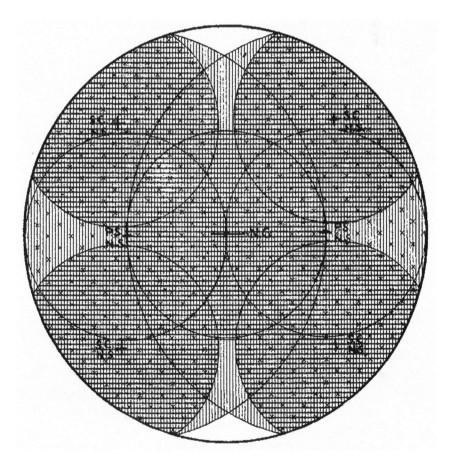

Figure 8.7 This diagram, based on a 1952 British publication, was intended to show that a "high degree" of access to neighborhood services could be secured "even at a low density." Source: Allaire, "Neighborhood Boundaries," 19.

The working out of neighborhood service provision seems a kind of micro-cosm of the regularized geographic distribution of services observed by the ge-ographer Walter Christaller in the 1930s. In Christaller's central place theory, the location and size of settlements is explained by the types of services these settle-ments offer and the range of their impact. The neighborhood has been thought of as being similar to the lowest order in the hierarchy. Central place theory does not explain the distribution of services within urban places, but where services converge within a hexagon, neighborhoods might form.

But the concept of a nested hierarchy of service areas and neighborhood sizes did not always work out as planned. People did not restrict their shopping behavior according to hierarchical arrangements that looked good on paper.[101] Trying to adapt service hierarchies to the neighborhood unit did not prove more successful. While it was believed that planning by neighborhood would help sit-uate services closer to where people lived, shopping conceived as a multilevel affair differentiating street corner, neighborhood, or town center often ended up omitting the smaller-scale stores.[102]

These service hierarchies, in which neighborhood-based services are sepa-rated from higher-order services that have a larger geographic range, have always been fundamental to neighborhood ideals, whether market-based, communist, 19th century or 21st century. Neighborhoods are supposed to be the locations of lower-order services like elementary schools and small shops; higher-order services, like theaters and hospitals, stretch beyond the neighborhood and are often linked to public infrastructure with a much broader range. The signifi-cant complication, of course, is that the ability of the neighborhood to sustain services, even "lower-order" ones, is never a sure thing. Perry had maintained that the market would sustain the commercial and service needs of the 5,000 residents of his neighborhood unit, but he did not foresee that the elementary school would be a service that struggled for survival. This is a dominant and re-curring narrative about neighborhood: the breakdown of its own servicing.

Applying the concept of neighborhood to rural areas was an attempt to consolidate daily life. A study of the disparate existence of one family in rural Wisconsin in 1921 traced the far-flung commutes—for meetings, trading, church, milk delivery, school—concluding that the "scattering" of daily life was "impairing the efficiency" of the family unit. And though the family was "a unit by itself," people were "looking for a larger group relationship." Though unre-lated to pedestrianism, the automobile was blamed as "one factor in this whole situation."[103]

Servicing the neighborhood center has been a special struggle, as keeping the center viable has meant extending its reach beyond the neighborhood. The focus of each New Deal–era Greenbelt town (initially conceived as a single neighbor-hood) was the well-serviced neighborhood center, broadened beyond the school

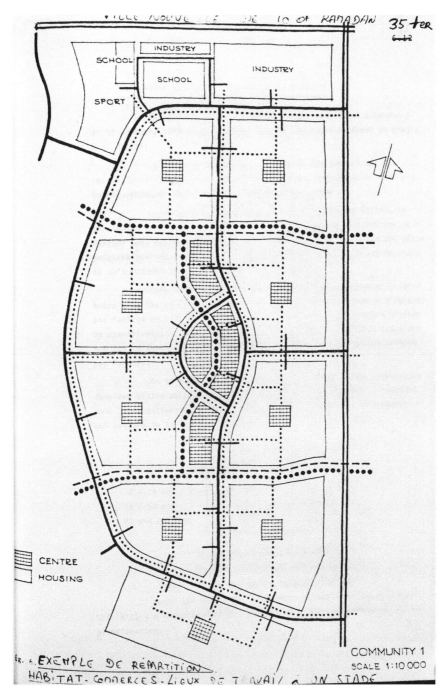

Figure 8.8 A neighborhood unit proposal for Cairo shows a variation on the service hierarchy theme: smaller centers for smaller units, and larger facilities shared by a cluster of neighborhoods. Source: Deboulet, *Stratification Sociale et Villes Nouvelles Autour du Caire.*

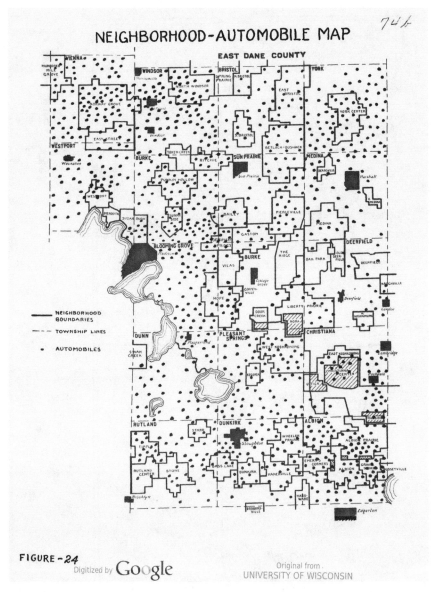

Figure 8.9 A 1921 study of rural Wisconsin painstakingly mapped the location of all automobiles against neighborhood boundaries, concluding that the automobile "must be 'domesticated' and made to do service for neighborhood and for community as well." Source: Kolb, "Rural Primary Groups," 96.

to include government offices, community buildings, and a shopping center, in addition to a school. Greenbelt, Maryland, originally with 2,831 residents, provides an interesting case study of the design, function, and viability of the neighborhood center as a complete service provider. The initial town-neighborhood was supposed to build outward from the center. At first, shops at the center were placed so that they were within one-half mile of every residence, and residents reported that the shopping center functioned as the social lifeblood of the neighborhood. Everyone shopped there; older people hung out there; and the center was convenient, accessible, and well run. Many shops were set up as co-ops. But when the population increased to 7,000, distance to the center was too much for the residents farther out, many of whom were a mile away. Despite creative attempts to service the entire area with food trucks and buses, the shopping experience at Greenbelt became "more than a local affair," and its role as the "social lifeblood" of the expanded town seemed lost.[104]

Unless there is a clear understanding about the service area of a center— that is, whether it is meant to service a whole city or a region or just the neighborhood—conflicts emerge when centers are not neighborhood-scaled (see color plate 18). This tension surfaced in postwar Europe. Housing was built in large complexes that eventually acquired services in the form of large health complexes, shopping centers, and sports facilities. But these large-format facilities tended to draw population from an area much larger than the immediate neighborhood, resulting in conflicts between mobility and consumption— nodes in a larger network pitted against neighborhood proximity and the identity it might have engendered.[105]

It was a similar story throughout Western Europe. Postwar neighborhoods were initially planned with their own shops and schools within walking distance, but in the decades since have experienced "viability problems." For one thing, larger stores built at the periphery of a neighborhood disrupted a more natural functional hierarchy that, for centuries, had integrated services within neighborhoods. Government planners did not have the ability to control all the relevant variables, so the usual issues of increased mobility, larger stores, consolidated schools, aging population, and population decline have meant that the neighborhood units are now in need of "renewal." The policy being pursued is to rekindle the original intent of a neighborhood center as the social and economic heart of a neighborhood.[106]

Mumford was frustrated by the failure to understand the difference between daily (neighborhood-based) and specialized activities. The latter had little to do with self-containment, and the attempt to claim otherwise not only was "naively specious" but also implied complacency about whether daily activities *should* be near one's home. Mumford reacted strongly to the idea that neighborhoods could be self-serviced because it was so often used as the basis of critique. His argument was that, for services, the distribution is scalar, and to argue otherwise was simply flawed economics. Because of the added transportation costs of dispersing facilities, there was no need to use vague ideas about political cohesion or face-to-face social interaction to motivate the need for localized services. It was possible to justify the need for neighborhood-based services "on economic terms alone." This did not imply self-containment, Mumford argued; even an entire city is never self-contained.[107]

For Mumford, the neighborhood unit was the "only practical answer to the giantism and inefficiency of the over-centralised metropolis."[108] The American Public Health Association similarly argued that neighborhoods that were "unified" would offer "stability," and in order to retain that unity, the neighborhood "should be physically self-contained in respect to most of the daily necessities of life." The city at large, beyond the neighborhood, would provide employment, cultural facilities, and transportation, but in the planned neighborhood, the dispatching of some facilities to neighborhoods would take congestion pressure off of more centralized places.[109]

But planned neighborhoods struggled with the ideal. The grocery stores planned for the neighborhoods of Columbia, Maryland, for example, proved financially unrealistic because the neighborhood population was too small (the 33 neighborhoods organized within the 10 villages of the 1960s new town of Columbia, Maryland, averaged 3,000 residents each), prices were not competitive, and people simply drove elsewhere for groceries. Chain stores were substituted. Outside of the controlled environment of a planned neighborhood unit, there was an additional hurdle to contend with: zoning, subdivision regulations, and other "city rules" that prevented local services in any case.[110]

Criticism of the neighborhood unit corresponded with a gradual wearing down of the servicing ideal associated with the planned neighborhood. The Urban Land Institute began advocating the "garden apartment community," a neighborhood of several hundred one- to three-story walk-up apartment buildings that were essentially bedroom neighborhoods. The amenities to be included were limited to "leisure-time" activities: a swimming pool and a clubhouse with a manager who could develop an activities program, with the caveat that such activities were voluntary: there was to be no "enforced togetherness."[111]

The effort to match neighborhood definition to service or "catchment" area created a highly rationalized understanding of what the neighborhood was supposed to be. In the 1950s in the U.S., neighborhood size could be based on school catchment areas of 1,200 for a nursery school–based neighborhood, 5,000 for an elementary school–based neighborhood, 25,000 for high school, and 75,000 for a junior college.[112] The American Planning Association advocated three neighborhood sizes: the face-block, the residential neighborhood (consisting of a few face-blocks that share services), and institutional neighborhoods, which combine several residential neighborhoods and encompass the catchment areas of larger institutions like hospitals and school systems. All were equally legitimate neighborhood definitions.

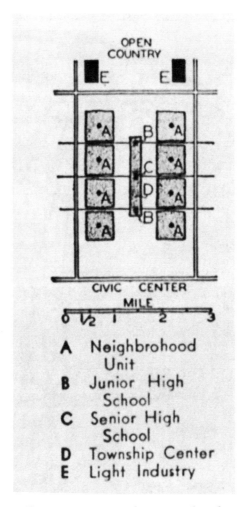

Figure 8.10 A proposal by José Sert, c. 1945, shows a simple and somewhat elegant service hierarchy oriented around the neighborhood unit. Source: De Chiara and Koppelman, *Urban Planning and Design Criteria.*

These sensibilities never died out. The New Urbanist Robert Gibbs developed a typology of neighborhood based on shopping, in which different levels of stores require different populations surrounding them. Corner stores (selling food and beverages) need 2,500 people; convenience stores (with a pharmacy, bakery, dry-cleaner) need 5,000; neighborhood shopping centers with grocery stores need 10,000 people; and so on. Within these target levels, different kinds of neighborhoods can be conceived. A neighborhood with a corner grocery store is like a "residential neighborhood," while a neighborhood with a convenience store is like an "institutional neighborhood." Of course, where

(a)

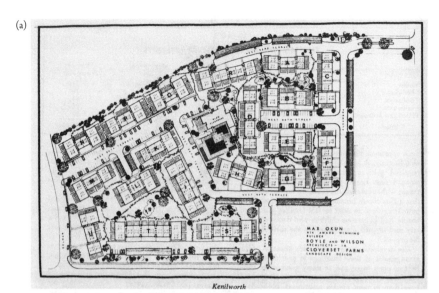

Kenilworth

(b)

Figure 8.11a and 8.11b Kenilworth is a "garden apartment community" built in the 1960s in Kansas City, Missouri, conceived as a complete neighborhood of apartments set among single-family homes. Image (b) shows the neighborhood now, wedged between single-family houses and strip malls. Source: (a) Norcross and Hysom, *Apartment Communities*; (b) Google Earth.

these neighborhood types are not constrained by a walkability requirement, where assumptions about the distances and densities required to access stores is opened up and a neighborhood center can be accessed from far distances, a very different notion of neighborhood and size results.[113] This is probably why HUD's 1980 "Neighborhood Identification" guide suggested a neighborhood population range of between 2,000 and 50,000 residents.[114]

Redefining Expectations

What do these market realities, straining something so basic as the servicing of the neighborhood, mean for neighborhood service provision? There are those who are unwilling to accept that neighborhoods should ever be thought of as incomplete; in fact some go in the opposite direction and declare that neighborhoods are not only about local needs and "lower-order" services, but they should also provide employment. In this view, jobs should not be thought of as a higher-order need drawn from a broader sphere than the neighborhood. This was the contention of the British architect John Turner, that the essence of neighborhood was the combining of home, work, and culture, and that the severing of the triage was a deliberate outcome of state-sponsored capitalism and the centralizing forces of technology and financial markets. The eclipsing of work out of neighborhoods has been particularly detrimental to those of limited resources.

The rise of the welfare state in capitalist societies might have led to a "decline in material dependence on neighbors"—but going forward, reinstalling neighbor interdependence seems to be an important strategy for the service-based neighborhood. Working outside of the system, start-ups and sharing economies are considered essential for bringing servicing, including jobs, back to the neighborhood. This includes "flexible manufacturing" and "trading networks," offered as a way to help sustain the work-home nexus and keep neighborhoods "working."[115] The informal barter economy not only supports neighborhood servicing but is believed to be both cause and effect of a shared attachment to neighborhood.[116]

But the emphasis on neighborhood as service provider, interdependent and collaborative or not, does have to be weighed against the reality that what often matters most to people about a neighborhood is not service, but lower crime rate and social homogeneity—the "who" rather than the "what."[117] Research has consistently found that, for neighborhoods rated "unsatisfactory," crime and social problems rank highest.[118] For parents, safety is more important than any other variable in predicting neighborhood satisfaction.[119] While people do tend to define their neighborhood on the basis of physical qualities,[120] preferences appear to be driven more by social factors. One caveat is that this depends on a resident's background and how long a person has lived in a neighborhood. (For new residents, preferences seem to be more about physical factors.) It is also true that neighborhood preferences are constantly changing, as new research shows high demand for walkable urban neighborhoods, which is largely a matter

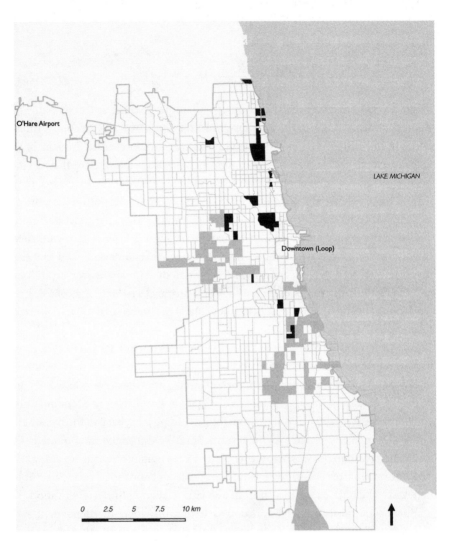

Figure 8.12 The combination of Walk Score and census tract data can be used as an indicator of how common the stable, diverse, walkable neighborhood is in 21st-century America. Out of the 3,505 tracts in the U.S. that held their diversity between 1970 and 2010, 484 of them also had high Walk Scores. The upshot: about 1% of census tracts in the U.S. are walkable, income diverse, and stable. The map shows Chicago, which fared slightly better: shaded areas are tracts that had top quartile income diversity in both 1970 and 2010 (about 12% of all tracts); those with the darkest shading—about 4% of all tracts—also had a high Walk Score (80 or above). Source: U.S. Census. Image: author.

of servicing.[121] Critics counter that residents who prioritize service functionality over social relations are overly interested in consumption and packaged lifestyles. Neighborhoods, it seems, can't win.

Whether possible or not, the stark reality is that neighborhoods in the U.S. are overwhelmingly not well serviced. Walk Score can be used to make this assessment. The score is based on business and amenity locations along street networks, which is essentially a measure of neighborhood access and functionality. The Walk Score algorithm assigns points (0 to 100) based on distance to amenities, weighted by category. For example, amenities within one-quarter mile (of a given origin) receive maximum points, while no points are awarded for amenities further than 1 mile. Amenity weights are based on empirical research on walking behavior. Grocery stores receive the strongest weight, followed by restaurants. A slightly lower weighting is assigned to banks, parks, coffee shops, schools, and bookstores.[122] Using a smaller version of neighborhood than the census tract—the census block group—there were 14,912 neighborhoods that had a Walk Score in 2013 of at least 80 or above. This level is considered to be a minimum for having the ability to access daily life needs on foot—that is, within the neighborhood. By this metric, just 8.5% of the 174,186 block group neighborhoods in the U.S. were walkable—that is, had an adequate level of services.

Notes

1. Cooley, *Social Organization*.
2. Mumford, "The Neighborhood and the Neighborhood Unit," 260.
3. La Gory and Pipkin, *Urban Social Space*; Stone, *Nippur Neighborhoods*.
4. McKenzie, "The Neighborhood II," 344, 348.
5. Fairfield, "Alienation of Social Control," 431. On the link between sociology and planning, see Buttimer, "Sociology and Planning."
6. For a critique see Pahl, *Patterns of Urban Life*; Greer and Kube, "Urbanism and Social Structure," 109, 111.
7. Wright, "The Interrelation of Housing and Transit," 51.
8. Wehrly, "Activities and Comment," 32.
9. Campleman, "Some Sociological Aspects of Mixed-Class Neighbourhood Planning," 2.
10. Mumford, "The Neighborhood and the Neighborhood Unit," 258.
11. This was revealed through a survey conducted in the East End of London in 1938. See Lammers, "The Birth of the East Ender."
12. Tannenbaum, "The Neighborhood," 362; Patricios, "Urban Design Principles," 28.
13. Ministry of Town and Country Planning, "Design of Dwelling." Section 2 concerns neighborhood planning.
14. Mann, "The Concept of Neighborliness," 164.
15. Felton, *Serving the Neighborhood*, 136; Looker, "Microcosms of Democracy," 355.
16. Galster, "What Is Neighbourhood?," 259; Taylor, "Social Order and Disorder of Street Blocks and Neighborhoods," 113.
17. Michigan Council of Defense, Civilian War Service Division, *Neighborhood War Clubs*, 10, 14, 16.
18. Bardet, "Social Topography."

19. Milgram, *The Individual in a Social World*; Cooley, *Social Organization*.
20. Taylor, "Social Order and Disorder of Street Blocks and Neighborhoods", 113; Alexander, *A Pattern Language*, 72.
21. Bardet, "Social Topography."
22. Martin, "Enacting Neighborhood," 366. Martin is here citing an observation by Aitken, "Mothers, Communities and the Scale of Difference"; Suttles, *The Social Construction of Communities*.
23. Elizabeth Roberts, "Neighbourhoods," paper given at History Workshop 23, University of Salford, November 1989, cited in Pearson, "Knowing One's Place," 222.
24. "The State of Your New York Block."
25. Guttenberg, "Planning and Ideology," 289.
26. Hall, *Cities of Tomorrow*, 123.
27. Stein, "Toward New Towns for America (Continued)," 353.
28. Rofe, "Space and Community," 118.
29. Stein, "Toward New Towns for America (Continued)," 390.
30. Dewey, "The Neighborhood, Urban Ecology, and City Planners"; Herbert, "The Neighbourhood Unit Principle."
31. Mann, *An Approach to Urban Sociology*, 155.
32. Herbert, "The Neighbourhood Unit Principle," 197.
33. Gans, "Planning for People, Not Buildings," 33.
34. Wellman, "The Unbounded Community," 799.
35. Wellman and Leighton, "Networks, Neighborhoods, and Communities," 364, 365, 366.
36. Bettencourt, "The Origins of Scaling in Cities."
37. Churchill, "Housing and Community Planning," 87.
38. Keller, *The Urban Neighborhood*, 145.
39. Webber, "Order in Diversity"; Kotler, *Neighborhood Government*.
40. Biddulph et al., "From Concept to Completion."
41. Warren and Warren, *The Neighborhood Organizer's Handbook*; Huckfeldt et al., "Alternative Contexts of Political Behavior." Cox did pathbreaking work on this subject, e.g., "The Voting Decision in a Spatial Context."
42. Ham and Manley, "Commentary," 2788.
43. This is the main basis of the rather acerbic critique of social mixing advanced by Lees, "Gentrification and Social Mixing." See also Cheshire, "Resurgent Cities, Urban Myths and Policy Hubris."
44. Sampson, *Great American City*; O'Brien Caughy et al., "Neighborhoods, Families, and Children"; Newburger et al., *Neighborhood and Life Chances*. Quote is from the Penn Institute for Urban Research website: http://penniur.upenn.edu/publications/neighborhood-and-life-chances-how-place-matters-in-modern-america.
45. Kim and Kaplan, "Physical and Psychological Factors," 313.
46. As reported in Forrest and Kearns, "Social Cohesion, Social Capital and the Neighbourhood," 2132.
47. Ivory et al., "The New Zealand Index of Neighbourhood Social Fragmentation."
48. Cortright, "Less in Common."
49. Brekelmans, *Nederlanders en bun buren*.
50. These stages were proposed by Grannis, *From the Ground Up*.
51. See Neighbours from Hell, http://www.nfh.org.uk; Problem Neighbours, http://www.problemneighbours.co.uk.
52. Abu-Ghazzeh, "Built Form and Religion," 55.
53. For a very antispace and -place argument, see Goetz and Chapple, "You Gotta Move," quote on 229.
54. Raine, "On Measuring Patterns of Neighbourly Relationships."
55. Sharkey, *Stuck in Place*, 166; Crisp, "'Communities with Oomph'?"
56. See, for example, Hillery, *Communal Organizations*.
57. Kuper, "Social Science Research and the Planning of Urban Neighbourhoods," 238.
58. Committee on City Planning and Zoning, *The President's Conference on Home Building and Home Ownership*, 8:104. See also Gillette, "The Evolution of Neighborhood Planning";

Central Housing Advisory Committee, Great Britain, and Ministry of Housing and Local Government, *Design of Dwellings*; Collison, "Town Planning and the Neighbourhood Unit Concept," 467.

59. Allaire, "Neighborhood Boundaries," 14–15.
60. Kuper, "Social Science Research and the Planning of Urban Neighbourhoods," 238.
61. See, for example, Todd and Wheeler, *Utopia*; Hayden, *Seven American Utopias*.
62. MOMA, "Look at Your Neighborhood," 2.
63. Keller, *The Urban Neighborhood*, 137.
64. Wekerle, "From Refuge to Service Center," 90.
65. Grigsby et al., "Residential Neighborhoods and Submarkets," 21.
66. See Galster, "What Is Neighbourhood?"
67. Fitzsimmons, "A Wish for More Community in Mixed-Income Units"; Chaskin and Joseph, "Contested Space Design Principles and Regulatory Regimes in Mixed-Income Communities in Chicago."
68. Chaskin and Joseph, "Contested Space Design Principles and Regulatory Regimes in Mixed-Income Communities in Chicago."
69. Bolt and Van Kempen, "Successful Mixing?," 367.
70. Freeman, "Displacement or Succession?"
71. Greenberg, *The Poetics of Cities*, 113.
72. Lunday, "Impact of African American Ethnicity on Neighborhood Design," 109.
73. Mumford, "What Is a City?," 187.
74. Cabot et al., *A Course in Citizenship*, 86, 88.
75. Guest et al., "Changing Locality Identification in the Metropolis"; Hawley, *Urban Society*, 198.
76. Llewelyn-Davies, "Town Design," 157.
77. Gibberd, *Town Design*, 204.
78. Ibid., 203.
79. Tetlow and Goss, *Homes, Towns and Traffic*, 93.
80. Gardner-Medwin and Connell. "New Towns in Scotland," 312.
81. Roach and O'Brien, "The Impact of Different Kinds of Neighborhood Involvement."
82. Ibid., 389, 390; McKenzie, "The Neighborhood II," 363.
83. Aronovici, *Housing the Masses, 249.*
84. McKenzie, "The Neighborhood III," 486; McKenzie, "The Neighborhood no. 5," 610.
85. Boger, "The Meaning of Neighborhood in the Modern City."
86. Chudacoff, "A New Look at Ethnic Neighborhoods."
87. See Rofe, "Space and Community," 121.
88. Pfeiffer, "Racial Equity in the Post–Civil Rights Suburbs?," 17.
89. Ericksen and Yancey. "Work and Residence in Industrial Philadelphia"; Yancey and Ericksen, "The Antecedents of Community."
90. Pendola and Gen, "Does 'Main Street' Promote Sense of Community?," 545; Hein, "Machi Neighborhood and Small Town."
91. Völker et al., "When Are Neighbourhoods Communities?"
92. Vaiou and Lykogianni, "Women, Neighbourhoods and Everyday Life," 741.
93. Botsman and Rogers, *What's Mine Is Yours*; Winter and Cooksey, "Where Goes the Neighborhood?"
94. Hohenberg and Lees, *The Making of Urban Europe*, 34.
95. Ibid.
96. Farr, *Sustainable Urbanism*, 131.
97. Editors, "Regional Plan of New York and Its Environs," 127.
98. Engelhardt, "The School-Neighborhood Nucleus," 88.
99. Adams et al., "Panel I," 79.
100. Gutnov, *The Ideal Communist City.*
101. Wassenberg, "The Netherlands."
102. Gardner-Medwin and Connell, "New Towns in Scotland."
103. Kolb, "Rural Primary Groups," 96.
104. Stein, "Toward New Towns for America (Continued)," 354–55.
105. Querrien and Devisme, "France."

106. Wassenberg, "The Netherlands." The neighborhood unit in early postwar planning in the Netherlands is detailed (in Dutch) in Blom et al., "De Typologie Van De Vroeg-Naoorlogse Woonwiken."

107. Mumford, "The Neighborhood and the Neighborhood Unit," 264, 266.

108. Ibid, 266.

109. American Public Health Association, *Planning the Neighborhood*. 1.

110. Talen, *City Rules*.

111. Norcross and Hysom, *Apartment Communities*, 7.

112. Bailly, *An Urban Elementary School for Boston*, cited in Park and Rogers, "Neighborhood Planning Theory, Guidelines, and Research."

113. Gibbs, *Principles of Urban Retail Planning and Development*; Park and Rogers. "Neighborhood Planning Theory, Guidelines, and Research."

114. Broden et al., "Neighborhood Identification."

115. Turner and Ward, *Housing by People*; Turner, "Rebuilding Working Neighbourhoods and the Rediscovery of Tradition," 13.

116. Garrioch and Peel, "Introduction."

117. Shlay, "Castles in the Sky," 620, 622.

118. Hur and Morrow-Jones, "Factors That Influence Residents' Satisfaction with Neighborhoods." See also Brower, *Good Neighborhoods*.

119. Cook, "Components of Neighborhood Satisfaction Responses from Urban and Suburban Single-Parent Women."

120. Sims, *Neighborhoods*.

121. Leinberger and Lynch, "The WalkUP Wake-Up Call"; Nelson, *Reshaping Metropolitan America*.

122. See Walkscore.com; Moudon et al. "Attributes of Environments".

9

Neighborhoods and Segregation

This chapter reviews the final, and most significant, debate about the neighborhood: its association with social segregation. Many have argued that the delineation of neighborhood is by definition a form of exclusion, and that if neighborhoods weren't identified in the first place, there would be less emphasis on social sorting and who is "in" and "out" of the neighborhood. There is no denying that the neighborhood, especially the planned neighborhood unit, was and is associated with segregation, sometimes explicitly. But it is important to remember that this was a practice much more pronounced in the 20th century than historically, as the record shows.

Whereas the proposed resolution for other types of debates has been more about negotiation (like accommodating both plan and process), the resolution of the segregation critique boils down to answering the critique head-on and seeking a proactive response to an undeniable problem. (As this chapter recounts, segregation by neighborhood is a serious and tenacious issue.) Proposed resolutions are (a) to make neighborhood-scale social diversity an explicit policy goal, furthered, for example, by supporting a variety of housing types within a neighborhood; and (b) to look for ways to successfully integrate smaller, more homogeneous neighborhoods set within larger, heterogeneous districts. Both of these proposals have long been on the table, but their usefulness is limited by neighborhood ambiguity. In both cases, it is again the physically defined neighborhood rather than the socially differentiated neighborhood that provides an identity through which diversity can be embraced.

Segregated by Definition

The social- and service-related challenges of neighborhoods reviewed in previous chapters are tied to a related and often stronger critique: that neighborhoods exist mainly for purposes of segregation and exclusion and are thus a societal problem, not a solution. Probably the majority of critiques of neighborhood are on this topic. In this view, neighborhoods are the embodiment of difference, sorting racial, ethnic, or economic privilege, one group from another. The neighborhood, by definition, "always involves exclusions and boundaries," and these self-interested enclaves sap energy from wider urban reforms.[1]

As the history of the neighborhood recounts, pre-20th-century neighborhoods were mostly a socially mixed affair. But toward the end of this time, as industrial urbanization gained force, segregated enclaves created by the wealthy fleeing the industrial city or the poor confined to it, became more common. It was a situation that anarchists and reformers exploited for political gain. In Europe in the Victorian Era, the segregation of neighborhoods into middle-class and working-class populations was famously denounced by Engels and other political contemporaries, with different interpretations about who was to blame. The Manchester Statistical Society complained in 1843 that the "comfortable class" was resettling in the outskirts, leaving "large tracts of the town . . . occupied solely by operatives." This was regarded as "unfavourable to the town as a community" because it separated the residences of "the employers and the employed." Rhetorically such separation was considered "equally inimical to the well-being of both."[2]

It is not always possible to determine what the historical levels of neighborhood segregation actually were. All those "below" the wealthy, such as artisans, factory workers, and domestic workers, were lumped together, and there was a tendency to focus on the elite enclaves of the wealthy even while the middle class and "all of the diverse strata of the working class" might have actually been highly "interspersed."[3] In the book *Unbounded Community: Neighborhood Life and Social Structure in New York City, 1830–1875*, Kenneth Scherzer makes the case that locality was not organized into identifiable neighborhoods, and social support had little to do with where one lived.[4] It is true that 19th-century reformers began the practice of delineating sections of the city as neighborhoods, because they were searching for a way to grasp the helter-skelter and injustice of the Western, industrialized city. Neighborhood was a device for making sense of it all, prompting the neighborhood enthusiast Robert Woods to declare in 1914, "The neighborhood is concretely conceivable; the city is not." Neighborhood was essentially "an analytical tool" that could help people "better decipher the undifferentiated chaos of the urban wilderness."[5]

Because neighborhoods were the portal through which to trace the segregation and spatial sorting of urban dwellers, naturally the issues of segregation and racial conflict were almost always discussed in neighborhood terms.[6] Keeping whites segregated and away from blacks was a matter of keeping them out of specific neighborhoods. As Zorbaugh put it, "There is no phenomenon more characteristic of city life, as contrasted with the life of the rural community or the village, than that of segregation." The neighborhood concept itself seemed to somehow facilitate this segregation, or at least the understanding of it. Historians traced the movement and consolidation of groups in and out of neighborhoods and interpreted these flows as having significant bearing on class formation.[7]

Thus began the tradition of defining neighborhoods based on segregation. The sociologist's view of the neighborhood would later include structural constraints (market forces, public policies, politics), but explorations of social homogeneity versus heterogeneity dominated.[8] The main parameters of neighborhood definition became degree of mix versus similarity of population from within; and from without, the degree of social difference with other neighborhoods. A standard geographer's definition of neighborhood was "a defined area within which there is an identifiable subculture to which the majority of its residents conform."[9]

Sociologists of the Chicago School pursued the topic of neighborhood social differentiation vigorously. Foremost among them was Robert Park, whose "mosaic of little worlds" were essentially "mosaics of segregated peoples."[10] A main topic of interest was assimilation—neighborhood as the primary vehicle through which the "Americanization" of immigrants could take place. According to classic urban ecology, immigrants first settled in Burgess and Hoyt's "zone in transition" (basically a ghetto) and then, seeking better accommodation, migrated to the "zone of workingmen's homes." But the model reflected a certain acceptance of the inevitability of differentiation and segregation, a proclamation that "competition forces associational groupings." Park and the Chicago School made clear that the result of "continuous processes of invasions and accommodations" was a subdivided residential pattern of varying classes and associated land values, mores, and degrees of "civic interest." Where one neighborhood might be "conservative, law-abiding, civic-minded," another would be "vagrant and radical." Such differentiation and segregation developed along racial, linguistic, age, sex, and income lines, forming units of communal life that they termed "natural areas."[11]

As the decades progressed, spatial patterning models became more complex. Sector and wedge models were added to explain similarity and patterning, looking for areas that could be considered organically unified. But the search for social homogeneity was always paramount. In the 1970s Hawkes brought in the question of distance from the city center in an effort to explain the social pattern of 351 census tracts in Baltimore. His model achieved what subsequent researchers have sought: finding "the spatially systematic variation of people in neighborhoods."[12]

The important point is that the Chicago School did not provide much support for the idea that neighborhoods could be viably mixed. It was the village—a freestanding neighborhood, not an urban one—that, according to R. D. McKenzie, represented the "dominance of neighborhood over kinship as a bond of union." There was something universal and hard-wired about the social makeup of the village, the result of "common human nature responding to common stimuli," so it was imbued with a natural form of social integration. But city neighborhoods, in contrast, did not have it; they instead thrived on differentiation along economic, racial, or cultural lines.[13]

McKenzie did not hold out much hope that the juxtapositions of rich and poor he discovered in the 1920s in Columbus, Ohio, would be possible elsewhere. In the Columbus case, economic circumstances had compelled dissimilar families to live next to each other. However, McKenzie confided, "in such regions there can be no positive neighborhood sentiment; hatred and avoidance prevail until opportunity arises for moving on."[14] In a search for a more authentic narrative, McKenzie worked hard to document "natural groupings" using consistency in attitudes, "morals," and voting behavior. Homogeneity was to be the basis of neighborhood definition and governance, although in the end McKenzie thought that the "very looseness" of society meant that neighborhoods were becoming less real and less important in any case.[15]

As sociologists of the early 20th century set in motion the idea that neighborhoods should be defined by homogeneity and that heterogeneous neighborhoods were intrinsically dysfunctional, planners planned the neighborhood accordingly. Clarence Perry's vision seemed a conscious attempt to expand and codify the segregationist impulses of neighborhood residents. His valid concerns about the need for better-designed living environments and the importance of neighborhood context (beyond the consideration of the housing unit alone) veered into language that was insulting, antipoor, and racist. He envisioned discrete, separated residential developments of homogeneous social character, insisting that "the great foe to community life is heterogeneity." Citing McKenzie, he argued that this homogeneity was "a natural phenomenon of urban life."[16] Perry utilized a village ideal explicitly defined by homogeneity. This required reconceptualization: the village in a modern city was bound not by traditional medieval economic localism but by sociocultural homogeneity (the Chicago School's "natural areas"), organized around a school and other neighborhood institutions. Whereas a village was surrounded by farm and forest, an urban neighborhood was surrounded by other neighborhoods, heightening the sense of social separation, competition, and, potentially, conflict.[17]

Planners objectified the homogeneous neighborhood and oriented their data-gathering approach accordingly. This extended not only to the mixing of people but to the mixing of land use as well (despite the fact that the evils of land use mixing had largely passed). The official planning manual, "Neighborhood Boundaries," outlined how the "demarcation" of neighborhoods should be wherever there is a "shift" from residential to commercial, or where there are "different characteristics of residential structures."[18] Planners seemed not to recognize the value of demarcating neighborhoods in a way that would capitalize on and help integrate and connect, a more heterogeneous—and therefore potentially more functional—pattern of land use. It became standard practice to exclude shops from "the boundaries of residential neighborhoods" and treat them instead as "special small planning units."[19] As for social mixing, neighborhoods that were not demarcated on the basis of "*established* social patterns" (original emphasis) were deemed "a failure" because they did not "make use of all the resources at hand for creation and maintenance of an improved environment." These "resources" were the "traditions, social groupings, and associations among the residents."[20]

Some proponents of the "neighborhood idea" felt no need to apologize for what they believed was its intrinsic homogeneity. A planner wrote in 1948 in city planning's main journal, " 'Heterogeneous neighborhoods' is not only a fanciful theory, but is the juxtaposition of two words with completely divergent meanings." An official with the British Ministry of Town and County Planning remarked in the same year, "We shall do little to create a civic spirit by shoveling all kinds of people together."[21] These statements reflect the position that homeowner perception was the only legitimate basis of neighborhood definition. On these terms planners and sociologists relied on a "socioeconomic brotherhood" for neighborhood definition, where residents of homeowners associations—isolationist by definition—enforced an understanding of neighborhood that was based on "homogeneous housing values and populations."[22]

It was not just sociologists and urban planners who promoted the segregated neighborhood. Residents and politicians found that unit-like neighborhoods "could abruptly change character in a way that the mixed space of preindustrial cities could not," and they worked this to their advantage. In one example, between 1910 and 1917 Baltimore implemented a law (the "West Ordinance") that purposefully kept people segregated into color-based neighborhoods. Where many neighborhood associations had been working to implement small improvements like sidewalks and street trees, groups in Baltimore used neighborhood as a way to maintain separation and a geographically bounded racial purity.[23] Baltimore's law was reminiscent of what was happening in other parts of the world that had fallen victim to Western colonialism.[24]

All manner of institutions have been complicit in using the neighborhood for segregationist goals. In the Depression era, the YMCA used the neighborhood as a way of getting youth away from dense inner cities. They called it "decentralization." Their 1938 pamphlet *From Building to Neighborhood* spelled out the importance of transitioning from a building-centered to a neighborhood-centered approach. The idea was wrapped up in something borrowed from "city planners and industrialists," whose interest was "spreading out to a more rural type of development in the future." The neighborhood was the vehicle through which boys could be part of the exodus, connected to "smaller groupings" via the neighborhood as opposed to "large masses" in concentrated downtowns.[25]

Most notorious was the redlining undertaken by the U.S. Home Owners Loan Corporation and the Federal Housing Authority. Incredibly, the agencies used an underwriting manual that called for investigating whether a neighborhood had a mix of "incompatible" social and racial groups.[26] The Residential Security Maps produced in the 1930s sorted the residential environment into blocks of grades from first to fourth (green, blue, yellow, red), impacting mortgage lending and sealing the fate of neighborhoods for decades (see color plate 19). Notably the rating of property for home financing purposes was a rating of *neighborhood*, not of individual property owners and their ability to meet financial obligations.[27] Planners and developers aided the process by putting in place the deed restrictions, zoning, subdivision regulations, and other land development controls that created the segregated neighborhoods of postwar suburbanization.[28]

The Census Bureau has long defined census tracts—the de facto definition of neighborhood—on the basis of social homogeneity. In a 1980 publication, the U.S. Department of Housing and Urban Development forcefully advocated that neighborhoods be defined on the basis of housing submarkets, since "realtors recognize this fact." Tracts "are designed to be homogeneous with respect to population characteristics, economic status, and living conditions," and "geographical shape and areal size are of relatively minor importance." Housing submarkets were considered "the best foundation for a conceptual definition of neighborhood" alongside "neighborhood associations" and "subdivisions," all of which were mostly driven by housing developers rather than any normative conception of neighborhood as a subset of a diverse society. The report also considered nonresidential uses to be unrelated to neighborhood formation, that the investigator should identify neighborhoods based on "clusters of residents with similar demographic characteristics," and that boundaries should be based on land use changes, including change from single-family to multifamily housing.[29] In these ways, official neighborhood definition was, and continues to be, intent on solidifying homogeneity.

Thus it is easy to understand why the neighborhood's most strident critics believe that neighborhoods exist *only* for the purpose of segregation—that is, that they arise only when there is social discordance among groups. By reducing "access and openness," they ultimately limit the economic opportunities of individuals, and as such they are "foreign to the essential urban quality of free association."[30] Supporting these claims are numerous examples rendered in built form, from suburban enclaves to inner-city neighborhoods of tenement housing that were carefully tucked away and out of site of social elites and business interests. This antiurban behavior creates walled-off, isolated neighborhoods that legitimize the critique.[31]

Also underscoring the equation that neighborhoods are synonymous with segregation is that neighborhood identity and neighborhood exclusion seem to be in lockstep, such that the stronger the sense of neighborhood, the more prone to turf consciousness and social segregation people seem to become. The 19th- and 20th-century Catholic parish in America exposed this linkage. John McGreevy's study of parish boundaries revealed the conflicted history of the strong geographical ties of parishioners—motivated by priests who urged them to invest and care for their parish neighborhoods—and the racism that ensued. While the strong neighborhood rootedness often had the benefit of delaying if not preventing flight to the suburbs, racism, it seems, played a significant role in the identity and tenacity of these geographically rooted and strongly bounded neighborhoods. Protestants and Jews, who fled to the suburbs more readily, might have been less invested in neighborhood and the effort to protect it.[32]

Neighborhoods provide identity and place-bound institutions essential to political causes,[33] but a neighborhood's renown can also foster feelings of superiority or inferiority. One study found that the reputation of a neighborhood alone could significantly impact social relationships and even personal well-being; the authors suggested that policymakers should put some effort into improving a neighborhood's reputation through "reputation management."[34] These status associations are indoctrinated at an early age. Parents have been known to restrict the movements of their children in an effort to keep them contained in the "right" neighborhood, such that telling a child not to cross a certain street might be as much about maintaining social status as protection from cars.[35] As recounted in books like *Not in My Neighborhood*, neighborhood becomes the mechanism through which fear and prejudice are manifested.

Taking Stock: Neighborhood Segregation in the 21st Century

How segregated are neighborhoods now? As an empirical matter, the situation in many parts of the world is that, while there have been significant gains in terms of mixing by race and ethnicity, neighborhoods are more economically segregated than ever. The segregation of the affluent, especially, is seen as dramatic because it translates to a reduction in support for public investment in cities and neighborhoods that are less well off.[36] In the U.S. the spatial clustering of "like-minded America" intensifies each time a family moves, creating what Bill Bishop calls the "Big Sort" at all geographic levels, political and economical separation like never before.[37] The paradox is that neighborhood is not only the harbor of all this sifting and sorting but also its means of reversal. Dissolving neighborhoods is not likely to accomplish social integration objectives.

It is important to note, however, that just because racial and ethnic segregation is steadily declining, and this trend will continue given the "diversity explosion" and resultant loss of a clear racial majority, that doesn't translate to a profusion of racially diverse neighborhoods. Segregation by race is even more prevalent than segregation by income; it's just that racial segregation has declined steadily since its peak in 1970.[38]

But recently, because of the trends, more attention has been paid to the data showing that income-based segregation at the neighborhood scale is increasing. A few statistics: lower-income households that live mostly around others with low incomes increased from 23% to 28% between 1980 and 2010; higher-income households that live mostly around others with high incomes doubled from 9% in 1980 to 18% in 2010.[39] In Toronto between 1970 and 2005, the proportion of middle-income neighborhoods fell from 66% to 29%, while the proportion of low-income neighborhoods from from 19% to 53%.[40] These changes are exacerbated by income inequality overall, which translates to income segregation by neighborhood. According to the Pew Research Center, between 1980 and 2010 there was a significant increase in the percentage of lower-income households living in majority lower-income tracts and upper-income households living in majority upper-income tracts.

Neighborhood income integration in the U.S. is unstable. The data show that most economically diverse neighborhoods do not remain so, because they become either more uniformly rich or more uniformly poor. According to the Urban Institute, only 18% of neighborhoods that were economically integrated in 1970 remained integrated in 2000.[41] One gets the impression that Americans are chasing each other around, sorting each other out in pursuit of either a better neighborhood or a more affordable one. The changes have led neighborhood proponents to take a fairly dour view of the "stages of neighborhood transition," which go from stable to declining: gradual decline, rapid decline, "total deterioration," or gentrifying and displacing.[42]

Cities in Asia and elsewhere, many of them hyperdense by Western standards, are also highly segregated. Neighborhood segregation in Hong Kong, for example, despite its high density and its high proportion of public housing, is at a level similar to that in the U.S. In fact, compared to the U.S., high-income households are even more isolated from low-income households than in the U.S.[43] The urban growth of Cairo, as another example, is characterized by walled or barricaded enclaves at the periphery, each a socially homogeneous, internalized neighborhood where the rich sequester themselves and the poor are isolated. This is not a new feature of urban growth, as Cairo has always been a city of enclaves. But where these enclaves used to be centrally located, they are now at the periphery, furthering class-based spatial division.[44]

Compared to Europe, racial segregation in the U.S.—especially black-white—is considered extreme. A common segregation index known as the "index of dissimilarity" gives a score between 0 (complete integration) and 100 (complete segregation).[45] Around 2000, cities in Western Europe had levels of 40 to 60, while in the U.S., black-white segregation in places like Chicago, New York, Detroit, Milwaukee, and Buffalo was between 80 and 90. By 2010 these levels in the U.S. had declined to the 70 to 80 range, still above Europe's. Part of the explanation for this is that European cities have much more socialized housing, counteracting the tendency for markets to homogenize housing. On the other hand, the differences apply only to certain cities (like Chicago) and only for black-white segregation, and European cities may be catching up due to housing sector marketization.[46]

While American neighborhoods are more racially integrated than they were in 1910, this is mostly because of the suburbanization of blacks rather than whites moving into inner-city black neighborhoods. As Jacob Vigdor and Edward Glaeser explain, "For every prominent example of a black neighborhood undergoing gentrification—in Harlem, Roxbury, or Columbia Heights—there are countless more neighborhoods witnessing no such trend. Instead, the dominant trend in predominantly black neighborhoods nationwide has been population loss."[47] Jackelyn Hwang and Robert Sampson show that, all else being equal, gentrification rates are lower in black neighborhoods.[48] Their study revealed the now conventional American urban story: rich neighborhoods stay rich, poor neighborhoods stay poor, and middle-income neighborhoods change up or down—with race determining to a large degree the direction of change.

The immigration of Hispanics and Asians is altering some of these dynamics in the U.S. The rapid growth of neighborhoods that include Hispanics and Asians in addition to blacks and whites means that the old invasion-succession model does not fully describe neighborhood dynamics and racial/ethnic change. For one thing, there are now "global neighborhoods" consisting of four rather than two racial/ethnic categories, and these neighborhoods may be able to hang on to their diversity longer. However, statistically, stable diversity is possible "if and only if black entry is preceded by a substantial presence of both Hispanic and Asian residents." In the last two decades of the 20th century, Hispanics and Asians were the "pioneer integrators" into all-white zones, apparently with less resulting white flight.[49]

While the study of neighborhood population dynamics tends to focus on segregation, there have been a few recent exceptions. Michael Poulsen et al. argue the need to study the internal complexity of residential neighborhoods despite their segregation on some dimensions, which is another way of arguing the importance of understanding diversity within rather than segregation without. They show the full complexity of ethnic sorting in London neighborhoods (which, incidentally, are nowhere near "the extremes" of U.S. segregation), and that within clustered populations, subgroups may not be segregated. Ethnic neighborhoods in London vary widely. While it has exclusively white suburbs, its ethnic neighborhoods are more about multiethnic diversity than group dominance.[50]

It is possible to gauge the stability of income diversity in U.S. neighborhoods using tract data between 1970 and 2010 and using the Simpson Diversity Index.[51] In 1970 the top quartile of census tracts was anything at or above a Simpson diversity score of 3.5648. There were 12,370 tracts (out of 49,493) that had this score. In 2010 the top quartile of census tracts was anything at or above a Simpson diversity score of 3.5911, a slight increase. There were 18,017 tracts (out of 72,063) that had this score. Comparing the 1970 and 2010 tracts, there were 3,505 tracts that held their diversity between those years.

Planning for Diversity

One response to the segregationist critique is to activate the counternarrative that planners, contrary to popular impression, have been strong proponents of neighborhood diversity. Neighborhood planning, rather than being a source of segregation, is actually an essential tool for countering it.

As already touched on, it is true that many neighborhood planners had unambiguous ideas about the importance of social mixing. The neighborhood, as Lewis Mumford wrote, was to be "an essential organ of an integrated city," where the guiding principle was that "the neighborhood should, as far as possible, be an adequate and representative sample of the whole."[52] Howard Hallman's summary of an intensive discussion that took place in Philadelphia in 1957–58 between professionals and citizens on the topic "What Neighborhoods Should Be Like," identified a universal rejection of the homogeneous suburban neighborhood. Planners and citizens wanted "greater social heterogeneity" and "greater variety" to "produce a better esthetic effect."[53] Planned neighborhood units often failed to live up to this standard, but it was not necessarily for lack of trying.

The settlement house movement of the late 19th and early 20th century must be singled out for its neighborhood-based diversity cause. The diverse neighborhood was defined as a "meeting place of the hospitality minded of all classes" and "a centre for every sort of neighborhood well-being on every sort of neighborhood terms."[54] Mary K. Simkhovitch's *Neighborhood: My Story of Greenwich House* recounts a world of intense caring about the socially mixed neighborhood as a place and a way of life. She wrote, "We were Protestant and Catholic, we were rich and poor, we were Republicans, Democrats, and Socialists, but this we can say, that differences melted away when we faced the facts of our community." Even race was transcended: "The race animosities that have sprung up elsewhere seem always to have been absent in our neighborhood."[55]

For many 20th-century planners and activists, neighborhoods were supposed to be dynamic and accommodate changes in family size, age, and income. This could help achieve what was "the one paramount factor that is essential to democracy": "the removal, as far as possible, of class consciousness." On this basis Levittown was critiqued almost immediately for its homogeneity and its "dead level" of development that excluded diverse uses and price points.[56] The widely distributed 1948 *Planning the Neighborhood* report argued that "diversified dwelling types" within one neighborhood "to meet the needs of different families . . . cannot be too emphatically stressed." The dwelling and family types that needed to be mixed within a neighborhood were worked out precisely (see Table 9.1).[57]

Planners, nonprofits, and government agencies have, for many decades now, instituted a plethora of strategies aimed at fostering socially mixed neighborhoods, mostly in terms of income mix. A partial list includes new mixed-income neighborhoods (HOPE VI), scattered-site housing, vouchers, community land trusts, inclusionary housing requirements, tax credits, bonus densities, transfer of development rights, condominium conversion ordinances, limits on the use of restrictive covenants, loans, grants, bond financing, tax abatement, tax-base sharing. This is only a small subset of the arsenal of policies and programs that have been devised with the aim of creating socially diverse neighborhoods in a society dominated by housing segregation.[58]

These deliberate neighborhood mixing policies have not always achieved their intended outcomes, however. As a result, not everyone agrees with the overall objective. Robert Sampson argued that the "theoretical assumptions" underlying mixed-income neighborhoods were suspect: that low-income residents benefit from high-income neighbors as models of behavior and educational attainment; that positive interaction and social support is dependent on residential proximity; that higher-income residents are willing to provide this social support via informal social control or organizational involvement; and that these improvements in social engagement and role-model provision will offset neighborhood instability resulting from attempts to mix up the population of a neighborhood. In addition, mixed-income policy "assumes a static equilibrium with regard to intervention effects"; it does not account for "interdependencies" among neighborhoods in terms of "social mechanisms"; and it ignores the macro-level political and social realms.[59]

Critical urban theorists don't think much of government-directed neighborhood-scale income mixing either. One line of criticism draws from

Table 9.1 **Land area and density for a neighborhood of 5,000 persons (1,375 families) with diversified dwelling types**

Population Composition		Proposed Dwelling Type	Dwelling Units (Families)		Required Neighborhood Land Area	
Type of Family	Percentage of Families		Percentage	Number	Square feet per Family	Total Acres
Families with minor children	52.0	1-family detached	26.0	357	8,440	69.0
		1-family row	26.0	357	3,740	30.3
Childless couples, single adults, and other adult households	48.0	1	20.0	275	2,195	13.8
			28.0	386	1,580	14.0
TOTAL	100.0		100.0	1,375		127.1

RESULTANT NEIGHBORHOOD DENSITY: 10.8 FAMILIES PER ACRE

Source: Adapted from American Public Health Association, *Planning the Neighborhood*, 68.

the literature on the politics of neighboring, where neighborhood social mixing becomes a problem because neighboring involves the "act of othering." Others see deliberate social mixing as a form of class structuring and a Band-Aid approach that treats the symptoms rather than the cause of segregation and concentrated poverty. In short, policies aimed at mixing incomes obscure the larger macro-level injustices going on.[60] Neoliberal policies offer only a "nominal form of redistribution" while ignoring "larger structural inequalities."[61] Rich and poor neighborhoods are an inevitability of income inequality, and attempts to mix incomes at the neighborhood scale are "on par with applying leeches to lower a fever."[62]

Probably everyone agrees that when it comes to socially mixed neighborhoods, there could be more nuance, sensitivity, and adjustment. There is a need to learn from decades of attempting to create mixed neighborhoods, whether via new high-end condos constructed in poor neighborhoods or subsidized housing in otherwise wealthy neighborhoods, and refine accordingly. Physical forms have been less than ideal: awkwardly placed new developments where the wealthy quickly retreat inside their homes, public space that is not accessible and badly designed, or services that never materialize.[63] Many still hold out hope that these missteps will not lead to complacency about the interrelated problems of all-wealthy and all-poor neighborhoods. As Joe Cortright urged, we should "stop demonizing the very changes that are, however slowly and awkwardly, moving us in the right direction."[64]

One lesson learned is that proximity alone does not always achieve a meaningful type of neighborhood integration. People in a diverse setting find other, nonspatial ways of maintaining what Park called "social distance." In addition, the desire for social mix varies widely depending on cultural background. For example, claims are made that Latinos seek sociability in a neighborhood that is way above the average American because "community interaction is a vital element of the Latino lifestyle," creating a need for "active and animated community gathering spaces." For Latinos, one author claimed, "the more dynamic the diversity" the better, preferring neighborhoods with the "multi" effect: multicultural, multisocial, multigenerational, multi-income, multitenure, multiuse, multihouse types, multidensity, multiarchitectural styles, multitechnology.[65]

There is new evidence that this openness to diversity is gaining wider traction. A recent Pew Community Survey found that one-half of Americans were open to living in diverse neighborhoods. In the 1970s young urban professionals openly discussed their desire to live in diverse neighborhoods and not in the suburbs,[66] an attitude that seems to have prevailed, as recurrent testimonials about the valuing of urbanism indicate. Still, diversity is rarely the basis of neighborhood definition. Without a strong counterposition for defining neighborhood, the homogeneity definition dominates.

Homogeneous Neighborhoods
in Heterogeneous Districts

A second response to the neighborhood segregation critique is to rethink the spatial parameters of neighborhood homogeneity. The argument is that what really matters is external connection, not internal similarity. How well neighborhoods connect to a larger metropolitan or even global domain should be the key concern, not their level of internal homogeneity. Pocket purity set in the midst of a wider diversity can be found at any scale. Sect-based "micro-segregation" is discernible within a single building.[67]

In fact, the argument goes, maybe some level of neighborhood homogeneity is needed as a way of maintaining order. By analogy, when the Burning Man festival grew and threatened to be unruly, organizers imposed zoning to create neighborhoods based on common interests (in marijuana, for example). These neighborhoods had already been loosely developing as "theme camps" that had formed "naturally," but it became necessary to formalize them to "facilitate harmony" between groups of people who had "developed different needs and different tolerances."[68] Potential segregation fallout is not an issue since the festival's aura safely envelops every subgroup.

Wider connection is the key to this model's success. For marginalized social groups, failure to make external linkages can be devastating. In 19th-century Washington, DC, small, intimate neighborhoods of black migrants formed around narrow alleys that were just behind the streets where Washington's middle and upper classes lived. Internally there was social support, vibrant life, and a sense of neighborhood. But the neighborhoods suffered from a lack of external connection, and disease flourished.[69] Modern equivalents, in different spatial form, are the segregated French *banlieue* and the American public housing project, places that lack social and often physical connection. In Washington's 19th-century alleys and 21st-century public housing projects, socially homogeneous, disconnected neighborhoods are marginalized.[70]

In many cases, race played (and continues to play) a definitive role in keeping homogeneous neighborhoods detached. Where race was less of a factor, small homogeneous clusters (neighborhoods) were capable of external connectedness. Scale helped, since historically the scale of social separation was small, such that if rich and poor lived in visibly distinct neighborhoods, they might be block-size, making the distances between them minimal. Even later, when industrial cities presented more zonal segregation, the segregation of wealthier people along a well-to-do street was never that far from the clustering of poor people along a more modest street, especially in smaller industrial cities.[71]

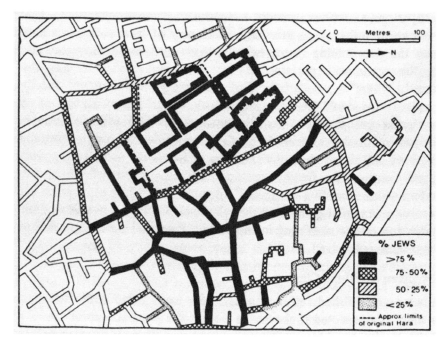

Figure 9.1 A map of ethnic population mixing in 17th-century Tunis shows the small scales at which homogeneity existed and the potential for regular interethnic contact. Source: Image after Sebag and Attal, *L'Évolution d'un Ghetto Nord-Africain*; Greenshields, "'Quarters' and Ethnicity."

A homogeneous neighborhood that exploited external relations was a neighborhood that did well. In early modern Europe, each neighborhood—parish, guild, quarter—was integrated in a larger hierarchy, ruled by collective agreement in a society where "individuals had rights and privileges not as individuals but as members of particular groups."[72] In the Islamic city, neighborhood form helped with connectedness. The relationship between self-contained *mahallehs* nested within a larger urban realm was "negotiated" by a hierarchical system of private courtyard, leading to semiprivate alley or cul-de-sac, to pedestrian network, to wider public street, to the public bazaar.[73]

The proximity of wealthy, pocket neighborhoods along fashionable main streets and around parks and squares, and adjacent poverty clusters in alleys, backyards, and other in-between spaces that were much smaller and less sanitary, was not exactly a recipe for social equality. These social patterns should not be interpreted as the good old days of social mixing, when everyone lived equally, or that divisions within the neighborhood or quarter, however small, were not impactful. One insidious mechanism for keeping neighborhood-level social mixing intact was the tradition of using "codes of deference" to maintain

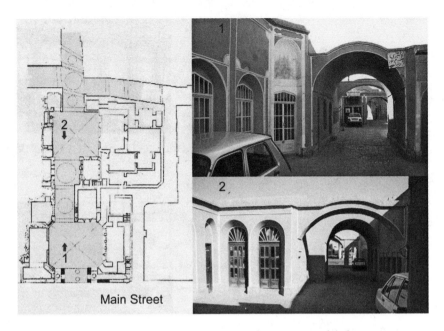

Figure 9.2 In this proposal, a neighborhood in Yazd, Iran, is remodeled to connect internalized courtyards to a main street network. Source: Nazemi, "Necessity of Urban Transformation in Introverted Historic Textures."

social separation whenever spatial segregation wasn't practical. (A stark example is the early American South, where blacks shared urban space, but the master-servant relationship kept social distances in place; the subordination of blacks "paradoxically lessened the need for a rigid system of housing segregation.")[74]

Yet theoretically the multilevel view of neighborhood as small homogeneous groups set in larger heterogeneous ones avoids the problem that diversity at a smaller scale translates to very different people being coerced to live—unnaturally—side by side. Larger district-type neighborhoods can thus be viewed as socially inclusive, even in the midst of socially homogeneous pockets. This played out in 20th-century London, where widened social networks resulted in an increasingly larger geographic concept of neighborhood in the East End. This expanded conception, in which being an East Ender suddenly had meaning where it previously had only included the street block, meant that all subcommunities had a sense of belonging to one commonly conceived place. Residents of this broadened local identity, encompassing diverse ethnicities and religions, famously stood together in solidarity to block an attempted fascist march through the neighborhood in 1936.[75]

Neighborhood planners helped conceptualize the ideal of an externally connected, socially homogeneous neighborhood. Hans Blumenfeld wrote in 1943 that "the specific task of city planning" is "coordination of many social units within one larger unit."[76] Albert Hunter noted that the ability to articulate an urban neighborhood's connection to the larger society—its external linkages— is what provides its explanation, not just its mere description. On this point, he admitted, he was merely drawing from Burgess's earlier insight: "To think of the neighborhood . . . in isolation from the rest of the city is to disregard the biggest fact about neighborhood."[77]

This was Suzanne Keller's view of things. Neighborhoods could be identified only if there was social or geographic isolation, or there was a historic or class identity—but this was not necessarily a problem. The city was composed of a mosaic of neighborhoods of different kinds and with different prospects, each with its own basket of resources and daily life encounters ranging from serene to violent, but "one has access to all the diverse pleasures of the metropolis with everything in its separate space as deemed desirable by the majority of the people."[78] Interconnected to a wider urban mosaic, this external linkage could be used to justify neighborhood homogeneity—that is, that neighborhoods function best when their inhabitants share interests, values, and institutions. There is nothing to worry about since "different neighborhoods," rich and poor, "are interdependent and essential parts of the larger whole."[79]

There is a useful ecological analogy. In "The Neighborhood Project," the naturalist David Sloan Wilson applies evolutionary science to "the cells" of a city—its neighborhoods. He explains, "An organism the size of a city must be multicellular. The cells are small groups of people with the authority to manage their own affairs." Their attachment to the neighborhood is an example of "biotope formation," the "habitat or locale to which an organism is attracted through some combination of learning, imprinting, and instinct."[80] These cells are essential to the ecosystem because "people come alive in small groups." It is where people "feel safe, known and liked as individuals."[81] Another analogy comes from computer science, where social networks are defined as "sets of vertices with more connections inside the set than outside." Successful neighborhoods might be conceived as "cohesive collections of nodes in a network," with varying "conductance scores."[82] A practical application is "Neighbor Networks," as formulated by the sociologist Rick Grannis, in which neighborhoods are defined by interaction along tertiary streets.[83]

The need to limit insularity is not only about helping those within a homogeneous neighborhood form and broaden external connections. The goal is aimed at the reverse too, helping a wider society gain entry into an otherwise insular neighborhood. Neighborhoods that are gated or enclosed might try to block this access, but they are nevertheless "infiltrated" on a daily basis, dependent on service workers, teachers, roads, police, and environmental resources that do not stop at a gate.[84]

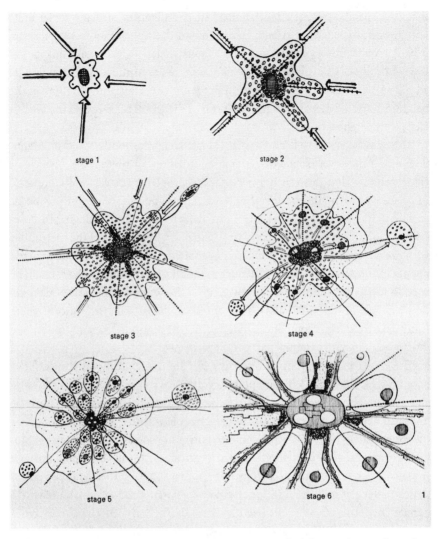

Figure 9.3 As cities evolve from a dense urban core to gradual decentralization brought about by congestion, neighborhoods become a fundamental part of the cellular dynamic of urban change.
Source: Johnson-Marshall, *Rebuilding Cities from Medieval to Modern Times.*

The modern idea that neighborhoods should be interdependent, organic parts of an organic whole is rooted in late 19th- and early 20th-century Progressive Era ideology. Wilbur C. Phillips proposed that each block of a city be given decision-making authority—a strategy that later morphed into machine politics—but it was supposed to be a system based on interdependence and cooperation rather than competition and power politics.[85] The idea offered a way of coping with urban complexity; an organic whole of interconnected groups instead of an

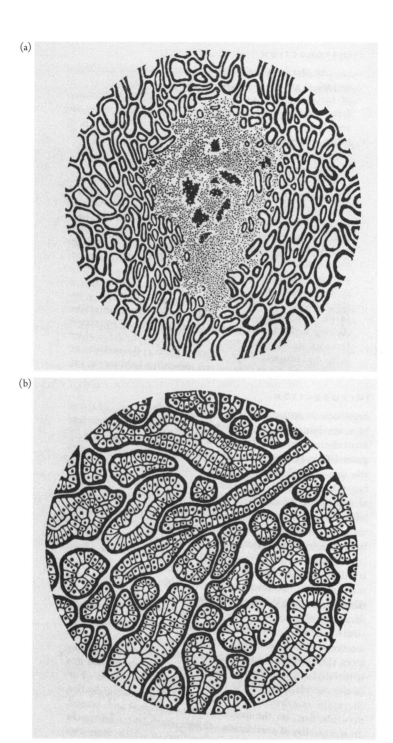

(a)

(b)

Figure 9.4a and 9.4b While neighborhoods are often thought of as the cells of a larger urban organism, the architect Eliel Saarinen used the analogy more controversially, to contrast "healthy" (b) and "diseased" (a) cells. Source: Saarinen, *The City*.

unconnected disarray of unattached individuals seemed a more realistic way of addressing the problems of the city.

Ethnically homogeneous neighborhoods have always seemed easier to endorse; income homogeneity, especially concentrated poverty, is less likely to be viewed positively. The self-selected clustering of ethnic groups is valued for its potential to strengthen social support networks, protect against discrimination, and preserve cultural heritage. Numerous studies have confirmed the vibrancy and positive affirmations of the ethnic enclave, starting with the writings of the Chicago School.[86] Louis Wirth's classic 1928 study, *The Ghetto*, painted a picture of communalism in an ethnically homogeneous neighborhood that, he believed, was as strong as modern cities could ever hope to achieve (similar to how one autobiography described the Jewish neighborhood as "a self-imposed ghetto, but a happy world").[87] In contrast to Mumford's "nightmare of the undefinable" or Warner's "weak and amorphous" urbanism, the ethnic neighborhood created place-based identity and helped residents cope with the intensity of the American metropolis. And in the midst of massive population change—ethnic immigration—the import of neighborhood was at its strongest.

Maybe ethnic homogeneity has been easier to legitimize because American ethnic neighborhoods were usually, despite their enclave status, diverse on some dimensions. By the end of the 19th century, it was not uncommon to have a minimum of two and often up to four or five ethnic groups in one urban block. Individual tenement buildings were likely to have a mix of ethnicities, and since people were unlikely to remain indoors (due to poor ventilation and crowding), interethnic contact was a necessity.[88] Even Burgess's immigrant "ghettos" were highly diverse and not socially isolated the way later black neighborhoods were. This diversity was seen as a strength. Mark Wild's *Street Meeting* provides evidence of the ethnoracially diverse neighborhoods of central Los Angeles that bloomed prior to World War II and offered constant resistance to "corporate reconstruction."[89]

To deal with the problems associated with homogeneity—segregation, isolation, exclusion—sociologists and planners proposed nested, self-governing "subcommunities," each corresponding to higher and higher levels of service provision.[90] In 2014 the Urban Institute made an adjustment to the terminology, proposing that neighborhoods themselves should be defined as districts composed of smaller homogeneous blocks clustering together. They termed their scheme "the mosaic district." The district-neighborhood would share larger facilities like parks, schools, and commercial streets, assets that would act as social seams to encourage important, though weaker, social ties. Such ties would not be the same as those that could occur among proximal neighbors at the subneighborhood scale, where residents would be bonded by income, ethnicity, or race.[91]

This has been proposed before. In Britain in the early 1950s, neighborhood unit proponents were arguing for "small one-class neighborhoods" of similar housing type that would usefully "accentuate their common problems and interests at the level of town affairs," where "one's personal social attitudes are not deeply involved."[92] The concept was later implemented in the British new town of Northampton, following "extensive discussions" with Peter Willmott, a British sociologist. Each enclave had "dwellings of a similar standard and more or less similar sorts of people to encourage mixing."[93] A version of this idea was also described in Julia Abrahamson's 1959 *A Neighborhood Finds Itself*. Neighborhoods were composed of subareas consisting of a group of blocks with identical housing types, such as three-story apartment buildings. The long list of activities these subareas were able to accomplish (e.g., lot cleanup, litter removal, playground enhancement, lighting strategies) was believed to foster identity, pride, and action.[94]

The modernist translation of homogeneous clusters set in heterogeneous districts seemed unsuccessful in terms of interconnection. In a 1943 article in *Architectural Forum* entitled "Planning with You," a variety of housing types were represented, each set within their own little subneighborhood context, but there was no obvious connection between them other than as-the-crow-flies proximity. As if to reinforce this separateness, the subneighborhood of the apartment building had its own cafeteria, nursery, and café. Open space and "nature" were used as a way of keeping small clusters of homogeneous groups within the neighborhood comfortably apart. The author explained that neighborhoods that have both single-family houses and apartments would be less likely to "clash" if the town regulations required "a minimum amount of ground space for each family," resulting in apartment buildings "set in miniature parks." And in typical modernist superblock fashion, the siting of building types was predicated on taking advantage of breezes, sunlight, and views, which trumped (and undermined) the creation of public life in the street. Such patterns, using similar rationales, were repeated in new towns like Columbia, Maryland, and Reston, Virginia.[95]

Thus it is not always clear what level of homogeneity within a heterogeneous district absolves the district of the segregation problem—or simply reinforces it. When late 19th-century cities "ballooned" and distinct homogeneous social groupings formed, they were at first seen as interdependent, together constituting a unified civic realm. But by the mid-1920s neighborhoods were no longer seen as complementary; they were instead translated as examples of segregation and conflict.[96]

The 20th century saw the prospect of homogeneous neighborhoods connected to wider realms broken down by an inability to access wider networks, even if those neighborhoods were highly proximal. This may be changing. Research shows that locating immigrant neighborhoods in places that are not remote but are near the city center does sometimes translate to "successful economic integration into the host society."[97] And, it may be that some aspects of the "new economy," especially those that promote "neighborhood globalization," are successfully integrating homogeneous neighborhoods into a wider transglobal world.[98]

Notes

1. On the homogeneity definition, even from within planning, see Park and Rogers, "Neighborhood Planning Theory, Guidelines, and Research"; Grigsby et al., "Residential Neighborhoods and Submarkets," 20; Garrioch and Peel, "Introduction," 672. See also Sennett, *The Fall of Public Man.*
2. Quoted in Chapman, "Review of *The Cutteslowe Walls* by Peter Collison," 237.
3. Ward, "Environs and Neighbours in the 'Two Nations,'" 135, 162.
4. Scherzer, *The Unbounded Community.*
5. Woods, "The Neighborhood in Social Reconstruction," 579; Conn, Steven. Americans Against the City: Anti-Urbanism in the Twentieth Century. Oxford: Oxford University Press, 2014.
6. Meyer, *As Long as They Don't Move Next Door.* See also Philpott, *The Slum and the Ghetto.*
7. Zorbaugh, *Gold Coast and the Slum,* 232; Garb, "Drawing the 'Color Line.'"
8. For example, Tate, *Research on Schools, Neighborhoods, and Communities.*
9. U.S. Department of Commerce, Bureau of the Census, "Geographic Terms and Concepts." For a current tract definition see "Defining Neighborhood," 429; Johnston et al., *Dictionary of Human Geography,* 540.
10. Park et al., *The City,* 40.
11. Ibid., 78–79.
12. Hawkes, "Spatial Patterning of Urban Population Characteristics," 1234.
13. McKenzie, "The Neighborhood II," 344, 348.
14. McKenzie, "The Neighborhood III," 486; McKenzie, "The Neighborhood no. 5" 610.
15. McKenzie, "The Neighborhood: Concluded," 785, 799.
16. Perry, "The Tangible Aspects of Community Organization," 563.
17. For more on the historical conflict and cooperation between adjoining neighborhoods, see Keating, "Chicagoland."
18. Allaire, "Neighborhood Boundaries," 15, 16.
19. Davidson County, Tennessee, "Planning Units in the Nashville Metropolitan Area," 1959, cited in Allaire, "Neighborhood Boundaries," 20.
20. Allaire, "Neighborhood Boundaries," 15, 16.
21. Wehrly, "Activities and Comment," 34; The author quotes S. L. G. Beaufoy in the *Journal of the Royal Institute of British Architects,* July 1948.
22. Galster and Hesser, "The Social Neighborhood," 236.
23. Boger, "The Meaning of Neighborhood in the Modern City," 236.
24. Nightingale, "The Transnational Contexts of Early Twentieth-Century American Urban Segregation." See also Nightingale, *Segregation.*
25. Gregg and Himber, *From Building to Neighborhood,* 7, 14.
26. Schill and Wachter, "The Spatial Bias of Federal Housing Law and Policy."
27. A point made by Ken Jackson in *Crabgrass Frontier.*
28. Weiss, *The Rise of the Community Builders.*
29. Broden et al., "Neighborhood Identification," 8, 21.
30. Madanipour, "How Relevant Is 'Planning by Neighbourhoods' Today?"; Smailes, *The Geography of Towns,* 128.
31. Hove, *Networking Neighborhoods.*
32. McGreevy, *Parish Boundaries.* See also the review by Kelly, "*Parish Boundaries.*" On the migration of American Jews (but not Catholics) out of urban neighborhoods, see Gamm, *Urban Exodus.*

33. Chauncey, *Gay New York.*

34. Kullberg et al., "Does the Perceived Neighborhood Reputation Contribute to Neighborhood Differences in Social Trust and Residential Wellbeing?"

35. Pietila, *Not in My Neighborhood*; Hunter, "The Urban Neighborhood."

36. Reardon and Bischoff, "Growth in the Residential Segregation of Families by Income." See also Reardon et al., "Income Inequality and Income Segregation."

37. Bishop, *The Big Sort.*

38. Fry and Taylor, "The Rise of Residential Segregation by Income."

39. Ibid.

40. Hulchanski, "The Three Cities within Toronto."

41. Tach et al., "Income Mixing across Scales."

42. For example, the stages found in Perlman, "Neighbourhood Organisation," 114.

43. Monkkonen and Zhang, "Socioeconomic Segregation in Hong Kong."

44. "Cairo's Metropolitan Landscape."

45. The dissimilarity indices for 318 U.S. cities using 2000 data can be found at www.censusscope. org. Indices for 100 cities using the 2005–9 American Community Survey can be found at http://www.psc.isr.umich.edu/dis/census/segregation.html.

46. Logan and Zhang. "Global Neighborhoods."

47. Fry and Taylor, "The Rise of Residential Segregation by Income"; Vigdor and Glaeser, "The End of the Segregated Century."

48. Hwang and Sampson, "Divergent Pathways of Gentrification."

49. Logan and Zhang, "Global Neighborhoods," 1070.

50. Poulsen et al., "Using Local Statistics and Neighbourhood Classifications to Portray Ethnic Residential Segregation." See also Philpott, *The Slum and the Ghetto.*

51. Its formal expression is $A = [N (N - 1)] / [\Sigma i\, n_i\, (n_i - 1)]$, where A is the diversity index, N is the total number of individuals (or housing units or households) for all categories, and n_i is the number of individuals (or other characteristic) in the ith category. I used spatially interpolated census tract data obtained from GeoLytics for the years 1970 and 2010 to find diverse neighborhoods. Because tract boundaries as well as tract identifying numbers can change between decades, normalization is required in order to compare tract data over time. The Geolytics Neighborhood Change Database accomplishes this normalization.

52. Mumford, "The Neighborhood and the Neighborhood Unit," 267, 269.

53. Hallman, "Citizens and Professionals Reconsider the Neighborhood," 121.

54. National Federation of Settlements, "A Letter from Robert A. Woods," 1.

55. Simkhovitch, *Neighborhood*, 100, 119.

56. See, for example, Aronovici, *Community Building*, 245.

57. American Public Health Association, *Planning the Neighborhood*, 2, 67.

58. Organizations like PolicyLink (http://www.policylink.org/) and and the Institute for Community Economics keep track of such policies and try to monitor their effects.

59. Sampson, "Notes on Neighborhood Inequality and Urban Design."

60. See for example Bond et al., "Mixed Messages about Mixed Tenures"; Bridge et al., *Mixed Communities.*

61. Conte and Li, "Neoliberal Urban Revitalization in Chicago."

62. Cheshire, "Resurgent Cities, Urban Myths, and Policy Hubris," 1241.

63. These design limitations were clear in this study: Davidson "Love Thy Neighbour?" See also Chaskin and Joseph, *Integrating the Inner City.*

64. Cortright, "Truthiness in Gentrification Reporting."

65. Cisneros and Rosales, *Casa y Comunidad*, 90, 95.

66. Parkman Center for Urban Affairs, *Young Professionals and City Neighborhoods.*

67. Flint et al., "Between Friends and Strangers."

68. DuBois, "Managing Diversity," cited in Smith et al., "Neighborhood Formation in Semi-Urban Settlements," 11.

69. Borchert, "Urban Neighborhood and Community"; Borchert, *Alley Life in Washington.*

70. Picone and Schilleci, "A Mosaic of Suburbs," 356, 363.

71. Mills and Wheeler, *Historic Town Plans of Lincoln*, 20.

72. Garrioch and Peel, "Introduction,'"" 668.

73. Kheirabadi, *Iranian Cities.*

74. Massey and Denton, *American Apartheid*, 40–41. See also Hanchett, *Sorting Out the New South City*.

75. Lammers, "The Birth of the East Ender."

76. Blumenfeld, "Form and Function in Urban Communities," 13.

77. Hunter, "The Urban Neighborhood"; Cottrell et al., *Ernest W. Burgess on Community, Family, and Delinquency*, 42.

78. Teaford, "Jane Jacobs and the Cosmopolitan Metropolis," 886.

79. Garrioch and Peel, "Introduction," 668.

80. Sommer, "Man's Proximate Environment," 61, 62. On proxemics see Hall, *The Hidden Dimension*.

81. Wilson, *The Neighborhood Project*, 384, 386.

82. Gleich and Seshadhri, "Neighborhoods Are Good Communities," 1.

83. Made possible because of the Census Bureau's Feature Classification Code; see Grannis, *From the Ground Up*.

84. For example, in Landman, "Gated Communities in South Africa."

85. Mooney-Melvin, *The Organic City*.

86. Dunn, "Rethinking Ethnic Concentration." On the benefits of ethnic diversity, see Wild, *Street Meeting*; Vervoort et al., "The Ethnic Composition of the Neighbourhood and Ethnic Minorities' Social Contacts."

87. Wirth, *The Ghetto*; Kops, *The World Is a Wedding*, 15.

88. Barrett, "Unity and Fragmentation"; Conzen, "Immigrants, Immigrant Neighborhoods, and Ethnic Identity."

89. Von Hoffman, *Local Attachments*, 4, 5.

90. Suttles, "Community Design,"

91. Tach et al., "Income Mixing across Scales."

92. Ibid.; Campleman, "Some Sociological Aspects of Mixed-Class Neighbourhood Planning," 199.

93. Patricios, "The Neighborhood Concept," 79.

94. Abrahamson, *A Neighborhood Finds Itself*.

95. "Planning with You," 79; "Mixed Neighborhood of Rental Housing," 87.

96. Mooney-Melvin, "Changing Contexts," 358.

97. Vaughan, "The Spatial Syntax of Urban Segregation," 235, 249; See also Nasser, "Southall's Kaleido-scape."

98. Laguerre, *Global Neighborhoods*.

10

Conclusion

This book began by asking whether the neighborhood could be reconstituted in a way that would make it more than a label and more than a social segregator, but at the same time not incompatible with 21st-century realities. After a century of trying to come to terms with a vastly changed definition and understanding of the neighborhood, can some version of the neighborhood as traditionally and historically understood be reinstated as real and meaningful? For those living in the undefined expanse of contemporary urbanism—which characterizes most of American cities—can the neighborhood come to be more than a shaded area on a map, more than a segregated housing tract, and more than a valentine?

The answer is yes, although such neighborhoods will not form spontaneously. The socially inclusive, well-serviced, self-governed, and noninsular 21st-century version of the historical neighborhood will require backing. But policies and actions that work toward the creation of neighborhoods that are more than lines on a map and more than social sequestering will have significant payoff: lessening displacement by meeting the demand for diverse neighborhoods, fostering a sense of ownership and caring that does not rest on exclusion, cultivating social and economic connection by situating connectivity in daily experience, and substituting place for homogeneity as the basis of neighborhood definition.

While it is important not to sentimentalize the past, historically neighborhoods satisfied many of these goals. They were well defined, often socially diverse, and a source of identity, economic life, social connection, and political power, even in societies dominated by authoritarianism, hierarchy, and inequality. As modern cities lost this localized sense of daily life, some urban dwellers were unaffected. But others, especially many urban planners and social scientists, saw the loss as a problem, and they tried to recover it. The debates that ensued showed that neighborhood planners often overstepped the bounds of what neighborhoods could do, while critics overstepped their repudiation of proposals.

With the positioning of neighborhood as valentine or social segregator, we entered the 21st century pressed to define what the neighborhood in any traditional sense of the term could be in the modern world. The ideal of neighborhood became wrapped up in issues of control, social determinism, segregation, exclusion, and injustice, on the one hand, but also identity, group protection, sense of community, empowerment, and the meeting of daily life needs on the other. Failure to resolve intrinsic tensions made the definition of neighborhood ambiguous. Over the course of the 20th century and into the 21st, the definition of neighborhood widened to be anything and everything, and this made it not only less meaningful but value-neutral: an exclusionary gated community had just as much claim to being a neighborhood as anything else.

The traditional understanding of neighborhood as the essential infrastructure of daily life was thus beaten down by a century's worth of negation—on the one hand, cavalierly equating neighborhood with any clump of housing, but on the other, trivializing the attempt to get the neighborhood back and render it in physical form. In an American context, with its vast stretches of single-use suburban housing tracts, neighborhoods might consist *only* of residences. (As one American scholar argued, a neighborhood with no services and an indeterminate location is "still a neighborhood.")[1] But such a definition, it should be recognized, is a historical anomaly.

Because of the seeming incongruity between a localized neighborhood existence and modern expectations and freedoms, normative theories about neighborhood were problematized. If neighborhoods were thought to need local control, local control could just as easily be seen as correlating with exclusion or a lessening of power. If neighborhoods were aimed at diversity, deliberate attempts to create diversity could be thwarted by homogeneity-seeking rules or by a general attitude that the pursuit of diverse neighborhoods was irrational. Neighborhoods might be planned so that they were better defined and perceived, but stronger neighborhood identity could also correlate with exclusion, and neighborhood form could be seen as a vehicle for capitalist exploitation, gentrification, and displacement. Neighborhoods might be the basis of compact urban form and therefore sustainability, but planned neighborhoods could also be seen as a rural concept realized only in tabula rasa form, in which case localized functionality would be illusory.

Some of these negative appropriations were justified. Neighborhood plans were often fraught with prejudices. One of the first mistakes of planners was believing that neighborhood constituency was restricted to families with children—as if childless couples, singles, or retired folks were not really the neighborhood type. But rather than reworking it, finding a more just and appropriate definition and refining it based on changing demographics and new urban challenges—while remaining committed to what the construct of the neighborhood traditionally was—critics of neighborhood plans seemed more interested in making the neighborhood obscure and irrelevant. Those still interested—planners with their physical plans and sociologists with their social interpretations—ceased to have a meaningful dialogue, and the dueling themes of "neighborhood prescribed" and "neighborhood rejected" competed for play over the course of the 20th century.

The 20th-century attempt to consciously plan the neighborhood back into existence was a reaction to the sense that the neighborhood had been lost to technological, economic, and social forces that undermined its relevance. Connectivity and heterogeneity pulled in opposite directions like never before, and the localized neighborhood became a means of social sorting rather than a means of congealing. Many argued that the rules of the game had become too different to reconstitute the neighborhood: there was no technological require-ment to live close, and institutions (churches, clubs) were no longer function-ing as the neighborhood-based, class cross-cutting social integrators they once were. It would also be difficult to reinstate the traditional neighborhood without recovering local networks of interdependence, especially economically based ones, which had been the basis of neighborhood-scale daily life for millennia.

But for proponents of the traditional understanding of neighborhood, these issues could be addressed not through anachronistic ideas that sentimentalized neighborhood life but instead by simply working toward a more explicit sense of what and where the neighborhood was. Over time, it was believed, this sense of neighborhood could be leveraged to gradually engender something approach-ing the historical experience of neighborhood—different from the localized networks of interdependence that were once essential, but no less capable of rendering urban life more *locally* meaningful. An explicit understanding of neigh-borhood would help to make local networks in some form work, to make access work, to make the sharing of services work, to make diversity work, to make DIY tactics work, to make local control work, to make "buying local" work, to make caring about the public realm work, to make collective visioning work. If any of these tasks were too far removed from the places that were daily experienced— the neighborhood—their effectuation would be harder.

A sense of neighborhood required *physical* definition. Before the 1960s, neigh-borhoods were routinely defined on the basis of their physicality, delineated by "physiographic space" like roads and topography, or on the basis of service areas that related population to service needs. But because these approaches were later seen as ignoring "the existence of close-knit social processes" or too preoccupied with "resource allocation issues," the physiographic and service area approaches were thrown over in favor of socially derived neighborhood definition based on resident surveys, "mental maps" and personal understanding.[2]

The social understanding of neighborhood is not something to ignore. Neighborhoods do intersect with multiple social realms, sometimes informal and sometimes having to do with authority and control, such as a block watch, a police precinct, a school district, a homeowner association, a church parish. But here again the physical neighborhood is needed: to pull these varied interests together and to open up the possibility of a place-based identity that can foster connection based on a diversity of social experience and not, solely, social sameness. Without neighborhood framing, social entities might stay disconnected and misaligned. In an earlier planning era, planners tried to foster these connections and alignments via the neighborhood unit, defining it as "an attempt to group the total components—social, physical, economic, visual—which overlay an area into a single, identifiable unit."[3] In the 21st century these components can no longer be so neatly corralled, but the instinct to promote connection by way of a physically defined neighborhood might not be so out of line.

There is still mistrust of physically defined neighborhoods because of the potential for misuse through control, determinism, segregation. And yet it may be the demise of neighborhood as an articulated, physical ideal that has led to confusion and resentment. Critics of social mixing policy are right to argue that governments have no real idea what they're after—in terms of targeted percentages and types of social mixing—in order to bring about an "urban renaissance."[4] But maybe it's a problem of neighborhood definition and the lack of a more conceptually clear idea about what neighborhoods are supposed to be.

After a century of grappling, it is now possible, this book concludes, to propose a resolution of debates and move forward, hopefully making neighborhood relevant once again for those who seek it. The resolution constitutes a modern interpretation of the historical neighborhood—neighborhoods that are identifiable and serviced but also diverse and connected, and with the added quality of self-determination. A traditional understanding of neighborhood in 21st-century terms—recapping the proposed resolutions of previous debates— translates to strong centers (rather than strong boundaries) in the form of centripetal public spaces and streets; internal and external connectivity that helps build a strong sense of neighborhood (which in turn facilitates localized control); support from both a plan and a process (an expression of physical ideals in tandem with a process for engagement); self-determination strengthened by neighborhood identity (in turn fostered by physical design); the promotion of social connection via the neighborhood's functionality; support and enabling of social diversity in multiple ways; and mechanisms for governance (like participatory budgeting and the consolidation of neighborhood-scale controls and expenditure).

These are the debate outcomes that offer a way of conceiving how a traditional, historical understanding of the neighborhood is possible in 21st-century terms.

Everyday Neighborhoods

The historical neighborhood and its decline, what emerged in response, and the resolution of the ensuing debates all factor into a proposal for the "everyday neighborhood"—a place-based, traditional conception of neighborhood that is not defined by insularity or exclusion and that at the same time strives for more standing than as a geographic adjective. For even though the literature on neighborhood is voluminous, there is room for normative thinking about what a neighborhood should be, how physical and social ideals might be combined, how historical experience can be learned from and applied, and how a century of debate can foster neighborhoods capable of providing an essential context for daily life.

The previous century's neighborhood unit debates inspired a spirited dialogue and a search for meaning and clarity, but the debates were left hanging, leaving no consistency or professional nomenclature as to what a neighborhood is or what it should be. What follows is a proposal to make manifest an unambiguous conception of neighborhood. The "everyday neighborhood" is what a neighborhood could be, if based on a traditional understanding that is at the same time cognizant of 21st-century constraints and demands. It leverages physical form to enable human connection, exchange, and sense of belonging, which in turn provides the capacity to act collectively. Toward this goal, an everyday neighborhood has the following eight qualities:

1. It has a name.
2. Residents know where it is, what it is, and whether they belong to it.
3. It has at least one place that serves as its center.
4. It has a generally agreed-upon spatial extent.
5. It has everyday facilities and services, although it is not self-contained.
6. It has internal and external connectivity.
7. It has social diversity within it, or it is open to its enabling.
8. It has a means of representation, a means by which residents can be involved in its affairs, and an ability to speak with a collective voice.

These are the essentials of an everyday neighborhood, derived from the historical record on neighborhoods, the endurance of certain characteristics, and the lessons learned from the planning debates that took place throughout the 20th century. It is a normative definition, and as such its goal is not to maximize the range of interpretations; its goal is to articulate a clear position and advance an argument. The existence of multiple conceptions of neighborhood—individualized, cognitive, digital, global—the allure of a looser, contested neighborhood

definition, and the complacency that neighborhoods are little more than valentines are countered with an aspirational view that neighborhoods could be
something more.

The proposal avoids Perry's mistake of being overly diagrammatic. An everyday neighborhood seeks a quality environment, but it can exist in many forms,
shapes, densities, and spatial configurations. To the degree that it has other hall-
marks of place quality—enclosure, bike lanes, traffic calming, transit access, and
the like—all the better, but these are separate endeavors with their own advocates and committed constituencies. If there is economic interdependence, that
is a special plus. It might even be a place where social expression is especially
accepted and valued. But these are separate considerations. In fact the inability
to conceive of alternative neighborhood forms that satisfy the above eight conditions has meant that neighborhood has been pigeonholed into a narrow conception (the much maligned "neighborhood unit") that undermines its viability.
The confusion caused by elevating specific forms over adherence to a set of core
principles has been profoundly damaging.

An everyday neighborhood provides a framework for other urban interventions. This sets it apart from most urban design proposals. For example, in 1979,
when Allan Jacobs and Donald Appleyard proposed an "urban design manifesto"
composed of five physical qualities essential to urban life, neighborhood was but
one quality on the list. They proposed livable streets and neighborhoods, minimum density and intensity of land use, the proximal integration of activities,
buildings that provide spatial definition, and building-type diversity. For everyday neighborhoods, things like livable streets, density levels, and mixed use
depend on neighborhood definition and control; they are not listed alongside it
as equal players. In other words, the emphasis is not on the component parts—
streets, coding, park design—but the contextualizing of those parts within a
neighborhood framework, without which engagement, acceptance of diversity,
and collective voice would be difficult.

Naming a neighborhood raises awareness and fosters a sense of identity and
ownership. No one is likely to rally around a census tract number or a housing
submarket or a "pedestrian shed" to care about a local place and take ownership. Without this framing, "improvement" or "placemaking" strategies appear
unidimensional and abstract, leading to individualized outcomes that, if detrimental to the neighborhood as a whole, have no effective political resistance (or
resistance is written off as a case of NIMBYism). Revitalization with the label
"neighborhood" attached to it can be simply about increasing property value,
with no recognition of how daily life is affected. But couching investments in
the context of neighborhoods as places with particular identities—everyday
neighborhoods—guards against these abstractions and their potential for perverse effects.

An everyday neighborhood also resolves the long-standing confusion that swirls around the social dimension of neighborhood. Above all, it does not rely on social relationships for its meaning and relevance in residents' lives. There is a sense of belonging to the neighborhood, but there are no friendship or even familiarity prerequisites. There is no implicit or assumed longing for a time when, absent technology-enabled communication, people relied on the neighborhood for associational life. On the other hand, if the neighborhood does emerge as socially meaningful for some residents, that is a bonus.

An everyday neighborhood focuses on the day-to-day practicality of neighborhood existence, prioritizing service over social functionality. These daily functions build opportunity for social connection, which is helpful but not absolute. More important is a sense of neighborhood as an agent for inspiring various forms of exchange.

Rather than obsessing over social connection or the engineering of relationships, an everyday neighborhood focuses on ensuring that form does not undermine human connection and instead makes it possible. The social bond that the neighborhood works toward is shared affection for space, not shared affection for other residents. It is a limited social goal, offering only a setting for familiar social encounters. Over time this is likely to build collective awareness.

An everyday neighborhood accepts social and land use diversity as positives. In neighborhoods where diversity is at the low end, residents do not block opportunities to advance it—the neighborhood's sense of identity and inclusive engagement provides a way for diversity to be contextualized as a net positive. There are no preset levels of diversity prescribed, but this does not mean that diversity can be anything. Open-ended definitions have been tried, for example where diversity is equated with the mixing of rural and urban qualities, but an "abundance of variety" in and of itself is unlikely to satisfy what an everyday neighborhood is meant to achieve: a better quality of everyday life.[5]

Difference is at the core of neighborhood, whether it characterizes a degree of internal social likeness or defines how one neighborhood is different from another. The diversity objective of the everyday neighborhood requires a constant search for balance, a middle ground between a neighborhood of strangers and a neighborhood of friends. Physical definition is essential to finding this balance. (It is worth noting that those who disdain proactive social mixing because of the associated displacement it provokes often find themselves advocating for just this kind of physical, identity-building focus.)[6] If the balance is found by having homogeneous groupings at the *sub*neighborhood level—small clusters of homogeneity set within larger, heterogeneous neighborhoods—that is one approach.

The diversity goal is critical because the inability to deal with social difference at a localized level—at the scale of a neighborhood—may be the single most significant problem facing Western cities. For American cities, it is the root cause of intractable urban problems from sprawl to inner-city disinvestment, from failing schools to environmental degradation. Everyday neighborhoods help counteract social sorting and thereby destabilize the complacent view that rich and poor neighborhoods are inevitable. The diversity goal is driven by the perversity of its opposite: concentrations of wealth that hoard resources and concentrations of poverty that aggregate disadvantage. Neighborhoods are implicated in this problem because income inequality translates to spatial segregation via the housing market. Unless actively countered, segregation self-perpetuates because, as familiarity with heterogeneity erodes, so too does support for policies that would counteract it.

Diversity is not for the purpose of paternalistic ideas about socialization, positive role models, or the supposed benefits of intergroup social contact. The calculus is more straightforward: resident income and wealth are positively correlated with neighborhood investment. Since resources—services and facilities, a quality public realm—are finite, wealth commands access to resources that the market, or political influence, obligingly follows. Disinvestment, on the other hand, is correlated with population loss (leading to closed schools and businesses), a deteriorating building stock, foreclosures, and failing schools. The only practical solution from a broader societal perspective—and in a Western, capitalist democracy—is to spread the wealth around and try to build more economically diverse neighborhoods.

An everyday neighborhood counters threats of decline with localized "durable investments" that work to increase neighborhood functionality.[7] Neighborhood-scale investment pushes back against the dominance of big capital, production building, and the consolidation of power and resources—a consolidation that has always worked against local control. A supportive neighborhood context and constituency enables small developers and plot-by-plot retrofitters, which has the added benefit of supporting the diversity goal.

Everyday neighborhoods provide a material counternarrative to the normalization of socially segregated neighborhoods, which are a historical anomaly. Neighborhood scholarship has been complicit in reinforcing the social segregation narrative, always focused on social similarity and its inverse, social difference, how one group bands together or differs from another, the processes of walling off and then filtering out, the strategies of exclusion and the fighting for inclusion, the degree to which difference is contained within, and the whole process of delineation and boundedness that forms the basis of homogeneity and difference. All of these are important processes to understand, but they are not the only reality. In fact everyday neighborhoods do not fit within the conventional metrics. They apply instead to diverse, not homogeneous, social groupings, and in this they fill the vacuum created by an inability—or unwillingness—to define and physicalize the socially diverse neighborhood.

An everyday neighborhood has an identity, but it is not insular; it seeks integration within the wider urban context, and this contributes to a healthy neighborhood ecosystem. Its external connectedness to a wider region is likely improved, somewhat paradoxically, by a stronger sense of internal identity. An everyday neighborhood provides the identity and empowerment necessary to capitalize on broader opportunities.

There is an intrinsic tension between social heterogeneity and social connection that an everyday neighborhood tries to overcome. It does this by providing a mediating public realm, a localized identity, and a chance to self-govern. Neighborhoods with a strong physical definition, which an everyday neighborhood exemplifies, have the potential to integrate diverse constituencies. Social homogeneity is regularly reinforced through physical means—gates, walls, singularity of use, and singularity of building type—but so is social diversity. A strong sense of a neighborhood's physical presence is necessary especially if local organizations are confined to single purposes, such as social services, affordable housing, small business. Having a clear neighborhood identity and definition helps broaden and consolidate a coalition of otherwise disconnected, though neighborhood-based, interests.

Everyday neighborhoods do not have a predetermined form, but the diversity principle does imply certain physical parameters. First, there needs to be a range of housing types and corresponding price points. To de-emphasize social difference, these housing types should be compatible, but this does not translate to sameness. In diverse neighborhoods—from the traditional Islamic neighborhood to the early 20th-century garden suburb—the principle is the same: a strong sense of neighborhood engenders a physical neighborhood coherence that masks the underlying diversity of housing sizes and thus levels of income.

Second, the physical form of an everyday neighborhood needs to support access (to services and facilities) via the walking or wheeled human body, since the requirement for a technological apparatus—a car—is an exclusionary tactic. Further, an everyday neighborhood prioritizes access for those for whom "accessibility" and "getting around" are especially important concerns: the elderly, the disabled, low-income populations, children. Such populations may not have access to Webber's "non-place urban realms" since their sense of distance is not elastic. For these locally oriented residents, the ability of neighborhoods to provide services is not trivial. As an added benefit, service functionality has the potential to make places, by being "locationally efficient," more affordable.[8]

Third, the goal that the everyday neighborhood makes social connection effortless translates to certain principles about neighborhood shape and form. The idea is to make social encounter easy, either when moving through space or when accessing points within space (e.g., services and facilities). The former objective translates to small blocks, narrower streets, and good street networks. The latter translates to proximity and the ability to work a neighborhood's "points" into daily routines (for shopping, education, jobs). Making these connections pleasing involves a second tier of interventions: quality public space, greening, complete streets, and the like. This is how social connection happens through the course of daily routine, through provision of the "mechanisms that permit people to accomplish things with greater effectiveness and pleasure."[9]

People have varying tolerances for this conscious connectivity. (Apparently in the U.S. it's about one-half of the population.)[10] A problem that ensues is that people resist the trade-offs necessary. It should be the case that if greater connectivity to people and resources is something not well tolerated, then access to resources will have to be surrendered. But some Americans try to have it both ways. (An advertisement for a development in Arizona sums up the conflicted desire perfectly: "Far from the crowds yet close to convenience.")[11] An everyday neighborhood is not about "crowds," but it does accept the correct translation between connectivity and convenience. The previous century of building was devoted to false expectations about escape and access, aided by highways, subsidies, and technology; the everyday neighborhood provides tangible benefits to overcome that contradiction.

One of these benefits is walkable access. Connectivity or access means a mix of uses, which delivers environmental advantages; close services means walkable cities, which in turn means less car travel and lower emissions, more opportunities for energy efficiencies, and lower land consumption and habitat loss. But there is also a social advantage, as use mix has an intimate, mutually reinforcing relationship to social diversity. Attempts to mix services without social diversity translate to "lifestyle centers" and other inauthentic brands of neighborhood that are increasingly difficult to push on a skeptical public.

A qualitatively better public realm—streets, sidewalks, parks, squares—helps social mix succeed because a physical environment in which people are satisfied will lessen the tendency to focus on social difference as something problematic. Public spaces become a point of pride and therefore—at least symbolically if not behaviorally—social connectors. Place-consciousness, facilitated by a sense of neighborhood, is meant to bind diversity, not isolate and exclude. If it is experienced as something more than individually conceived "place utility" and one's own "action space," that might be possible.

It is important to recognize how different this conceptualization of neighborhood is—the idea that diversity and the services it requires are facilitated by neighborhood delineation. Most often, neighborhoods have been defined in the reverse way, where social homogeneity defines neighborhoods for the purpose of service provision—that is, the ability to identify service areas based on common social characteristics. As previously argued, the demarcation of neighborhood has almost always involved a search for bounded areas of social homogeneity.[12]

An everyday neighborhood leverages its diversity to help it become identifiable and distinct. The uniqueness of neighborhood is both physical and social, the latter including behaviors: ways of gathering, ways of interacting, ways of conducting daily life. While this uniqueness makes it resistant to corporate branding, the diverse internal elements need an "interpretive frame" through which they can contribute to neighborhood identity.[13] That frame is an identifiable neighborhood, with a name, focal point, and spatial extent oriented around one or more centers. Set in that context, the physical parts of the human habitat—from small elements like trash cans (what Harvey Molotch calls "urban instrumentation") to large elements like parks and housing complexes—find relevance and value.[14]

Without neighborhood framing, urban parts are merely unanchored objects floating in space, their interrelation and contribution to a neighborhood's sense of purpose and uniqueness left untapped. For those who romanticize "nonplanning," neighborhood framing is a way to appreciate the "fragmented, random, incongruent" pieces of urbanism without giving in to the anarchy and hopelessness nonplanning represents.[15] Urban complexity—appreciated by Mumford as "social theater," by Jacobs as "street ballet," and by Whyte as the "urban stage"—is better valued and purposed within the conceptualizing framework of a neighborhood. This might also extend to the world of "big data," where atomized humans and their actions do not necessarily join to create collective awareness. Neighborhood consciousness is needed to stitch together small decisions and connect the small acts of participation into something larger.

A common theme of the neighborhood ideal is that its primary facilities, like schools, serve more than one function. An everyday neighborhood supports multifunctionality because multiuse is neighborhood-supporting, broadening the reach of a single building or place. Examples are multifunctional schools, multifunctional parks and libraries (that service the recreational and library needs of schools), senior centers connected to elementary schools or nursery schools, and school auditoriums functioning as community theaters. The relationship is reciprocal: neighborhood consciousness makes mixed services possible, and mixed services elevate neighborhood consciousness.

Neighborhood identity facilitates collective voice and the ability of residents to engage meaningfully. Identity, in turn, is strengthened by a sense of being "in" or "out" of a particular place, implying boundaries. This is a dilemma, as identity and boundedness may create problems for individuality, while potentially bolstering exclusion. The subordination of individual flexibility for the sake of collective need seems as intractable as the idea of excluding someone from neighborhood membership. The solution is to rely on the centripetal force of neighborhood centers—public spaces and commercial streets—where neighborhood membership is a matter of being within the spatial extent of a neighborhood-defining resource.

Under the swelling pressure of market demand, the forces of disruption and displacement will be a constant threat to the everyday neighborhood. Supply will not meet demand, and the very diversity and identity that define it will strain to stay in place. There are government planning strategies available to overcome this fallout, including both sticks (inclusionary zoning) and carrots (density bonuses), but these are external and top-down. The solution is to combine whatever government strategies are available and effective with a more homegrown effort. Self-preservation needs to be woven into the neighborhood's own agenda, the formulation of which requires a strong identity, a sense of empowerment, and the valuing of diversity as a collective enterprise. This building up and leveraging of neighborhood identity needs to be a conscious urban planning strategy.

But what is missing are the tools, language, methods, and experience to accomplish this. What is needed are neighborhood-building strategies that are incremental, resident controlled, and, if required, planner enabled. Mostly the experience with "building" neighborhoods has been the tabula rasa variety. Proponents of the neighborhood unit never learned the art of creating neighborhoods from existing fabric; instead their vision started with complete land clearance: understandable if complete control is the goal. (The costs of acquiring parcels naturally meant that the neighborhood unit on unencumbered and cheaper areas at the periphery held the most promise for quick deployment.) What is needed now are everyday neighborhoods in a broad range of contexts, starting with the disaggregated, sometimes depleted landscape of existing cities.

A Two-Part Strategy

Part 1: Delineation

The first task is to take a new approach to delineating neighborhoods. Planners, the professional keepers of the neighborhood ideal, could start things off by giving neighborhoods a physical basis and tangible meaning based on the location of neighborhood centers and their surrounding spatial extents (see color plate 20). Neighborhood boundaries, defined by the spatial reach of neighborhood centers, would necessarily overlap (as shown in the example below).

The task of delineation should make use of all the resources at hand: surveys, historical description, existing maps, bounding features like highways and rivers, street patterns, schools and centers, oral histories, market area

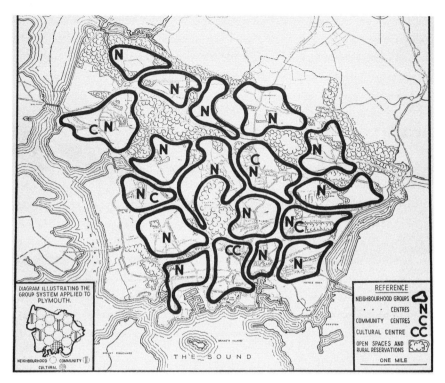

Figure 10.1 Planners in Plymouth, U.K., proposed neighborhood and community "groupings" in their 1945 plan to rebuild their city, which was heavily bombed during World War II. Source: Scotland, *A Handbook of the Plymouth Plan.*

research—whatever intelligence is available to demarcate neighborhood centers and the areas around them that they affect. Planners should make themselves deeply familiar with all forms of delineation: the post office definition of neighborhood, the police precinct definition of neighborhood, the school board definition of neighborhood. In identifying potential centers, they could take a cue from Mumford's playbook: "The spotting and inter-relationship of schools, libraries, theaters, and community centers is the first task in defining the urban neighborhood and laying down the outlines of an integrated city."[16]

Since many places are in a weak neighborhood identity-building position because of their physical form—unlike the well-honed neighborhood definition of a gated or unit neighborhood—municipal planners will need to initiate this process wherever neighborhood is not explicitly defined. They need to play a role in elevating whatever latent sense of neighborhood can be found, helping residents leverage their assets and "find" their definition if no clear definition exists.

Most important, and unlike most social science research or the Home Owners' Loan Corporation redlining maps of the 1930s, planners need to resist defining neighborhoods solely on the basis of social similarity. They should not be averse to defining neighborhoods based on patterns of diversity, perhaps by including two sides of a commercial street within the same neighborhood. They might also look for ways to include homogeneous pockets of social similarity within the broader extent of heterogeneous neighborhoods.

Once planners have proposed neighborhood centers and the areas around them, the proposal should be widely publicized and shared, leading to open debate and critique. Planners should absorb these comments and critiques and refine the delineations accordingly. They will have to work out a method for arbitrating disputes.

Between the DIY urbanism of *Urbanism without Effort*, the absence of planners in fostering Charles Montgomery's *Happy City*, and the recurring lament "Where, actually, are the planners when it comes to planning cities?," figuring out the delineation of neighborhoods—jump-starting the process—may be one activity for which planners still have some expertise and credibility.[17] If done right, neighborhood delineation might emerge as an effective way for planners to push back against the idea that all urban planners actually do is "mask, manage or soften" capital accumulation.[18]

Part 2: Activation

Once neighborhood delineation is agreed upon, it is up to residents to act on it. The activation is necessarily bottom-up and resident controlled, but planners should help facilitate it. Cities are not likely to install a system of neighborhood governance unless such a system is already in place (which is rare). In the U.S. any semblance of "neighborhood" governance is either the investment-protection focus of homeowners associations or larger, anonymous districts controlled by elected council members or aldermen. What, then, could planners do to activate neighborhood-scale governance, activism, and control for these newly delineated neighborhoods?

One idea would be a "carrot" approach whereby neighborhood residents who self-organize and come forward are given whatever support they need to help them formulate a future-oriented neighborhood plan. (There might need to be some ground rules about not developing plans that are exclusionary in focus; a related approach was initiated in Seattle.)[19] Individuals willing to put in time and energy would need to be identified. (Planners in the 1940s knew that getting neighborhood participation jump-started required finding residents who could be the neighborhood's "spark plug.")[20] Such individuals would need to be recognized as having the capacity and authority to speak for the neighborhood.

Another idea is to charge residents with a specific task. Resident control of the neighborhood is motivated when there is a tangible issue to respond to. To keep things proactive and positive rather than reactive and defensive, that "issue" might revolve around ownership and control of neighborhood public space— the centers. The public spaces of an everyday neighborhood are fundamental to it, as they provide the identity-sustaining glue that helps diversity—in terms of both use and people—succeed. In an everyday neighborhood, the sharing of public space is habitual.

As a practical matter, an initial charge might be to catalog where and in what condition all publicly owned space (land and buildings) in the neighborhood is located, whether or not defined as a center. Once known, residents could evaluate what the neighborhood's requirements for public space are and whether those needs are being met. Are the requirements for children's play, senior activities, and family recreation understood and accommodated? Planners should stand ready to facilitate this evaluation, which might include initiating a participatory budgeting process.

From there, neighborhood residents might also develop an understanding of all public actions affecting their neighborhood. This includes zoning and other regulations, street improvements and closings, infrastructure investments, and policies like tax increment districts. An everyday neighborhood knows what the content, effect, and underlying assumptions of the rules, investments, and policies affecting it are. Only with this understanding can they then work to change them.[21]

Everyday neighborhoods can't be built as blueprints, nor by edict. But they can be encouraged to form where they are inchoate and helped to self-govern where they lack governing capacity. Most important, they can be given the tools and capacity to take charge of their own destinies. If neighborhood residents can work toward an identity and sense of ownership—in places where neighborhoods are wanted and needed—such neighborhoods will stand as living testaments to the possibility that the neighborhood, in its traditional sense of localized experience, can be more than a valentine, more than a segregator, and still relevant.

Notes

1. "Defining Neighborhood," 429.
2. Mutter and Westphal, "Perspectives on Neighborhoods as Park-Planning Units," 152.
3. Allaire, "Neighborhood Boundaries," 20.
4. Lees, "Gentrification and Social Mixing."
5. Smith, "Residential Neighborhoods as Humane Environments." On hidden forms of variety see Clay, *Close-Up*.

6. See, for example, the arguments made in Permentier et al., "Neighbourhood Reputation and the Intention to Leave the Neighbourhood."

7. Sharkey, "Making Our Assumptions about Integration Explicit." See also Turner, "Place Matters Even More Than We Thought."

8. Wekerle, "From Refuge to Service Center." On location efficiency, see the website of the Center for Neighborhood Technology, http://www.cnt.org/; Webber, *Explorations into Urban Structure*.

9. Molotch, "Design Decency at the Urban Front."

10. Pew Research Center, "Table 3.1 Preferred Community."

11. The unwillingness to give up urban convenience for a rural lifestyle is the very definition of sprawl.

12. This, for example, was the approach taken in Mutter and Westphal, "Perspectives on Neighborhoods as Park-Planning Units."

13. See, for example, Tach, "More than Bricks and Mortar."

14. Molotch, "Design Decency at the Urban Front."

15. Fontenot, Anthony. "Notes toward a History of Non-Planning."

16. Mumford, "What Is a City?", 185.

17. Gleye, "City Planning versus Urban Planning," 11.

18. Brenner, "Open City or the Right to the City?," 45.

19. Residents were given funding to develop a plan if the neighborhood was willing to take on additional density.

20. Howard, "Democracy in City Planning," 526, 527, 529.

21. One example: Sandy Sorlien's "Neighborhood Conservation Kit" is a method for getting residents directly involved in proposing a new zoning code for their neighborhood.

ACKNOWLEDGMENTS

First I want to thank Andrés Duany, who, early on, supported the idea that this book was in fact needed. Second I want to thank Doug Farr, a steadfast friend and tireless champion of the idea that neighborhoods matter.

Many people have sustained me in this five-year venture, and I am deeply grateful to have had so much support. A few people need special mention: Sandy Sorlien (her work on the Neighborhood Conservation Code is inspirational), Samantha Singer for helping put together an exhibition on neighborhoods at the University of Chicago, Richard Harris for his sharing of bibliographic resources, Sungduck Lee for her graphical talents, Lucas Penido and Olivia Jia at the University of Chicago for their amazing research abilities, Eran Ben-Joseph for enabling a neighborhoods course at MIT, Julia Koschinsky for her support in countless ways, and Alexandra Dauler and Hayley Singer at Oxford University Press for their help in getting this book over the finish line.

I am deeply thankful for the everyday support I receive from my children Emma, Lucie and Thomas, my son-in-law Ryan, my sisters and brothers, my parents, and most of all, my husband Luc. Zot van jou.

BIBLIOGRAPHY

Abbot, Carl. "The Neighborhoods of New York, 1760–1775." *New York History* 55, no. 1 (1974): 35–54. doi:10.2307/23169562.

Abercrombie, Patrick, and J. H. Forshaw. *The County of London Plan.* London: Macmillan, 1943.

Abrahamson, Julia. *A Neighborhood Finds Itself.* New York: Harper, 1959.

Abrahamson, Mark. *Urban Enclaves: Identity and Place in America.* Contemporary Social Issues. New York: St. Martin's Press, 1996.

Abu-Ghazzeh, Tawfiq M. "Built Form and Religion: Underlying Structures of Jeddah Al-Qademah." *Traditional Dwellings and Settlements Review* 5, no. 2 (1994): 49–59. doi:10.2307/41757170, 55.

Abu-Lughod, Janet L. "The Islamic City—Historic Myth, Islamic Essence, and Contemporary Relevance." *International Journal of Middle East Studies* 19, no. 2 (1987): 155–76. doi:10.1017/S0020743800031822.

Ackerman, Frederick L. "Houses and Ships." *American City* 19 (1918): 85–86.

Adams, Frederick J., Svend Riemer, Reginald Isaacs, Robert B. Mitchell, and Gerald Breese. "Panel I: The Neighborhood Concept in Theory and Application." *Land Economics* 25, no. 1 (1949): 67–88. doi:10.2307/3144878.

Adams, John S. "Residential Structure of Midwestern Cities." *Annals of the Association of American Geographers* 60, no. 1 (1970): 37–62. doi:10.2307/2569119.

Adams, Thomas. *Outline of Town and City Planning: A Review of Past Efforts and Modern Aims.* New York: Russell Sage Foundation, 1936.

Adams, Thomas. *Recent Advances in Town Planning.* New York: Macmillan, 1932.

Addams, Jane. "A Modern Lear." *Survey* xxix, November 2 (1912): 131–137.

Agnew, John A. "The Danger of a Neighborhood Definition of Community." *Community Education Journal* 7, no. 3 (1980): 30–31.

Aitken, Stuart C. "Mothers, Communities and the Scale of Difference." *Social & Cultural Geography* 1, no. 1 (2000): 65–82.

Alberti, Leon Battista. *The Ten Books of Architecture: The 1755 Leoni Edition.* New York: Dover, 1986.

Alexander, Christopher. A City is Not a Tree. *Architectural Forum* 122, (1965): April, 58-62; May, 58-61.

Alexander, Christopher. *A Pattern Language: Towns, Buildings, Construction.* New York: Oxford University Press, 1977.

Ali, Tanveer. "This Is Where Chicagoans Say the Borders of Their Neighborhoods Are." *Chicago Visualized,* September 28, 2015. http://www.dnainfo.com/chicago/20150928/loop/this-is-where-chicagoans-say-borders-of-their-neighborhoods-are.

Allaire, Jerrold. "Neighborhood Boundaries." Information Report No. 141. Chicago: American Society of Planning Officials, December 1960. American Planning Association. https://www.planning.org/pas/reports/report141.htm.

American Institute of Architects. *America at the Growing Edge: A Strategy for Building a Better America*. Report of the National Policy Task Force. Washington, DC: American Institute of Architects, 1972.

American Planning Association, Frederick R. Steiner, and Kent Butler. *Planning and Urban Design Standards*. Hoboken, NJ: Wiley, 2006.

American Public Health Association. *Planning the Neighborhood*. Standards for Healthful Housing. Chicago, 1948. Hathi Trust Digital Library. http://hdl.handle.net/2027/mdp.39015007191813.

Anselin, Luc. "Local Indicators of Spatial Association—LISA." *Geographical Analysis* 27, no. 2 (1995): 93–115.

Appleyard, Donald. "Livable Streets: Protected Neighborhoods?" *Annals of the American Academy of Political and Social Science* 451 (September 1, 1980): 106–17.

Appleyard, Donald. "Towards an Imageable Structure for Residential Areas." MCP thesis, Massachusetts Institute of Technology, 1958. http://dspace.mit.edu/handle/1721.1/72298.

Aravantinos, A. "Planning Objectives in Modern Greece." *Town Planning Review* 41, no. 1 (1970): 41–62. doi:10.2307/40102683.

Arendt, Randall, and American Planning Association. *Crossroads, Hamlet, Village, Town: Design Characteristics of Traditional Neighborhoods, Old and New*. Revised ed. Planning Advisory Service Report No. 523/524. Chicago: American Planning Association, 2004.

Arnold, Joseph L. "The Neighborhood and City Hall: The Origin of Neighborhood Associations in Baltimore, 1880–1911." *Journal of Urban History* 6, no. 1 (1979): 3–30. doi:10.1177/009614427900600101.

Arnstein, Sherry R. "A Ladder of Citizen Participation." *Journal of the American Institute of Planners* 35, no. 4 (1969): 216–24.

Aronovici, Carol. *Community Building: Science, Technique, Art*. Garden City, NY: Doubleday, 1956.

Aronovici, Carol. *Housing the Masses*. New York: J. Wiley & Sons, Chapman & Hall, 1939.

Ayad, Irene Erika. "Louis I. Kahn and Neighborhood Design: The 'Mill Creek Redevelopment Area Plan,' 1951–1954." PhD dissertation, Cornell University, 1995.

Bacon, Edmund N. "Urban Redevelopment—An Opportunity for City Rebuilding." In *Planning*, 18–24. Chicago: American Society of Planning Officials, 1949.

Bailey, Nick. "How Spatial Segregation Changes over Time: Sorting Out the Sorting Processes." *Environment and Planning A* 44, no. 3 (2012): 705–22. doi:10.1068/a44330.

Bailey, Nick, and Madeleine Pill. "The Continuing Popularity of the Neighbourhood and Neighbourhood Governance in the Transition from the 'Big State' to the 'Big Society' Paradigm." *Environment and Planning C: Government and Policy* 29, no. 5 (2011): 927–42. doi:10.1068/c1133r.

Bailly, Paul Charles. 1959. *An Urban Elementary School for Boston*. Cambridge, MA: Massachusetts Institute of Technology Press.

Baker, Beth. *With a Little Help from Our Friends: Creating Community as We Grow Older*. Nashville, TN: Vanderbilt University Press, 2014.

Banerjee, Tridib, and William C. Baer. *Beyond the Neighborhood Unit: Residential Environments and Public Policy*. Environment, Development, and Public Policy. New York: Plenum Press, 1984.

Bar, Doron, and Rehav Rubin. "The Jewish Quarter after 1967: A Case Study on the Creation of an Ideological-Cultural Landscape in Jerusalem's Old City." *Journal of Urban History* 37, no. 5 (2011): 775–92. doi:10.1177/0096144211415634.

Bardet, Gaston. "Social Topography: An Analytico-Synthetic Understanding of the Urban Texture." *Town Planning Review* 22, no. 3 (1951): 237–60. doi:10.2307/40102188.

Bardet, Jean-Pierre. *Rouen au 17eme et 18eme Siècle*. Paris: Sedes, 1995.

Barnett, Jonathan. *An Introduction to Urban Design*. New York: HarperCollins, 1982.

Barrett, James R. "Unity and Fragmentation: Class, Race, and Ethnicity on Chicago's South Side, 1900–1922." *Journal of Social History* 18, no. 1 (1984): 37–55. doi:10.1353/jsh/18.1.37.

Barron, Hal S. "And the Crooked Shall Be Made Straight: Public Road Administration and the Decline of Localism in the Rural North, 1870–1930." *Journal of Social History* 26 (1992): 81–103. http://dx.doi.org/10.1353/jsh/26.1.81.

"A Basic Guide to ABCD Community Organizing." Accessed June 30, 2014. https://resources. depaul.edu/abcd-institute/publications/publications-by-topic/Documents/A%20 Basic%20Guide%20to%20ABCD%20Community%20Organizing(3).pdf

Beidler, Kyle Joseph. "Sense of Place and New Urbanism: Towards a Holistic Understanding of Place and Form." PhD dissertation, Virginia Polytechnic Institute and State University, 2007.

Belanger, Elizabeth. "The Neighborhood Ideal: Local Planning Practices in Progressive-Era Women's Clubs." *Journal of Planning History* 8, no. 2 (2009): 87–110. doi:10.1177/ 1538513209333274.

Bell, Wendell. "Social Areas: Typology of Neighborhoods." In *Community Structure and Analysis*, ed. Marvin B. Sussman, 61–92. New York: Crowell, 1959.

Benevolo, Leonardo. *The History of the City*. Cambridge, MA: MIT Press, 1981.

Bertagnin, Mauro, Ilham Khuri-Makdisi, and Susan Gilson Miller. "A Mediterranean Jewish Quarter and Its Architectural Legacy: The Giudecca of Trani, Italy (1000–1550)." *Traditional Dwellings and Settlements Review* 14, no. 2 (2003): 33–46. doi:10.2307/41758017.

Bestor, Theodore C. *Neighborhood Tokyo*. Studies of the East Asian Institute, Columbia University. Stanford, CA: Stanford University Press, 1989.

Bettencourt, Luís M. A. "The Origins of Scaling in Cities." *Science* 340 (2013): 1438–41. doi:10.1126/science.1235823.

Bickel, Robert, Cynthia Smith, and Teresa Eagle. "Poor, Rural Neighborhoods and Early School Achievement." *Journal of Poverty* 6, no. 3 (2002): 89–108. doi:10.1300/J134v06n03_04.

Biddulph, Michael, Bridget Franklin, and Malcolm Tait. "From Concept to Completion: A Critical Analysis of the Urban Village." *Town Planning Review* 74, no. 2 (2003): 165–93. doi:10.2307/ 40112551.

Bishop, Bill. *The Big Sort: Why the Clustering of Like-Minded America Is Tearing Us Apart*. Boston: Mariner Books, 2009.

Bliss, Geoff. "Forgotten History: The Cincinnati Social Unit Experiment." *Global Grid*, April 26, 2013. http://www.globalsiteplans.com/environmental-design/forgotten-history-the-cincinnati-social-unit-experiment-2/.

Bloem, Brigitte A., Theo G. Van Tilburg, and Fleur Thomése. "Starting Relationships with Neighbors after a Move Later in Life: An Exploratory Study." *Journal of Housing for the Elderly* 27, nos. 1–2 (2013): 28–47. doi:10.1080/02763893.2012.724374.

Blom, Anita, Bregit Jansen, and Marieke van der Heiden. "De Typologie Van De Vroeg-Naoorlogse Woonwiken." April 2004. Cultural Heritage Agency of the Netherlands. http://cultureeler-fgoed.nl/sites/default/files/publications/typologie-van-de-vroeg-naoorlogse-woonwijken. pdf.

Blommaert, Jan, James Collins, and Stef Slembrouck. "Polycentricity and Interactional Regimes in 'Global Neighborhoods.'" *Ethnography* 6, no. 2 (2005): 205–35. doi:10.1177/ 1466138105057557.

Blumenfeld, Hans. "Form and Function in Urban Communities." *Journal of the American Society of Architectural Historians* 3, nos. 1–2 (1943): 11–21. doi:10.2307/901248.

Blumenfeld, Hans. "'Neighborhood' Concept Is Submitted to Questioning." *Journal of Housing*, December 1948, 299.

Boger, Gretchen. "The Meaning of Neighborhood in the Modern City: Baltimore's Residential Segregation Ordinances, 1910–1913." *Journal of Urban History* 35, no. 2 (2009): 236–58. doi:10.1177/0096144208327915.

Bolt, Gideon, and Ronald Van Kempen. "Successful Mixing? Effects of Urban Restructuring Policies in Dutch Neighbourhoods." *Tijdschrift Voor Economische En Sociale Geografie* 102, no. 3 (2011): 361–68. doi:10.1111/j.1467-9663.2011.00668.x.

Boltanski, Luc, and Eve Chiapello. *The New Spirit of Capitalism*. Translated by Gregory Elliott. London: Verso, 2007.

"Bombelek—Joint Runner-up Entry for E12 Sweden, Kalmar." *Bustler*, January 28, 2014. http:// www.bustler.net/index.php/article/bombelek_-_runner-up_entry_for_e12_sweden_ kalmar/.

Bond, L., E. Sautkina, and A. Kearns. "Mixed Messages about Mixed Tenures: Do Reviews Tell the Real Story? *Housing Studies* 26, no. 11 (2010): 69–94.

Borchert, James. *Alley Life in Washington: Family, Community, Religion, and Folklife in the City*. New ed. Urbana: University of Illinois Press, 1980.

Borchert, James. "Urban Neighborhood and Community: Informal Group Life, 1850–1970." *Journal of Interdisciplinary History* 11, no. 4 (1981): 607–31. doi:10.2307/203145.

Botsman, Rachel, and Roo Rogers. *What's Mine Is Yours: The Rise of Collaborative Consumption*. New York: HarperBusiness, 2010.

Boulton, Jeremy. *Neighbourhood and Society: A London Suburb in the Seventeenth Century*. Cambridge, UK: Cambridge University Press, 2005.

Eaton, Ruth. *Ideal Cities: Utopianism and the (Un) Built Environment*. New York: Thames & Hudson, 2002.

Bowden, Leonard W. "How to Define Neighborhood." *Professional Geographer* 24, no. 3 (1972): 227–28. doi:10.1111/j.0033-0124.1972.00227.x.

Bradford, Calvin. "Financing Home Ownership: The Federal Role in Neighborhood Decline." *Urban Affairs Review* 14, no. 3 (1979): 313–35. doi:10.1177/107808747901400303.

Brekelmans, J. *Nederlanders en bun buren* [Dutch people and their neighbors]. Amsterdam: Synovate, 2008.

Brenner, Neil. "Open City or the Right to the City?" *Topos: The International Review of Landscape Architecture and Urban Design* 85 (2013): 43–45.

Bridge, G., T. Butler, and L. Lees. *Mixed Communities: Gentrification by Stealth?* Bristol, UK: Policy Press, 2012.

Broden, Thomas, Ronn B. Kirkwood, John Roos, and Thomas Swartz. "Neighborhood Identification: A Guidebook for Participation in the U.S. Census Neighborhood Statistics Program." Washington, DC: U.S. Department of Housing and Urban Development, April 1980. Hathi Trust Digital Library. http://hdl.handle.net/2027/mdp.39015063088903.

Brody, Jason. "Constructing Professional Knowledge: The Neighborhood Unit Concept in the Community Builders Handbook." PhD dissertation, University of Illinois at Urbana-Champaign, 2009.

Brody, Jason. "The Neighbourhood Unit Concept and the Shaping of Land Planning in the United States 1912–1968." *Journal of Urban Design* 18, no. 3 (2013): 340–62. doi:10.1080/13574809.2013.800453.

Brommer, Bea, and Dirk de Vries. "Historische Plattegronden van Nederlandse Steden, Deel 4: Batavia." *Archipel*, no. 1 (1994): 1–25.

Brooke, John L. "On the Edges of the Public Sphere." *William and Mary Quarterly*, 3rd series, 62, no. 1 (2005): 93–98. doi:10.2307/3491623.

Brower, Sidney N. *Good Neighborhoods: A Study of In-Town and Suburban Residential Environments*. Westport, CT: Praeger, 1996.

Brown, B., D. Perkins, and G. Brown. "Place Attachment in a Revitalizing Neighborhood: Individual and Block Levels of Analysis." *Journal of Environmental Psychology* 23, no. 3 (2003): 259–71.

Bruce, Robert, Patricia Mooney-Melvin, and Zane L. Miller. *Making Sense of the City: Local Government, Civic Culture, and Community Life in Urban America*. Columbus: Ohio State University Press, 2001.

Burke, Jill. "Visualizing Neighborhood in Renaissance Florence Santo Spirito and Santa Maria Del Carmine." *Journal of Urban History* 32, no. 5 (2006): 693–710. doi:10.1177/0096144206287094.

Bursik, Robert J., Jr., and Harold G. Grasmick. *Neighborhoods and Crime: The Dimensions of Effective Community Control*. Lanham, MD: Lexington Books, 2002.

Buslik, Marc S. "Dynamic Geography: The Changing Definition of Neighborhood." *Citiscape* 14, no. 2 (2012): 237–42.

Buttimer, Anne. "Social Space in Interdisciplinary Perspective." *Geographical Review* 59, no. 3 (1969): 417–26. doi:10.2307/213485.

Buttimer, Anne. "Sociology and Planning." *Town Planning Review* 42, no. 2 (1971): 145–80. doi:10.2307/40102739.

Cabot, Ella Lyman, Fannie Fern Andrews, Fanny E. Coe, Mabel Hill, and Mary McSkimmon. *A Course in Citizenship*. Boston: Houghton Mifflin, 1914. Hathi Trust Digital Library. http://hdl.handle.net/2027/nyp.33433081977864.

"Cairo's Metropolitan Landscape: Segregation Extreme—Failed Architecture." Failed Architecture. Accessed February 21, 2015. http://www.failedarchitecture.com/cairos-metropolitan-landscape-segregation-extreme/.

Campleman, Gordon. "Some Sociological Aspects of Mixed-Class Neighbourhood Planning." *Sociological Review* 43 (January 1951): 191–200.

Carías, Allan-Randolph Brewer. *La Ciudad Ordenada*. Caracas: Criteris Editorial, 2006.

Carvalho, Máyra, R. Varkki George, and Kathryn H. Anthony. "Residential Satisfaction in Condominios Exclusivos (Gate-Guarded Neighborhoods) in Brazil." *Environment and Behavior* 29, no. 6 (1997): 734–68. doi:10.1177/0013916597296002.

Castells, Manuel. *The Urban Question: A Marxist Approach*. Social Structure and Social Change 1. Cambridge, MA: MIT Press, 1977.

Celik, Zeyneb. *Urban Forms and Colonial Confrontations: Algiers under French Rule*. Berkeley: University of California Press, 1997.

Center for Applied Research in the Apostolate. "Catholic Data, Catholic Statistics, Catholic Research." 2015. http://cara.georgetown.edu/frequently-requested-church-statistics/.

Center for Neighborhood Technology. http://www.cnt.org/. Accessed July 10, 2018.

Central Housing Advisory Committee, Great Britain, and Ministry of Housing and Local Government. *Design of Dwellings*. London: HMSO, 1944.

Chandigarh: The City Beautiful. "Le Corbusier's Master Plan." . Accessed July 10, 2018.

Chapman, Dennis. "Review of *The Cutteslowe Walls* by Peter Collison." *Town Planning Review* 34, no. 3 (1963): 237–38. doi:10.2307/40102398.

Chaskin, Robert J. "Neighborhood as a Unit of Planning and Action: A Heuristic Approach." *Journal of Planning Literature* 13, no. 1 (1998): 11–30. doi:10.1177/088541229801300102.

Chaskin, Robert J., and Mark L. Joseph. "Contested Space Design Principles and Regulatory Regimes in Mixed-Income Communities in Chicago." *Annals of the American Academy of Political and Social Science* 660, no. 1 (2015): 136–54. doi:10.1177/0002716215576113.

Chaskin, Robert J., and Mark L. Joseph. *Integrating the Inner City*. Chicago: University Of Chicago Press, 2015.

Chauncey, George. *Gay New York: Gender, Urban Culture, and the Making of the Gay Male World*. New York: Basic Books, 1995.

Checkoway, Barry. "Two Types of Planning in Neighborhoods." *Journal of Planning Education and Research* 3, no. 2 (1984): 102–9. doi:10.1177/0739456X8400300209.

Chen, C. Z. "Some Ancient Chinese Concepts of Town and Country." *Town Planning Review* 19, nos. 3–4 (1947): 160–63. doi:10.2307/40101895.

Chermayeff, Serge, and Christopher Alexander. *Community and Privacy: Toward a New Architecture of Humanism*. Garden City, NY: Doubleday, 1963.

Cheshire, Paul C. "Resurgent Cities, Urban Myths and Policy Hubris: What We Need to Know." *Urban Studies* 43, no. 8 (2006): 1231–46. doi:10.1080/00420980600775600.

Chesson, Meredith S. "Households, Houses, Neighborhoods and Corporate Villages: Modeling the Early Bronze Age as a House Society." *Journal of Mediterranean Archaeology* 16, no. 1 (2003): 79–102.

Chicago Commons Association. *Chicago Commons: Twenty-Fifth Year, 1894–1919*. Chicago, Illinois, 1920. Hathi Trust Digital Library. http://hdl.handle.net/2027/mdp.39015010472457.

"Chicago Neighborhood Guide." Newberry Library. Accessed October 30, 2016. http://www.newberry.org/chicago-neighborhood-guide.

Chicago Plan Commission. *Building New Neighborhoods*. Chicago: Chicago Plan Commission, 1943.

Chicago Plan Commission. *Rebuilding Old Chicago: City Planning Aspects of the Neighborhood Redevelopment Corporation Law*. Chicago: Chicago Plan Commission, 1941.

Chow, Julian. "Differentiating Urban Neighborhoods: A Multivariate Structural Model Analysis." *Social Work Research* 22, no. 3 (1998): 131–42. doi:10.1093/swr/22.3.131.

Chudacoff, Howard P. "A New Look at Ethnic Neighborhoods: Residential Dispersion and the Concept of Visibility in a Medium-Sized City." *Journal of American History* 60, no. 1 (1973): 76–93. doi:10.2307/2936330.

Churchill, Henry S. "Housing and Community Planning." Seminar Address to Planning and Housing Division, School of Architecture, Columbia University. *Pencil Points*, May 1943, 87.

Cisneros, Henry G., and John Rosales. *Casa y Comunidad: Latino Home and Neighborhood Design.* Washington, DC: BuilderBooks, 2006.

City Planning Commission of Portland, Oregon. "Portland City Planning Commission." 1919. Hathi Trust Digital Library. http://babel.hathitrust.org/cgi/imgsrv/image?id=mdp.39015 023500260;seq=3;width=680.

Clampet-Lundquist, Susan. "HOPE VI Relocation: Moving to New Neighborhoods and Building New Ties." *Housing Policy Debate* 15, 2 (2004): 415–447.

Clarence Stein S. *Toward New Towns for America.* Liverpool, UK: University Press of Liverpool, 1951.

Clay, Grady. *Close-Up: How to Read the American City.* Reprint ed. Chicago: University of Chicago Press, 1980.

Cleveland Historical. "Aerial, 1937." http://clevelandhistorical.org/files/show/658#. VY2XKediQ28. Accessed July 10, 2018.

Cody, Jeffrey W. "American Planning in Republican China, 1911–1937." *Planning Perspectives* 11, no. 4 (1996): 339–77. doi:10.1080/026654396364808.

Cole, J. P. "Some Town Planning Problems of Greater Lima." *Town Planning Review* 26, no. 4 (1956): 242–51. doi:10.2307/40101581.

Collins, Christiane Crasemann, George R. Collins, and Camillo Sitte. *Camillo Sitte: The Birth of Modern City Planning: With a Translation of the 1889 Austrian Edition of His City Planning according to Artistic Principles.* Mineola, NY: Dover, 2006.

Collison, Peter. "Town Planning and the Neighbourhood Unit Concept." *Public Administration* 32, no. 4 (1954): 463–69. doi:10.1111/j.1467-9299.1954.tb01221.x.

Common Ground. "Parish Maps." https://www.commonground.org.uk/parish-maps/. Accessed July 10, 2018.

Conn, Steven. *Americans against the City: Anti-Urbanism in the Twentieth Century.* Oxford: Oxford University Press, 2014.

Conte, Julia, and Janet Li. "Neoliberal Urban Revitalization in Chicago." *Advocates' Forum,* 2013, 19–30.

Conzen, Kathleen Neils. "Immigrants, Immigrant Neighborhoods, and Ethnic Identity: Historical Issues." *Journal of American History* 66, no. 3 (1979): 603–15. doi:10.2307/1890298.

Cook, Christine C. "Components of Neighborhood Satisfaction Responses from Urban and Suburban Single-Parent Women." *Environment and Behavior* 20, no. 2 (1988): 115–49. doi:10.1177/0013916588202001.

Cooley, Charles Horton. *Social Organization: A Study of the Larger Mind.* New York: C. Scribner's Sons, 1909.

Copquin, Claudia Gryvatz. *The Neighborhoods of Queens.* New Haven, CT: Yale University Press, 2007.

Cortright, Joe. "Less in Common." *City Reports,* September 6, 2015. http://cityobservatory.org/less-in-common/.

Cortright, Joe. "Truthiness in Gentrification Reporting." *City Commentary,* October 29, 2015. http://cityobservatory.org/truthiness-in-gentrification-reporting/.

Cottrell, L., A. Hunter, and J. Short, eds. *Ernest W. Burgess on Community, Family, and Delinquency: Selected Writings.* Chicago: University of Chicago Press, 1973.

Coulton, Claudia. "Defining Neighborhoods for Research and Policy." *Cityscape* 14, no. 2 (2012): 231–36.

Coulton, Claudia J. "Finding Place in Making Connections Communities: Applying GIS to Residents' Perceptions of Their Neighborhoods." Urban Institute, March 30, 2010. http://www.urban.org/publications/412057.html.

Coulton, Claudia, Brett Theodos, and Margery A. Turner. "Residential Mobility and Neighborhood Change: Real Neighborhoods under the Microscope." *Cityscape: A Journal of Policy Development and Research* 14, no. 3 (2012). http://www.huduser.org/portal/periodicals/cityscpe/vol14num3/Cityscape_Nov2012_res_mobility_neigh.pdf.

Cowan, Robert. *The Dictionary of Urbanism.* Tisbury, MA: Streetwise Press, 2005.

Cox K. R. "The Voting Decision in a Spatial Context." In *Progress in Geography: Volume 1,* ed. C. Board, R. J. Chorley, P. Haggett, and D. R. Stoddarty, 81–117. London: Edward Arnold, 1969.

Cox, Kevin R., and Andrew Mair. "Locality and Community in the Politics of Local Economic Development." *Annals of the Association of American Geographers* 78, no. 2 (1988): 307–25. doi:10.1111/j.1467-8306.1988.tb00209.x.

Crisp, Richard. "'Communities with Oomph'? Exploring the Potential for Stronger Social Ties to Revitalise Disadvantaged Neighbourhoods." *Environment and Planning C: Government and Policy* 31, no. 2 (2013): 324–39. doi:10.1068/c11122.

Crum, Eric, and Dillon Mahmoudi. "Badass-ness Map." Accessed October 30, 2014. http://dillonm.io/files/PortlandBadassnessMap2011March.pdf.

Cullen, Gordon. *Concise Townscape*. London: Architectural Press, 1961.

Cunningham, James V., Roger S. Ahlbrandt, Rose Jewell, and Robert Hendrickson. "The Pittsburgh Atlas Program: Test Project for Neighborhoods." *National Civic Review* 65, no. 6 (1976): 284–89. doi:10.1002/ncr.4100650605.

Curbed NY. "Neighborhood Names Archives." https://ny.curbed.com/tag/neighborhood-names. Accessed July 10, 2018.

Curran, Winifred, and Trina Hamilton. "Just Green Enough: Contesting Environmental Gentrification in Greenpoint, Brooklyn." *Local Environment* 17, no. 9 (2012): 1027–42. doi:10.1080/13549839.2012.729569.

Dahir, James. "Greendale Comes of Age: The Story of Wisconsin's Best Known Planned Community as It Enters Its Twenty-First Year." Manuscript prepared for Milwaukee Community Development Corporation, Milwaukee, WI, 1958.

Dahir, James. *The Neighborhood Unit Plan, Its Spread and Acceptance: A Selected Bibliography with Interpretative Comments*. New York: Russell Sage Foundation, 1947.

Daniels, John. *America via the Neighborhood*. Americanization Studies. New York: Harper & Brothers, 1920.

Davidson, Mark. "Love Thy Neighbour? Social Mixing in London's Gentrification Frontiers." *Environment and Planning A* 42, no. 3 (2010): 524–44. doi:10.1068/a41379.

Davies, W. K. D., and D. T. Herbert. *Communities within Cities: An Urban Social Geography*. London: Belhaven Press, 1993.

Dear, Michael, and Steven Flusty. "Postmodern Urbanism." *Annals of the Association of American Geographers* 88, no. 1 (1998): 50–72. doi:10.2307/2563976.

De Chiara, Joseph, and Lee Koppelman. *Urban Planning and Design Criteria*. 3rd ed. New York: Van Nostrand Reinhold, 1982.

Debord, Guy. *Guide Psychogeographique de Paris: Discours sur les Passions d'Amour*. Copenhagen: Permild and Rosengreen, 1957.

Deboulet, Agnès. *Stratification Sociale et Villes Nouvelles Autour du Caire: Perspectives d'une Politique d'urbanisme*. Nanterre: Université Paris-X, 1984.

Deering, Tam. "Social Reconstruction through Neighborhood and Town Planning." *Social Forces* 10, no. 2 (1931): 227–29. doi:10.2307/2570253.

"Defining Neighborhood." *National Civic Review* 73, no. 9 (1984): 428–29. doi:10.1002/ncr.4100730902.

Dehaene, Michiel. "Surveying and Comprehensive Planning: The 'Co-ordination of Knowledge' in the Wartime Plans of Patrick Abercrombie." In *Man-Made Future: Planning, Education and Design in Mid-20th Century Britain*, ed. Iain Boyd Whyte, 26–47. Milton Park, Abingdon, UK: Routledge, 2007.

De Marco, Allison, and Molly De Marco. "Conceptualization and Measurement of the Neighborhood in Rural Settings: A Systematic Review of the Literature." *Journal of Community Psychology* 38, no. 1 (2010): 99–114. doi:10.1002/jcop.20354.

Deshen, Shlomo. "Social Control in Israeli Urban Quarters." In *The Changing Middle Eastern City*, ed. Gerald Henry Blake and Richard I. Lawless, 149–66. London: Croom Helm, 1980.

Dewey, Richard. "The Neighborhood, Urban Ecology, and City Planners." *American Sociological Review* 15, no. 4 (1950): 502–7. doi:10.2307/2087309.

Dongtan New Town Urban Space Design. Seoul: Korea Land Corporation, 2008.

Dorren, Gabrielle. "Communities within the Community: Aspects of Neighbourhood in Seventeenth-Century Haarlem." *Urban History* 25, no. 02 (1998): 173–88. doi:10.1017/S0963926800000791.

Dougill, Wesley. "Educational Buildings: Their Relation to the Town Plan." *Town Planning Review* 16, no. 1 (1934): 1–15.

Dougill, Wesley. "Wythenshawe: A Modern Satellite Town." *Town Planning Review* 16, no. 3 (1935): 209–15. doi:10.2307/40101182.

Downs, Anthony. *Neighborhoods and Urban Development*. Washington, DC: Brookings Institution Press, 1981.

Duany, Andres. "Chapter 25 Commentary." In *Charter of the New Urbanism*, 2nd ed., ed. Emily Talen and Congress for the New Urbanism, 231–38. New York: McGraw-Hill, 2013.

Duany, Andres, and Elizabeth Plater-Zyberk. "Neighborhoods and Suburbs." *Design Quarterly*, no. 164 (April 1, 1995): 10–23. doi:10.2307/4091349.

Duany, Andres, and Elizabeth Plater-Zyberk. *Towns and Town-Making Principles*. New York: Rizzoli, 2006.

DuBois, Harley K. "Managing Diversity: The Zoning of Black Rock City." *Burning Man Journal*, May 25, 2010. http://blog.burningman.com/2010/05/building-brc/managing-diversity-the-zoning-of-black-rock-city/.

Dunbar, R. "Neocortex Size as a Constraint on Group Size in Primates." *Journal of Human Evolution* 22 (1992): 469–93.

Duneier, Mitchell. *Ghetto: The Invention of a Place, the History of an Idea*. New York: Farrar, Straus and Giroux, 2016.

Dunn, Kevin M. "Rethinking Ethnic Concentration: The Case of Cabramatta, Sydney." *Urban Studies* 35, no. 3 (1998): 503–27.

Düring, Bleda Serge. "Constructing Communities: Clustered Neighbourhood Settlements of the Central Anatolian Neolithic ca. 8500–5500 Cal. BC." PhD dissertation. Leiden University, 2006. https://openaccess.leidenuniv.nl/handle/1887/4340.

Durose, C., and V. Lowndes. "Neighbourhood Governance: Contested Rationales within a Multi-level Setting: A Study of Manchester." *Local Government Studies* 36 (2010): 341–59.

Eben Saleh, Mohammed Abdullah. "Planning and Designing for Defense, Security and Safety in Saudi Arabian Residential Environments." *Journal of Architectural & Planning Research* 18, no. 1 (2001): 39–58.

Eckardt, Frank. "Germany: Neighbourhood Centres—A Complex Issue." *Built Environment* 32, no. 1 (2006): 53–72. doi:10.2307/23289486.

Eckstein, Nicholas A. "Addressing Wealth in Renaissance Florence: Some New Soundings from the Catasto of 1427." *Journal of Urban History* 32, no. 5 (2006): 711–28. doi:10.1177/0096144206287095.

Editors. "Regional Plan of New York and Its Environs." *Town Planning Review* 15, no. 2 (1932): 123–36. doi:10.2307/40101044.

Elliott, James. *The City in Maps: Urban Mapping to 1900*. London: British Library Publishing Division, 1987.

Ellis, Joyce M. *The Georgian Town, 1680–1849*. New York: Palgrave Macmillan, 2001.

Engelhardt, N. L., Jr. "The School-Neighborhood Nucleus." *Architectural Forum* 10, no. 4 (1943): 88–90.

Ericksen, Eugene P., and William L. Yancey. "Work and Residence in Industrial Philadelphia." *Journal of Urban History* 5, no. 2 (1979): 147–182.

Fairfield, John D. "Alienation of Social Control: The Chicago Sociologists and the Origins of Urban Planning." *Planning Perspectives* 7 (1992): 418–34. http://dx.doi.org/10.1080/02665439208725758.

Farr, Douglas. *Sustainable Urbanism: Urban Design with Nature*. A Wiley Book on Sustainable Design. Hoboken, NJ: Wiley, 2008.

Faure, Alain. "Local Life in Working-Class Paris at the End of the Nineteenth Century." *Journal of Urban History* 32, no. 5 (2006): 761–72. doi:10.1177/0096144206287098.

Federal Housing Administration. "Successful Subdivisions Planned as Neighborhoods for Profitable Investment and Appeal to Home Owners." Land Planning Bulletin 1. Washington, DC: Superintendent of Documents, 1940.

Feinstein, Otto. *Ethnic Groups in the City*. Lexington, MA: Heath Lexington Books, 1971.

Felton, Ralph A. *Serving the Neighborhood.* New York: Council of Women for Home Missions, Missionary Education Movement, 1920. Hathi Trust Digital Library. http://hdl.handle.net/2027/nnc1.cr60993855.

Fischer, K. F. "Canberra: Myths and Models." *Town Planning Review* 60, no. 2 (1989): 155–94. doi:10.2307/40112789.

Fisher, Robert. *Let the People Decide: Neighborhood Organizing in America.* Boston: Twayne, 1984.

Fitzsimmons, Emma Graves. "A Wish for More Community in Mixed-Income Units." *New York Times,* May 20, 2010. http://www.nytimes.com/2010/05/21/us/21cnchousing.html.

Flint, Shlomit, Itzhak Benenson, and Nurit Alfasi. "Between Friends and Strangers: Micro-Segregation in a Haredi Neighborhood in Jerusalem." *City & Community* 11, no. 2 (2012): 171–97. doi:10.1111/j.1540-6040.2012.01397.x.

Fogelson, Robert M. *The Fragmented Metropolis: Los Angeles 1850–1930.* Berkeley: University of California Press, 1993.

Fontenot, Anthony. "Notes toward a History of Non-Planning." *Places Journal,* January 2015. https://doi.org/10.22269/150112.

Forrest, Ray, and Ade Kearns. "Social Cohesion, Social Capital and the Neighbourhood." *Urban Studies* 38, no. 12 (2001): 2125–43. doi:10.1080/00420980120087081.

Fox, Cybelle, and Thomas A. Guglielmo. "Defining America's Racial Boundaries: Blacks, Mexicans, and European Immigrants, 1890–1945." *American Journal of Sociology* 118, no. 2 (2012): 327–79. doi:10.1086/666383.

Freeman, Lance. "Displacement or Succession? Residential Mobility in Gentrifying Neighborhoods." *Urban Affairs Review* 40, no. 4 (2005): 463–91. doi:10.1177/1078087404273341.

Frolic, B. Michael. "The Soviet City." *Town Planning Review* 34, no. 4 (1964): 285–306. doi:10.2307/40102409.

Fry, Richard, and Paul Taylor. "The Rise of Residential Segregation by Income." Pew Research Center's Social & Demographic Trends Project, August 1, 2012. http://www.pewsocial-trends.org/2012/08/01/the-rise-of-residential-segregation-by-income/.

Fung, K. "Satellite Town Development in the Shanghai City Region." *Town Planning Review* 52, no. 1 (1981): 26–46. doi:10.2307/40103418.

Gabaccia, Donna R. "Sicilians in Space: Environmental Change and Family Geography." *Journal of Social History* 16, no. 2 (1982): 53–66. doi:10.1353/jsh/16.2.53.

Gallion, Arthur B. *The Urban Pattern: City Planning and Design.* New York: Van Nostrand, 1963.

Galton, Antony. "On the Ontological Status of Geographical Boundaries." In *Foundations of Geographic Information Science,* ed. Matt Duckam, Michael F. Goodchild and Michael Worboys, 151–71. London: Taylor and Francis, 2003.

Galster, George C. "What Is Neighbourhood? An Externality-Space Approach." *International Journal of Urban & Regional Research* 10, no. 2 (1986): 243.

Galster, George C., and Garry W. Hesser. "The Social Neighborhood: An Unspecified Factor in Homeowner Maintenance?" *Urban Affairs Review* 18, no. 2 (1982): 235–54. doi:10.1177/004208168201800205.

Gamm, Gerald. *Urban Exodus: Why the Jews Left Boston and the Catholics Stayed.* Cambridge, MA: Harvard University Press, 2001.

Gans, Herbert J. "Planning for People, Not Buildings." *Environment and Planning A: Economy and Space* 1, no. 1 (1969): 33–46. https://doi.org/10.1068/a010033.

Gans, Herbert J. "Gans on Granovetter's 'Strength of Weak Ties.'" *American Journal of Sociology* 80, no. 2 (1974): 524–27.

Garb, Margaret. "Drawing the 'Color Line': Race and Real Estate in Early Twentieth-Century Chicago." *Journal of Urban History* 32, no. 5 (2006): 773–87. doi:10.1177/0096144206287099.

Gardner-Medwin, R., and F. J. Connell. "New Towns in Scotland." *Town Planning Review* 20, no. 4 (1950): 305–14. doi:10.2307/40101976.

Garrioch, David. *Neighbourhood and Community in Paris, 1740–1790.* Cambridge Studies in Early Modern History. Cambridge, UK: Cambridge University Press, 1986.

Garrioch, David. "Sacred Neighborhoods and Secular Neighborhoods Milan and Paris in the Eighteenth Century." *Journal of Urban History* 27, no. 4 (2001): 405–19. doi:10.1177/ 009614420102700402.

Garrioch, David, and Mark Peel. "Introduction: The Social History of Urban Neighborhoods." *Journal of Urban History* 32, no. 5 (2006): 663–76. doi:10.1177/0096144206287093.

Gaubatz, Piper. "Looking West towards Mecca: Muslim Enclaves in Chinese Frontier Cities." *Built Environment* 28, no. 3 (2002): 231–48. doi:10.2307/23288454.

Gaube, Heinz. *Iranian Cities*. New York: New York University Press, 1979.

Gehl, Jan. *Life Between Buildings: Using Public Space*. New York: Van Nostrand Reinhold, 1987.

Gibberd, Frederick. 1967. *Town Design*. Revised ed. London: Architectural Press, 1967.

Gibbs, Robert J. *Principles of Urban Retail Planning and Development*. Hoboken, NJ: Wiley, 2012.

Gillette, Howard. "The Evolution of Neighborhood Planning from the Progressive Era to the 1949 Housing Act." *Journal of Urban History* 9, no. 4 (1983): 421–44. doi:10.1177/ 009614428300900402.

Gleich, David F., and C. Seshadhri. "Neighborhoods Are Good Communities." Internet Archive. November 30, 2011. http://archive.org/details/arxiv-1112.0031.

Gleye, Paul H. "City Planning versus Urban Planning: Resolving a Profession's Bifurcated Heritage." *Journal of Planning Literature* 30, no. 1 (2015): 3–17. doi:10.1177/0885412214554088.

Goetz, Edward G., and Karen Chapple. "You Gotta Move: Advancing the Debate on the Record of Dispersal." *Housing Policy Debate* 20, no. 2 (2010): 209–36. doi:10.1080/ 10511481003779876.

Goering, John M. "The National Neighborhood Movement: A Preliminary Analysis and Critique." *Journal of the American Planning Association* 45, no. 4 (1979): 506–14. doi:10.1080/ 01944367908976998.

Goodman, Percival, and Paul Goodman. *Communitas: Means of Livelihood and Ways of Life*. 2nd ed., revised. New York: Vintage Books, 1960.

Gopnik, Adam. "The Secret Lives of Cities." *New Yorker*, October 5, 2015. http://www.newyorker. com/magazine/2015/10/05/naked-cities.

Gordon, Norman J. "China and the Neighborhood Unit." *American City*, October 1946, 112–13.

Goss, Anthony. "Neighbourhood Units in British New Towns." *Town Planning Review* 32, no. 1 (1961): 66–82. doi:10.2307/40102302.

Grabar, Henry. "Nabe or Hood? A Brief History of Shortening 'Neighborhood.'" *Citylab*, August 27, 2012. http://www.theatlanticcities.com/neighborhoods/2012/08/nabe-or-hood-brief-history-shortening-neighborhood/3074/.

Grannis, Rick. *From the Ground Up: Translating Geography into Community through Neighbor Networks*. Princeton, NJ: Princeton University Press, 2009.

Grannis, Rick. "T-Communities: Pedestrian Street Networks and Residential Segregation in Chicago, Los Angeles, and New York." *City & Community* 4, no. 3 (2005): 295–321. doi:10.1111/j.1540-6040.2005.00118.x.

Graziosi, Giovani H. "Urban Geospatial Digital Neighborhood Areas: Urban Geodna." PhD dissertation, Rutgers University, 2012.

Greater Minnesota Housing Fund. *Building Better Neighborhoods: Creating Affordable Homes and Livable Communities: A Collaborative Project*. St. Paul: Greater Minnesota Housing Fund, 2001.

Green, Norman E. "Aerial Photographic Analysis of Residential Neighborhoods: An Evaluation of Data Accuracy." *Social Forces* 35, no. 2 (1956): 142–47. doi:10.2307/2573361.

Greenbaum, Paul E., and Susan D. Greenbaum. "Territorial Personalization Group Identity and Social Interaction in a Slavic-American Neighborhood." *Environment and Behavior* 13, no. 5 (1981): 574–89. doi:10.1177/0013916581135003.

Greenberg, Mike. *The Poetics of Cities: Designing Neighborhoods That Work*. Urban Life and Urban Landscape Series. Columbus: Ohio State University Press, 1995.

Greenfield, Adam. *Against the Smart City*. 1.3 ed. New York: Do Projects, 2013.

Greenshields, T. H. "'Quarters' and Ethnicity." In *The Changing Middle Eastern City*, ed. Gerald Henry Blake and Richard I. Lawless, 120–40. London: Croom Helm, 1980.

Greer, Scott, and Ella Kube. "Urbanism and Social Structure: A Los Angeles Study." In *Community Structure and Analysis*, ed. Marvin B. Sussman, ed. 93–114. New York: Crowell, 1959..

Gregg, Abel J., and Charlotte Himber. *From Building to Neighborhood*. New York: Association Press, 1938. Hathi Trust Digital Library. http://hdl.handle.net/2027/wu.89097246854.

Grigsby, William, Morton Baratz, George Galster, and Duncan Maclennan. "Residential Neighborhoods and Submarkets: Some General Concepts." *Progress in Planning* 28, part 1 (1987): 20–24. doi:10.1016/0305-9006(87)90015-8.

Grunsfeld, Ernest A., and Louis Wirth. "A Plan for Metropolitan Chicago." *Town Planning Review* 25, no. 1 (1954): 5–32. doi:10.2307/40101561.

Guerrieri, Veronica, Daniel Hartley, and Erik Hurst. "Endogenous Gentrification and Housing Price Dynamics." University of Chicago, Booth School of Business, January 28, 2013. http://faculty.chicagobooth.edu/erik.hurst/research/gentrification_jpube_final_publish.pdf.

Guest, Avery M., Barrett A. Lee, and Lynn Staeheli. "Changing Locality Identification in the Metropolis: Seattle, 1920–1978." *American Sociological Review* 47, no. 4 (1982): 543–49. doi:10.2307/2095198.

Gulyani, Sumila, and Ellen M. Bassett. "The Living Conditions Diamond: An Analytical and Theoretical Framework for Understanding Slums." *Environment and Planning A* 42, no. 9 (2010): 2201–19. doi:10.1068/a42520.

Gutman, Marta. *A City for Children: Women, Architecture, and the Charitable Landscapes of Oakland, 1850–1950*. Chicago: University of Chicago Press, 2014.

Gutnov, A. È. *The Ideal Communist City*. I Press Series on the Human Environment. New York: G. Braziller, 1971.

Guttenberg, Albert Z. "Planning and Ideology." *Journal of Planning History* 8, no. 4 (2009): 287–94. doi:10.1177/1538513209338895.

Habib, Farah, Hamed Moztarzadeh, and Vahideh Hodjati. "The Concept of Neighborhood and Its Constituent Elements in the Context of Traditional Neighborhoods in Iran." *Advances in Environmental Biology* 7, no. 9 (2013): 2270–78.

Hakim, Besim S. *Arabic-Islamic Cities: Building and Planning Principles*. Emergent City Press, 2008.

Hall, Edward T. *The Hidden Dimension*. New York: Anchor, 1990.

Hall, Peter. *Cities of Tomorrow*. London: Blackwell, 1989.

Hallman, Howard W. "Citizens and Professionals Reconsider the Neighborhood." *Journal of the American Institute of Planners* 25, no. 3 (1959): 121–27. doi:10.1080/01944365908978319.

Hallman, Howard W. *The Organization and Operation of Neighborhood Councils: A Practical Guide*. Westport, CT: Praeger, 1977.

Ham, Maarten van, and David Manley. "Commentary: Neighbourhood Effects Research at a Crossroads. Ten Challenges for Future Research." *Environment and Planning A* 44, no. 12 (2012): 2787–93. doi:10.1068/a45439.

Hanchett, Thomas W. *Sorting Out the New South City: Race, Class, and Urban Development in Charlotte*. Chapel Hill: University of North Carolina Press, 1998.

Harbeson, John F. "Design in Modern Architecture." *Pencil Points*, March 1930, 244–251.

Harris, Chauncy D., and Edward L. Ullman. "The Nature of Cities." *Annals of the American Academy of Political and Social Science* 242 (1945): 7–17.

Harvey, David. *Social Justice and the City*. Johns Hopkins Studies in Urban Affairs. Baltimore: Johns Hopkins University Press, 1973.

Harvey, David. *The Urban Experience*. Baltimore: Johns Hopkins University Press, 1989.

Haselberger, Lothar, David Gilman Romano, Elisha Ann Dumser, and D. Borbonus. *Mapping Augustan Rome*. Portsmouth, RI: Journal of Roman Archaeology, 2002.

Hawkes, Roland K. "Spatial Patterning of Urban Population Characteristics." *American Journal of Sociology* 78, no. 5 (1973): 1216–35.

Hawley, Amos Henry. *Urban Society: An Ecological Approach*. New York: Ronald Press, 1971.

Hayden, Dolores. "The Potential of Ethnic Places for Urban Landscapes," *Places* 7, no. 1 (1991): 11–17.

Hayden, Dolores. *Seven American Utopias: The Architecture of Communitarian Socialism, 1790–1975*. Cambridge, MA: MIT Press, 1979.

Healey, Patsy. "Urban Planning in a Venezuelan City: Five Plans for Valencia. Content, Concepts and Context." *Town Planning Review* 46, no. 1 (1975): 63–82. doi:10.2307/40103082.

Heeger, H. P. "The Dutch Solution to the Problem of a Residential Environment." *Planning and Development in the Netherlands* 11, no. 1 (1979): 3–16.

Hegemann, W., W. W. Forster, and R. C. Weinberg. *City Planning, Housing*. New York: Architectural Book Publishing, 1936.

Hegemann, Werner, and Elbert Peets. *The American Vitruvius: An Architects' Handbook of Civic Art*. New York: The Architectural Book Publishing Co., 1922.

Hein, Carola. "Machi Neighborhood and Small Town—The Foundation for Urban Transformation in Japan." *Journal of Urban History* 35, no. 1 (2008): 75–107. doi:10.1177/0096144208322463.

Herbert, Gilbert. "The Neighbourhood Unit Principle and Organic Theory." *Sociological Review* 11, no. 2 (July 1963): 165–213. doi:10.1111/1467-954X.ep13629152.

Hess, Daniel Baldwin, Hiroaki Hata, and Ernest Sternberg. "Pathways and Artifacts: Neighborhood Design for Physical Activity." *Journal of Urbanism: International Research on Placemaking and Urban Sustainability* 6, no. 1 (2013): 52–71. doi:10.1080/17549175.2013.765904.

Hester, Randolph T. *Planning Neighborhood Space with People*. New York: Van Nostrand Reinhold, 1984.

Hilberseimer, Ludwig. *The New City: Principles of Planning*. Classic Reprint. Chicago: Paul Theobald, 1944.

Hillery, George A. *Communal Organizations: A Study of Local Societies*. Chicago: University of Chicago Press, 1968.

Hillier, Bill, Richard Durdett, John Peponis, and Alan Penn. "Creating Life: Or, Does Architecture Determine Anything?" *Architecture and Behavior* 3, no. 3 (1987): 233–250.

Hillier, B., A. Penn, J. Hanson, T. Grajewski, and J. Xu. "Natural Movement: Or Configuration and Attraction in Urban Pedestrian Movement." *Environment and Planning B: Planning and Design* 20 (1993): 29–66.

Hipp, John R., and Adam Boessen. "Egohoods as Waves Washing across the City: A New Measure of 'Neighborhoods.'" *Criminology* 51, no. 2 (2013): 287–327. doi:10.1111/1745-9125.12006.

Historic American Buildings Survey. No. NJ-1235. School Street–Monroe Street Neighborhood. http://www.loc.gov/pictures/collection/hh/. Accessed July 10, 2018.

Hohenberg, Paul M., and Lynn Hollen Lees. *The Making of Urban Europe*. Revised ed. Cambridge, MA: Harvard University Press, 1995.

Hojnacki, William P. "What Is a Neighborhood?" *Social Policy* 10, no. 2 (1979): 47–52.

Holt, John Bradshaw. "Report of a Reconnaissance Survey of Neighborhoods and Communities of Caswell County, North Carolina with Recommendations." Washington, DC: Department of Agriculture, Bureau of Agricultural Economics. 1940. Hathi Trust Digital Library. http://hdl.handle.net/2027/coo.31924013730944.

Hooker, George E. "City Planning and Political Areas." *National Municipal Review* 6 (May 1917): 341–42.

Hoolhorst, Drew. "Moving to San Francisco." *Bold Italic*. Accessed July 10, 2018. https://thebold-italic.com/moving-to-san-francisco-the-bold-italic-san-francisco-fd5762a7c6e7

Hoover, Robert C., and Everett L Perry. *Church and City Planning: Suggestions for Coordination*. New York: Bureau of Research and Survey, National Council of the Churches of Christ in the U.S.A., 1955.

Hove, Erik van. *Networking Neighborhoods. Social Problems and Social Issues*. Columbia: University of South Carolina Press, 2001.

Howard, John T. "Democracy in City Planning." *Antioch Review* 4, no. 4 (1944): 518–30. doi:10.2307/4609039.

Hoyt, Homer. "Rebuilding American Cities after the War." *Journal of Land & Public Utility Economics* 19, no. 3 (1943): 364–68. doi:10.2307/3158915.

Huckfeldt, Robert, Eric Plutzer, and John Sprague. "Alternative Contexts of Political Behavior: Churches, Neighborhoods, and Individuals." *Journal of Politics* 55 (1993), 365–81. http://dx.doi.org/10.2307/2132270.

Hulchanski, J. David. "The Three Cities within Toronto: Income Polarization among Toronto's Neighbourhoods, 1970–2005." Toronto: University of Toronto Cities Centre, 2007. http://3cities.neighbourhoodchange.ca/wp-content/themes/3-Cities/pdfs/three-cities-in-toronto.pdf. Accessed July 10, 2018.

Hunter, Albert. "The Urban Neighborhood: Its Analytical and Social Contexts." *Urban Affairs Review* 14, no. 3 (1979): 267–88. doi:10.1177/107808747901400301.

Hur, Misun, and Hazel Morrow-Jones. "Factors That Influence Residents' Satisfaction with Neighborhoods." *Environment and Behavior* 40, no. 5 (2008): 619–35. doi:10.1177/0013916507307483.

Hwang, Jackelyn, and Robert J. Sampson. "Divergent Pathways of Gentrification: Racial Inequality and the Social Order of Renewal in Chicago Neighborhoods." *American Sociological Review* 79, no. 4 (2014): 726–51. doi:10.1177/0003122414535774.

I Grow Chicago. "Peace Campus." http://www.igrowchicago.org/about-us/peace-house/. Accessed July 10, 2018.

Institute of Transportation Engineers. "Designing Walkable Urban Thoroughfares: A Context Sensitive Approach." 2010. http://library.ite.org/pub/e1cff43c-2354-d714-51d9-d82b39d4dbad.

Isaacs, Reginald R. "Are Urban Neighborhoods Possible?" *Journal of Housing*, July 1948, 177.

Ivory, Vivienne, Karen Witten, Clare Salmond, En-Yi Lin, Ru Quan You, and Tony Blakely. "The New Zealand Index of Neighbourhood Social Fragmentation: Integrating Theory and Data." *Environment and Planning A* 44, no. 4 (2012): 972–88. doi:10.1068/a44303.

Jackson, Kenneth. *Crabgrass Frontier: The Suburbanization of the United States*. New York: Oxford University Press, 1985.

Jacobs, Jane. *The Death and Life of Great American Cities*. New York: Vintage, 1961.

Jakle, John A., Stanley D. Brunn, and Curtis C. Roseman. *Human Spatial Behavior: A Social Geography*. North Scituate, MA: Duxbury Press, 1976.

"Jakriborg, juni 2005 c." CC BY-SA 3.0. Wikimedia Commons. June 8, 2005. https://commons.wikimedia.org/wiki/File:Jakriborg,_juni_2005_c.jpg#/media/File:Jakriborg,_juni_2005_c.jpg.

Jezierski, Louise. "Neighborhoods and Public-Private Partnerships in Pittsburgh." *Urban Affairs Review* 26, no. 2 (1990): 217–49. doi:10.1177/004208169002600205.

Jin, Wu. "The Historical Development of Chinese Urban Morphology." *Planning Perspectives* 8, no. 1 (1993): 20–52. doi:10.1080/02665439308725762.

Johnson, Donald Leslie. "Origin of the Neighbourhood Unit." *Planning Perspectives* 17, no. 3 (2002): 227–45. doi:10.1080/02665430210129306.

Johnson-Marshall, Percy. *Rebuilding Cities from Medieval to Modern Times*. New Brunswick, NJ: Aldine Transaction, 2010.

Johnston, R. J., Derek Gregory, Geraldine Pratt, and Michael Watts, eds. *The Dictionary of Human Geography*. 4 edition. Oxford, UK; Malden, Mass: Wiley-Blackwell, 2000.

Jones, Diana Nelson. "Boundaries Blur in Many City Neighborhoods; Residents Confused about Names, Where Their Homes Are Located." *Pittsburgh Post-Gazette*, June 5, 2006.

Jones, Rees L. *Golf Course Developments*. Technical Bulletin 70. Washington: ULI, 1974.

Joseph, Miranda. *Against the Romance of Community*. Minneapolis: University of Minnesota Press, 2002.

Jun, Kyu-Nahm, and Juliet A. Musso. "Explaining Minority Representation in Place-Based Associations: Los Angeles Neighborhood Councils in Context." *Journal of Civil Society* 3, no. 1 (2007): 39–58. doi:10.1080/17448680701390737.

Kadushin, Charles, and Delmos J. Jones. "Social Networks and Urban Neighborhoods in New York City." *City & Society* 6, no. 1 (1992): 58–75. doi:10.1525/city.1992.6.1.58.

Kark, Ruth, and Michal Oren-Nordheim. *Jerusalem and Its Environs: Quarter, Neighborhoods, Villages, 1800–1948*. Israel Studies in Historical Geography. Detroit, MI: Wayne State University Press.

Kasinitz, Philip. "The Gentrification of 'Boerum Hill': Neighborhood Change and Conflicts over Definitions." *Qualitative Sociology* 11, no. 3 (1988): 163–82.

Kaufman, Joanne. "Researching Your Future Neighbors." *New York Times*, November 7, 2014. http://www.nytimes.com/2014/11/09/realestate/researching-your-future-neighbors.html.

Kazimee, Bashir A., and James Mcquillan. "Living Traditions of the Afghan Courtyard and Aiwan." *Traditional Dwellings and Settlements Review* 13, no. 2 (2002): 23–34. doi:10.2307/41757892.

Keating, Ann Durkin. "Chicagoland: More Than the Sum of Its Parts." *Journal of Urban History* 30, no. 2 (2004): 213–30. doi:10.1177/0096144203258353.

Keeble, Lewis B. *Principles and Practice of Town and Country Planning*. London: Estates Gazette, 1952.

Keene, Derek, and Vanessa Harding. *A Survey of Documentary Sources for Property Holding in London Before The Great Fire*. London: London Record Society, 1985.

Keith, Kathryn. "The Spatial Patterns of Everyday Life in Old Babylonian Neighborhoods." In *The Social Construction of Ancient Cities*, ed. Monica L. Smith, 56–80. Washington, DC: Smithsonian Books, 2003.

Keller, Suzanne Infeld. *The Urban Neighborhood: A Sociological Perspective*. Studies in Sociology. New York: Random House, 1968.

Kelling, George L., and James Q. Wilson. "Broken Windows." *Atlantic Monthly* 3 (1982): 29–38.

Kellogg, Paul Underwood. *The Pittsburgh Survey; Findings in Six Volumes*. New York: Russell Sage Foundation, 1909.

Kelly, Timothy. "*Parish Boundaries: The Catholic Encounter with Race in the Twentieth-Century Urban North*. By John T. McGreevy (Chicago: University of Chicago Press, 1996, vi plus 362pp. $27.50)." *Journal of Social History* 32, no. 2 (1998): 480–882. doi:10.1353/jsh/32.2.480.

Keyvanian, Carla. "Concerted Efforts: The Quarter of the Barberini Casa Grande in Seventeenth-Century Rome." *Journal of the Society of Architectural Historians* 64, no. 3 (2005): 292–311. doi:10.2307/25068166.

Kheirabadi, Masoud. *Iranian Cities: Formation and Development*. Austin: University of Texas Press, 1991.

Kiang, Heng Chye. "Visualizing Everyday Life in the City: A Categorization System for Residential Wards in Tang Chang'an." *Journal of the Society of Architectural Historians* 73, no. 1 (2014): 91–117. doi:10.1525/jsah.2014.73.1.91.

Kim, J. and R. Kaplan. Physical and Psychological Factors in Sense of Community: New Urbanist Kentlands and Nearby Orchard Village. *Environment and Behavior* 36 (2004): 313–340.

King, Angela. "Mapping Your Roots: Parish Mapping." In *Boundaries of Home: Mapping for Local Empowerment*, ed. Doug Aberley, 31–34. New Catalyst Bioregional Series. Gabriola Island, BC: New Society, 1993.

Kinkela, David. "The Ecological Landscapes of Jane Jacobs and Rachel Carson." *American Quarterly* 61, no. 4 (2009): 905–28. doi:10.1353/aq.0.0115.

Kinney, Nancy T., and William E. Winter. "Places of Worship and Neighborhood Stability." *Journal of Urban Affairs* 28, no. 4 (2006): 335–52. doi:10.1111/j.1467-9906.2006.00299.x.

Klaus, Susan L. *A Modern Arcadia: Frederick Law Olmsted Jr. and the Plan for Forest Hills Gardens*. Amherst: University of Massachusetts Press, 2004.

Knight Foundation. "No Barriers Project." http://www.knightfoundation.org/grants/201550682. Accessed July 10, 2018.

Koenigsberger, Otto H. "New Towns in India." *Town Planning Review* 23, no. 2 (1952): 94–132. doi:10.2307/40101227.

Kolb, John H. "Rural Primary Groups: A Study of Agricultural Neighborhoods." PhD dissertation, University of Wisconsin, 1921. http://hdl.handle.net/2027/wu.89009643263.

Kops, Bernard. *The World Is a Wedding*. New York: Coward-McCann, 1963.

Kostof, Spiro. *The City Shaped*. London: Thames & Hudson, 1991.

Kotler, Milton. *Neighborhood Government: The Local Foundations of Political Life*. Indianapolis, IN: Bobbs-Merrill, 1969.

Krase, Jerome. "Italian American Urban Landscapes: Images of Social and Cultural Capital." *Italian Americana* 22, no. 1 (2004): 17–44. doi:10.2307/29776910.

Krieger, Nancy. "A Century of Census Tracts: Health and the Body Politic (1906–2006)." *Journal of Urban Health* 83, no. 3 (2006): 355–61. doi:10.1007/s11524-006-9040-y.

Krier, Leon. *The Architecture of Community*. 2nd ed. Washington, DC: Island Press, 2011.

Krier, Léon. *Houses, Palaces, Cities*. AD Profile 54. London: Architectural Design AD Editions, distributed by St. Martin's Press, 1984.

Kullberg, Agneta, Toomas Timpka, Tommy Svensson, Nadine Karlsson, and Kent Lindqvist. "Does the Perceived Neighborhood Reputation Contribute to Neighborhood Differences in Social Trust and Residential Wellbeing?" *Journal of Community Psychology* 38, no. 5 (2010): 591–606. doi:10.1002/jcop.20383.

Kuper, Leo. "Social Science Research and the Planning of Urban Neighbourhoods." *Social Forces* 29, no. 3 (1951): 237–43. doi:10.2307/2572411.

La Gory, Mark, and John Pipkin. *Urban Social Space.* Belmont, CA: Wadsworth, 1981.

Laguerre, Michel S. *Global Neighborhoods: Jewish Quarters in Paris, London, and Berlin.* Albany: State University of New York Press, 2009.

Lammers, Benjamin J. "The Birth of the East Ender: Neighborhood and Local Identity in Interwar East London." *Journal of Social History* 39, no. 2 (2005): 331–44. doi:10.1353/jsh.2005.0143.

Landman, Karina. "Gated Communities in South Africa: The Challenge for Spatial Planning and Land Use Management." *Town Planning Review* 75, no. 2 (2004): 151–72. doi:10.2307/40112598.

Lang, Jon. *Urban Design: A Typology of Procedures and Products.* Illustrated with over 50 Case Studies. Oxford: Routledge, 2005.

Larice, Michael Angelo. "Great Neighborhoods: The Livability and Morphology of High Density Neighborhoods in Urban North America." PhD dissertation, University of California, Berkeley, 2005.

Lavedan, Pierre. *Histoire de l'urbanisme à Paris.* Paris: Henri Laurens, 1975.

Lebel, Alexandre, Robert Pampalon, and Paul Y. Villeneuve. "A Multi-Perspective Approach for Defining Neighbourhood Units in the Context of a Study on Health Inequalities in the Quebec City Region." *International Journal of Health Geographics* 6 (July 5, 2007): 27. doi:10.1186/1476-072X-6-27.

Lee, Chang-Moo, and Kun-Hyuck Ahn. "Is Kentlands Better Than Radburn? The American Garden City and the New Urbanist Paradigms." *Journal of the American Planning Association* 69, no. 1 (2003): 50–71.

Lee, Terence. "Urban Neighbourhood as a Socio-Spatial Schema." *Human Relations* 21 (1968): 241–67. http://dx.doi.org/10.1177/001872676802100303.

Lees, Loretta. "Gentrification and Social Mixing: Towards an Inclusive Urban Renaissance?" *Urban Studies* 45, no. 12 (2008): 2449–70. doi:10.1177/0042098008097099.

Leinberger, Christopher B., and Patrick Lynch. "The WalkUP Wake-Up Call: Boston." George Washington University School of Business, 2015. http://www.smartgrowthamerica.org/documents/walkup-wake-up-call-boston.pdf.

Lesger, Clé, and Marco H. D. Van Leeuwen. "Residential Segregation from the Sixteenth to the Nineteenth Century: Evidence from the Netherlands." *Journal of Interdisciplinary History* 42, no. 3 (2012): 333–69.

Lewis, Harold MacLean. *Planning the Modern City.* New York: J. Wiley, 1949.

Liang, Samuel Y. "Where the Courtyard Meets the Street: Spatial Culture of the Li Neighborhoods, Shanghai, 1870–1900." *Journal of the Society of Architectural Historians* 67, no. 4 (2008): 482–503.

Lis, Catharina, and Hugo Soly. "Neighborhood Social Change in West European Cities." *International Review of Social History* 38 (1993): 1–30.

"Little Grids: How Small-Scale Utilities Could Solve America's Infrastructure Woes." *Global Urbanist*, March 12, 2015. http://globalurbanist.com/2015/03/12/little-grids.

Liu, Yishi. "Other Modernities: The Rise of a Japanese Colonial Capital City, 1932–1937." *Traditional Dwellings and Settlements Review* 20, no. 1 (2008): 17–18. doi:10.2307/41758548.

Llewelyn-Davies. *Urban Design Compendium.* London: English Partnerships & The Housing Corporation, 2000.

Llewelyn-Davies, Richard. "Town Design." *Town Planning Review* 37, no. 3 (1966): 157–72. doi:10.2307/40102517.

Logan, John R., and Charles Zhang. "Global Neighborhoods: New Pathways to Diversity and Separation." *American Journal of Sociology* 115, no. 4 (2010): 1069–109.

Looker, Benjamin. "Microcosms of Democracy: Imagining the City Neighborhood in World War II–Era America." *Journal of Social History* 44, no. 2 (2010): 351–78. doi:10.1353/jsh.2010.0069.

Lott, J. Bert. *The Neighborhoods of Augustan Rome.* Cambridge, UK: Cambridge University Press, 2004.

Low, Setha. *Behind the Gates: Life, Security, and the Pursuit of Happiness in Fortress America.* New York: Routledge, 2004.

Lowndes, Sullivan H., V. "How Low Can You Go? Rationales and Challenges for Neighborhood Governance." *Public Administration* 86 (2008): 53–74.

Lu, Duanfang. "Building the Chinese Work Unit: Modernity, Scarcity, and Space, 1949–2000." PhD dissertation, University of California, Berkeley, 2003.

Lu, Duanfang. *Remaking Chinese Urban Form: Modernity, Scarcity and Space.* London: Routledge, 2011.

Lu, Duanfang. "Travelling Urban Form: The Neighbourhood Unit in China." *Planning Perspectives* 21, no. 4 (2006): 369–92. doi:10.1080/02665430600892138.

Lunday, Elizabeth Austin. "Impact of African American Ethnicity on Neighborhood Design." *Urban Land* 64, no. 10 (2005): 109.

Lydon, Mike, Anthony Garcia, and Andres Duany. *Tactical Urbanism: Short-Term Action for Long-Term Change.* 2nd ed. Washington, DC: Island Press, 2015.

Lynch, Kevin. *The Image of the City.* Cambridge, MA: MIT Press, 1960.

Mabie, Hamilton Wright. "Ethics and the Larger Neighborhood." Paper delivered before the University of Pennsylvania, March 12, 1914. Hathi Trust Digital Library. http://hdl.handle.net/2027/wu.89046147765.

Macfarlane, Patrick W. "Planning an Arab Town: Kuwait on the Persian Gulf." *Journal of the Town Planning Institute,* April 1954, 110–13.

Madanipour, Ali. "How Relevant Is 'Planning by Neighbourhoods' Today?" *Town Planning Review* 72, no. 2 (2001): 171–91. doi:10.2307/40112446.

Maki, Fumihiko. *Investigations in Collective Form.* St. Louis, MO: School of Architecture, Washington University, 1964.

Manbeck, John B.. *The Neighborhoods of Brooklyn.* New Haven, CT: Yale University Press, 1998.

Mann, Peter H. *An Approach to Urban Sociology.* International Library of Sociology and Social Reconstruction. London: Routledge & K. Paul, 1965.

Mann, Peter H. "The Concept of Neighborliness." *American Journal of Sociology* 60, no. 2 (1954): 163–68.

Mannarini, Terri, Stefano Tartaglia, Angela Fedi, and Katiuscia Greganti. "Image of Neighborhood, Self-Image and Sense of Community." *Journal of Environmental Psychology* 26, no. 3 (2006): 202–14. doi:10.1016/j.jenvp.2006.07.008.

Manzano, Roberto J. "Community: Name Change for Former Section of Van Nuys Bolstered Sense of Neighborhood Identity, Residents Say at Anniversary Event." *Los Angeles Times,* September 26, 1999.

Marans, Robert W. "Neighborhood Planning: The Contributions of Artur Glikson." *Journal of Architectural & Planning Research* 21, no. 2 (2004): 112–24.

Marcus, Abraham. *The Middle East on the Eve of Modernity: Aleppo in the Eighteenth Century.* New York: Columbia University Press, 1989.

Marcus, Lars. "Social Housing and Segregation in Sweden—From Residential Segregation to Social Integration in Public Space." "The Spatial Syntax of Urban Segregation," ed. Laura Vaughan. Special issue of *Progress in Planning* 67, no. 3 (2007): 251–63. doi:10.1016/j.progress.2007.03.001.

Marcuse, Peter. "The Grid as City Plan: New York City and Laissez-Faire Planning in the Nineteenth Century." *Planning Perspectives* 2 (1987): 287–310.

Martin, Deborah G. "Enacting Neighborhood." *Urban Geography* 24, no. 5 (2003): 361–85. doi:10.2747/0272-3638.24.5.361.

Martin, Deborah G. "'Place-Framing' as Place-Making: Constituting a Neighborhood for Organizing and Activism." *Annals of the Association of American Geographers* 93, no. 3 (2003): 730–50. doi:10.1111/1467-8306.9303011.

Massey, Douglas S. and Nancy A. Denton. *American Apartheid: Segregation and the Making of the Underclass.* Cambridge: Harvard University Press, 1993.

Mattern, Shannon. "Methodolatry and the Art of Measure: The New Wave of Urban Data Science." *Places Journal,* November 2013. https://placesjournal.org/article/methodolatry-and-the-art-of-measure/.

McBride, Amanda Moore, and Eric Mlyn. "Innovation Alone Won't Fix Social Problems." *Chronicle of Higher Education.* Accessed July 10, 2018. https://www.chronicle.com/article/Innovation-Alone-Won-t-Fix/151551

McCann, Eugene J. "Framing Space and Time in the City: Urban Policy and the Politics of Spatial and Temporal Scale." *Journal of Urban Affairs* 25, no. 2 (2003): 159–78. doi:10.1111/1467-9906.t01-1-00004.

McGovern, Stephen J. "Philadelphia's Neighborhood Transformation Initiative: A Case Study of Mayoral Leadership, Bold Planning, and Conflict." *Housing Policy Debate* 17, no. 3 (2006): 529–70. doi:10.1080/10511482.2006.9521581.

McGreevy, John T. *Parish Boundaries: The Catholic Encounter with Race in the Twentieth-Century Urban North.* Historical Studies of Urban America. Chicago: University of Chicago Press, 1996.

McKenzie, R. D. "The Neighborhood: A Study of Local Life in the City of Columbus, Ohio. II." *American Journal of Sociology* 27, no. 3 (1921): 344–63.

McKenzie, R. D. "The Neighborhood: A Study of Local Life in the City of Columbus, Ohio. III." *American Journal of Sociology* 27, no. 4 (1922): 486–509.

McKenzie, R. D. "The Neighborhood: A Study of Local Life in the City of Columbus, Ohio." *American Journal of Sociology* 27, no. 5 (1922): 588–610.

McKenzie, R. D. "The Neighborhood: A Study of Local Life in the City of Columbus, Ohio—Concluded." *American Journal of Sociology* 27, no. 6 (1922): 780–99.

McKnight, John. "Neighborhood Necessities: Seven Functions That Only Effectively Organized Neighborhoods Can Provide." *National Civic Review* 102, no. 3 (2013): 22–24. doi:10.1002/ncr.21134.

McKnight, John, and Peter Block. *The Abundant Community: Awakening the Power of Families and Neighborhoods.* San Francisco: Berrett-Koehler, 2010.

Media History of New York. Blog. "Census Tract Map 1950." Word Press, September 7. 2011. https://mediahistoryny.files.wordpress.com/2011/09/census-tract-map-1950.jpg.

Meegan, Richard, and Alison Mitchell. "'It's Not Community Round Here, It's Neighbourhood: Neighbourhood Change and Cohesion in Urban Regeneration Policies." *Urban Studies* 38, no. 12 (2001): 2167–94. doi:10.1080/00420980120087117.

Mehaffy, Michael, Sergio Porta, Yodan Rofè, and Nikos Salingaros. "Urban Nuclei and the Geometry of Streets: The 'Emergent Neighborhoods' Model." *Urban Design International* 15, no. 1 (2010): 22–46.

Mehaffy, Michael W., Sergio Porta, and Ombretta Romice. "The 'Neighborhood Unit' on Trial: A Case Study in the Impacts of Urban Morphology." *Journal of Urbanism: International Research on Placemaking and Urban Sustainability* 8, no. 2 (2015): 199-217. doi:10.1080/17549175.2014.908786.

Meyer, Stephen Grant. *As Long as They Don't Move Next Door: Segregation and Racial Conflict in American Neighborhoods.* Lanham, MD: Rowman & Littlefield, 2001.

Meyer, William B. "The Poor on the Hilltops? The Vertical Fringe of a Late Nineteenth-Century American City." *Annals of the Association of American Geographers* 95, no. 4 (2005): 773–88. doi:10.2307/3694012.

Michigan Council of Defense, Civilian War Service Division. *Neighborhood War Clubs: Michigan's Block Plan.* 1942. Hathi Trust Digital Library. http://hdl.handle.net/2027/mdp.39015071128337.

Milgram, Stanley. *The Individual in a Social World: Essays and Experiments.* Addison-Wesley Series in Social Psychology. Reading, MA: Addison-Wesley, 1977.

Miller, Stephen R. "Legal Neighborhoods." 37 *Harvard Environmental Law Review* 105 (2013): 106–166. Available at SSRN: https://ssrn.com/abstract=2013565

Miller, Susan Gilson, Attilio Petruccioli, and Mauro Bertagnin. "Inscribing Minority Space in the Islamic City: The Jewish Quarter of Fez (1438–1912)." *Journal of the Society of Architectural Historians* 60, no. 3 (2001): 310–27. doi:10.2307/991758.

Miller, Zane. "The Role and Concept of Neighborhood in American Cities." In *Community Organization for Urban Social Change: A Historical Perspective*, ed. Robert Fisher and Peter Romanofsky, 3–32. Westport, CT: Greenwood Press, 1981.

Miller, Zane L. *Visions of Place: The City, Neighborhoods, Suburbs, and Cincinnati's Clifton, 1850–2000.* Urban Life and Urban Landscape Series. Columbus: Ohio State University Press, 2001.

Mills, D. R., and R. C. Wheeler. *Historic Town Plans of Lincoln, 1610–1920.* U.K.: Lincoln Record Society, 2010.

Ministry of Town and Country Planning. "Design of Dwelling." London: His Majesty's Stationery Office. 1944.

Minnery, John R., Jon Knight, John Byrne, and John Spencer. "Bounding Neighbourhoods: How Do Residents Do It?" *Planning Practice and Research* 24, no. 4 (2009): 471–93.

Mirgholami, Morteza, and Sidh Sintusingha. "From Traditional Mahallehs to Modern Neighborhoods: The Case of Narmak, Tehran." *Comparative Studies of South Asia, Africa and the Middle East* 32, no. 1 (2012): 214–37.

Misra, Tanvi. "The Tricky Task of Rating Neighborhoods on 'Livability.'" *CityLab*, February 12, 2015. http://www.citylab.com/housing/2015/02/the-tricky-task-of-rating-neighborhoods-on-livability/385392/.

"Mixed Neighborhood of Rental Housing, Washington." *Architectural Forum*, October 1943, 79–87.

Molotch, Harvey. "Design Decency at the Urban Front." *Cities Papers*, July 23, 2014. http://cities-papers.ssrc.org/design-decency-at-the-urban-front/.

Museum of Modern Art (MOMA), New York, NY. *Look at Your Neighborhood.* https://www.moma.org/momaorg/shared//pdfs/docs/press_archives/928/releases/MOMA_1944_0014_1944-03-28_44328-12.pdf. Accessed July 10, 2018.

Monkkonen, Paavo, and Xiaohu Zhang. "Socioeconomic Segregation in Hong Kong.." Working Paper. Berkeley: Institute of Urban and Regional Development, University of California. Accessed July 11, 2013. https://iurd.berkeley.edu/wp/2011-03.pdf.

Mooney-Melvin, Patricia. "Before the Neighborhood Organization Revolution: Cincinnati's Neighborhood Improvement Associations, 1890–1940." In *Making Sense of the City: Local Government, Civic Culture, and Community Life in Urban America*, ed. Robert Bruce Fairbanks, Patricia Mooney-Melvin, and Zane L. Miller, 95–118. Columbus: Ohio State University Press, 2001.

Mooney-Melvin, Patricia. "Changing Contexts: Neighborhood Definition and Urban Organization." *American Quarterly* 37, no. 3 (1985): 357–67. doi:10.2307/2712662.

Mooney-Melvin, Patricia. *The Organic City: Urban Definition and Community Organization, 1880–1920.* Lexington: University Press of Kentucky, 1987.

Morrish, William R., and Catherine R. Brown. *Planning to Stay: Learning to See the Physical Features of Your Neighborhood.* Minneapolis, MN: Milkweed Editions, 2000.

Moudon, Anne Vernez, Chanam Lee, Allen D. Cheadle, Cheza Garvin, Donna B. Johnson, Thomas L. Schmid, and Robert D. Weathers. "Attributes of Environments Supporting Walking." *American Journal of Health Promotion* 21, no. 5 (2007): 448–59.

Moudon, Anne Vernez. "Housing and Settlement Design Series Working Paper: Spatial Structures." Cambridge, MA: Massachusetts Institute of Technology, 1978.

Mouzon, Steve. *Original Green.* Blog. www.originalgreen.org/blog. Accessed July 10, 2018.

Mullin, John Robert. "Henry Ford and Field and Factory: An Analysis of the Ford Sponsored Village Industries Experiment in Michigan, 1918-1941. *Journal of the American Planning Association* 48, no. 4 (1982): 419–431.

Mumford, Lewis. *The City in History: Its Origins, Its Transformations, and Its Prospects.* New York: Harcourt, Brace & World, 1961.

Mumford, Lewis. "The Neighborhood and the Neighborhood Unit." *Town Planning Review* 24, no. 4 (1954): 256–70. doi:10.2307/40101548.

Mumford, Lewis. "Planning for the Phases of Life." *Town Planning Review* 20, no. 1 (1949): 5–16. doi:10.2307/40101922.

Mumford, Lewis. "What is a City?" *Architectural Record,* November, 1937. Reprinted in Richard T. LeGates and Frederic Stout (Eds.), *The City Reader*: 93–96. London: Routledge, 2000.

Mutter, L. R., and Joanne M. Westphal. "Perspectives on Neighborhoods as Park-Planning Units." *Journal of Architectural & Planning Research* 3, no. 2 (1986): 149–60.

Myers, Garth Andrew. "Designing Power: Forms and Purposes of Colonial Model Neighborhoods in British Africa." *Habitat International* 27, no. 2 (2003): 193–204. doi:10.1016/S0197-3975(02)00045-0.

Nasser, N. "Southall's Kaleido-scape: A Study in the Changing Morphology of a West London Suburb." *Built Environment* 30 (2004): 76–103.

National Federation of Settlements. "A Letter from Robert A. Woods." Boston: National Federation of Settlements and Neighborhood Centers, October 1920. Hathi Trust Digital Library. http://hdl.handle.net/2027/wu.89099295396, 1.

Nazemi, Pourya. "Necessity of Urban Transformation in Introverted Historic Textures: The Ancient Persian City of Yazd." *Journal of Planning History* 13, no. 1 (2014): 50–67. doi:10.1177/1538513213507538.

Nelson, Arthur C. *Reshaping Metropolitan America: Development Trends and Opportunities to 2030.* Washington, DC: Island Press, 2013.

Nelson, George. "Architects of Europe Today." *Pencil Points*, 1935, 406–11.

Neutra, Richard J. "Peace Can Gain from War's Forced Changes." *Pencil Points*, July 1942, 596–605.

Newburger, Harriet B., Eugenie L. Birch, and Susan M. Wachter, eds. *Neighborhood and Life Chances: How Place Matters in Modern America.* Philadelphia: University of Pennsylvania Press, 2013.

Newcombe, Vernon Z. "A Town Extension Scheme: At Karachi." *Town Planning Review* 31, no. 3 (1960): 219–29. doi:10.2307/40178357.

The New York Times. 1988. "New York Gazetteer," November 20, 1988. https://www.nytimes.com/1988/11/20/news/new-york-gazetteer.html. Accessed July 10, 2018.

Nhà xuất bản Thế giới and Philippe Le Failler. *Cartes anciennes de Hanoi et des environs.* Hanoi: Nhà xuất bản Thế giới, 2008.

Nightingale, Carl H. *Segregation: A Global History of Divided Cities.* Chicago: University of Chicago Press, 2012.

Nightingale, Carl H. "The Transnational Contexts of Early Twentieth-Century American Urban Segregation." *Journal of Social History* 39, no. 3 (2006): 667–702. doi:10.1353/jsh.2006.0008.

Nolan, James, and Norman Conti. "Neighborhood Development and Crime: Situational Policing." Paper presented at the annual meeting of the American Sociological Association, San Francisco, August 14, 2004. http://citation.allacademic.com/meta/p_mla_apa_research_citation/1/0/9/3/2/pages109323/p109323-1.php.

Nolen, John. *New Ideas in the Planning of Cities, Towns and Villages.* New York: American City Bureau, 1919.

Norcross, Carl, and John Hysom. *Apartment Communities: The Next Big Market. A Survey of Who Rents and Why.* Washington, DC: Urban Land Institute, 1968.

Norris, Nathan. "The Neighborhood School," in: Congress for the New Urbanism and Emily Talen (Ed.), *Charter of the New Urbanism*, pp. 158–159. New York: McGraw-Hill, 2013.

NUSA—Neighborhoods U.S.A. Accessed March 14, 2014. http://www.nusa.org/.

Nyden, Philip, John Lukehart, Michael T. Maly, and William Peterman. "Chapter 1: Neighborhood Racial and Ethnic Diversity in U.S. Cities." *Cityscape: A Journal of Policy Development and Research* 4, no. 2 (1998): 1–17.

Nyden, Philip, Michael Maly, and John Lukehart. "The Emergence of Stable Racially and Ethnically Diverse Urban Communities: A Case Study of Nine U.S. Cities." *Housing Policy Debate* 8, no. 2 (1997): 491–533.

Nyström, Louise, and Mats Johan Lundström. "Sweden: The Life and Death and Life of Great Neighbourhood Centres." *Built Environment* 32, no. 1 (2006): 32–52. doi:10.2307/23289485.

O'Brien Caughy, Margaret, Patricia O'Campo, and Anne E. Brodsky. "Neighborhoods, Families, and Children: Implications for Policy and Practice." *Journal of Community Psychology* 27, no. 5 (1999): 615–33. doi:10.1002/(SICI)1520-6629(199909)27:5<615::AID-JCOP8>3.0.CO;2-F.

Onnela, Jukka-Pekka, Samuel Arbesman, Marta C. González, Albert-László Barabási, and Nicholas A. Christakis. "Geographic Constraints on Social Network Groups." *PLoS ONE* 6, no. 4 (2011). doi:10.1371/journal.pone.0016939.

Osofsky, J. D. "The Impact of Violence on Children." *Future of Children/Center for the Future of Children, the David and Lucile Packard Foundation* 9, no. 3 (1999): 33–49.

Pahl, R. E. *Patterns of Urban Life. Aspects of Modern Sociology, the Social Structure of Modern Britain.* Harlow, UK: Longman, 1970.

Painter, Joe. "The Politics of the Neighbour." *Environment and Planning D: Society and Space* 30, no. 3 (2012): 515–33. doi:10.1068/d21110.

Palmitessa, James R. "Arbitration of Neighborhood Ties and Honor: Building and Property Disputes before the Six-Man Council of Prague, 1547–1611." *Sixteenth Century Journal* 34, no. 1 (2003): 123–45. doi:10.2307/20061316.

Panerai, Philippe, Jean Castex, and Jean-Charles Depaule. *Urban Forms: The Death and Life of the Urban Block.* London: Architectural Press, 2004.

Pannell, Clifton W. "Past and Present City Structure in China." *Town Planning Review* 48, no. 2 (1977): 157–72. doi:10.2307/40103265.

Park, Robert E., Ernest W. Burgess, and Morris Janowitz. *The City: Suggestions for Investigation of Human Behavior in the Urban Environment.* Reprint ed. Chicago: University of Chicago Press, 1925.

Park, Yunmi, and George O. Rogers. "Neighborhood Planning Theory, Guidelines, and Research: Can Area, Population, and Boundary Guide Conceptual Framing?" *Journal of Planning Literature,* October 9, 2014. doi:10.1177/0885412214549422.

Parkman Center for Urban Affairs. *Young Professionals and City Neighborhoods.* 1977. http://archive.org/details/youngprofessiona00park.

Patel, Mayur, Jon Sotsky, Sean Gourley, and Daniel Houghton. "The Emergence of Civic Tech: Investments in a Growing Field." Knight Foundation, December 2013. http://www.knightfoundation.org/media/uploads/publication_pdfs/knight-civic-tech.pdf.

Patricios, Nicholas N. "The Neighborhood Concept: A Retrospective of Physical Design and Social Interaction." *Journal of Architectural & Planning Research* 19, no. 1 (2002): 70–90.

Patricios, Nicholas. "Urban Design Principles of the Original Neighborhood Concepts." *Urban Morphology* 6, no. 1 (2002): 21–32.

Pearsall, Hamil. "Moving Out or Moving In? Resilience to Environmental Gentrification in New York City." *Local Environment* 17, no. 9 (2012): 1013–26. doi:10.1080/13549839.2012.714762.

Pearson, Robin. "Knowing One's Place: Perceptions of Community in the Industrial Suburbs of Leeds, 1790–1890." *Journal of Social History* 27, no. 2 (1993): 221–44. doi:10.1353/jsh/27.2.

Pecar, Marina. "Bosnian Dwelling Tradition: Continuity and Transformation in the Reconstruction of Sarajevo." *Traditional Dwellings and Settlements Review* 11, no. 1 (1999): 49–55. doi:10.2307/41757731.

Peets, Elbert. "Current Town Planning in Washington." *Town Planning Review* 14, no. 4 (1931): 219–37. doi:10.2307/40101105.

Pendola, Rocco, and Sheldon Gen. "Does 'Main Street' Promote Sense of Community? A Comparison of San Francisco Neighborhoods." *Environment and Behavior* 40, no. 4 (2008): 545–74. doi:10.1177/0013916507301399.

Perlman, Janice. "Neighbourhood Organisation: America Learns from the Third World." *Built Environment* 5, no. 2 (1979): 111–18. doi:10.2307/23285927.

Permentier, Matthieu, Maarten van Ham, and Gideon Bolt. "Neighbourhood Reputation and the Intention to Leave the Neighbourhood." *Environment and Planning A* 41, no. 9 (2009): 2162–80. doi:10.1068/a41262.

Perry, Clarence Arthur. "City Planning for Neighborhood Life." *Social Forces* 8, no. 1 (1929): 98–100. doi:10.2307/2570059.

Perry, Clarence Arthur. *Neighborhood and Community Planning: Regional Survey of New York and Its Environs.* Vol. 7. New York: Regional Plan of New York and Its Environs, 1929.

Perry, Clarence Arthur. "The Rehabilitation of the Local Community." *Social Forces* 4, no. 3 (1926): 558–62.

Perry, Clarence Arthur. "The School as a Factor in Neighborhood Development." New York: Russell Sage Foundation, 1914. Hathi Trust Digital Library. http://hdl.handle.net/2027/uc2.ark:/13960/t7cr5qj3x.

Perry, Clarence Arthur. "The Tangible Aspects of Community Organization." *Social Forces* 8, no. 4 (1930): 558–64.

Perry, Clarence. *Wider Use of the School Plant.* New York: Russell Sage Foundation, 1910.

Perry, Clarence Arthur, New York Regional Plan Association, and Russell Sage Foundation. *The Rebuilding of Blighted Areas: A Study of the Neighborhood Unit in Replanning and Plot Assemblage*. New York: Regional Plan Association, 1933.

Perry, Clarence Arthur. *Housing for the Machine Age*. New York: Russell Sage Foundation, 1939.

Pew Research Center. "Table 3.1 Preferred Community." June 12, 2014. http://www.people-press.org/2014/06/12/preferred-community/.

Pfeiffer, Deirdre. "Racial Equity in the Post–Civil Rights Suburbs? Evidence from US Regions 2000–2012." *Urban Studies*, December 19, 2014. doi:10.1177/0042098014563652.

Philpott, Thomas Lee. *The Slum and the Ghetto: Immigrants, Blacks, and Reformers in Chicago*. Belmont, CA: Wadsworth, 1991.

Picone, Marco, and Filippo Schilleci. "A Mosaic of Suburbs: The Historic Boroughs of Palermo." *Journal of Planning History* 12, no. 4 (2013): 354–66. doi:10.1177/1538513213498482.

Pietila, Antero. *Not in My Neighborhood: How Bigotry Shaped a Great American City*. Chicago: Ivan R. Dee, 2010.

"Planning with You." *Architectural Forum* 79 (August 1943): 65–80.

Plater-Zyberk, Elizabeth, Gianni Longo, Peter J. Hetzel, Robert Davis, and Andres Duany. *The Lexicon of the New Urbanism*. Miami, FL: Duany Plater-Zyberk, 2000.

Poulsen, Michael, Ron Johnston, and James Forrest. "Using Local Statistics and Neighbourhood Classifications to Portray Ethnic Residential Segregation: A London Example." *Environment and Planning B: Planning and Design* 38, no. 4 (2011): 636–58. doi:10.1068/b36094.

President's Conference on Home Building and Home Ownership. *Report of the Committee on City Planning and Zoning*. Washington, DC, 1931.

Prevost, Lisa. "Using Data to Find a New York Suburb That Fits." *New York Times*, July 18, 2014. http://www.nytimes.com/2014/07/20/realestate/using-data-to-find-a-new-york-suburb-that-fits.html.

Proshansky, Harold M., Abbe K. Fabian, and Robert Kaminoff. "Place-Identity: Physical World Socialization of the Self." *Journal of Environmental Psychology* 3, no. 1 (1983): 57–83. https://doi.org/10.1016/S0272-4944(83)80021-8.

Providence Public Schools and Rhode Island College. *Neighborhoods: Curriculum Guide, Grades K–3*. Providence Social Studies Curriculum Project. Distributed by ERIC Clearinghouse, 1970. https://eric.ed.gov/?id=ED048163. Accessed July 10, 2018.

Querrien, Anne, and Laurent Devisme. "France: Centrality or Proximity, Consumption or Culture?" *Built Environment* 32, no. 1 (2006): 73–87. doi:10.2307/23289487.

Raine, J. W. "On Measuring Patterns of Neighbourly Relationships." *Socio-Economic Planning Sciences* 13, no. 1 (1979): 27–33. doi:10.1016/0038-0121(79)90006-5.

Rayner, Alan David. "Space Cannot Be Cut—Why Self-Identity Naturally Includes Neighbourhood." *Integrative Psychological and Behavioral Science* 45, no. 2 (2011): 161–84. doi:10.1007/s12124-011-9154-y.

Reardon, S.. and K. Bischoff. "Growth in the Residential Segregation of Families by Income, 1970-2009." US2010 Research Brief. New York: Russell Sage Foundation, 2011.

Reardon, Sean F., and Kendra Bischoff. "Income Inequality and Income Segregation." *American Journal of Sociology* 116, no. 4 (2011): 1092–153. doi:10.1086/657114.

Reinhardt, Kathleen. "Theaster Gates's Dorchester Projects in Chicago." *Journal of Urban History* 41, 2 (2015): 193-206. doi:10.1177/0096144214563507.

Reps, John W. "Town Planning in Colonial Georgia." *Town Planning Review* 30, no. 4 (1960): 273–85. doi:10.2307/40102287.

Richman, Alan, and Francis Stuart Chapin. *A Review of the Social and Physical Concepts of the Neighborhood as a Basis for Planning Residential Environments*. Chapel Hill: Department of City and Regional Planning, University of North Carolina, 1977.

Roach, Mary Joan, and David J. O'Brien. "The Impact of Different Kinds of Neighborhood Involvement on Residents' Overall Evaluations of Their Neighborhoods." *Sociological Focus* 15, no. 4 (1982): 379–91.

Robinson, Charles Mulford. "The Remaking of Our Cities: A Summing Up of the Movement For Making Cities Beautiful While They Become Busy And Big – A Chain of Great Civic Improvements Which Mark a New Era of Urban Development." *The World's Work* 12, October (1906): 8046–8050.

Rofe, Yodan. "Space and Community—The Spatial Foundations of Urban Neighborhoods: An Evaluation of Three Theories of Urban Form and Social Structure and Their Relevance to the Issue of Neighborhoods." *Berkeley Planning Journal* 10, no. 1 (1995). http://www.escholar-ship.org/uc/item/8691z2bp.

Rohe, William M. "From Local to Global: One Hundred Years of Neighborhood Planning." *Journal of the American Planning Association* 75, no. 2 (2009): 209–30. doi:10.1080/01944360902751077.

Romano, Dennis. "Gender and the Urban Geography of Renaissance Venice." *Journal of Social History* 23, no. 2 (1989): 339–53. doi:10.2307/3787884.

Rose, Dina R. "Social Disorganization and Parochial Control: Religious Institutions and Their Communities." *Sociological Forum* 15 (2000): 339–358.

Rosenthal, David. "Big Piero, the Empire of the Meadow, and the Parish of Santa Lucia: Claiming Neighborhood in the Early Modern City." *Journal of Urban History* 32, no. 5 (2006): 677–92. doi:10.1177/0096144206287100.

Rothschild, Nan A. *New York City Neighborhoods: The 18th Century.* San Diego: Academic Press, 1990.

Saarinen, Eliel. *The City: Its Growth, Its Decay, Its Future.* Boston: MIT Press, 1965.

Saginaw (MI) Public Schools. *Elementary Social Studies Curriculum Guide: Grade 2. Neighborhoods.* Distributed by ERIC Clearinghouse, 1983. https://eric.ed.gov/?q=Elementary+Social+Stu dies+Curriculum+Guide%3a+Grade+2.+Neighborhoods&id=ED241443. Accessed July 10, 2018.

Sampson, Robert J. *Great American City: Chicago and the Enduring Neighborhood Effect.* Chicago: University of Chicago Press, 2012.

Sampson, Robert J. "Notes on Neighborhood Inequality and Urban Design." *Cities Papers,* July 23, 2014. http://citiespapers.ssrc.org/notes-on-neighborhood-inequality-and-urban-design/.

Sanchez-Jankowski, Martin. *Cracks in the Pavement: Social Change and Resilience in Poor Neighborhoods.* Berkeley: University of California Press, 2008.

Sandalack, B. A., F. G. Alaniz Uribe, A. Eshghzadeh Zanjani, A. Shiell, G. R. McCormack, and P. K. Doyle-Baker. "Neighbourhood Type and Walkshed Size." *Journal of Urbanism: International Research on Placemaking and Urban Sustainability* 6, no. 3 (2013): 236–55. doi:10.1080/17549175.2013.771694.

Sanderson, Dwight, and Warren S. Thompson. "The Social Areas of Otsego County." Ithaca, NY: Cornell University, Agricultural Experiment Station, 1923. Hathi Trust Digital Library. http://hdl.handle.net/2027/wu.89097127500.

"San Jose Strong Neighborhoods." Accessed July 19, 2013. http://www.strongneighborhoods.org/.

Santos, Simone M., Dora Chor, and Guilherme Loureiro Werneck. "Demarcation of Local Neighborhoods to Study Relations between Contextual Factors and Health." *International Journal of Health Geographics* 9 (June 29, 2010): 34. doi:10.1186/1476-072X-9-34.

Scharlach, Andrew. "Creating Aging-Friendly Communities in the United States." *Ageing International* 37 (2012): 25–38.

Scherzer, Kenneth A. "Neighborhoods." In *The Encyclopedia of New York City,* ed. Kenneth T. Jackson, 886–87. New Haven, CT: Yale University Press, 1995.

Scherzer, Kenneth A. *The Unbounded Community: Neighborhood Life and Social Structure in New York City, 1830–1875.* Durham, NC: Duke University Press, 1992.

Schill, Michael H., and Susan Wachter. "The Spatial Bias of Federal Housing Law and Policy: Concentrated Poverty in Urban America." *University of Pennsylvania Law Review* 143, no. 5 (1995): 1285–1342.

Schlumbohm, Jürgen. "'Traditional' Collectivity and 'Modern' Individuality: Some Questions and Suggestions for the Historical Study of Socialization. The Examples of the German Lower and Upper Bourgeoisies around 1800." *Social History* 5, no. 1 (1980): 71–103.

Schubert, Dirk. "The Neighbourhood Paradigm: From Garden Cities to Gated Community." In *Urban Planning in a Changing World: The Twentieth Century Experience,* ed. Robert Freestone, 118–38. London: E&FN Spon, 2000.

Schwab, William A. "Alternative Explanations of Neighborhood Change: An Evaluation of Neighborhood Life-Cycle, Composition, and Arbitrage Models." *Sociological Focus* 21 (1988): 81–93. http://dx.doi.org/10.1080/00380237.1988.10570970.

Schwartz, Edward A., and Institute for the Study of Civic Values. *The Neighborhood Agenda.* Philadelphia: Institute for the Study of Civic Values, 1982.

Schweitzer, Mary M. "The Spatial Organization of Federalist Philadelphia, 1790." *Journal of Interdisciplinary History* 24, no. 1 (1993): 31–57. doi:10.2307/205100.

Scotland, Andrew. *A Handbook of the Plymouth Plan.* London: Nisbet, 1945.

Sebag, Paul, with Robert Attal. *L'Évolution d'un Ghetto Nord-Africain: La Hara de Tunis.* Paris: Presses universitaires de France, 1959.

Sell, James Lee. "Territoriality and Children's Experience of the Neighborhood." PhD dissertation, University of Arizona, 1983.

Sendut, Hamzah. "The Structure of Kuala Lumpur: Malaysia's Capital City." *Town Planning Review* 36, no. 2 (1965): 125–38. doi:10.2307/40102464.

Sennett, Richard. *The Fall of Public Man.* Reissue ed. New York: Norton, 1992.

Sennett, Richard. *The Uses of Disorder: Personal Identity and City Life.* New York: Norton, 1992.

Seoul City Government. "Administrative Districts." http://web.archive.org/web/20080220203429/http://english.seoul.go.kr/gover/organ/organ_03adm.htm. Accessed July 10, 2018.

Sert, José Luis, and International Congresses for Modern Architecture. *Can Our Cities Survive? An ABC of Urban Problems, Their Analysis, Their Solutions.* Cambridge, MA: Harvard University Press, 1942.

Sharkey, Patrick. "Making Our Assumptions about Integration Explicit." NYU Furman Center: The Dream Revisited, January 2014. http://furmancenter.org/research/iri/sharkey.

Sharkey, Patrick. *Stuck in Place: Urban Neighborhoods and the End of Progress toward Racial Equality.* Chicago: University of Chicago Press, 2013.

Shiber, Saba George. *The Kuwait Urbanization: Documentation, Analysis, Critique.* Published by the author, 1964.

Shlay, Anne B. "Castles in the Sky: Measuring Housing and Neighborhood Ideology." *Environment and Behavior* 17, no. 5 (1985): 593–626. doi:10.1177/0013916585175003.

Silva, Jennifer. *Coming Up Short: Working-Class Adulthood in an Age of Uncertainty.* Oxford: Oxford University Press, 2013.

Silver, Christopher. "Neighborhood Planning in Historical Perspective." *Journal of the American Planning Association* 51, no. 2 (1985): 161–74. doi:10.1080/01944368508976207.

Simkhovitch, Mary Kingsbury. *Here is God's Plenty: Reflections on American Social Advance.* New York: Harper and Brothers, 1949.

Simkhovitch, Mary Kingsbury. *Neighborhood: My Story of Greenwich House.* New York: Norton, 1938. Hathi Trust Digital Library. http://hdl.handle.net/2027/mdp.39015027424558.

Simkhovitch, Mary Kingsbury. *The Settlement Primer.* Boston: National Federation of Settlements, 1926. Hathi Trust Digital Library. http://hdl.handle.net/2027/mdp.39015005273860, 12.

Simmel, Georg. "The Metropolis and Mental Life" (1902). In *The Sociology of Georg Simmel*, KH Wolff (ed./transl.): pp. 409–24. New York: Free Press, 1964.

Sims, William R. *Neighborhoods: Columbus Neighborhood Definition Study.* Columbus, OH: Department of Development, 1973.

Sinha, Jill Witmer, Amy Hillier, Ram A. Cnaan, and Charlene C. McGrew. "Proximity Matters: Exploring Relationships among Neighborhoods, Congregations, and the Residential Patterns of Members." *Journal for the Scientific Study of Religion* 46, no. 2 (2007): 245–60. doi:10.1111/j.1468-5906.2007.00354.x.

Sit, Victor F. S. "Soviet Influence on Urban Planning in Beijing, 1949–1991." *Town Planning Review* 67, no. 4 (1996): 457–84. doi:10.2307/40113418.

Skjaeveland, Oddvar and Tommy Garling. "Effects of Interactional Space on Neighbouring." *Journal of Environmental Psychology"* 17 (1997): 181–198.

Slidell, John B. "The Shape of Things to Come? An Evaluation of the Neighborhood Unit as an Organizing Scheme for American New Towns." Chapel Hill: Center for Urban and Regional Studies, University of North Carolina, 1972.

Smail, Daniel Lord. *Imaginary Cartographies: Possession and Identity in Late Medieval Marseille.* Ithaca, NY: Cornell University Press, 2000.

Smailes, Arthur E. *The Geography of Towns.* Chicago: Aldine, 1966.

Small, Mario Luis. "Is There Such a Thing as 'the Ghetto'?" *City* 11, no. 3 (2007): 413–21. doi:10.1080/13604810701669173.

Smith, C. J. "Residential Neighborhoods as Humane Environments." *Environment and Planning A* 8, no. 3 (1976): 311–26. doi:10.1068/a080311.

Smith, Kathryn Schneider. *Washington at Home: An Illustrated History of Neighborhoods in the Nation's Capital.* Baltimore: Johns Hopkins University Press, 2010.

Smith, Michael E., Ashley Engquist, Cinthia Carvajal, Katrina Johnston-Zimmerman, Monica Algara, Bridgette Gilliland, Yui Kuznetsov, and Amanda Young. "Neighborhood Formation in Semi-Urban Settlements." *Journal of Urbanism: International Research on Placemaking and Urban Sustainability* 8, no. 2 (2015): 173-198. doi:10.1080/17549175.2014.896394.

Snyder, Mary G. *Fortress America: Gated Communities in the United States.* New ed. Washington, DC: Brookings Institution Press, 1999.

Social Geographies—The Social Inclusion of Certain Groups in Communities. "Neighbourhoods and Communities." Accessed July 16, 2013. https://sites.google.com/site/socialgeography1/neighbourhoods-and-communities.

Sommer, Robert. "Man's Proximate Environment." *Journal of Social Issues* 22, no. 4 (1966): 59–70.

Song, Yan, Barry Popkin, and Penny Gordon-Larsen. "A National-Level Analysis of Neighborhood Form Metrics." *Landscape and Urban Planning* 116 (August 2013): 73–85. doi:10.1016/j.landurbplan.2013.04.002.

Sorensen, Andre, and Carolin Funck, eds. *Living Cities in Japan: Citizens' Movements, Machizukuri and Local Environments.* London: Routledge, 2009.

Sorkin, Michael. "Love Thy Neighbor(hood)." *Cities Papers*, July 23, 2014. http://citiespapers.ssrc.org/love-thy-neighborhood/.

Sorlien, Sandy. "Neighborhood Conservation Kit." *Street Trip into the Heart of Town*, n.d. Blog. http://street-trip.com/neighborhood-conservation-kit/.

Southworth, Michael, and Peter M. Owens. "The Evolving Metropolis: Studies of Community, Neighborhood, and Street Form at the Urban Edge." *Journal of the American Planning Association* 59, no. 3 (1993): 271–287.

Spain, Daphne. *How Women Saved the City.* Minneapolis: University of Minnesota Press, 2001.

Spreiregen, Paul D. *Urban Design: The Architecture of Towns and Cities.* New York: McGraw-Hill, 1965.

Stangl, Paul, and Jeffery M. Guinn. "Neighborhood Design, Connectivity Assessment and Obstruction." *Urban Design International* 16, no. 4 (2011): 285–96.

"The State of Your New York Block." *New York Times*, February 17, 2015. http://www.nytimes.com/interactive/2015/02/18/nyregion/19stateofblock.html.

Stein, Clarence S. "City Patterns, Past and Future." *Pencil Points* 23 (1942): 52–56.

Stein, Clarence S. "Toward New Towns for America." *Town Planning Review* 20, no. 3 (1949): 203–82. doi:10.2307/40101963.

Stein, Clarence S. "Toward New Towns for America (Continued)." *Town Planning Review* 20, no. 4 (1950): 319–418. doi:10.2307/40101978.

Stein, Rachel E. "Neighborhood Scale and Collective Efficacy: Does Size Matter?" *Sociology Compass* 8, no. 2 (2014): 119–28. doi:10.1111/soc4.12127.

Steiner, Jesse F. "Is the Neighborhood a Safe Unit for Community Planning?" *Social Forces* 8, no. 4 (1930): 492–93.

Stephenson, Gordon. "Town Planning: Contemporary Problem of Civil Design." *Town Planning Review* 20, no. 2 (1949): 125–43. doi:10.2307/40101946.

Stern, Robert A.M. and John M. Massengale. *The Anglo-American Suburb.* London: Architectural Design, 1981.

Stieber, Nancy. *Housing Design and Society in Amsterdam: Reconfiguring Urban Order and Identity, 1900-1920.* Chicago: University of Chicago Press, 1998.

Stilgoe, John R. *Borderland: Origins of the American Suburb, 1820-1939.* New Haven: Yale University Press, 1988.

Stone, Elizabeth C. *Nippur Neighborhoods.* Chicago: Oriental Institute of the University of Chicago, 1987.

Suttles, Gerard. "Community Design: The Search for Participation in a Metropolitan Society." In *Metropolitan America in Contemporary Perspective*, ed. Amos Henry Hawley and Vincent P. Rock. New York: Sage, 1975.

Suttles, Gerald D. *The Social Construction of Communities*. Studies of Urban Society. Chicago: University of Chicago Press, 1972.

Suttles, G. D. *The Social Order of the Slum: Ethnicity and Territory in the Inner City*. Chicago: University of Chicago Press, 1968.

Sweetser, Frank Loel. *Neighborhood Acquaintance and Association: A Study of Personal Neighborhoods*. New York: Columbia University, 1941.

Tach, Laura M. "More than Bricks and Mortar: Neighborhood Frames, Social Processes, and the Mixed-Income Redevelopment of a Public Housing Project." *City & Community* 8, no. 3 (2009): 269–99. doi:10.1111/j.1540-6040.2009.01289.x.

Tach, Laura, Rolf Pendall, and Alexandra Derian. "Income Mixing across Scales: Rationale, Trends, Policies, Practice, and Research for More Inclusive Neighborhoods and Metropolitan Areas." Urban Institute, January 24, 2014. http://www.urban.org/publications/412998.html.

Tajbakhsh, Kian. *The Promise of the City: Space, Identity, and Politics in Contemporary Social Thought*. Berkeley: University of California Press, 2000.

Talen, Emily. "Affordability in New Urbanist Development: Principle, Practice, and Strategy." *Journal of Urban Affairs* 32, no. 4 (2010): 489–510. doi:10.1111/j.1467-9906.2010.00518.x.

Talen, Emily. *City Rules: How Regulations Affect Urban Form*. Washington, DC: Island Press, 2012.

Talen, Emily, and Congress for the New Urbanism, eds. *Charter of the New Urbanism*. 2nd ed. New York: McGraw-Hill, 2013.

Talen, Emily, and Julia Koschinsky. "Compact, Walkable, Diverse Neighborhoods: Assessing Effects on Residents." *Housing Policy Debate* 24, no. 4 (2014): 717–750. doi:10.1080/10511482.2014.900102.

Tannenbaum, Judith. "The Neighborhood: A Socio-Psychological Analysis." *Land Economics* 24, no. 4 (1948): 358–69. doi:10.2307/3159288.

Tate, William F., ed. *Research on Schools, Neighborhoods, and Communities: Toward Civic Responsibility*. Lanham, MD: Rowman & Littlefield, 2012.

Tatsuhiko, S. "The urban systems of Chang'an in the Sui and T'ang dynasties," in: M. A. J. Beg (Ed.) *Historic Cities of Asia*, pp. 159–200. Kuala Lumpur: Percetakan Ban Huat Seng, 1986.

Taylor, Ralph B. "Defining Neighborhoods in Space and Time." *Cityscape* 14, no. 2 (2012): 225–30.

Taylor, Ralph B. "Social Order and Disorder of Street Blocks and Neighborhoods: Ecology, Microecology, and the Systemic Model of Social Disorganization." *Journal of Research in Crime and Delinquency* 34, no. 1 (1997): 113–55. doi:10.1177/0022427897034001006.

Taylor, Ralph B., Stephen D. Gottfredson, and Sidney Brower. "Neighborhood Naming as an Index of Attachment to Place." *Population and Environment* 7, no. 2 (1984): 103–25. doi:10.1007/BF01254780.

Teaford, Jon C. "Jane Jacobs and the Cosmopolitan Metropolis: 2012 UHA Presidential Address." *Journal of Urban History* 39, no. 5 (2013): 881–89. doi:10.1177/0096144213479311.

Tetlow, John, and Anthony Goss. *Homes, Towns and Traffic*. New ed. London: Faber & Faber, 1970.

Thadani, Dhiru A., ed. *The Language of Towns and Cities: A Visual Dictionary*. New York: Rizzoli, 2010, 76.

Thale, Christopher. "Assigned to Patrol: Neighborhoods, Police, and Changing Deployment Practices in New York City before 1930." *Journal of Social History* 37, no. 4 (2004): 1037–64. doi:10.1353/jsh.2004.0070.

Thiis-Evenson, Thomas, and Scott Campbell (transl.). *Archetypes of Urbanism: A Method for the Esthetic Design of Cities*. Oslo: Universitetsforlaget, 1996.

Tocqueville, Alexis de. *Democracy in America*. Vol. 1. 1835. Reprint ed. New York: Knopf, 1994.

Todd, Ian, and Michael Wheeler. *Utopia: An Illustrated History*. New York: Harmony, 1979.

Tripp, Herbert Alker. *Town Planning and Road Traffic*. Ann Arbor, MI: University of Michigan Library, 1943.

Turner, Alan, and Jonathan Smulian. "New Cities in Venezuela." *Town Planning Review* 42, no. 1 (1971): 3–27. doi:10.2307/40102722.

Turner, John. "Rebuilding Working Neighbourhoods and the Rediscovery of Tradition." *Traditional Dwellings and Settlements Review* 2, no. 1 (1990): 13. Doi:10.2307/41757742.

Turner, John F. C., and Colin Ward. *Housing by People: Towards Autonomy in Building Environments.* London: Marion Boyars, 2000.

Turner, Margery Austin. "Place Matters Even More Than We Thought: New Insights on the Persistence of Racial Inequality." *Poverty & Race,* July–August 2013. http://www.prrac.org/full_text.php?text_id=1445&item_id=14145&newsletter_id=130&header=Race+%2F+Racism&kc=1.

Tyng, Alexandra. *Beginnings: Louis I. Kahn's Philosophy of Architecture,* New York: John Wiley & Sons, 1984.

U.K. National Archives, Office for National Statistics. "Parishes and Communities." April 7, 2010. http://www.ons.gov.uk/ons/guide-method/geography/beginner-s-guide/administrative/england/parishes-and-communities/index.html.

Underhill, Jack A. "Soviet New Towns, Planning and National Urban Policy: Shaping the Face of Soviet Cities." *Town Planning Review* 61, no. 3 (1990): 263–85. doi:10.2307/40112920.

University of Washington, University Extension Division. "The Social and Civic Center." Seattle: University of Washington, 1912. Hathi Trust Digital Library. http://hdl.handle.net/2027/loc.ark:/13960/t23b6sb8v.

Unwin, Raymond. *Town Planning in Practice: An Introduction to the Art of Designing Cities and Suburbs.* London: T. F. Unwin, 1909.

Urban Land Institute Community Builders' Council. *The Community Builders Handbook.* Washington, DC: Urban Land Institute. 1960.

U.S. Department of Commerce, Bureau of the Census. "Geographic Terms and Concepts: Census Tract." 1980. http://www.census.gov/geo/reference/gtc/gtc_ct.html.

Uzzell, David, Enric Pol, and David Badenas. "Place Identification, Social Cohesion, and Environmental Sustainability." *Environment and Behavior* 34, no. 1 (2002): 26–53. doi:10.1177/0013916502034001003.

Vaiou, Dina, and Rouli Lykogianni. "Women, Neighbourhoods and Everyday Life." *Urban Studies* 43, no. 4 (2006): 731–43. doi:10.1080/00420980600597434.

Vaughan, Laura. "The Spatial Syntax of Urban Segregation." *Progress in Planning* 67, no. 3 (2007): 205–94. https://doi.org/10.1016/j.progress.2007.03.001.

Vervoort, Miranda, Henk Flap, and Jaco Dagevos. "The Ethnic Composition of the Neighbourhood and Ethnic Minorities' Social Contacts: Three Unresolved Issues." *European Sociological Review* 27, no. 5 (2011): 586–605. doi:10.1093/esr/jcq029.

Vidyarthi, Sanjeev. "Inappropriately Appropriated or Innovatively Indigenized? Neighborhood Unit Concept in Post-Independence India." *Journal of Planning History* 9, no. 4 (2010): 260–76. doi:10.1177/1538513210384457.

Vigdor, Jacob L., and Edward L. Glaeser. "The End of the Segregated Century: Racial Separation in America's Neighborhoods, 1890–2010." Civic Report 66. Manhattan Institute, January 2012. http://www.manhattan-institute.org/html/cr_66.htm#06.

Vinh, Tan. "Frelard or Balmont? So Hip, It Defies Definition—Microhoods. A Look at Changing Neighborhoods, a Block at a Time." *Seattle Times,* September 18, 2008.

Völker, Beate, Henk Flap, and Siegwart Lindenberg. "When Are Neighbourhoods Communities? Community in Dutch Neighbourhoods." *European Sociological Review* 23, no. 1 (2007): 99–114. doi:10.1093/esr/jcl022.

Von Hoffman, Alexander. *Local Attachments: The Making of an American Urban Neighborhood, 1850–1920.* Baltimore: Johns Hopkins University Press, 1994.

Walker, Mabel L., and Henry Wright. *Urban Blight and Slums: Economic and Legal Factors in Their Origin, Reclamation, and Prevention.* Harvard City Planning Studies 12. Cambridge, MA: Harvard University Press, 1938.

Wann, David. "Neighborhoods on Purpose." Cohousing Association of the United States, March 15, 2014. http://www.cohousing.org/on_purpose. Accessed July 10, 2018.

Ward, Colin. *The Child in the City.* New York: Pantheon, 1979.

Ward, David. "Environs and Neighbours in the 'Two Nations' Residential Differentiation in Mid-Nineteenth-Century Leeds." *Journal of Historical Geography* 6, no. 2 (1980).

Ward, Edward J. "Where Suffragists and Anti's Unite." In *American City,* vol. 10. January–June 1914. Accessed July 10, 2013. http://babel.hathitrust.org/cgi/imgsrv/image?id=mdp.39015068229676;seq=529;width=680.

Ward, Josi. "Dreams of Oriental Romance." *Buildings & Landscapes* 20, no. 1 (2013): 19–42.

Warner, Sam Bass. *American Urban Form: A Representative History*. Urban and Industrial Environments. Cambridge, MA: MIT Press, 2012.

Warner, Sam Bass. *Streetcar Suburbs: The Process of Growth in Boston, 1870–1900*. 2nd ed. Cambridge, MA: Harvard University Press, 1962.

Warren, Donald I. "The Functional Diversity of Urban Neighborhoods." *Urban Affairs Review* 13, no. 2 (1977): 151–80. doi:10.1177/107808747701300202.

Warren, Rachelle B., and Donald I Warren. *The Neighborhood Organizer's Handbook*. Notre Dame, IN: University of Notre Dame Press, 1977.

Wassenberg, Frank. "The Netherlands: Adaptation of the Carefully Planned Structure." *Built Environment* 32, no. 1 (2006): 12–31. doi:10.2307/23289484.

Webber, Melvin M. "Order in Diversity: Community without Propinquity." In *Cities and Space: The Future Use of Urban Land*, ed. Lowdon Wingo Jr., 23–56. Baltimore: Johns Hopkins University Press, 1963.

Webber, M.M. (Ed). *Explorations into Urban Structure*, Philadelphia: University of Pennsylvania Press, 1964.

Webber, Richard. "The Metropolitan Habitus: Its Manifestations, Locations, and Consumption Profiles." *Environment and Planning A* 39, no. 1 (2007): 182–207. doi:10.1068/a38478.

Weber, Rachel, Thea Crum, and Eduardo Salinas. "The Civics of Community Development: Participatory Budgeting in Chicago." *Community Development* 46, no. 3 (2015): 261–78. doi:10.1080/15575330.2015.1028081.

Wehrly, Max S. "Activities and Comment: Comment on the Neighborhood Theory." *Journal of the American Institute of Planners* 14, no. 4 (1948): 32–34. doi:10.1080/01944364808979081.

Weiss, Linda, Danielle Ompad, Sandro Galea, and David Vlahov. "Defining Neighborhood Boundaries for Urban Health Research." *American Journal of Preventive Medicine* 32, no. 6, Supplement (2007): S154–S159. doi:10.1016/j.amepre.2007.02.034.

Weiss, Marc A. *The Rise of the Community Builders: The American Real Estate Industry and Urban Land Planning*. Washington, DC: Beard Books, 2002.

Wekerle, Gerda R. "From Refuge to Service Center: Neighborhoods That Support Women." *Sociological Focus* 18, no. 2 (1985): 79–95. doi:10.2307/20831352.

Wellman, Barry. "The Unbounded Community: Neighborhood Life and Social Structure in New York City, 1830–1875 (Book Review)." *American Journal of Sociology* 99, no. 3 (1993): 798–800.

Wellman, Barry, and Barry Leighton. "Networks, Neighborhoods, and Communities Approaches to the Study of the Community Question." *Urban Affairs Review* 14, no. 3 (1979): 363–90. doi:10.1177/107808747901400305.

Wenger, Yvonne. "Saving Sandtown-Winchester: Decade-Long, Multimillion-Dollar Investment Questioned." *Baltimore Sun*, May 10, 2015. http://www.baltimoresun.com/news/maryland/baltimore-city/west-baltimore/bs-md-ci-sandtown-winchester-blight-20150510-story.html.

Whitehead, Mark. "Love Thy Neighbourhood—Rethinking the Politics of Scale and Walsall's Struggle for Neighbourhood Democracy." *Environment and Planning A* 35, no. 2 (2003): 277–300. doi:10.1068/a35127.

Whitten, Robert Harvey. "A Research into the Economics of Land Subdivision, with Particular Reference to a Complete Neighborhood Unit for Low or Medium Cost Housing." Syracuse, NY: Syracuse University School of Citizenship and Public Affairs, 1927. Hathi Trust Digital Library. http://hdl.handle.net/2027/mdp.39015063533957, 1.

Whitten, Robert Harvey, and Thomas Adams. *Neighborhoods of Small Homes: Economic Density of Low-Cost Housing in America and England*. Harvard City Planning Studies, no. 3. Cambridge, MA: Harvard University Press, 1931.

Wiebe, Mark. "People Define a Neighborhood." *Kansas City Star*, April 9, 1998.

Wild, Mark. *Street Meeting: Multiethnic Neighborhoods in Early Twentieth-Century Los Angeles*. Berkeley: University of California Press, 2008.

Williams, Albert L. "A Plan for a Co-operative Neighborhood." Madison, WI: Democrat Printing Company, 1912. Hathi Trust Digital Library. http://hdl.handle.net/2027/wu.89069256071.

Williams, Keith. *Blurred Lines*. Blog. Accessed February 5, 2014. http://ny.curbed.com/tags/blurred-lines.

Wilson, Catharine Anne. "Reciprocal Work Bees and the Meaning of Neighbourhood." *Canadian Historical Review* 82, no. 3 (2001): 431–464.

Wilson, David Sloan. *The Neighborhood Project: Using Evolution to Improve My City, One Block at a Time*. New York: Little, Brown, 2011.

Winter, Benjamin, and Jacqueline Cooksey. "Where Goes the Neighborhood?" MFA Design Thesis, Parsons The New School for Design, 2012.

Wirth, Louis. *The Ghetto*. 1928. Chicago: University of Chicago Press, 1956.

Wolch, Jennifer R., Jason Byrne, and Joshua P. Newell. "Urban Green Space, Public Health, and Environmental Justice: The Challenge of Making Cities 'Just Green Enough.'" *Landscape and Urban Planning* 125 (May 2014): 234–44. doi:10.1016/j.landurbplan.2014.01.017.

Wolfe, Charles R. "Streets Regulating Neighborhood Form: A Selective History." In *Public Streets for Public Use*, ed. Anne Vernez Moudon, 110–122. New York: Columbia University Press, 1991.

Wolfe, Charles R. *Urbanism without Effort*. Washington, DC: Island Press, 2013.

Wolfe, Chuck. "Re-visioning Neighborhood and the City, Then and Now." My Urbanist, November 20, 2010. http://www.myurbanist.com/archives/4885#sthash.vS5bURqu.dpuf.

Wood, Joseph S. "'Build, Therefore, Your Own World': The New England Village as Settlement Ideal." *Annals of the Association of American Geographers* 81, no. 1 (1991): 32–50. doi:10.2307/2563669.

Woodruff, Andy. "Crowdsourced Neighborhood Boundaries, Part One: Consensus." *Bostonography*, July 2, 2012. http://bostonography.com/2012/crowdsourced-neighborhood-boundaries-part-one-consensus/.

Woods, Robert A. "The Neighborhood in Social Reconstruction." *American Journal of Sociology* 19, no. 5 (1914): 577–91. doi:10.2307/2763126.

Woods, William K. "Neighborhood Innovations." *National Civic Review* 77, no. 5 (1988): 473–75. doi:10.1002/ncr.4100770511.

Wright, Henry C. "The Interrelation of Housing and Transit." In *American City*, vol. 10. January–June 1914. http://babel.hathitrust.org/cgi/imgsrv/image?id=njp.32101077275962;seq=59;width=1020.

Wycherley, R. E. "Hellenistic Cities." *Town Planning Review* 22, no. 3 (1951): 177–205. doi:10.2307/40102185.

Xiong, V. C. *Sui-Tang Chang'an: A Study in the Urban History of Medieval China*. Ann Arbor, MI: University of Michigan Press, 2000.

Yancey, William L., and Eugene P. Ericksen. "The Antecedents of Community: The Economic and Institutional Structure of Urban Neighborhoods." *American Sociological Review* 44, no. 2 (1979): 253–62.

Yeomans, Alfred B., and City Club of Chicago. *City Residential Land Development: Studies in Planning. Competitive Plans for Subdividing a Typical Quarter Section of Land in the Outskirts of Chicago*. Publications of the City Club of Chicago. Chicago: University of Chicago Press, 1916.

York, Abigail M., Michael E. Smith, Benjamin W. Stanley, Barbara L. Stark, Juliana Novic, Sharon L. Harlan, George L. Cowgill, and Christopher G. Boone. "Ethnic and Class Clustering through the Ages: A Transdisciplinary Approach to Urban Neighbourhood Social Patterns." *Urban Studies* 48, no. 11 (2011): 2399–415. doi:10.1177/0042098010384517.

Youssoufi, Samy, and Jean-Christophe Foltête. "Determining Appropriate Neighborhood Shapes and Sizes for Modeling Landscape Satisfaction." *Landscape and Urban Planning* 110 (February 2013): 12–24. doi:10.1016/j.landurbplan.2012.09.005.

Zack, Dan. "To Connect or Not to Connect?" *PlannerDan*, September 20, 2013. http://www.plannerdan.com/2013/09/to-connect-or-not-to-connect.html. Accessed July 10, 2018.

Zorbaugh, Harvey Warren. *The Gold Coast and the Slum: A Sociological Study of Chicago's Near North Side*. Chicago: University of Chicago Press, 1929.

INDEX

Page numbers in *italics* indicate illustrations. Published works will be found under the author's name rather than the title.